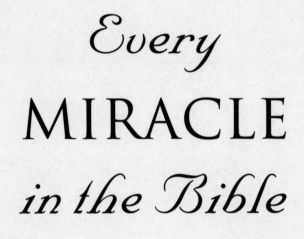

Every
MIRACLE
in the Bible

Every
MIRACLE
in the Bible

LARRY RICHARDS

Illustrated by
Paul Gross

THOMAS NELSON PUBLISHERS
Nashville

Library of Congress Cataloging-in-Publication Data

Richards, Larry, 1931–
    Every miracle in the Bible / Larry Richards ;
illustrated by Paul Richards.
      p.   cm.
    Includes indexes.
    ISBN 0-7852-4531-6
    1. Miracles—Biblical teaching.   2. Bible—Criticism,
interpretation, etc.   I. Title.
BS680.M5R53   1997
231.7′3—dc21   97-39584
                                              CIP

Printed in the United States of America

5 6 7 8—03

CONTENTS

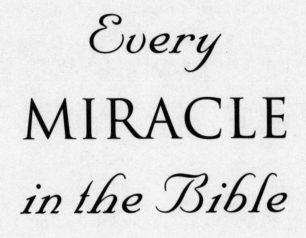

Every

MIRACLE

in the Bible

❖

CHAPTER 1

CAN MIRACLES HAPPEN?

THE GRAND MIRACLES OF SCRIPTURE

Genesis 1—2; John 1:1–3; Romans 1:1–4

A suspicious Gideon said it well. "O my lord, if the LORD is with us, why then has all this happened to us? And where are all His miracles which our fathers told us about, saying, 'Did not the LORD bring us up from Egypt?' "

At times we wonder too. Where are all the miracles we read about in the Bible? At such times we need to hear the testimony of Scripture, which affirms, "You are the God who does wonders" (Psalm 77:14). The more clearly we see God as the God who does wonders, the more confident we will be when we face troubled times.

I. THE GRAND MIRACLES OF SCRIPTURE

Three "grand miracles" described in Scripture shape the Christian understanding of God. These grand miracles are defining events—happenings which stamp the Christian faith as unique. These three miracle are so central to our faith that, if any one of them were taken away, our faith could no longer be called "biblical" or "Christian."

The three grand miracles of Scripture are:

- the miracle of Creation,
- the miracle of the Incarnation, and
- the miracle of the Resurrection.

THE MIRACLE OF CREATION

Any person who sets out to understand the meaning of life realizes that his or her inquiry must begin with the question of origins. Where did this universe in which we live come from? And, how did human beings originate?

The reason our quest has to begin here is simply because the answer we give to these two most basic questions will shape the answers we give to every other question about life.

VARIOUS BELIEFS ABOUT ORIGINS AND THEIR IMPLICATIONS

Ancient Middle Eastern beliefs were expressed in religious terms. The people of the ancient world understood that the issue of origins was vital, and they struggled to suggest answers. Their answers were given religious form, in that they invented myths to explain where the world came from and to explain man's role in the world.

A popular myth in Mesopotamia portrayed the universe as the body of a god who had been killed in a cosmic struggle. Human beings had sprung from his drops of blood and they had been forced to work for all time for the victorious deity.

The Egyptians had at least five creation myths. These myths featured gods giving birth to other gods, with the universe an almost accidental by-product. In one of the myths, human beings sprang from the lewd sex act of one of their pagan gods.

In another ancient tradition, human beings were made after a rebellion by lower gods forced the higher gods to create man to do the labor which these lower gods refused to do.

In each of these belief systems, man's role was to toil and then to die, with little or no hope of an afterlife.

Today, of course, these ancient myths are rejected as naïve. They belong to the realm of superstition, surviving only as academic curiosities. Yet the questions the people of the ancient world sought to answer still remain with us. And the answers we give still shape our basic attitudes toward life and death.

Ancient Western beliefs were expressed in philosophical terms. In the West, the Greeks saw matter as co-eternal with the gods. Human beings were part of the material creation. Philosophers probed to find ways that men might live in harmony with an essentially impersonal universe, in which fate ruled the destiny of gods and men alike.

As elements of that impersonal universe, men and women were thought to live for a brief time before they slipped away into the realm of the dead. Wisdom demanded that human beings learn the limits imposed on them as creatures in the natural world. Their lives should be marked by moderation. The common belief was that if any part of man remained after death, it was doomed to wander endlessly in a dark and shadowy realm filled with misery.

In each world, Eastern and Western, beliefs about the origin of the universe and man's relationship to the material universe shaped the culture's basic attitudes toward life and death.

Modern beliefs about origins are stated in "scientific" terms. In the modern world, the ancient religious answers and philosophic approaches to the question of origins have been set aside in favor of the claim to "scientific" certainty. Those who hold the contemporary view of origins admit that the universe had a beginning, in some unexplained cosmic "big bang" explosion. But contemporary theory goes on to affirm that the matter and energy unleashed in this cataclysmic event is the only reality. Everything that exists today was formed by processes that operate in the material universe in conformity with known or as-yet-unknown natural laws.

According to this view, simple one-celled living creatures were generated spontaneously by the interaction of chemicals which existed in primordial seas. Gradually, over millions of years, these simple one-celled living things became more and more complex. Ultimately, life developed into the vast array of plants and animals that exists today. Human beings, like other members of the animal kingdom—so this theory goes—are no more than accidents, coming into existence by chance. In essence, mankind is no different from the apes, horses, or dogs which evolved through this same process.

This contemporary "scientific" view of the origin of the universe—and especially its explanation of the origin of human beings—has serious implications.

First, if human beings are nothing more than the products of a purposeless process, it is foolish to speak of life after death. If the material universe is in fact the only reality, then when the body dies the "person" no longer exists.

Second, if the material universe is the only reality, there can be no ethical or moral absolutes. Each society and individual is free to work out whatever system he wishes, and none can stand in judgment, saying one way is "right" and the other "wrong." Ethics and morality are merely matters of whether one way or another is "better," in that it provides a society or an individual with more benefits [pleasures?] than harm [pain?].

The biblical view of origins. The biblical view of origins stands in bold contrast to each of the theories outlined above. Scripture presents one God, who has existed eternally. It affirms that this God chose to create the material universe, and that it came into existence by his agency.

Genesis 1 tells the story of the creation of living things, again by God's will and design. Genesis 2 then goes into detail about the separate, special creation of human beings as creatures made in God's image and likeness and assigned dominion over the earth by the Creator Himself.

As the biblical story unfolds, it provides answers for our most basic questions about life. The Bible portrays human beings as the continuing objects of God's love. It promises that biological death is not the end. Each person, self-conscious and aware, will survive death to meet a destiny shaped by his or her response during this lifetime to the God who loves each one completely.

What is perhaps most striking about the Bible's answer to the question of origins is that it has no roots in any belief system of the ancient world. Each attempt to portray Scripture's vision of one supreme Creator God as a derivative of ancient faith fails totally. The Bible's explanation of origins burst as a striking revelation into a world which had forgotten the one true God. And it stands today as the only account of origins which offers an adequate explanation of life as we experience it as well as a foundation for hope beyond our earthly existence.

AN EVALUATION OF THE CONTEMPORARY "SCIENTIFIC" VIEW OF ORIGINS

There are really only two viable modern views concerning origins. The dominant view—that all that exists "evolved"—is presented as truth proven by "science." To most people in our culture, evolutionary theory is thought to provide an accurate, factual, and true explanation of origins. Yet, this materialistic explanation is not as reliable as most assume.

In a recent novel, Michael Crichton, who believes that evolution offers the only realistic explanation of origins, has one of his characters explain some of the problems with that theory which trouble scientists today:

"After Watson and Crick in 1953, we knew that genes were nucleotides arranged in a double helix. Great. And we knew about mutation. So by the late twentieth century, we have a theory of natural selection which says that mutations arise spontaneously in genes, that the environment favors the mutations that are beneficial, and out of this selection process evolution occurs. It's simple and straightforward. God is not at work. No higher organizing principle involved. In the end, evolution is just the result of a bunch of mutations that either survive or die. Right?"

"Right," Arby said.

"But there are problems with that idea," Malcolm said. "First of all, there's a time problem. A single bacterium—the earliest form of life—has two thousand enzymes. Scientists have estimated how long it would take to randomly assemble those enzymes from a primordial soup. Estimates run from forty billion years to one hundred billion years. But the earth is only four billion years old! So, chance alone can't account for it, particularly since we know bacteria actually appeared at least four hundred million years after the earth began. That's very fast—which is why some scientists have declared life on earth must be of extraterrestrial origin. Although I think that's just evading the issue."

"Okay . . ."

"Second, there's the coordination problem. If you believe the current theory, then all the wonderful complexity of life is nothing but the accumulation of chance events—a bunch of genetic accidents strung together. Yet when we look closely at animals, it appears as if many elements must have evolved simultaneously. Take bats, which have echolocation—they navigate by sound. To do that, many things must evolve. Bats need a specialized apparatus to make sounds, they need specialized ears to hear echoes, they need specialized brains to interpret the sounds, and they need specialized bodies to dive and swoop and catch insects. If all these things don't evolve simultaneously, there's no advantage. And to imagine all these things happen purely by chance is like imagining that a tornado can hit a junkyard and assemble the parts into a working 747 airplane. It's very hard to believe" (*The Lost World*, 1996, 226–227).

Irreducibly complex systems and evolution. The problem Crichton is referring to is developed in a 1996 book by biochemist Michael J. Behe, *Darwin's Black Box*. Aside from the fact that there is no existing scientific evidence of any such changes as evolutionists postulate, Behe points out that many biological systems are *irreducibly complex*.

By irreducibly complex, he means that most biological systems are integrated units. You cannot take away one element of the system and still have the system work. For instance, a mousetrap has a platform, a spring, a holding bar, a catch, and a hammer. It is designed to do one thing: to kill a mouse. If you take away any part of the trap—the spring, for example—the mousetrap simply will not work as designed and is therefore useless.

If we go back to Crichton's illustration of the bat, the system that enables it to fly and catch insects fits the criterion of an *irreducible complexity*. Take away the bat's ability to make specialized sounds, and its entire system is useless. Or take away the ability to hear echoes. Or any of the other elements. Take away *any* element—and the system fails. Each element must be present at the same time for the biological system to give the bat any advantage.

How then can evolution take place by a system of small changes—each of which provides some advantage to the creature—if no advantage exists unless all the elements of a complex system are present and working at the same time?

Irreducibly complex systems and design. What is even more disturbing to evolutionary theory is the fact that nature's irreducibly complex systems seem to be *designed to accomplish a specific purpose*. That is, *there is a purposeful arrangement of the parts*.

No one coming across a mousetrap would imagine that it had been put together without a specific purpose in mind. In the same way, irreducibly complex systems by their nature *imply a design*.

How then can an evolutionist, looking at the multitudes of irreducibly complex systems in living creatures, even imagine that these systems are the product of chance? Every living thing bears the unmistakable stamp of design, and this implies a Designer.

Some have tried to get around this problem by assuming that evolution took place not by gradual changes but by giant leaps, or quantum changes in entire systems. There is an obvious problem with this notion. Such leaps would have to take place not in one individual creature, but in at least one male and one female of the species at the same time and same place if the change were to be transmitted to offspring. But even aside from this, University of Georgia geneticist John McDonald has noted a serious problem. He writes,

The results of the last 20 years of research on the genetic basis of adaptation has led us to a great Darwinian paradox. *Those [genes] that are obviously variable within natural populations do not seem to lie at the basis of many major adaptive changes, while those genes that seemingly do constitute the foundation of many, if not most, major adaptive changes apparently are not variable within natural populations* (Quoted in Behe, *Darwin's Black Box*, 37).

For example, genes that control the length of a bat's wings are variable in natural populations. Changes in length can and do take place. But genes that control the bat's ability to generate sounds, hear echoes, and interpret them, etc., do not exhibit variability. The irreducibly complex systems of living creatures simply do not change, and thus their existence is unexplainable by evolutionary theory.

The "intelligent design" movement. The January 6, 1997, issue of *Christianity Today* noted that challenges to Darwin are rooted in the growing awareness that the high level of complexity found in life forms could not have resulted from chance occurrences, as Darwinists believe. This, plus the fact that these complex systems display all the characteristics of purposive design, has led to the emergence of an "intelligent design" movement in the scientific community. This movement has aroused vigorous opposition, and has even been labeled "scientific heresy" by some.

Interestingly, the reason for the opposition is *not* that the facts and observations on which the movement is based are flawed. Law professor Phillip Johnson, author of *Darwin on Trial*, observed that "materialists do not challenge his [Behe's] facts. They just dismiss the logical inference from the facts as philosophically unacceptable" (*Christianity Today*, Jan. 6, 1997, 64).

Is evolutionary theory really "scientific?" The common assumption that the evolutionists' account of origins is scientific while the biblical account is a matter of faith is seriously flawed. Evolution proposes that the origin of all things, from our earth to the various living forms found on it, can be explained by the operation of natural processes which operate consistently throughout the universe and for all time.

Evolutionary theory was proposed by Darwin, who suggested possible mechanisms by which changes in living creatures might take place. His ideas, extended by his disciples, were quickly accepted by the scientific world. Initial arguments favoring the theory seemed impressive, and evidence to support it was quickly provided by partisans in many scientific disciplines. Paleontologists presented fossils; biologists traced similarities in animal forms.

But the early promise of proof of the theory remains unfulfilled. No fossil evidence has been provided that shows transition from one distinct life form to another. When superficial similarities were looked beyond, evidence pointed *away from* rather than toward direct-line evolution with family and genus. Today

our growing knowledge of microbiology and of complex biological structures is rapidly demonstrating more and more flaws in basic evolutionary assumptions. And now proponents of the growing "intelligent design" movement are providing more and more evidence which points to the likelihood that living creatures have a Designer.

Even the older references to "simple, one-celled animals" has been debunked, as microbiologists learn how complex single-cell creatures really are. When scientists are confronted with the facts about origins but refuse to question their commitment to the evolutionary view, it is clear that evolution is as much a "faith" for the materialist as is creation for the theist.

Eugenie Scott, executive director of the National Center for Science Education, made this very clear when she labeled intelligent design theorists as heretics, and declared, "You can't call it science if you allow in supernatural explanations" (*Christianity Today*, Jan. 6, 1997, 65).

In essence, the materialist argues that it is valid to reason from evidence provided by science . . . if you accept only conclusions that support materialist assumptions. Any evidence which points toward God and the supernatural is ruled out as "unscientific."

A flawed faith. There are many additional lines of scientific evidence to which we might appeal to demonstrate that the evolutionary explanation of origins by the materialists is fatally flawed. The line of evidence above is intended to show two things: (1) that we need not accept evolution as a "scientific fact," and (2) that evolutionary assumptions are actually rooted in faith rather than science.

The tragedy is that while many modern scientists are beginning to question evolutionary assumptions, most people assume that the evolutionary account of origins is a fact rather than a dubious theory. As a result, many even in our churches operate with a flawed God-concept. Rather than seeing God through the lens of creation's grand miracle, as the One who acts freely in our world of space and time, many limit God to a distant and shadowy "spiritual" realm where he has little impact on daily life. How different such a God is from the God of creation. For the God of creation is powerful, active in our world, unlimited in his freedom, able to help and heal us NOW.

GOD AS CREATOR: OUR RESPONSE TO THE FIRST GRAND MIRACLE

Psalm 77:14 reminds us, "You are the God who does wonders; / You have declared Your strength among the peoples." The psalmists go on to remind us often that we are to nurture our awareness that our God is One who does wonders.

- "I will praise You, O Lord, with my whole heart; / I will tell of all Your marvelous works" (Ps. 9:1).
- "Come and see the works of God; / He is awesome in His doing toward the sons of men" (Ps. 66:5).
- "We give thanks to You, O God, we give thanks!/ For Your wondrous works declare that Your name is near" (Ps. 75:1).
- "We will not hide them from their children, / Telling to the generation to come the praises of the LORD, / And His strength and His wonderful works that He has done" (Ps. 78:4).
- "That they may set their hope in God, / And not forget the works of God, / But keep His commandments" (Ps. 78:7).
- "Remember His marvelous works which He has done, / His wonders, and the judgments of His mouth" (Ps. 105:5).
- "He has made His wonderful works to be remembered" (Ps. 111:4).

How are we to "remember" this first of his grand miracles, creation, and how will nurturing an awareness of it affect our lives?

Creation described (Genesis 1, 2). Theologians describe the creation of the material universe as taking place *ex nihilo.* In the beginning, nothing existed except God. Then God spoke, and the entire material universe came into being. The myriads of stars, the earth, the moon, were all designed by God and brought into being by his power. The varied forms of life that exist on our earth's surface were also designed by God, and brought into being by him.

Some have interpreted the Genesis story to affirm that God directly created each breed of dog or cat, every strain of wheat, each different color of tulip. What the creation story actually teaches is that God created every "kind" of living creature, enabling them to reproduce only with others of the same "kind" (Gen. 1:21, 24, 25). Within the genetic code of each "kind" that God created there existed from the beginning the possibility of wonderful variations of size, shape, and color. The many breeds of animals and strains of vegetation that exist today developed from and within these original "kinds."

The emphasis within the theory of evolution on natural selection can and does account for this kind of variation in the natural universe. But it was God who created the original kinds from which the variety has sprung. There has been no "evolution" of the original kinds, nor has there been reproduction across kinds, as if a mammal mated with a bird or reptile.

But most important, Scripture's creation story sets the creation of human beings apart from the creation of all other animal life. Only human beings are made, as Genesis 1:26 declares, "in Our image, according to Our likeness." While sharing our physical nature with the animal creation, human beings possess a unique spiritual nature that has its origin in God's gift of his own image-likeness. Like God, human beings are persons. And Scripture's clear testimony is that each person, like God, is destined to exist as a self-aware individual, with his or her own personal identity, on into eternity.

The biblical account of creation thus makes unique claims about origins which have dramatic impact on our view of the world and life's meaning.

"In the beginning, God . . . . "

Some implications of the biblical account of creation. The material universe was created by God. According to Scripture, God is distinct from, and greater than, the universe he created. It follows that the material universe is subject to him, and that God is not limited in his ability to act by any "natural laws" that operate in the universe. Given a God who created and shaped all that exists, there is no reason to suppose that this all-powerful being cannot act in any way that he chooses within his own creation.

The existence of "natural law" within the material universe is no barrier to God's performing miracles which seem to us to "violate" natural law. God is free to act in any way he chooses, for he is sovereign over all he has made.

Human beings, as a special creation of God, are special to him. The sacred history recorded in Scripture is actually salvation history—an account of what God has done to bring salvation from sin and sin's consequences to humanity. The love of God for human beings, demonstrated over and over again in his Word, helps us to understand why God *should* perform miracles. Miracles are not random expressions of God's power, performed simply because God can do them. Miracles are an integral part of salvation history, linked to God's purposes and serving as vivid expressions of his love.

Thus, belief in the grand miracle of creation provides a solid basis for belief in the lesser miracles and wonders that Scripture reports. If we see God as the God of creation, sovereign over all he has made—and understand that all he does is linked with his salvation purpose—we will not shrink from belief in the "little" miracles the Bible records.

Why doubt that the God who brought into being all that exists should find it difficult to divide the waters of the Red Sea? Why question whether the God who formed the eye should be able to give sight to a man who was born blind? Or that the God whose sovereignty is clearly affirmed by his creation can act as he chooses in his world today?

If we approach the question of miracles and wonders with the assumption of the materialists—that all that exists can be accounted for without reference to the supernatural—we will rule out the possibility of miracles. But if we approach them in the firm conviction that God created and rules the universe, we will at least be open to the possibility of miracles. As we examine the miracles of Scripture, we should recognize that each is linked with God's deep love for humanity and his salvation purpose. Then we will come to understand the distinctives that set biblical miracles apart from "magic" signs and pagan superstitions.

THE MIRACLE OF THE INCARNATION

Christian faith is centered in the person of Jesus Christ. Jesus is considered special by most people. Even Muslims acknowledge him as a prophet. And he is given a place on every list of humankind's great religious leaders. In his own time, Jesus was acknowledged to have special powers and to perform miracles. But in the world in which he spent his earthly ministry, Jesus' miracles would not have been viewed as absolute proof of his divinity.

FIRST-CENTURY MAGIC AND MAGICIANS

In the hellenistic world, distinctions between magic and religion were not very clear. The words *magos*, *magicus*, and *mageia* were used with a variety of meanings, ranging from

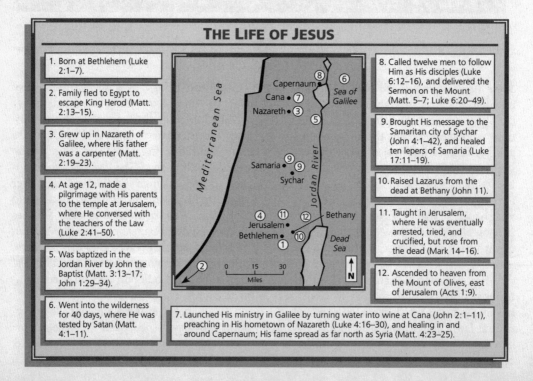

THE LIFE OF JESUS

1. Born at Bethlehem (Luke 2:1–7).

2. Family fled to Egypt to escape King Herod (Matt. 2:13–15).

3. Grew up in Nazareth of Galilee, where His father was a carpenter (Matt. 2:19–23).

4. At age 12, made a pilgrimage with His parents to the temple at Jerusalem, where He conversed with the teachers of the Law (Luke 2:41–50).

5. Was baptized in the Jordan River by John the Baptist (Matt. 3:13–17; John 1:29–34).

6. Went into the wilderness for 40 days, where He was tested by Satan (Matt. 4:1–11).

8. Called twelve men to follow Him as His disciples (Luke 6:12–16), and delivered the Sermon on the Mount (Matt. 5–7; Luke 6:20–49).

9. Brought His message to the Samaritan city of Sychar (John 4:1–42), and healed ten lepers of Samaria (Luke 17:11–19).

10. Raised Lazarus from the dead at Bethany (John 11).

11. Taught in Jerusalem, where He was eventually arrested, tried, and crucified, but rose from the dead (Mark 14–16).

12. Ascended to heaven from the Mount of Olives, east of Jerusalem (Acts 1:9).

7. Launched His ministry in Galilee by turning water into wine at Cana (John 2:1–11), preaching in His hometown of Nazareth (Luke 4:16–30), and healing in and around Capernaum; His fame spread as far north as Syria (Matt. 4:23–25).

Mediterranean Sea

Capernaum
Cana
Nazareth
Sea of Galilee
Jordan River
Samaria
Sychar
Jerusalem
Bethlehem
Bethany
Dead Sea

0   15   30
Miles

N

the religious to witchcraft. In Rome, magic was viewed as subversive. Chaldean astrologers were driven from Rome in 33 B.C. on the grounds that they were magicians, and in 13 B.C. Augustus ordered all books on occult subjects burned. In A.D. 16 magicians and astrologers were expelled from Italy, an edict reinforced in A.D. 69 and 89.

These facts remind us that in the first century magic was taken seriously, or it would not have been outlawed. The repeated edicts against magic tell us that it was widely practiced. It is no surprise that in the world of the first century persons might present themselves to others as magoi, possessors of special powers.

How magi worked their magic. Magicians generally used spells to aid or attack others. An example is this spell, included by Lewis and Reinhold in their *Roman Civilization Sourcebook II* (New York: 1955), evoked against a charioteer named Eucherius:

I conjure you up, holy beings and holy names; join in aiding this spell and bind, enchant, thwart, strike, overturn, conspire against, destroy, kill, and break Eucherius, the charioteer and all his horses tomorrow in the circus at Rome. May he not leave the barriers well, may he not be quick in the contest, may he not outstrip anyone; may he not make the turns well; may he not win any prizes; and, if he has pressed someone hard, may he not come off the victor; and, if he follows someone from behind, may he not overtake him; but may he meet with an accident, may he be bound, may he be broken, may he be dragged along by your power in the morning and afternoon races. Now! Now! Quickly! Quickly!

Marlene LeFever, a senior editor at Cook Communications, teaches a Sunday school class in a little town outside Colorado Springs known for its covens of witches. One Easter Sunday when she told the story of the Resurrection, a nine-year-old girl in her class said in awe, "He must have been a really powerful warlock." Her immediate reaction to the miracle story was to assume that it was accomplished by magic.

In the first century, stories of Jesus' miracles might have suggested to many people just what the resurrection story implied for the nine-year-old in Marlene's class: Jesus must be a powerful sorcerer or magician.

FIRST-CENTURY CONCEPTS OF THE "DIVINE MAN"

The overlap of magic and religion in the first-century world allowed for another explanation for the miraculous. An individual might possibly be a true miracle worker, whose acts depended not on his mastery of occult practice but on true superiority of being. One example of the significance of this distinction is found in Porphyry's *Life of Plotinus.* Before mentioning Plotinus's feats, the author took care to establish his subject as a "divine man" who possessed a divine guiding spirit. Porphyry wrote,

Plotinus possessed by birth something more than is accorded to other men. An Egyptian priest who had arrived in Rome and, through some friend, had been presented to the philosopher, became desirous of displaying his powers to him, and he offered to evoke a visible manifestation of Plotinus's presiding spirit. Plotinus readily consented and the evocation was made in the Temple of Isis, the only place, they say, which the Egyptian could find pure in Rome.

At the summons, a divinity appeared, not a being of the spirit ranks, and the Egyptian exclaimed, "You are singularly blessed; the guiding-spirit within you is none of the lower degree, but a God." It was not possible, however, to interrogate or even to contemplate this God any further, for the priest's assistant, who had been holding the birds to prevent them from flying away, strangled them, whether through jealousy or in terror. Thus, Plotinus had for indwelling spirit a being of the more divine degree, and he kept his own divine spirit unceasingly intent upon that inner presence. (Cited in Plotinus, *The Enneads,* tr. Stephen MacKenna, London: 1965, p. 8.)

Porphyry then went on to describe several feats which he argued must be viewed as miracles rather than as magical manipulations because of Plotinus's obvious superiority to ordinary men.

The world of the first century was well acquainted with the idea that a person with a special relationship to a deity might perform miracles. To the first-century mind, one did not have to *be* God to do the kind of works ascribed to Jesus by the early Christians.

JEWISH CONCEPTS OF THE SPIRIT WORLD

It is notable that the Old Testament does not describe the kinds of miracles that Jesus performed with regularity. For example, there is no mention in the Old Testament of a prophet restoring a cripple's legs, or giving sight to the blind, or walking on water, or casting out a demon. So it is clear that Jesus' miracles had to be explained in some way peculiar to Jewish culture and theology.

The authenticity of the miracles is attested by the reaction of Jesus' opponents. They didn't deny the reality of miracles that large crowds had witnessed. They couldn't deny what so many knew to be true from personal experience. So instead of trying to cast doubt on the miracles themselves, Christ's opponents attempted to create doubt about the *meaning of the miracles.*

The Jewish leaders didn't accuse Jesus of magic. Christ used none of the incantations or materials associated with magic in the ancient world. And the Jewish leaders couldn't account for the miracles on the basis that Jesus had a unique relationship with God without being forced to acknowledge his spiritual authority. So the leaders devised another tactic. They began to whisper that "this fellow does not cast out demons except by Beelzebub, the ruler of the demons" (Matt. 12:24).

In first-century Judaism, much religious literature focused on the supernatural world, which was populated by angels and demons (See *Every Good and Evil Angel in the Bible,* Nelson, 1997). So it was not far-fetched to imply that while Jesus' powers were supernatural, they originated in the dark side of the spiritual realm, and that Satan energized Jesus and enabled him to work his miracles.

Jesus quickly brought this charge into the open and refuted it. If Jesus cast out demons by the power of the prince of demons, he reasoned, Satan must be fighting against himself! This meant Satan's kingdom would surely fall apart from internal strife (Matt. 12:25, 26).

In fact, by casting out demons Jesus entered Satan's own "house" (realm) and *bound* Satan, so that even the devil could not successfully oppose Christ's actions (Matt. 12:29)! Jesus' opponents had to come up with a better explanation than this to explain the source of Jesus' powers.

This survey of beliefs about miracle workers in the first century helps us identify the compelling issue raised by Jesus' miracles. The issue was not, "Did they happen?" It was not, "Can the miracles be explained away as hallucinations or the product of mass hysteria?" The issue was, and is, *Who can this miracle-working person be?"*

In the context of the first-century world, the miracles Jesus worked led Jew or pagan to focus on the person of Jesus. Could Jesus be a magician? Could he be someone like Plotinus, who had a special relationship with a deity? Could he be an emissary of Satan, empowered by demons?

In answer to this issue raised by Jesus' miracles, the Gospel writers and apostles offered a unique response. Jesus was none of these. Jesus was God the Creator come into his universe in the flesh. Jesus was God incarnate: truly human, fully God.

This answer, as uncomfortable as it was to the Jewish religious leaders of the first century, is plainly taught in the Old Testament as well as in the New!

JESUS' MIRACLES IDENTIFIED HIM AS THE MESSIAH

At one point in Jesus' ministry, the disciples of his cousin, John the Baptist, came to Christ and asked him if he were really the Messiah. John had been thrown into prison by Herod the tetrarch (Matt. 14:3–12) and had begun to wonder about Jesus. Like other Jews of his time, John had expected the Messiah to throw off the yoke of Roman oppression and establish an earthly kingdom. When Jesus failed to meet these expectations, even such a person of faith as John the Baptist began to doubt.

Jesus answered his cousin by telling John's disciples to "go and tell John the things which you hear and see" (Matt. 11:4). Christ then described what he was doing in terms linked in Isaiah 29:18, 35:4–6, and especially in Isaiah 61:1, to the ministry of the promised Messiah.

The blind see and the lame walk; the lepers are cleansed and the deaf hear; the dead are raised up and the poor have the gospel preached to them (Matt. 11:5).

No Old Testament man of God performed the kind of miracles which Jesus did regularly. These miracles clearly identified him as the Christ, the Messiah whom God had promised to send as a Savior for his people. No one who knew the Old Testament prophecies—no one who witnessed the miracles that Jesus performed—should have had any question about his identity as the Messiah. But there is even more than this.

❖

Healing miracles connected Jesus to Isaiah's description of the Messiah.

THE OLD TESTAMENT IDENTIFIED THE MESSIAH AS GOD

The specific miracles that Jesus performed identified him as the Messiah. And the Old Testament identified the Messiah as God.

James Smith examined 73 key Old Testament prophecies about the Messiah. He identified 13 of these which teach the deity of the Messiah.

1. "For I know that my Redeemer lives, and he shall stand at last on the earth" (Job 19:25). The role of the Redeemer was clearly messianic. Here Job expressed confidence that the Redeemer "lives" even in Job's own time, and that he will "stand at last on the earth."

2. " 'Behold, I send My messenger, and he will prepare the way before Me. And the Lord, whom you seek, will suddenly come to His temple, even the Messenger of the covenant, in whom you delight. Behold, he is coming,' says the Lord of Hosts" (Mal. 3:1). The promised Messiah, the Messenger of the covenant, is to be the Lord himself, who will "suddenly come to His temple."

3. "Of old You laid the foundation of the earth, and the heavens are the work of Your hands" (Ps. 102:25). This verse, from the messianic Psalm 102, is quoted in Hebrews 1:10–12 as addressed by God to Jesus. The psalm goes on to affirm the eternity of the Messiah as well as his identity as the Creator himself.

4. "Your throne, O God, is forever and ever; a scepter of righteousness is the scepter of Your kingdom" (Ps. 45:6). This verse is from another messianic psalm. It is also applied to Jesus in Hebrews 1. Here the ruler of the messianic kingdom promised in the Old Testament is identified as God himself.

5. "For unto us a child is born, unto us a Son is given; And the government will be upon his shoulder. And his name will be called Wonderful, Counselor, Mighty

God, Everlasting Father, Prince of Peace" (Isa. 9:6). This pivotal Old Testament verse pointed out that the child born in fulfillment of the Messiah prophecies is to be "a Son . . . given." The fact that this son is God the Son is underlined by the titles given him in this verse. The one born as a human being is in reality the "Mighty God," the "Everlasting Father." This last term translated as "Father (source) of Eternity," placed the Messiah outside of time as the God who existed before Creation took place.

6. "Behold, the virgin shall conceive and bear a Son, and shall call his name Immanuel" (Isa. 7:14). Written about 700 years before Christ's birth, this verse described a conception that will take place without a human father, the offspring of which would be a son named Immanuel. In Hebrew the name Immanuel means "With us is God." Through a virgin birth, God will come in the flesh to be "with us" as a true human being.

7. "But you, Bethlehem Ephrathah, though you are little among the thousands of Judah, yet out of you shall come forth to Me the One to be Ruler in Israel, whose goings forth are from of old, from everlasting" (Mic. 5:2). This verse identified the Messiah's birthplace and affirmed his pre-existence.

8. "I will be his Father, and he shall be My son" (2 Sam. 7:14). This phrase from the Davidic covenant indicated that the Messiah, who is David's descendant, was also to be God's Son, a theme also addressed in the following several passages.

9. "I will declare the decree: the Lord has said to Me, You are My Son, today I have begotten You" (Ps. 2:7).

10. "I will make him My firstborn, the highest of the kings of the earth" (Ps. 89:27). Here the word "firstborn" is used in the technical sense of "heir."

11. "Out of Egypt I called My son" (Hos. 11:1). This verse is quoted in Matt. 2:15 and applied to the journey of Jesus and

his family to and from Egypt when threatened by King Herod.

12. "Afterward the children of Israel shall return and seek the Lord their God and David their king" (Hos. 3:5). The Hebrew in this verse identified the Lord (here Yahweh, God's personal name) with the person of "David their king." Christ the descendant of David, who as Messiah fulfilled the promises given to David, is the Yahweh (Lord) of the Old Testament.

13. "Their king will pass before them, with the Lord at their head" (Mic. 2:13). Here again the Hebrew identified the messianic king with the Lord, Yahweh of the Old Testament. The messianic king and Yahweh are one and the same (James Smith, *What the Bible Teaches about the Promised Messiah*, Nelson, 1993).

Thus, hundreds of years before the birth of Jesus, the writers of the Old Testament predicted that a person would be born of a virgin. That person was to be God himself, yet at the same time the human descendant of King David. He and he alone would fulfill all the prophecies concerning Israel's Messiah. This person would be the Son of God—indeed, God the Son, who is the Yahweh of the Old Testament—who has existed forever and is himself the source of eternity.

In spite of the testimony of Jesus' miracles to his identity as the Messiah—and in spite of the testimony of Scripture to the Messiah's identity as God incarnate—Israel's leaders refused to accept Jesus Christ for who he is.

THE NEW TESTAMENT IDENTIFIED JESUS AS GOD THE SON

The New Testament, in complete harmony with the Old, gives a decisive answer to the issue raised by Jesus' miracles: "Who is he?" The answer is that Jesus is God come in the flesh. John's Gospel begins with this great affirmation:

In the beginning was the Word, and the Word was with God, and the Word was God. He was in the beginning with God. All things were made through Him, and without him nothing was made that was made. . . . And the Word became flesh and dwelt among us, and we beheld his glory, the glory as of the only begotten of the Father, full of grace and truth (John 1:1–3, 14).

This great affirmation is repeated throughout the Scriptures, which tell us that "God so loved the world that he gave his only begotten Son, that whoever believes in him should not perish but have everlasting life" (John 3:16). Colossians and Hebrews add their testimony to the first century's Hellenistic and Jewish populations that Jesus is indeed God in the flesh.

He is the image of the invisible God, the firstborn over all creation. For by him all things were created that are in heaven and that are on earth, visible and invisible. . . . All things were created through him and for him. And he is before all things, and in him all things consist (Col. 1:15–17).

God, who at various times and in various ways spoke in time past to the fathers by the prophets, has in these last days spoken to us by His Son, whom also He has appointed heir of all things, through whom He made the worlds; who being the brightness of His glory and the express image of His person, and upholding all things by the word of His power, when He had by Himself purged our sins, sat down at the right hand of the Majesty on high (Heb. 1:1–3).

Similar passages and references can be multiplied. Together they leave no doubt that the early Christians had a decisive and stunning answer to the issue posed by Jesus' miracles: "Who is this man?" The answer, found in the Old Testament and affirmed by Christ

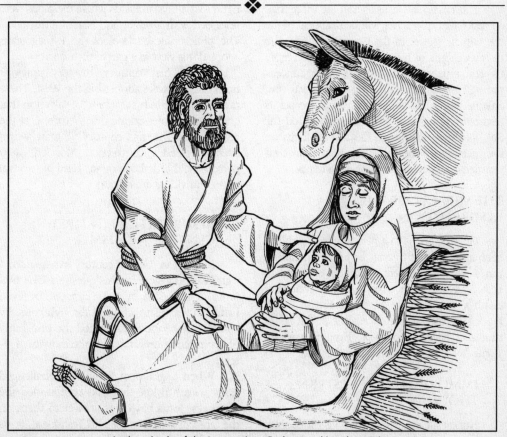

In the miracle of the Incarnation, God entered into humanity.

himself and the apostles is, "Jesus Christ is God the Son; God come in human flesh."

Compared with the grand miracle of Incarnation—the miracle that IS Jesus Christ—the miracles performed by Jesus pale to relative insignificance. Why should we be surprised, if God the Creator walked among us as a human being, that he should be able to straighten bent limbs or give hearing to the deaf? Why doubt that, if God the Creator walked among us as a human being, he could still a storm with a gesture, walk on water as easily as on land, or expel the demons that tormented helpless victims?

If we accept this grand miracle, the Incarnation of Jesus, the credibility of all other miracles follows naturally and easily—especially when we link those miracles with salvation history and the purposes which God's Son came to accomplish.

Those who see Jesus as nothing more than a great religious teacher will be skeptical of the the miracle stories in the Gospels. Those who dismiss claims of his deity will tend to ignore the real issue which his miracles raise, concentrating instead on explaining them away. But anyone who looks to Scripture and accepts its testimony that Jesus is the Messiah—God the Son incarnate in human flesh—will focus on the meaning of the miracles rather than concentrate on whether or not they were real.

THE MIRACLE OF THE RESURRECTION

What happens to a person after death has been a concern of human beings from earliest times. No clearly defined beliefs emerged in East or West, other than the hope that after death a person might enter a realm in which he or she could experience some of the better things of earthly existence. Even this was a vague hope, by no means shared by all.

IMMORTALITY IN WESTERN THOUGHT

Homer's *Iliad* opens with a vision of souls being cast into Hades. For Homer the soul

(*psyche*) bore a resemblance to the physical body, but it was drained of all that made the individual vital and real. Death meant passage to a dreary world where shadows passed their time in weary, meaningless wanderings. The only meaningful immortality a person might gain was won by accomplishments that caused him or her to be remembered.

In the face of this grim expectation, some people feigned indifference. Many tombstones in the Roman world bore the initials NFFNSNC, standing for a Latin phrase which means, "I was not, I was, I am not, I care not."

In time, the belief that the afterlife involved reward and punishment emerged in the West. Its full development is seen in Virgil's *Aeneid*. The poet depicted the dead carried across the river Styx by the boatman Charon, to face a court which would send them either to the left, to Tartarus the place of punishment, or to the right, to the Elysian Fields where the pious were rewarded with a bright and beautiful existence. The philosophical school of the Pythagoreans adopted this view as a part of their doctrine.

In the first century, mystery religions from the East were adopted in the West. These promised their initiates a kind of salvation that guaranteed a blessed afterlife. Yet none of the religions of the first-century Roman world even imagined a resurrection. Most educated persons held little hope of any kind of survival of the individual after death.

RESURRECTION IN FIRST-CENTURY JUDAISM

Judaism in the first century experienced a significant division on this question. The majority of Jews, led by the Pharisees, believed firmly in the resurrection of the righteous. By contrast, the Sadducees denied the possibility of resurrection or survival of the individual after death.

When a group of Sadducees challenged Jesus with a riddle that had confounded the Pharisees, Jesus based his answer to them on the tense of a verb in the Old Testament. Jesus pointed out that God had said to Moses, "I am the God of Abraham. . . ." (Mark 12:26). Because God said "I am" rather than "I was" proves that the long-dead Abraham still was self-conscious and "alive" in Moses' time! Jesus also noted that any assumption that the resurrected would live the same kind of life people have now is unwarranted. "When they rise from the dead, they neither marry nor are given in marriage" (Mark 12:25).

Thus, while in Judaism there was no clear idea of what life after death would be like, there was at least a belief in resurrection. The awareness that God intended to raise human beings from the dead was not clearly defined until later in Old Testament times. On this point, one scholar commented:

The OT emphasizes the blessings of living on earth in obedient, intimate relationship with the Lord. In most cases, the "salvation" spoken of in the OT is deliverance from some present enemy or trouble. Yet it would be a mistake to conclude that the OT is a stranger to the doctrine of resurrection, or that OT saints enjoyed no such hope. In fact, saints who "died in faith" did look forward to a better country, to a city God would one day found (Heb. 11:8–16).

Many OT references may allude to the possibility of resurrection (cf. Gen. 3:22–24; Deut. 32:39; 2 Kings 2:11,12). Other statements, whose meaning may not be perfectly clear, still make sense only in the context of a belief in resurrection (cf. Job 19:25–27; Ps.16:9–11).

When we reach the prophets, we see this belief expressed clearly and confidently. One day death will be defeated (Isa. 25:8), and "your dead will live" as their bodies rise when "the earth gives birth to her dead" (Isa. 26:19). Daniel is very explicit. Those who "sleep in the dust of the earth will awake; some to everlasting life, others to shame and everlasting contempt" (Dan. 12:2, 3) (*Richards' Complete Bible Handbook*, 1987, 299).

Yet, belief in resurrection was focused in the distant future, when history reached God's appointed end. Resurrection was a hope. Then suddenly, in Christ, resurrection became an experienced reality!

THE RESURRECTION OF JESUS

This third of the grand miracles is so essential to Christian faith that the apostle Paul wrote, "If Christ is not risen, then our preaching is empty and your faith is also empty" (1 Cor. 15:14). It is striking that the teaching of every book of the New Testament is rooted in the firm conviction that Jesus Christ died a real death, and three days later was literally, physically raised from the dead.

In the opening verses of Romans, Paul linked the second and third of the grand miracles. Paul was an apostle of that gospel "which He [God] promised before through His prophets in the Holy Scriptures, concerning His Son Jesus Christ our Lord, who was born of the seed of David according to the flesh, and declared to be the Son of God with power according to the Spirit of holiness, by the resurrection from the dead" (Rom. 1:1–4). Jesus' resurrection from the dead was the final, decisive proof that He is Who He claimed to be: the human descendant of David and yet at the same time God the Son.

The resurrection of Jesus is also unmistakable confirmation of God's intention to raise believers in Jesus. Christ is the firstfruits—an image drawn from the Old Testament. Worshipers presented to the Lord the first crops to ripen in thankfulness for the harvest to follow (1 Cor. 15:20, 23). Jesus' resurrection is the guarantee that we too will rise.

This, the third of the three grand miracles of the Bible, was undoubtedly the most compelling to men and women of the first century. No one in the Roman Empire had even imagined a future resurrection. They had hoped for some kind of survival after death, but their hope was at best vague and uncertain. And then the Christian gospel broke through the darkness with its promise of full restoration to life!

The anguish of separation from loved ones could now be soothed by the expectation of seeing them once again. And death lost its most fearsome qualities in the promise that we will awake from it as from a sleep, restored and whole.

The resurrection of Jesus is perhaps the most disturbing of the grand miracles. To the materialist, who believes that this universe is the total reality, death is absolute finality. The materialist believes the person and his body are indistinguishable. Once the body dies, the person no longer exists.

Yet Jesus arose. And this forces us to make a choice.

- We can perceive reality as the materialist does. Or we can accept Scripture's perspective, and adopt a view of reality shaped by history's three grand miracles.
- We can accept Scripture's doctrine of creation and believe in a God who exists apart from and over the material universe.
- We can accept Scripture's report of the Incarnation, and put our faith in Jesus as God the Son, come among us as a human being.
- And we can accept Scripture's triumphant proclamation of Jesus' resurrection, believing God's promise that all who trust Jesus as Savior will share in the new life He has won.

So we see again as we begin our review of the miracles of Scripture that the real issue is not whether they happened. No one who approaches miracles with the materialist's assumption will accept miracle stories as true. And one who approaches miracles with his or her perspective shaped by belief in the three grand miracles of the Scriptures will have no doubt that God could do what the Bible records.

II. OBJECTIONS TO MIRACLES

The word *miracle* is not an easy term to define. This is especially true because we use the word so loosely. A baseball team that wins its last five games to reach the playoffs is likely to generate headlines about a "miracle finish." And many a sincere believer has asked God for "a miracle" when a loved one is seriously ill.

So before we look at objections that have been raised about miracles in general and especially about biblical miracles, we need to have at least a working definition of what a miracle is. For now, let's adopt the following general definition. Essentially, what we mean by a miracle—and what critics of miracles object to—is the idea that there have been or are . . .

extraordinary events
caused by God
which have religious significance.

The empty tomb affirms that Jesus was who He said He was, and believers can be assured they will be raised to eternal life.

HISTORIC ASSAULTS ON MIRACLES

Trench, in his *Notes on Miracles,* traced objections that have been raised to the stories of Jesus' miracles.

The Jewish leaders of Christ's own time attacked Jesus' miracles. They couldn't deny that what Jesus did constituted extraordinary events. There were too many witnesses. Nor could they doubt that the events had religious significance. So the Pharisees started a rumor that Jesus' miracles were not caused by God but by the devil (Matt. 12:24). If Satan were the source of his power to cast out demons, Jesus answered, Satan would be fighting against his own, and unable to maintain his authority (Matt. 12:26). Thus, the charge is foolish and inconsistent.

The heathen in the first centuries of the Christian era argued that similar wonders had been performed by men like Aesculapius and Apollonius. Hierocles, who was governor of Bythnia in the last decade of the first century, argued that "we do not account him who has done such things for a god, only for a man beloved of the gods: while the Christians, on the contrary, on the ground of a few insignificant wonder-works, proclaim their Jesus for a God."

This attack focused on the religious significance of the miracles as argued by early Christians. The critics did not doubt that such wonders had been done. They argued that others also performed such feats through powers bestowed by pagan gods.

This attack is not relevant today, since no contemporary miracles are being "played off" against Christ's.

The philosopher Spinoza in the 17th century argued that the idea of miracles was absurd. He believed the universe was uncreated, and that "God" is identical with the material universe. His attack was rooted in the conviction that the universe operates by fixed, immutable, natural laws. Miracles [i.e., extraordinary events] to Spinoza were violations of natural law and therefore impossible, and belief in them was irrational.

Spinoza's argument begs the question. He starts from the anti-supernaturalist premises that "God" and nature are identical and that the laws of nature are immutable. Anyone who begins with these assumptions will, of course, decide that belief in miracles is irrational. Spinoza's belief in a pantheistic universe, not the force of his arguments, determined his conclusions.

The skeptic philosopher David Hume in the 18th century agreed that as extraordinary events, miracles are violations of natural law. He also argued that natural laws are unalterably uniform. But rather than base his argument on a philosophical assumption as Spinoza did, Hume argued from experience.

Hume declared that what we call natural laws are defined by what we human beings observe to be regular occurrences. Because all of us experience events governed by natural laws as regular occurrences, we have to give great weight to the idea that they are unalterable.

Miracles, on the other hand, are by definition extraordinary events. As such, they could be experienced by very few persons. Thus, we have little evidence for miracles and should give little weight to miracle stories. What Hume argued is not that miracles are impossible, but that they are *incredible.*

The problem with Hume's argument is that he must *assume* uniformity of experience of natural laws. Suppose we were to live in a country where dogs are black. We set out to prove that *all* dogs are black, and so we survey everyone in the land. We ask them if they have seen dogs, and they say "Yes." We ask if they have seen anything other than a black dog, and they say "No." Finally, we add up our results. A total of 1,300,012 people have seen dogs. And all the dogs they have seen are black.

Can we conclude that all dogs are black? Not at all—only that no one we surveyed has ever seen anything other than a black dog.

Now suppose that we happen on a visitor from another country, and ask him if he has seen a dog. He answers, "Yes." Then we ask if all dogs he has seen are black, and he tells us, "No. In my country there are white dogs, black dogs, and spotted dogs."

If we were to use Hume's criteria, we would have to label this man's report incredible and unworthy of belief. Why? Because the weight of the evidence [1,300,012 to 1] is that all dogs are black. We must discount the one report of white and spotted dogs.

But what if we were to meet other people from that country who also report seeing white, black, and spotted dogs? How many witnesses would we need to consider the possibility that other than black dogs exist? Would we accept 1,300,012 to 10? Or 1,300,012 to 100? Or to 1000?

C. S. Lewis pointed out the fallacy of Hume's argument:

Now of course we must agree with Hume that if there is absolutely "uniform experience" against miracles, if in other words they have never happened, why then they never have. Unfortunately we know the experience against them to be uniform only if we know that all the reports of them are false. And we can know all the reports to be false only if we know already that miracles have never occurred. In fact, we are arguing in a circle (C. S. Lewis, *Miracles*, 102).

Hume never intended to survey every person who has ever lived. He only intended to count up those who had not witnessed a miracle and to use that number to insist that any miracle report was false. Hume had *decided beforehand* that reports of miracles found in Scripture and in other sources must be false.

The rationalist Paulus in the early 19th century focused his attention on the idea that Jesus' miracles were extraordinary events. He denied this, suggesting there was a rational explanation for what the Bible records. Rather than heal an impotent man at the pool of Bethesda, for instance, Jesus detected an imposter. Christ was not walking on the water but on the shore of Lake Galilee. It only appeared to the disciples that he was walking on the water.

This approach, which makes Jesus out to be the consummate trickster or the apostles to be unbelievably naïve, has few adherents today.

The theologian Bultmann in the 20th century recast miracle stories as myth. The third criterion of a miracle as defined earlier is that it has religious significance. The European theologian Bultmann argued that the miracle stories have significance that transcends history, and so serve as myths intended to convey deep spiritual truths. Such stories become articles of faith, and as such the issue of objective verification is irrelevant. All that can and, indeed, needs to be established is that the early disciples believed these stories and the spiritual truths they conveyed.

While Bultmann's argument seems to suggest that the historicity of miracles is irrelevant, he was actually determined to deny the miracle stories any possible claim to objective reality. This bias is shown by Geisler in his excellent book on miracles:

It is evident that the basis of Bultmann's antisupernaturalism is not evidential, nor even open to real discussion. It is something he holds no matter how many witnesses are cited. The dogmatism of his language is revealing. Miracles are "incredible," "irrational," "no longer possible," "meaningless," "utterly inconceivable," "simply impossible," "intolerable." Hence, the "only honest way" for modern people is to hold that miracles are "nothing else than spiritual" and that the physical world is "immune from interference" in a supernatural way. This is not the language of one open to historical evidence for a miracle. It looks more like a mind that does not wish to be "confused" with the facts! (Geisler, *Miracles and the Modern Mind*, 72).

How different Bultmann's approach to miracles is from that of the New Testament, which affirms that its writers have not conveyed "cunningly devised fables" (2 Pet. 1:16), but have spoken only of that to which they and many others were eyewitnesses (compare Acts 1:3; 1 John 1:3).

Contemporary philosophers have continued the attack on miracles, but their arguments tend to be refinements of those discussed above. Their arguments seem to reflect their assumptions rather than to prove their positions.

For some of the critics, miracles cannot happen because natural law cannot be violated. But this argument assumes that the material universe is all that exists or that, if there is a God, he is unable to act in the material realm.

Other critics argue that miracles need not be believed because it can never be proven that they have occurred. This argument rules out ahead of time the testimony of Scripture or any other witness to miracles. It is tantamount to saying, "Even if you see a miracle, I do not have to and will not believe your report."

Sophisticated statements of these two basic positions may sound compelling when couched in philosopher's words. But the fact remains that the issue of belief in miracles will be settled long before the arguments are addressed. We will either be committed to a concept of God that is defined by the three grand miracles of Creation, Incarnation, and Resurrection. Or we will adopt the evolutionist's materialistic view of reality.

If we are committed to the concept of God defined by the grand miracles, the idea that extraordinary events with religious significance should be caused by God will not surprise us. If we adopt the materialist's approach, we will deny this possibility, using those arguments which make us most comfortable with our choice.

If we believe in the God of Scripture, no compelling argument against miracles will force us to doubt their reality.

III. THE MEANING OF MIRACLES

We have already established the fact that the Gospel reports of Christ's miracles raise the issue of Jesus' identity. In a similar way, Old Testament miracle stories raise the issue of our concept of God.

MIRACLES AS A GROUP RAISE QUESTIONS ABOUT OUR CONCEPT OF GOD

Old Testament miracles force us to ask such questions as these: "Is it possible that God exists, or is the material universe the only reality?" "Is the material universe eternal or does it have a source?" "What is God's relationship with the material universe?" "What are the possibilities of God using events to punish or reward human beings?"

The testimony of the Old Testament's miracle stories supports Scripture's teaching that, as Creator, God is the source of the material universe, distinct from it, and totally free to act within it on behalf of his people.

Similarly, the Gospel miracle stories raise the issue of Jesus' identity. First-century men and women were forced to ask, "Is Jesus a magician or sorcerer? Is he a 'divine man,' whose superiority and closeness to God enable him to work wonders? Or is he God incarnate, as he claims?"

The miracles Jesus performed did not in themselves answer these questions. But they did impel those who heard the stories to make some decision about Jesus' identity. And in examining that issue, each person was confronted with Scripture's affirmation of all three grand miracles which shape the Christian's concept of God.

1. God created all things.
2. The Creator God became incarnate in Jesus.
3. God incarnate died, and was raised from the dead.

EACH INDIVIDUAL MIRACLE HAS ITS OWN RELIGIOUS SIGNIFICANCE

The story of Sodom and Gomorrah illustrates the priority of religious significance. At the same time that we affirm the larger significance to Scripture's miracle stories as a whole, we also have to affirm that there is intrinsic meaning to be found in every miracle reported in Scripture. We have already defined a "miracle" as "an extraordinary event caused by God which has religious significance." Now let's focus on this truth: *The religious significance of any miracle is of primary importance.*

Each miracle story in Scripture, studied in the context of its time and in view of God's salvation purpose, has its own special significance. In studying miracles, we might focus on the significance of the setting of Sodom and Gomorrah (Gen. 19). They lay in a valley formed by a major fault in the earth's crust. In that valley, deposits of bitumen and pitch abounded.

With this information, we could easily see how the two cities might be destroyed by fire falling from heaven. A massive shift along the fault line would cause an earthquake, filling the air with inflammable materials. Thunderstorms generated by the dust hurled into the sky would generate lightning and ignite that material, causing the entire valley to be scorched in a great firestorm.

But if we emphasized only their geologic setting in an attempt to make the event more credible to the modern mind, we would miss the meaning of Sodom and Gomorrah. The event was extraordinary not because it involved a violation of natural law, but because the Lord predicted it to Abraham (Gen. 18)

Fire destroyed Sodom and Gomorrah.

and explained that he was about to cause it because of the sins of the men of those cities. The religious significance of the miracle is that God is the moral judge of our universe and that he will punish sins.

Biblical terms for miracles help us identify their religious significance. One thing that will help us determine the significance of miracles is the vocabulary used to describe them.

OLD AND NEW TESTAMENT WORDS FOR MIRACLES

Each testament has specialized vocabulary for identifying miracles. It is important to know what each of these words tells us about the miracles they describe.

Pala´. This word is used about 70 times in the Old Testament. It means "to be marvelous or wonderful." The root usually refers to God's acts, either in shaping the universe or acting in history on behalf of his people. The word focuses our attention on people's reaction when they are confronted by a miracle. The believer sees the awesome power of the God who has invaded time and space to do something too wonderful for humans to duplicate (*Expository Dictionary of Bible Words,* Zondervan, 444).

One authority says of *pala´,*

Preponderantly, both the verb and substantive refer to the acts of God, designating either cosmic wonders or historical achievements on behalf of Israel. That is, in the Bible the root *pl´* refers to things that are unusual, beyond human capacity. As such, it awakes astonishment (*pl´*) in man. Thus, the "real importance of the miraculous for faith (is)—not in its material factuality, but in its evidential character . . . it is not, generally speaking, the especially abnormal character of the event which makes it a miracle; what strikes men forcibly is a clear impression of God's care or retribution within it" (Eichrodt). We may add that it is essential that the miracle is so abnormal as to be unexplainable except as showing God's care or retribution (*Theological Wordbook of the Old Testament,* Moody, 1980, 723).

A number of English words are used to render *pala´,* including "wonder," "miracle," "wondrous works," "wonderful works," and "wonderful things."

Mopet. This Hebrew word occurs only 36 times in the Old Testament. It also means "wonder" or "miracle." It is used especially to recall God's mighty acts in Egypt performed to free his people from slavery. *Mopet* is also used of the punishments and the provision that show God's continuing care of Israel throughout history.

The *Theological Wordbook of the Old Testament* points out that *mopet* is frequently used with a third Hebrew word for miracle, `ot. The two together are typically translated "signs and wonders."

In Deuteronomy 13, *mopet* refers to a prediction required from anyone claiming to be a prophet. Depending on whether the `ot (sign) or *mopet* (wonder) actually happens, the would-be prophet is either authenticated or shown up as a false prophet.

Mopet standing alone is normally rendered as "wonder" or "wonders" in English versions of the Bible.

`ot. This Hebrew word means "miraculous sign." It has a wide range of meanings. The word is used to designate the heavenly bodies as "signs" which distinguish the seasons (Gen. 1:14) and to designate a signboard or standard (Num. 2:2). However, nearly all of its 80 occurrences in the Hebrew Old Testament carry the meaning of a miraculous sign, indicating a clear and unmistakable act of God. As noted above, `ot is frequently used with *mopet,* and the two together are rendered "signs and wonders."

Several other Hebrew words are used to describe miracles. For example, miracles are "mighty things" (*yalla*), or "mighty deeds" (*giborah*) which are the unmistakable works (*maasheh*) of God. We will examine these Hebrew words in more detail as we go on to look at every miracle in the Bible.

Dunamis. A number of Greek words are associated with miracles in the New Testament. Of the three major New Testament terms, *dunamis* identifies a miracle as a spontaneous expression of God's power. Like the other two primary miracle terms in the New Testament, this word portrays a miracle as a clear violation of what first-century people understood of natural law. God's acts of power were so unmistakably extraordinary that none who observed a miracle could mistake it.

Semeion. This Greek word means "a sign, wonder, or miracle." The basic meaning of the word indicates a sign by which one recognizes a particular person or thing. When the *semeion* has a marvelous or extraordinary dimension, it is generally translated "miraculous sign." The *Expository Dictionary of Bible Words* notes that this word "emphasizes the authenticating aspect of the miracle as an indication that supernatural power is involved."

Teras. This word, translated "wonder," or "wonders," is found only 16 times in the NT, in each case connected with *semeion* as "signs and wonders." In Greek literature, *teras* denoted some terrible appearance which evoked fright and horror, and which contradicted the order of the universe. The Septuagint [a Greek translation of the Hebrew Old Testament completed in the second century B.C.] uses *teras* to translate *mopet,* thus indicating a token, sign, or miracle. Both the Old Testament word and its New Testament equivalent are linked with God's revelation of himself to human beings.

In addition to these three basic New Testament terms for miracles or wonders, the apostle John especially refers to Jesus' miracles as "works" (*ergon*), emphasizing that a particular event occurred through the active agency of God.

The biblical vocabulary of miracles helps us to define more sharply what a miracle is.

A miracle is an extraordinary event (*pala`, teras*). This event may involve violation of what we consider natural laws, as did the parting of the Red Sea and Jesus' raising of Lazarus. But an event doesn't have to violate natural law in order to be extraordinary. The ancient Middle East was familiar with swarms of locusts. But the swarm which appeared in Egypt in the time of Moses came at the exact time Moses predicted. A clear judgment on

Pharaoh, this was one of a series of devastating plagues (Ex. 10:1f). These factors marked this swarm of locusts and several of the other plagues on Egypt as extraordinary.

A miracle is an event caused by God (*pala´, dunamis, ergon*). The nature and timing of the event, along with its religious significance or an associated revelation, make it unmistakably clear that God has acted in our world of space and time.

A miracle is an event with religious significance (´*ot, semeion*). It is not a random but a purposeful act of God. For instance, the series of miraculous plagues God imposed on Egypt had at least four distinctive religious functions:

First, the plagues focused Israel's faith, for from that time on God was identified with these acts performed on behalf of his people (Ex. 6:7). God exercised his power to fulfill his ancient covenant promises to the children of Abraham.

Two other purposes are seen in the fact that it would be through the plagues that the Egyptians not only would be confronted with the knowledge of who Yahweh is but also would allow Israel to leave Egypt (Ex. 7:5).

Fourth, the plagues served as a judgment on the gods of Egypt (Ex. 12:12). The powerlessness of human religious invention would be displayed as the living God exercised his power.

Each of these purposes is clearly linked with God's revelation of his nature. The false images of believer and unbeliever alike are shattered as God steps from the mysterious beyond to enter our here and now. The God of miracle must be responded to and not ignored, for the God of Scripture is no being of tenuous spirituality whose influence is limited to a mystic, immaterial setting.

For believers, this affirmation of God's reality and power is comforting, and the psalms constantly call on worshippers to remember and tell of his works. As David expressed it, "Tell of all his wonderful acts. . . . Remember the wonders he has done, his miracle" and "declare . . . his marvelous deeds among all peoples" (1 Ch. 16:9, 12, 24). God can be counted on by his people (*Expository Dictionary of Bible Words*, 444).

IV. DO MIRACLES HAPPEN TODAY?

In an interview, Kim Kwong Chan, co-author of *Protestantism in Contemporary China*

(1994), gave his explanation of why the Chinese church is growing so rapidly. His first reason was the ideological vacuum in China. His second was the intimate love, caring, and concern that Christianity provides. And then he said, "There are the miracles." Kim went on to add,

When I travel to the interior of China, the Christian communities all claim they've seen and experienced miracles.

One typical example: An old Christian woman in one village decided, after her eightieth birthday, to start preaching the gospel. She went to the village where her daughter lived and began to preach there. Some villagers who had been afflicted with various incurable diseases, like cancer, came to this woman. When she prayed for them, many were suddenly healed.

Then two more people came to ask for healing, and she prayed, and they were healed. Then three more families. After this woman left, these villagers decided her God was very good. So they abandoned their idols and decided to believe in this Jesus.

But they didn't know how to believe. So they sent one person to nearby towns to look for a place where people worshiped Jesus. When they finally found such a church, they told the pastor, "We have nearly 80 people in our village who want to believe in Jesus. But we don't know how to believe in Jesus."

After that a new church was started. I hear such stories all the time in my travels (*Christian History*, Vol. XV, No. 4, 44).

To many Christians, such a report would be occasion for rejoicing. "How wonderful that God is still at work," they might exclaim. But other Christians would look on grimly, convinced that the miracles recorded in the Gospels and in Acts are not to be expected—or believed—in our day.

WHY SOME DOUBT THAT REPORTS OF CONTEMPORARY MIRACLES ARE CREDIBLE

The Christian skeptic's position is stated carefully by Benjamin B. Warfield. Warfield did not doubt the biblical miracle stories.

What he argued was that such wonders "belonged exclusively to the Apostolic age." Warfield wrote,

These gifts were not the possession of the primitive Christian as such; nor for that matter of the Apostolic Church or the Apostolic age for themselves; they were distinctively the authentication of the Apostles. They were part of the credentials of the Apostles as the authoritative agents of God in founding the church. Their function thus confined them to distinctively the Apostolic Church, and they necessarily passed away with it (B. B. Warfield, *Counterfeit Miracles,* 1918, 6).

Warfield argued his case on two grounds. First, he affirmed that the New Testament teaching as to the origin and nature of miracles supported his position, and second, he cited testimony from later ages that the miraculous gifts had ceased.

We must be careful in developing our arguments on either ground. First, those who accept Scripture's testimony as true may differ in their understanding of it. Many would argue that while the New Testament miracles did serve to authenticate Christ and the apostles as God's messengers, this was not their *only* function.

One major function of the miracle stories in the Gospels—and thus one of Christ's purposes in performing them—was to compel the hearer to deal with the issue of Jesus' identity. We might also argue that another role of Gospel miracles was to unveil the compassionate character of God as one who deeply loves those who suffer and who are oppressed by sickness or Satan.

Surely, there is no basis to argue that this latter function of miracles "confined them distinctively to the apostolic age." In every age, human beings need reminders that God cares. Through our fallible exegesis of the Scriptures, we should not place limits on God's freedom to act.

Second, the argument that the testimony of later ages shows that miraculous gifts no longer operate is patently false. Kim Kwon Chan's report is just one of thousands of reports of extraordinary events with religious significance that believers have credited to God. Whether these reports are true and factual may be questioned. But the existence of the reports themselves certainly may not be.

It seems unwise to begin any exploration of miracles with the assumption that the biblical reports are true, but that all other reports are false. Those who believe firmly in the God who reveals himself in Creation, Incarnation, and Resurrection should never place limits on his freedom to do extraordinary things anywhere in the world—or in our own experience.

BIBLICAL INSIGHTS ON THE QUESTION OF MODERN MIRACLES

The Gospel of Mark closes with the following passage.

And He said to them, "Go into all the world and preach the gospel to every creature. He who believes and is baptized will be saved; but he who does not believe will be condemned. And these signs will follow those who believe: In My name they will cast out demons; they will speak with new tongues; they will take up serpents; and if they drink anything deadly, it will by no means hurt them; they will lay hands on the sick, and they will recover."

So then, after the Lord had spoken to them, He was received up into heaven, and sat down at the right hand of God. And they went out and preached everywhere, the Lord working with them and confirming the word through the accompanying signs. Amen (Mark 16:15–20).

Those who challenge the idea of modern miracles point out that verses 9–20 in this chapter are not found in the two Greek manuscripts generally considered the most reliable. They argue that these verses were added later by someone other than Mark, and thus should not be considered Scripture.

Whatever the case, these verses do help us identify the events which proponents of modern miracles are likely to point to as supernatural events—casting out demons, speaking with "new tongues," and healings.

No one seems to argue that the kind of miracles that marked the Exodus period or the time of Elijah are being performed today. But many, like Kim Kwon Chan, do report miraculous healings. In fact, it is healing which, over the past 150 years, has often been the focus of the debate over contemporary miracles.

But before we look more closely at the question of miraculous healing, there are a few things that we should consider.

MIRACLES HAVE NEVER BEEN COMMONPLACE OCCURRENCES

Miracles have not been evenly distributed throughout sacred history. In fact, nearly all recorded miracles took place during two relatively brief periods.

The first of these periods was the time of the Exodus from Egypt and the conquest of Canaan. A flurry of devastating miracle-judgments forced Pharaoh to release his Hebrew slaves. The travels of Israel to Canaan and their conquest of the land was also supported by miraculous interventions. These miracles made such an impression that throughout the Old Testament God is frequently identified as the wonder-working Redeemer of his people.

These miracles made a great impression on Israel, and they are referred to many times in Israel's history. It's hard to believe that all these miracles took place within a span of about fifty years!

A second flurry of miracles was associated with the ministries of Elijah and Elisha. Some 21 miracles which God performed through these two prophets are recorded in the books of 1 and 2 Kings. These events also occurred in a span of just a few decades!

The time from Abraham to Christ covered about two thousand years. It's clear that most followers of the Lord who lived during these centuries did not witness miracles.

The third period of miracles recorded in Scripture extended from the time when Christ began his public ministry through the book of Acts. The miracles reported during this time were limited to a span of just three to four decades! While some of the early church fathers reported miracles, these reports were rare. They do not constitute a major emphasis in the writings of Christians who argued for Christianity against pagan critics.

It is helpful to remember that, whatever we may believe about contemporary miracles, Scripture does not support the notion that miracles are a necessary or even frequent supplement to faith.

MIRACLES SHOULD NOT BE CONFUSED WITH GOD'S ANSWERS TO PRAYER OR WITH DIVINE PROVIDENCE

We've defined a miracle as an extraordinary event caused by God which has religious significance. It's important to limit our concept of miracles to the truly extraordinary.

Christians believe that God answers prayer. But answers to prayer aren't miracles. A person with cancer for whom the church gathers to pray, and who experiences a sudden remission, has not experienced a miracle. Yes, we can credit God with the healing. But to the extent that God worked through the body's own resources or medical treatment, the recovery was not a miracle.

The Catholic church, which traditionally has been more open to contemporary miracles than Protestants, realized that it was necessary to define conditions under which a healing could be termed miraculous. Those conditions were defined in the 18th century by Pope Benedict XIV.

1. The sickness or disability must be serious.
2. At the time of the healing, the patient should not be improving or suffering from a condition that might be expected to improve.
3. The patient should not be taking orthodox medical treatment at the time.

4. The healing should be sudden and instantaneous.
5. The cure must be perfect and complete.
6. The cure should not occur at a time when a crisis due to natural causes has affected the patient or the illness.
7. The cure must be permanent.

One example of a cure that meets these standards is the documented case of Vittorio Michelli. In 1962 Michelli suffered from a cancerous tumor on his left hip. The hip bone disintegrated, and the bone of his upper left leg was left floating in tissue. During a visit to the shrine at Lourdes, Michelli felt a sensation of heat moving through his body, and he began to improve.

Back at home, he went to his doctors and insisted that his hip be x-rayed. The tumor had shrunk. Over the next several months the tumor disappeared. But what was unheard of in medical history was that the hip bone had regenerated—something considered impossible! That we can call a miracle.

John Wimber, the founder of the Vineyard movement and a leading proponent of modern miracles, told of a woman he met in South Africa whom cancer had reduced to 85 pounds. He and a friend prayed for her, but with little confidence. As he reported in *Christianity Today* (Oct. 7, 1996, 51),

That night she woke up with a vibrant, tingling feeling throughout her body. For the next four hours her body was full of intense heat. She tried to call out to her husband in the next room but couldn't raise her voice loud enough for him to hear.

Alone and frightened, she crawled into the bathroom, her body racked with pain. At the time she thought, "O my God. My body is coming apart and I'm dying." Without knowing it, she eliminated from her body a number of large tumors. Finally, exhausted, she fell back asleep. She didn't know if she'd wake up.

But a half an hour later she woke up incredibly refreshed. Later her husband woke up to the smell of freshly brewed coffee. "What are you doing!" he asked, astonished to see his wife on her feet and preparing breakfast.

She replied with sudden understanding: "God has healed me."

Two days later she reported to her doctors, who gave her a clean bill of health. They couldn't find a cancer in her body. God had completely delivered her of it.

Extraordinary events like these two can be considered miracles. But many recoveries we experience as answers to prayer should not be placed in the "miracle" category.

We can say the same about providential occurrences. The book of Esther provides a clear example of God's providential care of his people. The existence of the Jewish people was threatened. A high official in the Persian court decided to avenge a supposed insult by a Jewish bureaucrat by wiping out the Jewish people. He cast lots to determine just the right day to approach the king. Finally every omen was positive, and he talked the king into ordering the execution of all Jews in the Persian Empire.

But that night the king was unable to sleep, so he had a secretary read to him from the royal archives. The secretary happened to read about a time when the very Jew who provoked the official's wrath exposed a plot against the king's life. When the king discovered this man had not yet been rewarded, he determined to correct the oversight immediately. And it also happened that the niece of the man who provoked the official had recently become queen, her race unrevealed! In the end, these events conspired to bring about the deaths of the scheming official and other enemies of the Jews, while the Jewish people were saved.

No one reading the book of Esther can fail to notice how every circumstance "just happened" to fit together neatly to provide for the Jews' deliverance. Yet not one of those circumstances was, in itself, extraordinary. Not one required an open or unmistakable intervention by God. The believer looks at the sequence of events and sees God's hand behind the scenes, arranging what happened to lead to his desired end. The unbeliever scoffs, pointing out that each event, however fortu-itous, took place naturally. Each follows the other in a chain of cause and effect which doesn't require "God" to explain.

Thus, we need to be careful in speaking of biblical or contemporary miracles. Answers to prayer which come through seemingly normal processes and unlikely chains of event which lead to fortunate outcomes may be credited to God's providential care. But they should not be called miracles.

Only extraordinary events which cannot be explained in any way other than by divine intervention merit consideration as miraculous.

PRACTICAL CONSIDERATIONS IN EVALUATING CLAIMS OF CONTEMPORARY MIRACLES

The Christian who believes in the God who has defined himself in the three grand miracles will not doubt that God is able to cause extraordinary events in the material universe. This does not mean that Christians naïvely accept every report of miraculous events as gospel. A belief in the possibility of contemporary miracles does not commit us to accept the validity of any modern miracle tales.

What should we consider in dealing with reports of modern miracles?

THERE ARE MIRACLE REPORTS WHICH ARE FALSE

The book of Acts tells of "a certain man called Simon, who previously practiced sorcery in the city and astonished the people of Samaria, claiming that he was someone great, to whom they all gave heed, from the least to the greatest, saying 'This man is the great power of God' " (Acts 8:9, 10). These verses remind us of several realities about miracle reports.

The reported miracle may be a counterfeit. Simon was not performing miracles but using "sorcery" to produce certain effects. As the term was used in the first century, "sorcery"

may have involved what we call "magic" or "illusion" today. Or "sorcery" might refer to events cause by a supernatural, demonic being. In neither case would the acts of Simon fit our definition of a miracle—an extraordinary event caused by God which has religious significance.

Those reporting the miracle might be deceived. It is possible to believe an event is a miracle—and to be totally deceived. Simon had deceived the entire population of Samaria, and thus was accorded a respect he didn't deserve. It's possible to believe sincerely in a miracle that we have supposedly observed, and still be wrong.

The motive of the supposed miracle-worker may be questionable. Simon used the so-called miracles that he performed to support his claim that "he was someone great." The more stridently a person claims miracle-working powers, the more likely it is that his motives and thus his claims should be questioned.

It's especially important to weigh miracle reports carefully and to apply the criterion established by Benedict XIV when "faith healers" come to town. God can heal, and he can give special gifts of healing to individuals. But faith healers who are unwilling to provide information which would allow their claims of healing miracles to be substantiated should not be respected as a "great power of God."

THE PRESENCE OR ABSENCE OF CONTEMPORARY MIRACLES NEITHER VALIDATES NOR INVALIDATES CHRISTIAN FAITH

It is important to keep the question of miracles in perspective. The grand miracles of Creation, Incarnation, and Resurrection are central to Christian faith. They define our understanding of who God is, and thus who it is in whom we believe.

But our faith in a God who is both our Creator and Redeemer does not rest on whether God performs miracles for us today.

We need to adopt the attitude of the three Hebrew officials in the Babylonian Empire who, when threatened with death in Nebuchadnezzar's fiery furnace, replied "Our God whom we serve is able to deliver us from the burning fiery furnace . . . But if not, let it be known to you, O King, that we do not serve your gods, nor will we worship the gold image which you have set up" (Dan. 3:17, 18).

God is able to perform miracles for us.

But if He chooses not to do so, we will still trust Him to the end.

MIRACLES ARE PERFORMED BY A SOVEREIGN GOD

John Wimber is a leading figure in the call for Christians to expect God to perform miracles today. In a moving article in *Christianity Today* (Oct. 7, 1996, 50), Wimber reflected on his own experience with life-threatening cancer:

When I began radiation treatments for my cancer, I discovered what it was like to walk through the valley of the shadow of death. As I spent weeks without eating solid food, I began to realize that the physical and emotional trauma coming my way could only be met by taking the hand of the Lord and walking with him.

. . .

Some Christians believe that we should never struggle with doubt, fear, anxiety, disillusionment, depression, sorrow, or agony. And when Christians do, it is because they're not exercising the quality of faith they ought to; periods of disillusionment and despair are sin.

If these ideas are true, then I'm not a good Christian. Not only have I suffered physically with health problems, but I also spent a great deal of time struggling with depression during my battle with cancer.

But I also found that the view from the valley gave me a focus on Christ that I wouldn't have gained any other way. Stars shine brighter in the desert. There are no obstructions, no distractions, no competing lights. The view from the valley isn't so bad because Jesus shines so clearly. I knew he was there even when I didn't always feel him close to me.

Wimber has now recovered from his cancer. And he realizes that God has healed him, even though through medical means. He also recognizes that others with just as much faith have died from a cancer like his. His conclusion provides a helpful reminder.

Two wonderful men from our Anaheim, California, congregation were diagnosed with cancer within weeks of my diagnosis. Harold Looney and Lynn Marang were both active servants in the church and very passionate in their worship of the Lord Jesus. We earnestly prayed in faith for their healings over the course of weeks and months, and in Lynn's case, well over a year. They had families that needed them and lives worth living. Yet in God's sovereign choice, he took each of them home to be with him. He chose to let me remain. I can't explain that. It's impossible to explain. The mystery of God's sovereign choice is the only answer.

As we come now to our study of biblical miracles, we want to affirm what Wimber calls "the mystery of God's sovereign choice."

- God does not perform miracles on demand.
- God may not perform miracles even when we believe they are most called for.
- But God, who created the world and who entered it to redeem us, performs miracles when to do so has served His sovereign purpose.

In examining the miracles of Scripture, we will discover something of what those purposes are. And we will develop a deeper trust in the God whose actions in our world display the unimaginable depth of His love for His people.

❖

CHAPTER 2

MIRACLES THAT SHAPED OUR LIVES

RELATIONSHIPS OF GOD AND MAN
Genesis 1—19

Some miracles touch our lives. Other miracles shape them. In fact, wonders reported in Genesis have molded our most basic understanding of the nature and meaning of our lives. Even more, Creation, the first of the cosmic miracles reported in Genesis, established the very nature of the universe in which we live. The miracle of humanity's origin defined human nature and mankind's relationship with God. The miracle of the Genesis Flood established forever the truth that ours is a moral universe, and God is its moral Judge.

When we compare the cosmic miracles reported in Genesis with pagan notions of how the world began and how human life originated, we are stunned to discover how completely the Genesis miracle reports have shaped Western civilization, and our own most basic beliefs.

I. MIRACLES IN THE BOOK OF GENESIS

The following events reported in Genesis fit the criterion of a miracle as "an extraordinary event caused by God which has religious significance."

1. The miracle of material creation—p. 28
2. The miracle of God's creation of Adam—p. 32
3. The miracle of God's creation of Eve—p. 36
4. The miracle of Enoch's translation—p. 38
5. The miracle of the Flood—p. 40
6. The miracle of Babel—p. 45
7. The miracle of the plagued Pharaoh—p. 48
8. The miracle of Sarah's conception—p. 50
9. The miracle of the blinded Sodomites—p. 52
10. The miracle of Sodom's destruction—p. 54
11. The miracle of Lot's wife—p. 55

THE MIRACLE OF MATERIAL CREATION   Genesis 1

In chapter 1, we identified the Creation as one of three grand miracles which are critical in defining the nature of God as he is revealed in Scripture. The main concern of this chapter was to show that the only alternative to creationism—the materialist view as presented in the theory of evolution—cannot be given credibility. The evolution theory claims to explain how the universe could have taken its present shape and how the many forms and varieties of life could have emerged. But its explanation is not merely unproven; it is fatally flawed. This leaves us with only one intellectually honest option: what exists has been designed and brought into being by an intelligent Creator.

This is exactly what Genesis 1 affirms.

THE DESCRIPTION OF CREATION IN GENESIS 1

Creation arose from an original state of nothingness. Most English versions of the Bible translate Genesis 1:1, "In the beginning God created the heavens and the earth. The earth was without form, and void, and darkness was on the face of the deep." It's clear from Scripture that the phrase "heaven and earth" is the usual biblical term for the universe. This meaning is clear from the use of the phrase in such verses as Genesis 14:19 and Psalm 121:2.

Unfortunately, most English renderings make it seem that God created the heavens and earth and then went about adding light, etc.

A notable exception to the translation of Genesis 1 found in typical English versions occurs in modern Jewish versions of Genesis. These read, "When God began to create . . ." and "In the beginning of God's creating the heavens and the earth. . . ." Nine hundred years ago the great Jewish commentator Rashi wrote,

The passage does not intend to teach the order of creation, to say that these [namely, the heaven and the earth] came first; because if it had intended to teach this, it would have been necessary to use the form *barishonha*.

What Genesis 1:1–3 actually does is to make a statement. When God set about creating the heavens and earth—the earth being unformed and void and space dark and empty—the Spirit was hovering over its vast expanse. *Then* God said, "Let there be light."

The means of creation (Genesis 1:3–25). The Genesis account repeats a pattern seen first in 1:3. "Then God said, 'Let there be light,' and there was light." This same formula, at times with the variation "and it was so," is found in verse 6, 9, 11, 14, 20, and 24. Without the need for any other agency, God simply spoke the material universe into existence! Psalm 33:6 declared, "By the word of the Lord the heavens were made, and all the host of them by the breath of his mouth." No wonder the psalmist added,

Let all the earth fear the Lord;
Let all the inhabitants of the world
　　stand in awe of him.
For he spoke and it was done;
he commanded, and it stood fast
　　(Ps. 33:8).

The sequence of creation (Genesis 1:3–27). One fascinating feature of the Genesis account is the sequence in which creation is described. Several things about the sequence are of interest.

1. *There is a clear pattern in the sequence.* This can be shown as follows:

Framework		Detail	
Day 1	Light and dark	Day 5	Creatures of water,
Day 2	Sea and sky		air
Day 3	Fertile earth	Day 6	Creatures of the
Day 4	Lights of day,		land
	night		Human beings

2. *The sequence is "scientific."* That is, the sequence in the Genesis account agrees with the stages for earth's development proposed by scientists on the basis of geologic and fossil evidence. The materialist supposes that natural causes account for the shape of the universe and for life in all its varied forms. But the materialist cannot define the mechanisms which caused their evolution. Yet all the evidence scientists have gathered has led materialists to adopt a sequence for creation which Moses wrote some 3,500 years ago, thousands of years before "science" even addressed the question!

Edwwyn Bevan, an evolutionist, has commented on Genesis 1, "The stages by which earth comes to be what it is cannot indeed be precisely fitted to the account which modern science would give of the process, but in principle they seem to anticipate the modern scientific account by a remarkable flash of imagination, which a Christian may also call inspiration."

The framework of creation: the "days" of Genesis 1. Bible scholars disagree as to how the six "days" in which Genesis 1 describes creation should be understood. At least six different theories have been put forward. (1) Creation took place in six, sequential 24-hour periods. (2) "Day" is figurative, probably representing what we call a geologic age. (3) "Day" is literal, but an age intervened between each of the Genesis 1 days. Thus God introduced vegetation in a 24-hour period, but He waited thousands of years for its varieties to develop before the next creative day. (4) God created in seven literal days a few thousand years ago, with coal, fossils, etc. created in place to give the appearance of age. (5) The six days are not days of creation at all. They are revelatory days, in which God revealed His works to Moses. (6) The six-day structure is a literary device used by the author to organize his material.

The repeated references in the Genesis text to morning and evening make some of these theories difficult to sustain. Yet Origen, and St. Augustine after him, argued that the days of God need have no human analogy (compare Ps. 90:4; Isa. 4:2). Whatever our personal convictions about the nature of the days, their use in Genesis 1 emphasizes the fact that God's creation took place in planned, logical stages. This reinforces the main truth that our universe has its origin in a being who carefully designed it and our earth, and then implemented that design.

THE UNIQUENESS OF THE GENESIS ACCOUNT

When archaeologists first discovered documents in the ancient Near East which recorded Babylonian and Egyptian creation myths, critics hurriedly counted the supposed similarities to the biblical account. Their assumption was that the writers of Scripture relied on earlier myths when "inventing" the Hebrew creation story.

However, the more these Middle Eastern creation accounts have been studied, the clearer it has become that the biblical account is unique. In fact, many elements of pagan cosmologies are directly confronted by the Genesis account.

A unique vision of God. In Genesis, God stands as the one and only true God. Other Near Eastern accounts are cluttered with gods and goddesses, who often are rivals of the high god of the pantheon.

A unique vision of emptiness. In Genesis, only God has being before He acts to create. Creation takes place in a void where nothing "is." The heavens and earth are formed by God's Word, coming into existence from nothing.

In the ancient Babylonian creation epic known as *Enuma elish,* the heavens and earth are formed from the body of a defeated rival god by a victorious deity. In Egyptian creation myths, an original deity is on earth when he creates three subordinate gods from his semen, who then exist in uncreated primordial waters.

A unique view of human beings. Most significant, in these other Near Eastern creation accounts, human beings are formed accidentally or as an afterthought. In Scripture, the creation of human beings is God's culminating act of creation. Humankind is special, made in God's image, created to inherit and care for the world which God has made.

Any similarities between the Genesis account and the creation myths of the ancient world are superficial at best. They do not show harmony with the sequence of life's appearance on earth which is evident in the Genesis account. Neither do they match the Bible's exalted presentation of God as unique and all-powerful.

❖

BIBLE BACKGROUND:

NEAR EASTERN CREATION MYTHS

In the Babylonian creation account known as *Enuma elish,* the material universe is formed by Marduk from the body of the slain goddess Tiamat. Tablet IV provides this description.

> he . . .
> turned back to Tiamat whom he had
>   bound.
> The lord trod on the legs of Tiamat,
> With his unsparing mace he crushed her
>   skull.
> When the arteries of her blood he had
>   severed,
> The North Wind bore (it) to places undis-
>   closed.
> On seeing this, his fathers were joyful and
>   jubilant,
> They brought gifts of homage, they to
>   him.
> Then the lord paused to view her dead
>   body,
> That he might divide the monster and do
>   artful works.
> He split her like a shellfish into two parts:
> Half of her he set up and ceiled it as sky,
> Pulled down the bar and posted guards.
> He bad them to allow not her waters to
>   escape.

An Egyptian creation myth that reflects a motif going back to at least 3,000 B.C. is detailed in the Pyramid Texts. An excerpt describing the creations of Ra pictures this superior deity as coming into being "in this earth" and then creating subsidiary deities.

> I conceived in my own heart; there came into being a vast number of forms of divine beings, as the forms of children and the forms of their children.
> [The text then mentions the sexual act by which the beings Shur and Tefnut were "spat" and "spewed" from Ra's mouth.] By my father Nun, the Primordial Waters, were they brought up, my Eye watching after them since the eaons when they were distant from me.
> After I had come into being as the only god, there were three gods aside from me. I came into being in this earth, but Shue and

Tenut rejoiced in Nun, the Primordial Waters, in which they existed.

The contrast between the gods of ancient myths and the God of Scripture is strikingly clear.

❖

THE RELIGIOUS IMPLICATIONS OF THE MIRACLE OF CREATION

Miracles are extraordinary events caused by God which have religious significance. Certainly creation fits the first two of these standards. But what are the implications of creation for faith?

Creation assures us that the universe is personal. There are really only two options: (1) Either the universe in which we live has been designed and brought into being by a supreme being, or (2) it has emerged randomly as the product of mere chance. If the first premise is true, existence has meaning beyond itself, and we can look to the Creator to discover what that meaning is. If the second assumption is true, existence is meaningless and we live in a universe that grinds on aimlessly toward an uncertain fate. If the universe is personal, there is hope that we might survive beyond the dissolution of our bodies. If the universe is impersonal, there is no hope for survival after death.

The Bible's affirmation of the miracle of creation assures us that the universe is personal rather than impersonal; that existence is meaningful rather than meaningless; that we can find this meaning by seeking to know the Creator; and that the possibility of life after death exists.

Creation portrays a trustworthy, caring God. Romans 1:20 asserts that God's invisible attributes are "clearly seen, being understood by the things that are made, even his eternal power and Godhead." The testimony of the creation is so overwhelming that every person intuitively recognizes God's existence. To deny God involves a suppression of known truth, and this act of denial is in itself a demonstration of human sinfulness (Rom. 1:18).

But the eye of faith learns much more about God from creation than his existence.

1. *Creation reveals a dependable God.* The creation—through its regular alternation of day and night, with season following season—reveals a God who is consistent in His works.

2. *Creation reveals a concerned God.* The vast complexity and multiple forms of animate and inanimate life are revealing. From the uniqueness of each snowflake to the individuality shown in the animal world, God's delight in creative expression and His concern for the individual are clearly displayed.

3. *Creation reveals a caring God.* Throughout Genesis 1 we read God's response to what He has done: "It is good." In the beauty and infinite variety of the universe, we catch a glimpse of a God who values the beautiful and the good. Surely our Creator is a God who *cares*.

Creation is one of the three grand miracles of Scripture. Together, these three miracles significantly define who God is. The Genesis account of creation stands as a unique vision of how our world came into being. Its striking contrast with ancient creation myths and with contemporary evolutionary theory challenges all to examine the implications of belief and disbelief, and to make a decision for or against God.

THE MIRACLE OF ADAM'S CREATION   *Genesis 1:26–31; Genesis 2:1–17*

While the creation of human beings is part of the Genesis creation account, it deserves to be treated as a distinct, separate, and extraordinary act of God. This account is given briefly in Genesis 1, and then in greater detail in Genesis 2.

THE TEXTUAL CHALLENGE TO EARLY GENESIS

In chapter 1 we looked briefly at the materialists' challenge to the Genesis account of creation, based on the theory of evolution. There we saw that evolution is hardly the "fact" which most people assume it to be. We also pointed out one of the fatal flaws which undermine its credibility.

Before we look at the Genesis account of mankind's creation, we need to note another challenge to Genesis. This challenge emerged in the 19th century as scholars began to argue against Mosaic authorship of the Pentateuch. They saw Genesis not as a revelation from God given through Moses, but as the patchwork creation of a religious document by human beings, completed centuries after its supposed date of composition. Rabbi Shlomo Riskin, dean of Israel's Ohr Torah institutions and chief rabbi of Efrat, commented on this attack:

What would eventually receive recognition as the Wellhausen School of Biblical Criticism plunged its teeth deep into the flesh of Jewish tradition. Its major hypothesis is that no fewer than four separate documents have contributed to the Torah [i.e., the Pentateuch]—commonly called J,E,P,D.

J stands for the first letter of God's four-letter name, and thus the sections where God appears with that appellation. E is for Elokim, the sections where God's name is Elokim. P is for the Priestly Code, and D for the Deuteronomist—author or editor of the last of the Five Books.

Based on a system of comparing the names of God as well as selected verses that sound redundant or dissimilar with other sections, and combined with conjectures about contemporaneous historical events, such biblical critics are direct heirs of the attempt to whittle the Bible down to human size that was originally called the Wissenschaft des Judentums (science of Judaism)

. . .

Now, long before the critics appeared, rabbinic tradition explained the distinctions between the two names. *Elokim* represents the universal God of nature, law and justice, while the four letter name represents the more personal God of compassion and human involvement. As to the narrative accounts, the supposed difference disappears if only we read the total narrative (*Jerusalem Post*, October 1, 1994).

Riskin went on to point out that the first chapter of Genesis sets the creation of human beings within the framework of the creation of the universe.

The second chapter of Genesis returns to the creation of human beings for a closer look at this special creature God has made. It looks in detail at what God has done, and in this, Genesis 2 helps us define original human nature. The shift from use of the name Elohim in Genesis 1 to Yahweh in Genesis 2 does not indicate a patchwork of two separate and different creation accounts. Rather, as Rabbi Riskin pointed out, this shift emphasizes the personal involvement of God in the creation of human beings.

All the major *assumptions* of the Wellhausen school—that writing did not exist in Moses' time, that Israelite religion evolved from polytheism to monotheism, that repetition and duplication prove separate authorship—have been discredited by the discovery of ancient Semitic literary documents. Yet the *conclusions* reached by that school, including the J,E,P,D documentary hypotheses on which Riskin comments, are still uncritically accepted by many contemporary scholars!

It is bizarre that such groundless methodologies are still used by many who reject Scripture's own affirmation that it is the revealed Word of God. We must take our stand with Rabbi Riskin, who concluded his article,

The Bible critics make a fatal error. They divest the Torah of context and subtext, examining the mechanics of the words while disregarding the majesty and the fire, the vision and the message.

What we must remember is that the Bible is not a book written by man. It emanates from God—a description not only of what humanity is, but what it must strive to become.

THE GENESIS 1 ACCOUNT OF THE CREATION OF MAN

The Genesis 1 account of man's creation begins with the statement of God's intention, "Let Us make man in our Image, according to Our likeness" (Gen. 1:26). The verse then goes on to express God's intention to "let him have dominion." Verse 27 tells us, "So God created man in his own image; in the image of God he created him; male and female he created them."

These verses are particularly significant.

1. *The use of the name Elohim* makes it clear that the one who created humankind is the same supreme being who created the universe.
2. *The name Elohim* is a plural noun. Together with plural pronouns, it indicates the personal nature of God and also suggests the trinitarian nature of God, which is fully revealed later.
3. *The terms image and likeness,* when used together, serve as a technical theological term. Only human beings are said in Scripture to be created in the image-likeness of God. This means that when trying to understand human nature, we cannot look to the animals to discern man's essence. We must look to God and evaluate humankind on the basis of man's resemblance to Him.
4. *The phrase "have dominion"* further sets humanity apart from the animal creation, which was created in the same Genesis "day" (the sixth). Mankind is not only different from earth's animals, but he is also set apart from them by his likeness to God and by the mission which mankind is assigned by the Lord.
5. *The phrase "male and female"* underlines the essential equality of man and woman. Each shares equally in the image of God. Each shares responsibility to care for the earth and its creatures.

The insights in Scripture's first overview of the extraordinary creation of man is further developed in the expanded description which occurs in Genesis 2.

THE GENESIS 2 ACCOUNT OF THE CREATION OF MAN

Genesis 2 comes back to the story of man's creation to provide a close-up look which develops additional details. Genesis 2:7 says,

And the Lord God formed man of the dust of the ground, and breathed into his nostrils the breath of life; and man became a living being.

The next section of Genesis, 2:8–17, describes a garden in which the Lord placed the first man, Adam. These verses also reveal much about the nature of God and the significance of man's creation in the image-likeness of God.

We especially note the following about Genesis 2:7:

1. *The text adds the personal name of Yahweh* (the Lord) to that of Elohim (God) in describing how God created man. Man was created by "the Lord God" (Yahweh Elohim). This addition emphasizes a personal investment in the miracle of man's creation which is not present in the creation of the material universe or the creation of other living things.

2. *God used pre-existing material,* the "dust of the ground," to make man's body. This shows that man is one with the universe in which we live.

3. *God breathed life into Adam* to make him a living being. This indicates that human nature is shaped by more than what can be accounted for physically. Human nature has a spiritual dimension. This dimension of being is not ascribed to any other creature in the animal kingdom.

4. *God planted a garden eastward in Eden* in which Adam was to live. The word *planted* focuses attention on God's design of Eden. The description of Eden provides clues as to the meaning of man's creation in the image-likeness of God. Each element of the garden's design provided Adam an opportunity to exercise capacities which he had received from God. These capacities remind us that human beings are persons who share with God all the attributes of personhood.

Some have interpreted the original image and likeness which God shared with Adam to be holiness. However Genesis 9:6 and James 3:9 base significant teaching on the assumption that even fallen human beings retain at

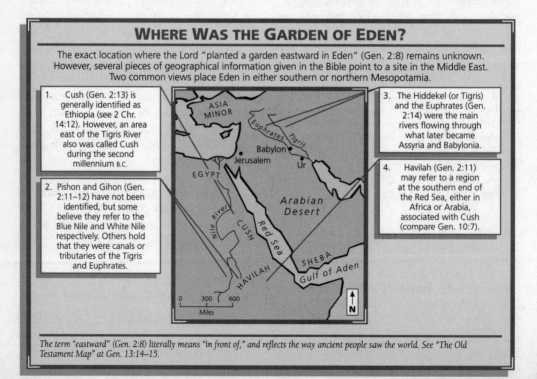

WHERE WAS THE GARDEN OF EDEN?

The exact location where the Lord "planted a garden eastward in Eden" (Gen. 2:8) remains unknown. However, several pieces of geographical information given in the Bible point to a site in the Middle East. Two common views place Eden in either southern or northern Mesopotamia.

1. Cush (Gen. 2:13) is generally identified as Ethiopia (see 2 Chr. 14:12). However, an area east of the Tigris River also was called Cush during the second millennium B.C.

2. Pishon and Gihon (Gen. 2:11–12) have not been identified, but some believe they refer to the Blue Nile and White Nile respectively. Others hold that they were canals or tributaries of the Tigris and Euphrates.

3. The Hiddekel (or Tigris) and the Euphrates (Gen. 2:14) were the main rivers flowing through what later became Assyria and Babylonia.

4. Havilah (Gen. 2:11) may refer to a region at the southern end of the Red Sea, either in Africa or Arabia, associated with Cush (compare Gen. 10:7).

ASIA MINOR
Euphrates
Tigris
Babylon
Jerusalem
Ur
EGYPT
Arabian Desert
Nile River
CUSH
Red Sea
SHEBA
Gulf of Aden
HAVILAH

0   300   600
Miles

N

The term "eastward" (Gen. 2:8) literally means "in front of," and reflects the way ancient people saw the world. See "The Old Testament Map" at Gen. 13:14–15.

least a reflection of God's image-likeness. It is better to understand image-likeness in terms of those things which make a human being a person: our reason, will, appreciation of beauty, ability to feel and to love, etc.

The *Teachers Bible Commentary* observes,

Remember that God's own personality was mirrored in Adam. Adam shared a capacity to appreciate. So the plantings of Eden included every tree "that is pleasant to the sight" (v. 9). God knew that man would be dissatisfied without work, so in the garden God let Adam "till it and keep it" (v. 15). God knew man's need for opportunity to use his intellectual capacities, so God brought the animals to the man "to see what he would call them; and whatever the man called every living creature, that was its name" (v. 19). God knew man's need for freedom to choose, so he placed a forbidden tree in the garden and commanded man not to eat fruit from it. This action once for all set man apart from creatures who live by instinct and demanded that he use his capacity to value and to choose.

In all these ways, then, the miracle of man's creation establishes a distinction between human beings and the rest of animal creation. The creation account lifts human beings up, setting them apart as special. Mankind is not only special within the created universe; he is special to God, as shown in the unique way in which the miracle of man's creation took place.

---- ❖ ----

BIBLE BACKGROUND:

MAN'S CREATION IN NEAR EASTERN MYTHS

Ancient Near Eastern creation myths assign a very different place to human beings than does Genesis. Tablet VI of the *Enuma Elish* gives this account.

When Marduk hears the words of the
   gods,
His heart prompts (him) to fashion artful
   works.
Opening his mouth, he addresses Ea
To impart the plan he had conceived in
   his heart:
"Blood will I mass and cause bones to be,
I will establish a savage, 'man' shall be his

name. Verily, savage-man I will create.
he shall be charged with the service of
   the gods
   That they might be at ease!
The ways of the gods I will artfully alter.

The Egyptian Pyramid Texts tell of Ra's loss of his eye. Fellow deities return Ra's lost eye. Man is derived from this incident in an unplanned and almost accidental manner. The text reads:

After I had united my members, I wept over them, and that was the coming into being of mankind, from the tears which came forth from my Eye.

---- ❖ ----

What a difference from the origin of humankind which Scripture describes and the exalted place that Scripture assigns to human beings.

IMPLICATIONS OF THE MIRACLE CREATION OF MANKIND

God's miraculous creation of Adam establishes Scripture's view of humankind. If we believe that human beings are nothing more than evolved animals, we will have a very different view of people and society than if we subscribe to the miracle of man's creation. In a materialistic society, the state and the "many" have clear priority over the individual, who exists to serve the collective. In this scheme of things, individuals are unimportant. The state or collective society has priority.

But if human beings are made in God's image, individuals are far more significant. Individual human beings have a worth and value that cannot be measured by the contribution they make to the state—or on the basis of race, education, or economic status. Only if human beings are God's direct and special creation is there a basis for the kind of respect and love each human being truly deserves.

One writer observed:

So what's at stake in the interpretation of Genesis is not merely the historicity of ancient narratives, or the doctrine of biblical inerrancy, or even the systems of theology based on an inerrant historical record of Creation, Fall, and Deluge. . . . From the perspective of a critical hermeneutics, what's ultimately at stake in the interpretation of Genesis is nothing less than the social order, its character and sanctions, as dependent on human nature, created and corrupt (James R. Moore, *Interpreting the New Creationism*, 113).

The way we view ourselves and other human beings will shape the way we relate to others. This will also affect the kind of society we build.

THE MIRACLE OF GOD'S CREATION OF WOMAN   *Genesis 2:18–25*

Genesis 1:27 states that God created man as male and female. Genesis 2 describes that creative work as taking place in two distinct steps. God first created Adam, giving him time to explore the Garden of Eden. At a later time God created Eve. Genesis reports,

And the Lord God said, "It is not good that man should be alone. I will make him a helper comparable to him." Out of the ground the Lord God formed every beast of the field and every bird of the air; and brought them to Adam to see what he would call them. And whatever Adam called each living creature, that was its name. So Adam gave names to all cattle, to the birds of the air, and to every beast of the field. But for Adam there was not found a helper comparable to him.

And the Lord God caused a deep sleep to fall on Adam, and he slept; and he took one of his ribs, and closed up the flesh in its place. Then the rib which the Lord God had taken from man he made into a woman, and he brought her to the man. And Adam said:

"This is now bone of my bones
And flesh of my flesh;
She shall be called Woman,
Because she was taken out of Man."

PREPARATION FOR THE CREATION OF WOMAN

After God stated His intention to create a "helper comparable to" Adam, Genesis describes God bringing every kind of animal and bird to Adam. The great Jewish commentator Rashi observed that this verse does not describe a new creation, but it elaborates on the making of animals referred to in Genesis 1:28.

The text should read, "Out of the ground God had formed every beast, and [now] He brought them to Adam."

Why is Adam's naming of the animals described in this text, following the statement of God's intention to create woman? To understand the reason for this insertion, we need to consider three things.

The revelation that God created animals "out of the ground" emphasizes further the distinction of all other members of the animal kingdom from humanity. Animals are of the earth only. They lack the God-given "breath of life" which transmitted God's image-likeness to man alone.

The naming of the animals has great significance. In Hebrew thought, a "name" was descriptive, intended to communicate something of the essential nature or character of the thing named. For Adam to name the animals implied a long process of study of each animal's habits and behavior. Adam became a careful observer of each creature's ways; then he chose a name which expressed its uniqueness.

Adam could find no "comparable helper" in spite of his careful research into the animal kingdom (Gen. 2:20). God had said it was not good for the man to be alone. The process of naming the animals taught Adam what God already knew: Adam could find among them no suitable companion to whom he could relate physically, intellectually, emotionally, or spiritually.

THE FULL EQUALITY OF MEN AND WOMEN

Full equality is seen in the statement of God's intent (Genesis 2:18). The verse expresses God's intention to make a "helper comparable to" Adam. Other English translations of the Hebrew phrase `etzr kenegdo` render it "a fitting helper for him" (RSV), an "aid fit for him" (Anchor Bible), "suitable helper" (NIV), and "a helper who is right for him" (God's Word). Unfortunately, each of these translations seems to suggest that woman was created *for the ben-*

God brought each creature before Adam, for him to name them.

❖

efit of man. Understood in this way, the text would support the assumption of many that females are by nature and by God's intent subordinate to males.

But this is *not* implied in the Hebrew phrase. In fact, this phrase guards against just this sort of misinterpretation of male-female relationships! Psalm 33:20 uses the exact word translated "helper" here in Genesis to describe God. The psalmist declared, "Our soul waits for the Lord; he is our help and our shield." Likewise, God is identified as man's helper (`*etzer*) in Exodus 18:4 and Psalm 70:5. Being a "helper" does not indicate subordination or that the person who helps exists for the benefit of the one being helped.

What Genesis 2:18 emphasizes is that only one who is fully a person—completely human as Adam was human and thus "comparable to him"—could meet the needs of Adam or any other human being.

Full equality is implied in the means God used to create woman (Genesis 2:22). God took a rib from Adam and used it as the basis for forming Eve. If God had made Eve as He formed Adam—from the dust of the earth—

there would have been no *essential connection* between man and woman. Woman would have been a separate and subsequent creation. By using Adam's rib, God further affirmed the identity of man and woman as humans who were equally possessors of the divine image-likeness.

Full equality was expressed in Adam's response to Eve (Genesis 2:23). Gordon Wenham, in the *Word Biblical Commentary,* noted that this verse scans as Hebrew poetry. He captured its essence when he described Adam as "in ecstasy," bursting into poetry on meeting his perfect helpmeet. Adam understood fully the fact that in Eve God had created a person who was "flesh of my flesh"—a person who shared with him all that it means to be human.

In the deepest sense, Adam and Eve—and the men and women who have descended from them—are not "different" but one.

IMPLICATIONS OF THE MIRACLE OF WOMAN'S CREATION

Materialists who adopt an evolutionary view of men and women tend to define male and female by their physical characteristics [men are stronger] and supposed evolutionary roles [women are nurturers, men hunters].

Christians who have misunderstood the message of woman's creation in Genesis 2 have tended to *limit* women's roles. Women are supposed to stay at home, rear children, and care for their husbands because God created them to be "helpers." For generations, this religiously based bias kept women in Western society from studying to be doctors or scientists.

Yet rightly understood, this miracle of God's creation of woman as a "helper comparable" to man emphasizes the equality of the sexes. God has gifted each sex with every capacity provided to humanity as a whole. Women do not come behind men in intellectual, emotional, or spiritual gifts. And only when we affirm, as Adam did, "This is now bone of my bones and flesh of my flesh," will we experience to the full all the wonderful ways in which God intends us to be helpers of one another.

THE MIRACLE OF ENOCH'S TRANSLATION   *Genesis 5:19–24; Hebrews 11:5*

This event is reported in a single verse nestled in the lengthy genealogy which traces Seth's descendants to Noah. The list names individuals and their offspring, indicating how long they lived. The entry for Enoch reads

Enoch lived sixty-five years, and begot Methuselah. After he begot Methuselah, Enoch walked with God three hundred years, and had sons and daughters. So all the days of Enoch were three hundred and sixty-five years. And Enoch walked with God; and he was not, for God took him (Gen. 5:21–24).

The Jewish rabbis have understood the phrase "and he was not" to mean that Enoch died. Noting the long lives of men before the Flood, some rabbis have suggested that the description of Enoch as one who "walked with God" is included to keep us from concluding that his relatively short life was ended as a divine judgment. The *Midrash* suggests that Enoch, although righteous, was likely to go

astray. So God cut his life short to avert that possibility.

However, the writer of the New Testament book of Hebrews has a very different explanation for the phrase "and he was not":

By faith Enoch was taken away so that he did not see death, "and was not found, because God had taken him," for before he was taken he had this testimony, that he pleased God (Heb. 11:5).

Thus, we have it on the authority of God's inspired Word that what Genesis actually describes is a miracle. Enoch was taken to be with the Lord without experiencing physical death.

ONE OTHER REFERENCE TO "ENOCH"

Another reference is made to "Enoch" in Jude 14, 15. This text speaks of "Enoch the seventh from Adam" prophesying. It also quotes Enoch's prophecy.

The difficulty is that the words quoted as those of Enoch are from a pseudepigraphic book, 1 Enoch, a Jewish religious treatise dating from the second or first century B.C. Some have assumed, because Jude quotes 1 Enoch, that Scripture authenticates this book—or at the least the content of the quote. However, other authorities have a different explanation:

The quotations are to be explained as necessary to the author's [the author of Jude] argument against the false teachers. . . . The author demonstrates that even these texts were misused by the heretics and he seeks to demonstrate that even the legends, when rightly interpreted, supported the orthodox view of the OT (Zondervan *Pictorial Encyclopedia of the Bible*, vol. 3, 734).

For this reason, we should not attempt to draw from Jude 14, 15 the kind of insights we can discern in the canonical texts which mention Enoch.

THE GENEALOGICAL SETTING OF THE MIRACLE STORY

The miracle of Enoch's translation is mentioned in a longer genealogy in Genesis 5.

This genealogy traces the family line of Adam's son Seth. It is notable for several reasons.

Long lives were ascribed to pre-Flood human beings. According to the text, it was not unusual for human beings before the Genesis flood to live eight or nine hundred years. There is no indication here that the numbers are meant to be figurative.

How could such lengthy lives be possible? Research has revealed that most diseases are linked to damage to various genes. This damage is transmitted from generation to generation. It does not seem unreasonable that the closer persons were to the perfect human gene pool in Adam and Eve, the less damage they would have experienced and the longer they would have lived. Another theory is that before the Flood a water vapor layer protected the earth from cosmic radiation, which has been linked to aging (compare Gen. 2:5 with Gen. 6:11, 12).

The Sumerian King List, an ancient Near Eastern document, names eight kings who ruled before "the Flood swept over (the earth)." The shortest length of rule cited for one of these kings is 18,600 years, and the longest 43,200! The document witnesses to a common tradition, showing that the life spans mentioned in Genesis 5 are conservative rather than exaggerated.

The length of lives cannot be "added up" to derive a date for creation. An attempt to do so by Bishop Usher in the 18th century led many people to believe the Bible teaches that creation took place in 4004 B.C. However, Hebrew genealogies typically do not list every person in a family line. And the Hebrew term translated as "son of" or "begat" is used of more distant descendants as well as one's children.

THE BIBLE'S DESCRIPTION OF ENOCH

It is clear from the comments about Enoch in Genesis and in Hebrews that his life and relationship with God was unusual.

He walked with God (Genesis 5:22, 24). Twice Genesis says that Enoch "walked with God." The same evaluation is given of Noah (Gen. 6:9). Malachi 2:6 indicates that priests were expected to walk with God, and Micah 6:8 indicates that what the Lord requires of His people is "to do justly, to love mercy, and to walk humbly with your God." The phrase in Genesis 5 clearly suggests Enoch's special intimacy with God and a life of piety.

The book of Hebrews adds that "before he was taken away, he had this testimony, that he pleased God."

THE BIBLE'S DESCRIPTION OF THE MIRACLE

Four phrases are used in Genesis and Hebrews to describe what happened to Enoch. The two accounts use phrases which stand in parallel:

Gen. 5	Heb. 11
he was not	he was not found
God took him	God had taken him

Each of these phrases is suggestive.

"He was not" (Genesis 5:24). Enoch ceased to exist as far as life on earth was concerned. He had spent about 365 years on earth. Then, suddenly, the life he had lived as a man came to an end.

For each of us, the time when we "are not" is fast approaching. We may leave our earthly life through the door of death or be caught up to join Jesus when he returns. But the one sure thing is that a day is coming when it will be said of us, "He was not."

When that time comes, how important it will be for the Lord to say of us that we "walked with God" during our days on earth.

"God took him" (Genesis 5:24). The phrase implies that God took Enoch *to be with Him*. The transition must have been an easy one for Enoch. He had spent his days living in fellowship with the Lord and walking with Him. Imagine how uncomfortable it would be to a person who is a stranger to the Lord to be suddenly brought into His presence. The more intimate our walk with the Lord here on earth, the more ready we will be to meet Him at the end of this life.

There is another implication of the phrase "God took him." Only God can make it possible for a human being to be with Him. It was only because of the promise of Christ's atoning death on Calvary that Enoch—a sinner like us—could be taken by God to be with Him.

"He was not found" (Hebrews 11:5). This phrase suggests that Enoch's contemporaries looked for him. He was not just gone; he was missed. A person who truly walks with God will be the kind of loving, caring individual whom others are drawn to and to whom they look for inspiration.

"God had taken him" (Hebrews 11:5). Hebrews speaks of the translation in the past tense. For Enoch the struggles of life on earth were over. Now and forever, Enoch was destined to enjoy endless life in the presence of the God with whom he had walked during his time on earth. For us the journey continues. But one day the journey will be over for us too. However great our trials and tragedies, they will be forgotten. Life will be past tense for us, as we enter an endless eternity.

We live in a day when we at last understand how God is able to forgive us so freely and to invite us into His presence. The death of Jesus lies in our past. The full benefits of His work lies ahead. Like Enoch, we lay hold of Him and all He has for us "by faith" (Heb. 11:5).

THE RELIGIOUS SIGNIFICANCE OF THE MIRACLE

There is much to consider in Scripture's description of Enoch and what God did for him. But there is also great significance in the miracle of translation itself.

After relating the story of creation (Gen. 1, 2), this first book of the Old Testament immediately tells the story of the Fall (Gen. 3). Adam and Eve sinned, and although they did

not lose the image-likeness of God, their natures were twisted and corrupted. Genesis 4 goes on to display the impact of the Fall in the stories of Cain—who murdered his brother Able in a fit of jealous anger—and of Lamech—who rejected the divine ideal for marriage by taking two wives. Lamech also tried to justify his killing of a young man who had injured him. These stories demonstrated clearly that Adam's offspring had inherited the first couple's sin nature and had wandered far from God.

If early Genesis left us there, with images of sin burned into our eyes, we might conclude that there is no hope. But Genesis 5 relates the miracle of Enoch's translation. Enoch, a human being like us—a sinner living in a sinful world—chose to walk with God. And God took Enoch to be with Him.

What a message of hope this miracle conveys! Yes, we have sinned. But God is loving and gracious. If we choose to walk with Him, He will accept us and take us to be with Him one day as well.

THE MIRACLE OF THE FLOOD
Genesis 6—8

Genesis 6—8 describes a cataclysmic Flood which God used to purge the earth of a humanity totally corrupted by sin. Only one man, Noah, had not given in to this immorality. Noah, like Enoch, "walked with God." This just man, "perfect in his generations" (Gen. 6:9), "found grace in the eyes of the Lord" (Gen. 6:8). Noah was given instructions for building a great floating ship, an ark. He and his sons were also given 120 years to complete its construction (Gen. 6:3).

When the ark was built and provisions had been stored aboard, God caused pairs of animals to enter the vessel. Noah, with his three sons and their wives, joined the animals aboard the ark. God then brought a devastating flood which wiped out humanity and "all flesh in which is the breath of life" (Gen. 6:17).

A year later the flood waters receded. Noah and his family left the ark to reenter a refreshed earth. According to Genesis, all earth's living things are descended from the life forms preserved on Noah's ark.

IS THERE SCIENTIFIC EVIDENCE OF SUCH A FLOOD?

In March 1929 Sir Leonard Wooley, who excavated Ur, published a report in the *London Times* that the expedition had discovered unmistakable evidence of the Flood. He wrote, "We were loath to believe that we had obtained confirmation of the Deluge of Genesis, but there is no doubt about it now."

Wooley was wrong. Although he is still quoted by some in support of the flood story, what Wooley found was evidence of a local flood with an impact far less than would have been created by the Flood described in Genesis.

Geologists today are committed to the doctrine of uniformitarianism. This theory insists that every feature on the earth's surface can be explained by natural processes which are at work even today. They ridicule the notion of the watery cataclysm. Some theologians have responded by arguing for a local flood. They argue that if the human race was limited to populating a relatively small area in Mesopotamia, God's intent of wiping out the race could have been achieved without a flood that covered the surface of the earth. This comment on the debate is typical of that reasoning:

Few biblical events have stirred more interest. Is the story a myth, or is it historical? Was the Flood universal, or local? When did it happen? How does it fit into the historic or prehistoric record? We know that:

1. No other story is so widely repeated in traditions of ancient peoples all over the globe as that of a judgmental flood.
2. Detailed tradition from the Mesopotamian Valley, where the Scripture locates Noah, has revealed striking supportive evidence (*Enuma elish*).
3. Some argue the Flood was world-wide (universal) with "all the high mountains under the entire heaven" (Gen. 7:19) covered to a depth of 20 feet (Gen. 7:20). Others argue this is phenomenological language, implying only that the

high ground in the writer's part of the world was inundated. Local Flood proponents argue that God's purpose, to judge a civilization which was likely localized in the great valleys of the Fertile Crescent, could be accomplished without universality.
4. Universalists see the Flood as a great catastrophe, with continental changes. The water vapor canopy of Genesis 2 fell to earth; quakes released subterranean waters on which the continents floated. The great weight of released waters resculptured the surface of the globe, thrusting up mountain ranges and depressing sea beds. This view is well presented in *The Genesis Flood*, by Whitcomb and Morris.
5. Local Flood proponents argue that a catastrophic flood would leave different evidence in the fossil record and rock strata. They interpret the words of Genesis 7 phenomenologically.
6. Neither group has solid evidence for dating the Flood, though suggestions range from 10 to 60 thousand years ago (*Richards Complete Bible Handbook* (Word), 38, 39).

If we leave aside the scientific debate and focus on the biblical text, there is much to learn from the miracle of the great Flood.

THE BIBLE'S DESCRIPTION OF THE GREAT FLOOD

The causes of the Flood (Genesis 6:5, 11). Genesis describes a corrupt civilization in which sin was institutionalized to the extent that "every intent of the thoughts of his [mankind's] heart was only evil continually" (Gen. 6:5). In this pre-Flood civilization, people freely acted on their intent and thoughts. Thus "the earth was corrupt before God, and the earth was filled with violence" (Gen. 6:11).

These conditions led God to determine "I will destroy man whom I have created from the face of the earth" (Gen. 6:7). There is no doubt that Genesis portrays the Flood as an act of divine judgment.

Coming at the point where it does in the sacred history, the Flood is a compelling witness to the moral character of God and His commitment to serve as the moral Judge of His universe. God may withhold His judgment out of love, to give us an opportunity to repent (Rom. 2:3, 4). But as the Genesis Flood reminds us, God *will* judge sin. And His judgments are severe.

(NOTE: The much debated identity of the "sons of God" referred to in Genesis 6:1–4 is thoroughly discussed in the companion volume, *Every Good and Evil Angel in the Bible*, also from Nelson.)

The choice of Noah (Genesis 6:8, 9). The description of Noah as a "just man, perfect in his generations" should not be taken to imply that Noah was sinless. He was not. Noah had chosen to walk with God (Gen. 6:9). To call him "just" indicates that he conducted himself in a righteous way. To call him "perfect in his generations" indicates that *in every respect* he tried to live a godly life.

Even so, God's choice of Noah was rooted in grace. The Jewish rabbis tend to interpret the phrase "Noah found grace in the eyes of the Lord" to indicate that God's favor was extended because Noah had earned it. It is far better to see Noah's godly character as *a result of God's grace.* Why did Noah live the kind of life described in verse 9? It was because Noah had "found grace" (verse 8)! Or perhaps we should say that God in grace had found Noah.

The ark Noah constructed (Genesis 6:14–16). The Genesis account gives very specific dimensions for the ark. It has been argued that the ark was too small to carry Noah's family, all the animals, and their food. Supposing the "cubit" (a unit of linear measure) Noah used was 24 inches rather than the more common 18-inch cubit, the ark, at 600 feet long, 100 feet wide, and 60 feet deep, would have a capacity of 3,600,000 cubic feet.

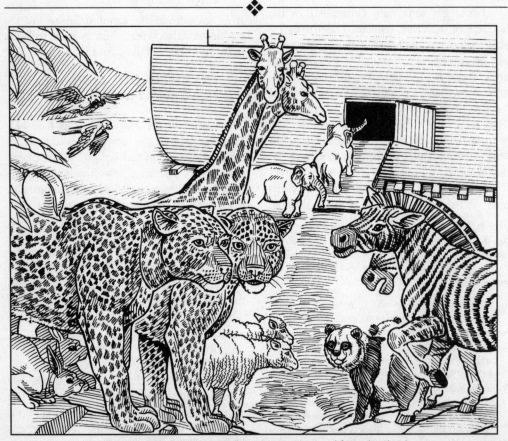

Through the ark, Noah and all creatures were saved from the Flood.

This would have been room for 2,000 cattle cars!

Earth today contains about 300 species (as distinct from sub-species) of land animals larger than sheep, about 750 species ranging in size from sheep to rats, and about 1,300 species smaller than rats. Two of each—plus seven pairs of ritually clean animals, with food for all—would have fit easily in the space available. Clearly, it would not have taken a miracle for the ark to hold the creatures and the necessary food to sustain life for the duration of the Flood.

The biblical description of the Flood itself (Genesis 7:11—8:14). There is no doubt, however, that the flood described in Genesis was a miracle. We can hardly imagine a more extraordinary act caused by God. No natural processes account for the things that happened.

According to Jewish exposition of the Hebrew text of Genesis 7:11, the "waters inundated the earth in a great seismic upheaval" while such torrential rains fell from heaven that they caused "complete havoc obscuring day and night." Genesis 7:19 indicates that the waters covered "all the high hills [Heb., mountains, *haharim*] under the whole heaven" to a depth of 15 cubits. The water level over all the earth's surface is thus said to have been at least 20 feet higher than the mountains!

This, of course, would have been possible only if before the Flood the earth's surface were smoother. The weight of the flood waters must have forced the upthrusting of earth's present mountain ranges and depressed the sea beds.

Another aspect of the Flood which emphasizes its miraculous nature is its length. It was five full months before waters receded enough for the ark to come to rest on the "mountains of Ararat" (compare Gen. 7:11 with 8:4).

The outcome of the Genesis Flood (Genesis 7:21–22; 8:20–22). The text indicates three results of the great Flood.

1. It accomplished God's intent of destroying the sinful civilization (Gen. 7:21–22). These

verses assert that "every man" who was on the dry land died.

2. It moved Noah to worship (Gen. 8:20). When Noah finally led his family from the ark, he sacrificed one of each from the seven pairs of clean animals that had entered the ark (Gen. 7:2, 3).

3. It culminated in God's promise not to destroy the human race, no matter how corrupt civilizations might become (Gen. 8:21, 22). This promise, however, was limited to "while the earth remains." At history's end a day of final judgment will come.

THE FLOOD ACCORDING TO THE EPIC OF GILGAMISH

A Sumerian account of a flood which destroyed mankind is contained in the Epic of Gilgamish, which predates the Genesis account by perhaps a thousand years. As in the Genesis story, the hero was warned by a deity to build a great boat to save himself and the animals. While the framework of the flood story is very close to the Genesis account, the moral tone and the concept of the gods displayed in the epic is strikingly different from the Genesis account.

The causes of the flood. Like Genesis, the Gilgamish Epic interpreted the flood as divine punishment. But rather than being a response to man's sin, the gods in the Epic decided to destroy mankind because man's buzzing irritated them.

The warning to Gilgamish. One of the gods, Ea, violated the intent of the council of the gods and warned Gilgamish. When Gilgamish asked how he could explain his project to others, Ea told him to deceive them about the intent of the gods.

> "Thou shalt then thus speak unto
> them:
> "I have learned that Enlil is hostile to
> me,

So that I cannot reside in your city,
Nor set my foot in Enlil's territory.
To the Deep I will therefore go
    down,
    To dwell with my lord Ea.
But upon you he will shower down
    abundance,
The choicests birds, the rarest fishes.
The land shall have its fill of harvest
    riches.
he who at dust ordered the husk-
    greens,
Will shower down upon you a rain
    of wheat."

When the ark was prepared and boarded, a terrible storm broke out. The flood of waters was so devastating that the gods themselves were terrified. The Epic states,

The gods were frightened by the
    deluge,
And, shrinking back, they ascended
    to the
    heaven of Anu.
The gods cowered like dogs
Crouched against the outer wall.

Finally the flood ended, and the gods reconsidered. In their irritation at humanity, they forgot that by man's offerings they were fed! When Gilgamish offered a sacrifice, the gods crowded greedily around. The gods promised never to destroy mankind again, but their motive was purely from self-interest and not of grace. The epic states,

The gods smelled the sweet savor,
The gods crowded like flies around
    the sacrificer.
When at length as the great goddess
    arrived,
She lifted up the great jewels which
    Anu had
    fashioned to her liking:
"Ye gods here, as surely as this lapis
Upon my neck I shall not forget,
I shall be mindful of these days,
    forgetting never."

FLOOD STORIES FROM AROUND THE WORLD

Some might argue it is not surprising that the Hebrews, Sumerians, Assyrians, and Babylonians shared a tradition of a great, destructive deluge. It is much harder to explain the fact that similar stories are found in the legends of peoples from around the world.

A comprehensive list of flood legends can be found in James Frazier's *Folklore in the Old Testament* (vol. 1, 1918). He discovered similar traditions in the Egyptian story of Toth, and the Greek tradition of Deucalion and Phyrrha. The Hindu legend of Manu relates how eight were saved from a worldwide flood, a story paralleled by the Chinese legend of Fah-he. Among the Hawaiians, the flood hero is called Nu-u; among the Mexican Indians, he is called Tezpi. Among our own Algonquin Indians, the hero is Manabozho.

Similar traditions are found in Sumatra, Figi, New Zealand, the Sudan, Greenland, and among the Kurnai tribe of Australian aborigines, and many others.

In these stories, the common theme is that the human race, with the exception of a few survivors, was wiped out at one time by a great flood. In these stories, the reason mankind was purged from the earth was divine displeasure over human sin.

The universality of these legends suggests that the miracle of the Genesis Flood made a deep impression on the human beings who descended, as all have, from Noah's sons and daughters-in-law. Through this racial memory, God declares that He rules a moral universe and that He most surely will judge man's sin.

THE RELIGIOUS SIGNIFICANCE OF THE MIRACLE OF THE GENESIS FLOOD

Probably no other miracle except for Creation itself has made such an impact on humanity, as demonstrated by the traditions of a world-wide flood which exist in many cultures. The story of this miracle serves as a present warning. God is a God of love. But God is also a God of justice. If we do not accept the love of God, we will surely experience His justice.

As Peter wrote in his second epistle, scoffers will say, "Where is the promise of his coming?" and continue in their sin, confident that "all things continue as they were from the beginning of creation" (2 Pet. 3:4). But all things have not continued the same! Peter wrote, "For this they willfully forget: that by the word of God the heavens were of old, and the earth standing out of water and in the water, by which the world that then existed perished, being flooded with water" (2 Pet. 3:5–6).

Today this world is reserved for another judgment—a judgment by fire. And the miracle of the Flood reminds all mankind that the day of God's judgment will appear.

THE MIRACLE OF BABEL   *Genesis 11:1–9*

The story of the Tower of Babel [Babylon] is told in a few brief verses. Yet it relates the last great judgment on mankind before the time of Abraham. The story reminds us that while God had destroyed sinful human civilization in the Flood, He had not put an end to sin. We can change the environment in which people live. But we cannot change fallen human nature. The stain of sin lies within us, not in outward circumstances.

After the Flood, the human family had "one language and one speech." When people multiplied, they determined to build a city and a tower "whose top is in heaven" as a symbol of human accomplishment and unity. This enterprise was contrary to God's earlier command to "fill the earth and subdue it" (Gen. 1:28). Rather than punish these builders, God "confused the language" they spoke and understood. Then those groups which did speak a common language were scattered "abroad over the face of all the earth."

This miracle had a universal impact, just like the others recorded in early Genesis. It affected all humankind and the development of peoples and nations. The miracle account also has great spiritual significance.

THE MOTIVES OF THE TOWER BUILDERS   *(Genesis 11:4)*

Genesis 11:4 reports the revealing words of the tower builders.

"Come, let us build ourselves a city, and a tower whose top is in the heavens; let us make a name for ourselves, lest we be scattered abroad over the face of the whole earth."

"Build ourselves a city." Hebrews 11:16 praised the Old Testament heroes of faith because they desired "a better, that is, a heavenly country. Therefore God is not ashamed to be called their God, for He has prepared a city for them." By contrast, the tower builders' concern was entirely focused on life in this world and what human effort could accomplish.

The society that developed after the Flood did not display the violence and intent to do evil described in Genesis 6:5 and 6:11. But man's proud and sinful nature had found a new form of expression.

"A tower whose top is in the heavens." Many scholars have noted that this tower was undoubtedly a ziggurat, a stepped tower similar to a pyramid with a temple on the top. Towers like this were found in all major Mesopotamian cities. The ziggurat of the temple of Marduk at Babylon was named Esaglia, meaning "whose top is [in] heaven." It measured 295 square feet at the base and rose to an equal height.

The name *Esaglia* tells us that the tower builders of Babel intended their structure to be a place of worship. In planning the building, they revealed a universal assumption. Human beings suppose that man by his own efforts can find God. This is contrary to the Bible's teaching that God must take the initiative. It is He who has reached down to reveal Himself to us.

There is really only one choice—to worship the gods of human invention or to worship the God of revelation. The men of Babel chose human religion.

"Let us make a name for ourselves." The tower was to be a spectacular achievement by which the builders would "make a name for" themselves. Their goal was not to glorify God in creating their religious structure but to gain fame and glory for themselves. Isaiah 2:17 commented on motives like those that drove the men of Babel:

> The loftiness of man shall be
>   bowed down,
> and the haughtiness of men shall
>   be brought low;
> the Lord alone will be exalted in that
>   day.

The day is coming when we will be ashamed of everything we did to exalt ourselves and to make a name for ourselves. How much better to devote ourselves to exalting the Lord, in preparation for that great day.

"Lest we be scattered abroad over the face of the whole earth." The tower builders expected their achievement to provide a basis for social unity. They could look with pride at the structure towering over the plains and find their identity in what they had done.

People today still struggle to find their own identity and relational bonds in their accomplishments. We define ourselves by our jobs. We feel closer to those who share the same work and have the same education, or who have gained enough wealth to live in the same neighborhood with us. But God calls us to find our identity and a basis for unity with others in who we are as persons created in His image and likeness (Gen. 1:26). We are also directed to find an even greater identity in a personal relationship with Jesus. Through Him we become children of God and brothers and sisters of other believers (Gal. 3:26–28).

GOD'S GRACIOUS RESPONSE TO THE TOWER BUILDERS
(Genesis 11:5–8)

In response to the tower builders, God planted a number of different languages in the minds of the inhabitants of the area. This led to total confusion, ultimately separating the peoples who spoke the different languages from one another. In one sense, this miracle was a judgment on the tower builders, who had rejected God's command to fill and subdue the earth. But in many ways, this "judgment" was a great blessing for humankind.

God examined the builders' work (11:5). There is more than a little irony in the phrase, "God came down" to see the tower. The skyscraper—in spite of all the claims of the builders that its top reached heaven—fell so far short that the Lord could hardly see it. He had to "come down" to look at it.

On one hand, the Genesis account is a sharp attack on the theology and mythology of Mesopotamia, a region which featured the mythical tower of Esagil. This miracle also refuted the notion that God could be reached in the temples atop the ziggurats. The greatest of the ancient Near Eastern temple towers were beneath the true God's notice.

More significantly, the phrase "come down" reminds us how futile is to try to im-

❖

The tower builders sought to reach up to heaven by their efforts.

press God through human effort. Titus 3:5 states, it is "not by works of righteousness which we have done, but according to his mercy he saved us." Our attempts to gain heaven must surely fail. Only by faith in the God who came down from heaven in Christ can we establish a personal relationship with Him.

God expressed concern for humankind's future (11:6). The verse reads, "indeed the people are one and they all have one language, and this is what they begin to do; now nothing that they propose to do will be withheld from them."

"The people are one and they all have one language." The builders had expressed concern that they might be scattered (11:4). They had failed to realize that the common language they spoke provided a bond that would hold them together. God, however, reminds us of the significance of language in facilitating unity of thought and intent.

"And this is what they begin to do." The plan to build the Tower of Babel revealed the direction in which the race was moving. Noah's descendants had focused on life in this world. In their arrogance, they thought they could reach any goal by self-effort. They were intent on making a name for themselves. Without God's intervention, they would have continued in the path they had chosen, moving further away from what God knew was best for them.

"Now nothing that they propose to do will be withheld from them." Human beings have wonderful abilities. It seems that nothing can interrupt the explosion of mankind's technological progress. We can build great cities, put libraries of information on a single silicon chip, and travel through space. It is this kind of progress that seemed to be in God's mind as he made this statement.

The key to interpretation of the passage is the phrase, "That they propose to do." The tower builders' focus was technological. They used the raw materials nature provided, made bricks and "bake(d) them thoroughly." Surely

with the tower finished, man's natural curiosity would have led to more and more inventions and discoveries.

But our generation demonstrates clearly that technological advances do not necessarily improve quality of life. In spite of all that man has created, the issues of injustice and crime have not been resolved. In every society, times of advance and prosperity are often followed by periods of decline and moral decay.

What might have been accomplished if our race, unified by a common language, had directed all its energies to building and making a name for itself? We cannot know for sure. But God's wise evaluation was that "nothing that they propose to do will be withheld from them." And that would not have been good for humankind.

GOD ACTED AND CONFUSED MAN'S LANGUAGE   *(Genesis 11:7)*

God's solution was simple. He impressed a number of different languages on the minds of the builders. One evening all went to bed speaking the same tongue; they awoke the next day speaking languages their neighbors no longer understood.

THE PRACTICAL CONSEQUENCES OF THE MIRACLE   *(Genesis 11:7, 8)*

The people were "scattered ... abroad from there, over the face of the whole earth" (11:8). Through this miracle, God's intent for mankind to populate the earth was implemented. The different language groups chose willingly to separate from each other.

It would be a mistake to interpret the actions of the builders of the Tower of Babel as *intentional rebellion* against the desire which God expressed at the creation of Adam and Eve. Many of our most serious sins do not grow out of intentional rebellion. Proverbs 21:2 reminds us that "Every way of a man is right in his own eyes, but the Lord weighs the heart." Rather than an act of rebellion, the intent of Noah's descendants to build the tower of Babel revealed a basic corruption of heart and motive which the Lord clearly discerned.

Men could no longer "understand one another's speech" (Genesis 11:7). This result of the miracle is more subtle but more far reaching that the scattering of the population. Language is more than a means of communicating. It determines the way we perceive and organize experiences—the way we think. English tenses carefully locate actions in the past, present, and future. Greek tenses emphasized the nature of the action—whether it was to be seen as continuing, as completed, as extending into the future—or whether a completed action had an impact on our present. Such a simple thing as this variation in the emphasis of tenses causes one language group to think differently than another group in society. And this difference can be multiplied by dozens of differences and hundreds of languages!

In confusing man's tongues, the Lord introduced a unique capacity for human beings to think about the world in a variety of different ways, expanding the possibilities for our race.

At the same time, the introduction of such significant differences makes clear communication difficult. Throughout history, human beings have focused on their differences as a cause for hostility and war. But the Lord determined that it would be better for the future of mankind to be divided by different languages than to be united by a common language. This would be better than all of mankind focusing on a common goal which could cause irreparable harm.

THE MIRACLE OF THE PLAGUED RULERS   Genesis 12:14–20; 20:1–18

Abraham is known in Scripture as a man of faith. Yet the Bible records two incidents in which Abraham failed to display trust in God, resorting to deceit to avoid imagined dangers. In each case, God himself intervened to protect Sarah from the consequences of Abra-

ham's failures. These two stories remind us that even the greatest of Scripture's heroes was marred by sin, as we are. Each also reminds us that God in grace will often, although not always, protect us from the consequences of our failures to trust Him.

ABRAHAM'S SIN AND ITS CAUSES (Genesis 12:11, 12; 20:10, 11)

When these miracles occurred, Abraham was living a nomadic life in Canaan, now called Palestine. Genesis 12 tells of a visit by Abraham to Egypt caused by a severe famine. Genesis 20 simply states that Abraham "stayed in Gerar," without explaining the reason. In each place, Abraham begged his wife and half-sister, Sarah, to pretend that they were not married. He was afraid the strangers among whom they had settled would kill him in order to take his beautiful wife.

In each case, the deceit led to a foreign ruler taking Sarah into his harem. In his action and his failure to speak up for his wife, Abraham sank to a low level of moral degradation. Why did Abraham lie and put his wife—and indeed the future which God had promised them—at such risk?

He let circumstances dictate his choice (Genesis 12:10). The circumstance that brought Abraham to Egypt was a famine in Canaan. God had led Abraham to Canaan and promised the land to his descendants (Gen. 12:7). There is no hint in the text that Abraham consulted the Lord when the famine struck Canaan. Apparently, Abraham let the circumstances dictate his actions, and he made the move to Egypt without seeking God's leading.

It is true that circumstances sometimes play a role in God's leading. But like Abraham, when we are divinely guided to a certain place in our lives, we should not be panicked by circumstances into hasty action.

He imagined what might happen (12:12). When Abraham and his party approached Egypt, he began to imagine the worst. Abraham knew Sarah was beautiful. And he imagined that "when the Egyptians see you . . . they will say, 'This is his wife,' and they will kill me, but they will let you live."

Abraham could neither predict nor control the future. But he based his request that Sarah lie on the basis of what he *imagined* the future might hold. How important it is to remember that our sovereign God controls the future. He remains free to make choices that are right rather than decisions which seem expedient.

He selfishly failed to consider others (12:13). Abraham begged his wife to consider him and to join in the lie "for my sake." But Abraham did not do himself what he asked from her. Abraham did not consider what it would mean to Sarah to be torn from her husband and taken into a strange man's harem.

When we are faced with difficult choices, we need to examine carefully not only our own motives but the impact of our decisions on others as well.

He acted in fear rather than in faith (20:10–11). In the second incident at Gerar, Abraham was asked "Why?" by Abimelech. "What did you have in view, that you have done this thing?" Abraham's answer was revealing. He replied, "I thought, surely the fear of God is not in this place; and they will kill me on account of my wife."

Two fallacies lie at the root of this kind of thinking. One is the notion that those who lack faith in God must be immoral. This simply is not true. There are many "good" people who try to do what's right by their own lights. To say that "all have sinned" does not mean that all people sin continually, or that all will do as much evil as they possibly can.

The second fallacy is to assume that because others do not believe in God, the Lord cannot influence their behavior. Abraham's God is a sovereign God, who is able to preserve His people in any circumstance. When fear keeps us from doing what we know is right, the problem is not in the circumstances but in our lack of faith.

GOD'S MIRACLES OF INTERVENTION   *(Genesis 12:17–20; 20:17–18)*

These miracles were not the spectacular type in which everyone recognized the hand of God. They were so ordinary that they would hardly have been recognized had not most people in the time of Abraham ascribed physical ills to supernatural sources.

Plagues struck Pharaoh and his court (Genesis 12:17–20). The Lord plagued Pharaoh with "great plagues because of Sarai, Abram's wife." Deuteronomy 28:59 identifies "extraordinary plagues—great and prolonged" as disciplinary punishments that God may use.

The Egyptians typically used some sort of magic to identify the source of such plagues. Perhaps God spoke to Pharaoh in a dream as he did some 20 years later to Abimelech. However he found out, Pharaoh fixed on Abraham as the reason he and his court were suffering. Abraham and Sarah were then sent away with all their possessions.

Abimelech's wife and servants became barren (20:17–18). Childlessness in the ancient world was not unusual. But in this case, *no women* in Abimelech's household could become pregnant. After a time, God revealed the cause of this curse to Abimelech in a dream.

Sarah and the kings were protected from committing adultery (12:19; 20:6). Although Sarah was taken into the harems of two kings, in neither case was she forced to have sex with the rulers. As God said to Abimelech, "I also withheld you from sinning against Me; therefore I did not let you touch her."

THE RELIGIOUS MESSAGE OF THE MIRACLE OF THE PLAGUED RULERS

There is much for us to learn by analyzing Abraham's mistakes and determining to avoid them. But there are additional messages for us in the account of these quiet, almost whispered miracles.

God's grace extends to sinners. Abraham's behavior in each case was inexcusable. Yet Abraham's failures did not cause God to withdraw His love or to rescind the covenant promises He had made to Abraham.

This is especially driven home by the promise given to Abraham that he would "be a blessing" to others (Gen. 12:2). In his attempts to deceive Pharaoh and Abimelech, Abraham had actually become a curse to each ruling house! Only God's intervention protected the two rulers and their subjects from greater suffering.

Miracles are evidence of God's grace, not of the holiness of any human being. One of the major theological dividing lines between Catholics and Protestants is the view of Catholics that miracles witness to the saintliness of persons associated with them. In the Catholic view, miracles authenticate one's faith. Thus John Milner argued that "the Catholic church, being always the beloved *spouse of Christ,* Rev. xxi.4, and continuing at all times to bring forth children of heroic sanctity, God fails not in this, anymore than in past ages, to illustrate her and them by unquestionable miracles." In order to be certified a "saint" by the Catholic church, definite evidence of miracles performed by the candidate or associated with him or her after death must be presented.

These two incidents involving Abraham remind us that association with miracles is not a guarantee of saintly character or spiritual superiority. Such miracles reaffirm God's grace to sinners, awakening thanksgiving for the Lord's kindness and mercy.

THE MIRACLE OF SARAH'S CONCEPTION   *Genesis 17:15–19; 18:10–14; 21:1–7*

God made great covenant promises to Abraham and his descendants. Yet as the years rolled on, Abraham's wife Sarah remained childless. Then, long after Sarah was past the child-bearing age, she became pregnant and gave birth to a son.

EVIDENCE THAT SARAH'S CONCEPTION WAS A MIRACLE

In the biblical world, barrenness was one of the greatest curses a woman could experience. Yet, six prominent Old Testament women were childless for much of their lives. Rebekah (Gen. 25:21) conceived after her husband Isaac prayed for her. Rachel (Gen. 29:31f) so despaired over her childlessness that she followed an ancient custom and had her maid Bilhah serve as a surrogate mother. Rachel eventually bore Joseph, whom God used to save His people from a terrible famine.

Manoah's wife (Judg. 13) was childless until told by God she would bear a son who would be named Samson. Hannah (1 Sam. 1) prayed desperately for a son. She later gave birth to Israel's last judge, the prophet Samuel. In the New Testament Elizabeth, who is described as "well advanced in years," bore John the Baptist after his birth was announced by an angel to her husband, Zacharias (Luke 1:5–25).

The common thread that runs through these stories of barren women is that each son they finally bore played a significant role in the spiritual history of God's people.

What sets the conception of Sarah apart as a miracle is more than the pre-announcement by the Lord (Gen. 17:16; 18:10) or the fact that Isaac was born "at the set time of which God had spoken" (Gen. 21:2). The truly miraculous part is revealed in the statement that "Sarah had passed the age of childbearing" (18:11). The Hebrew text says, literally, "the manner of women had ceased to be with Sarah." This delicate circumlocution meant that Sarah had stopped having her menstrual cycle. She had gone through menopause, and her womb had dried up. It was physically impossible for Sarah to have a child.

Sarah's conception of Isaac, while he was produced from her egg and Abraham's seed, was a truly extraordinary event. The Hebrew text implies that God was the cause of this miracle (compare Gen. 17:16; 18:14). "The Lord did for Sarah as He had spoken" (Gen. 21:1), and performed a miracle.

REACTIONS TO GOD'S ANNOUNCEMENT OF THE MIRACLE

Commentators have been fascinated by one aspect of this miracle story. When God told Abraham that he would become the father of a son by Sarah, "Abraham fell on his face and laughed, and said in his heart, 'Shall a child be born to a man who is one hundred years old? And shall Sarah, who is ninety years old, bear a child?'" (Gen. 17:17). Later, when Sarah heard the Lord in the guise of a human visitor make the same promise, the text reminds us of Sarah's sterile condition and says, "Therefore Sarah laughed within herself, saying, 'After I have grown old, shall I have pleasure?'" (Gen. 18:12).

In each of these two cases, the same Hebrew word is used for "laughed." Yet the Lord rebuked Sarah for her laughter but did not rebuke Abraham. Why?

The view of the Jewish sages. Jewish biblical scholars, many from the first and second centuries, argued that God rebuked Sarah because her laugh was "incredulous" (*Rashi*), indicating utter disbelief (*Midrash Aggadah*). In contrast, Abraham's laughter was a jubilant outburst, which according to Rashi, showed that he was "gratefully overjoyed."

This interpretation is rooted in the tremendous respect accorded to Abraham in Judaism. Although the word for "laugh" is the same in each verse, it is impossible to entertain the idea that this first of the patriarchs was flawed.

❖

BIBLE BACKGROUND:

ABRAHAM'S MERITS

The common teaching indicated that all Israel participated in the merits of the patriarchs—of Abraham in particular. These merits made prayers acceptable, protected people from danger, helped them in war, were a substitute for each person's lack of merit, expiated sins, appeased the wrath of God, warded off God's punishment, saved people from *Gehinnom,* and assured them a share in God's eternal kingdom (Joachim Jeremias, *Jerusalem,* 300).

Given this doctrine, it is no wonder that the rabbis and sages were unwilling to criticize Abraham or ascribe any but the most gracious motives to his actions.

❖

The evidence from Scripture. There is reason to believe that in spite of the use of the same word for laughter, Abraham's and Sarah's response to the announcement truly was different.

Abraham's laughter was linked with worship (Genesis 17:17). When Abraham received God's promise he "fell on his face." This represented deep respect and worship in Old Testament times. The text places worship immediately before Abraham's laughter. Thus Abraham's joyful laughter should be understood as an act of worship rather than an expression of doubt.

Psalm 126:2 records a parallel to Abraham's reaction: "Then our mouth was filled with laughter, and our tongue with singing. Then they said among the nations, 'The Lord has done great things for them.'"

Sarah's laughter earned her a rebuke (Genesis 18:13, 14). Sarah's denial that she laughed along with God's pointed question, "Is anything too hard for the Lord?" make it clear that her reaction was different from Abraham's.

The New Testament emphasized Abraham's faith (Romans 4:20, 21). The New Testament declared that Abraham "did not waver at the promise of God through unbelief." Unlike Sarah, he was "fully convinced that what God had promised, he was also able to perform."

Before we are too hard on Sarah, however, we need to remember that Abraham knew he was speaking with the Lord when the promise was given to him. Sarah overheard Abraham talking with angels, who appeared to be human beings. While we know that nothing is too hard for the Lord, we would probably react like Sarah if mere mortals were to promise us miracles!

RELIGIOUS SIGNIFICANCE OF THE MIRACLE OF SARAH'S CONCEPTION

Genesis 1-11 describes miracles which emphasize God's control over the physical universe. These were cosmic miracles, with direct impact on all mankind. The miracle described here, like that of the closing of the womb of Abimelech's women, is a miracle on a far smaller scale. At first glance, it seems the miracle involved in Sarah's giving birth to Isaac was almost a private miracle and that only the aging couple were affected.

But this extraordinary event is far more significant than that. God had told Abraham that the covenant promises He had made to him would be transmitted through his offspring. God was intent on creating a covenant people who would be the agency through which he revealed himself to all humanity and through which the Savior would come. The

The birth of Isaac began the fulfillment of God's promise to Abraham.

miracle happened to be a great blessing to the childless Sarah. But God performed it to accomplish a grander purpose.

Miracles are performed to fulfill God's purposes; they don't usually happen simply because we "need" them. God is gracious and loving in meeting our needs. But He will normally do so through natural rather than supernatural means.

THE MIRACLE OF THE BLINDED SODOMITES   *Genesis 19:9–11*

For centuries the name *Sodom* has been associated with depravity and sexual perversion. The Bible describes the valley in which Sodom and its associated cities were located as "well watered" and "like the garden of the Lord, like the land of Egypt as you go toward Zoar." The beautiful and fertile Jordan valley would have provided the people of Sodom with plenty of food, perhaps even agricultural wealth.

But in spite of the ideal conditions in which they lived, the people of the plain were unusually corrupt. Genesis reveals that the Lord told Abraham that "the outcry against Sodom and Gomorrah is great, and . . . their sin is grave" (Gen. 18:20). Two investigating angels paid a visit to Sodom. The men of the city gathered, intent on homosexual gang rape of the two visitors. The implication is that the "outcry against Sodom" had been made by earlier travelers who were treated in similar fashion.

But the cloaked angels had been invited into the home of Lot, Abraham's nephew. When the crowd attempted to break into Lot's house, the angels blinded them so they couldn't find the door. This is the first of three miracles reported in the account of Sodom's destruction.

The angels brought Lot and his wife and daughters to safety, then sent a rain of fire on the cities. The fiery destruction of the cities of the plain is the second miracle.

As Lot and his family fled from Sodom, Lot's wife looked back and was turned into a pillar of salt. This is the third miracle. We need to look at each of these.

ANGELS INVESTIGATE THE OUTCRY AGAINST SODOM AND GOMORRAH   *(Genesis 18:20, 21; 19:1–22)*

Angels are associated in Scripture with the divine moral law, and especially with the later giving of the Mosaic Law (Acts 7:53; Gal. 3:19, 20). Two angels were sent to investigate Sodom and Gomorrah. They did so by entering the city of Sodom dressed as ordinary travelers. The way they were treated provided evidence of the truth of complaints against the city and its sin.

Lot's righteousness was established by his hospitality (Genesis 19:1–4). Showing hospitality to strangers was a primary moral value in the biblical world. Lot's insistence that the two travelers stay with him along with his preparation of a special meal for them mirrored Abraham's treatment of strangers (Gen. 18:1–8). In the context of the times, Lot's welcome was evidence of his righteous character (compare Gen. 18:23–24).

The Sodomites' wickedness was established by their behavior (19:4–11). That night the men of Sodom gathered outside Lot's house, demanding that he turn the two travelers over to them. The phrase "that we may know them" means "to have sex with them." One Jewish commentary on Genesis quotes several sages on the matter, noting that "this interpretation is based on the fact that *yada,* know, is used in Scripture as a delicate term for carnal knowledge and marital intimacy. In this case the Sodomites wished to vent their lust upon the visitors" (*Bereishis,* Mesorah Publications, Vol. 1, 682).

Just as Lot's hospitality established his righteousness, the behavior of the "men of Sodom—both old and young, all the people from every quarter" (19:4)—established their

wickedness. Based on this evidence, God's subsequent destruction of the city is seen to be just.

BIBLE BACKGROUND:

WHAT WAS THE REAL SIN OF SODOM?

Jewish commentators have tended to downplay the behavior described in Genesis 19, suggesting that the Sodomites' real sin was their lack of hospitality. The great rabbi *Ramban* even suggested that their purpose in gang raping visitors was to prevent the impoverished from coming into their fertile valley. "Although they were notorious for every kind of wickedness their fate was sealed because of their persistent selfishness in not supporting the poor and needy (see Ezek. 16:49)."

While the sin of Sodom was not limited to illicit passion, most references in Scripture to Sodom's sin emphasize the sex sin (compare Jer. 23:14; 2 Pet. 2:6). Jude 1:7 cites "Sodom and Gomorrah, and the cities around them" which, "having given themselves over to sexual immorality and gone after strange flesh, are set forth as an example."

The weight of the evidence is that their attempted homosexual rape of the angels was the culminating sin which fully expressed the wickedness and corruption of the society. (For an unambiguous description of Scripture's attitude toward homosexuality, see Romans 1:21–26).

Lot's futile attempt to save his visitors (19:6–11). Typically, a miracle is unnecessary if its purposes can be achieved by ordinary means. In this case, Lot's efforts to protect his guests were useless.

Lot tried moral persuasion (19:7). He begged his neighbors not to "do so wickedly."

Lot offered his daughters in his guests' place (19:8). This shocking offer reflects both the sanctity of the host-guest relationship in biblical times and the devastating effect of living in a sinful society. Even Lot—who was "oppressed by the filthy conduct of the wicked," which "tormented his righteous soul from day to day by seeing and hearing their lawless deeds" (2 Pet. 2:7, 8)—was debased by his association with them.

Lot's wicked offer has troubled the sages. *Tanchuma* suggested Lot wanted to keep his daughters for himself (compare v. 36). The *Mishna Horayos* suggested that the prevention of perversion takes priority over the prevention of natural forms of immorality. Several rabbinic authorities suggested Lot's offer was insincere, for Lot knew that the men of Sodom would not accept, and he hoped only to gain time. Yet the horror of the offer itself, whatever Lot's intent, reminds us that we cannot make sinners our constant companions without being corrupted by them to some extent.

Lot tried to interpose his body (19:9). The crowd reviled Lot and "pressed hard against" him. The phrase suggests physical violence against Lot. When Lot's efforts proved futile and the Sodomites were about to break down his door, the angels acted.

The miracle and its nature (19:11). The text indicates the angels "struck the men . . . with blindness." The word translated "blindness" suggests a temporary disorientation or delusion, in which a person may "see" but not know what he sees. It seems the men of Sodom did not realize what had happened to them, for they "became weary trying to find the door."

With Lot and his family temporarily secure, the angels told him they were about to destroy the city and urged him to leave. When Lot lingered (Gen. 19:16), the angels transported the family outside the city and urged them to hurry to safety.

How good of God to intervene with miracles when all our efforts fail or when we hesitate to go His way.

THE MIRACLE OF SODOM'S DESTRUCTION   *Genesis 19:23–25*

At dawn, when Lot entered a nearby city named Zoar, "then the Lord rained brimstone and fire on Sodom and Gomorrah, from the Lord out of the heavens." In this rain of fire, the sinful cities and all their inhabitants were destroyed.

THE LOCATION OF SODOM AND THE OTHER SINFUL CITIES
(Genesis 13:11; 18:1, 28)

The biblical text locates Sodom and the other cities which were destroyed in the Jordan River valley, within sight of the heights of Mamre where Abraham lived. Early archaeologists suggested the ruins of these cities now lie under the southern basin of the Dead Sea. In recent years, Willem C. van Hatem and others have suggested the cities may be represented by fire-blackened ruins along wadis (dry riverbeds) in the foothills just south of the Dead Sea. There is no question, however, about the general location of these cities.

The area around Sodom and Gomorrah had natural deposits of asphalt, a flammable, semisolid mixture of bitumens (Gen. 14:10).

The destruction by fire and brimstone (19:24). There is no mystery about how the cities of the plain were destroyed. Archaeologist M. G. Kyle described it succinctly.

There is a stratum of marl mingled with free sulfur. It is a burned out region of oil and asphalt. A great

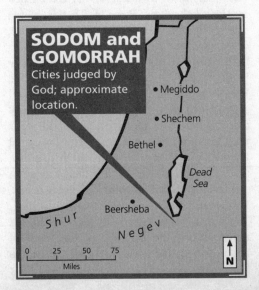

SODOM and GOMORRAH
Cities judged by God; approximate location.

• Megiddo

• Shechem

Bethel •

Dead Sea

Beersheba

Shur

Negev

0   25   50   75
Miles

N

rupture in the strata occurred. At the proper time God kindled the gases. A great explosion took place. The salt and the sulfur were thrown into the heavens red hot, so it did literally rain fire and brimstone from heaven.

Why should the destruction of these cities be considered a miracle? Like an earthquake in California, Sodom might have been destroyed at any time.

Its extraordinary nature. To say that an event is "extraordinary" does not mean that no natural agents can be used. What marked the destruction of Sodom as extraordinary was its occurrence as a judgment on sin (Gen. 18:20), its pre-announcement by God (Gen. 18:21–23), and its timing—immediately after Lot had safely left the city (Gen. 19:23, 24).

Its direct divine intervention. The angels told Lot the Lord had sent them to destroy the city (Gen. 19:13). The text also states that "then the Lord rained brimstone and fire" (Gen. 19:24). God apparently used the angels as instruments to carry out His will. As the one commanding the action, God was considered fully responsible for it.

Its lasting religious significance. The Bible refers back to the destruction of Sodom 28 times, 10 of them in the New Testament. Of these, four speak of the sins of Sodom. Six references in Ezekiel use "Sodom" as a caustic synonym for the northern Hebrew kingdom of Israel, while Revelation 11:8 refers to human civilization as "the great city which spiritually is called Sodom."

The other 17 specific biblical references point to Sodom as a grim reminder of the certainty of divine judgment on sin.

In addition, Luke 17:28–31 emphasizes the suddenness and unexpectedness of the day on which "it rained fire and brimstone from heaven and destroyed them all" (v. 29). Up until that day, the people of Sodom were completely focused on their life here on earth, eating and drinking, buying and selling, planting and building. In the same way, Jesus taught, people will be occupied with the affairs of this world when he returns again to judge mankind as Sodom was judged.

Most significantly, Jesus said of the cities where He taught and performed His miracles and subsequently was rejected, "I say to you that it will be more tolerable in that Day for Sodom than for that city" (Luke 10:12; compare Matt. 10:15; 11:24; Mark 6:11).

This last statement, often repeated in the Gospels, is a healthy reminder. While homosexuality and other sins call for divine judgment, all sins are forgivable, and the saved sinner's life can be redirected to holy ways. Paul reminded the Corinthians that "neither fornicators, nor idolaters, nor adulterers, nor homosexuals, nor sodomites, nor thieves, nor covetous, nor drunkards, nor revilers, nor extortioners will inherit the kingdom of God." But Paul immediately went on to add, "And such were some of you. But you were washed, but you were sanctified, but you were justified in the name of the Lord Jesus and by the Spirit of our God (1 Cor. 6:9–11). The far greater sin is to be exposed to the Christ of the gospel— and to refuse to acknowledge Him as Lord.

As we deal with the question of homosexuality in our day, we should remember that *all* have sinned. The critical issue is not which sins are worse than others, but what will the sinner do with Christ. He will wash, sanctify, justify, and transform all who receive Him.

THE MIRACLE OF LOT'S WIFE
Genesis 19:26

As Lot and his family hurried toward the hills and away from doomed Sodom, according to the biblical account, "his wife looked back behind him, and she became a pillar of salt."

THE NATURE OF THE MIRACLE

There is a question about whether the fate of Lot's wife should be considered a miracle. The text gives no details, and many Bible students have speculated about the exact nature of this event. Deuteronomy 29:22 notes that this entire area around the Dead Sea was "sulfur and salt." The Jewish sage Ibn Ezra suggested the bones of Lot's wife were burned and then encrusted with salt that fell with the sulfur. Lockyer suggests she was probably "struck by lightning and covered and stifled by sulphurous matter and vapors, transforming her into a pillar of salt."

Another theory suggests that an earthquake thrust up a mound of salt from the underground deposits in the area and that Lot's wife was entombed in this pillar. Another possibility is that as Lot's wife looked back toward the cities, she fell into one of the slime pits in the area, where her body was encrusted with salt.

It is interesting that in the first century both the Jewish historian Josephus and the early church father Clement of Rome were shown a pillar identified by local guides as "Lot's wife."

Both Jewish and Christian teachers agree that the death of Lot's wife was an extraordinary event caused by God and that it had religious significance. In this sense, at least, it must be considered a minor miracle.

WAS THE DEATH OF LOT'S WIFE A DIVINE JUDGMENT?

The view that the death of Lot's wife was a divine judgment is deeply rooted in Judeo-Christian tradition.

Suggested reasons for the judgment. The problem for commentators has been to determine a *reason* for the judgment. The *Midrash,* reasoning much as did Job's friends, notes that if Lot's wife had been righteous she would not have come to harm. The sage *Ralbag* thought that her looking back showed compassion on the wicked, which was a sin. *Abarbanel* says she was in the rear trying to save the family wealth when the sulfur and fire overtook her. *Radak* says she had little faith and so looked back to see if the angel's words were true.

Lockyer explains why she was turned into a pillar of salt by arguing that the phrase "she looked back" indicates motive. He says, "God read the motive of her heart (19:26) and

knew of her regret on having to leave the sinful pleasures of Sodom." Looking back was an indication of "incurable rebellion."

In these explanations offered for why Lot's wife died, the commentators go far beyond anything indicated in the biblical text.

A biblical reason for the judgment. The one clear statement we have in Scripture is found in Genesis 19:17. The angels told the family, "Do not look back, or stay anywhere on the plain. Escape to the mountains, lest you be destroyed." So the one certain fact we have is that in looking back Lot's wife disobeyed the angels who were eager to save the family.

THE RELIGIOUS SIGNIFICANCE OF THE MIRACLE

The death of Lot's wife raises a significant question. Does such slight disobedience as merely looking back call for punishment so serious? The story of Lot's wife, intertwined as it is with the story of Sodom, serves as a solemn warning. We human beings are prone to make distinctions between "little" and "big," between "venal" and "mortal" sins. But the disobedience by Lot's wife of a clear command from God was no less a sin than the wicked behavior of the men of Sodom. And any sin, involving as it does rebellion against the will of God, is deserving of death.

So the story of Lot's wife is a helpful reminder. We need not search for arguments to prove that her sin was great and serious. We need simply to remember that in agreeing that Sodom's greater sins called for punishment, we condemn ourselves for our own lesser sins. It is only by the forgiving grace of God that any of us are enabled to stand, purified, in the presence of our Lord.

JESUS' APPLICATION OF THE STORY (LUKE 17:28-32)

Jesus spoke about the unexpected and sudden nature of His second coming, warning that His return would bring terrible judgments on the earth. He used both the Genesis

Flood (Gen. 6—8) and the destruction of Sodom as images of what will happen to a sinful humankind when He returns. So Jesus urged immediate flight from doomed civilization at the first signs of His coming. The need to flee will be so urgent that a person working in the field must not go home even to snatch up food or clothing. And in this context Jesus said, "remember Lot's wife."

The only way to escape the fate of sinners is to run to Christ, without looking back to check on what we have left behind.

CHAPTER 3

❖

MIRACLE UPON MIRACLE!

FROM EGYPT TO SINAI

Exodus 3—20

No period in history has witnessed an outburst of miracles like those compressed into the span of a few brief years around 1400 B.C. During those few years miracles turned the wealthy land of Egypt into a wasted ruin, freed and commissioned a race of slaves as God's chosen people, and shook a flaming mountain as God delivered a Law which continues to shape mankind's moral vision more than three milleniums later.

Perhaps most significantly, the outburst of miracles that marked Israel's Exodus from Egypt indelibly identified God as One who is able to act in this world on behalf of His own.

The Exodus miracles provided Israel with unmistakable evidence of the reality of God. Today, too, the Exodus miracles remind us that God is real, that God is present, and that God has all power.

The impact of this brief period is reflected in both the opening and the conclusion of Psalm 105, the body of which traces the history of the patriarchs and celebrates the miracles by which the Lord redeemed Israel from slavery in Egypt.

Oh, give thanks to the LORD!
Call upon His name;

Make known His deeds among the
  peoples!
Sing to Him, sing psalms to Him!
Talk of all His wondrous works!
Glory in His holy name;
Let the hearts of those rejoice who
  seek the LORD!
Seek the LORD and His strength
Seek His face forevermore!
Remember His marvelous works
  which He has done,
His wonders, and the judgments
  of His mouth,
O seed of Abraham His servant,
You children of Jacob, His chosen
  ones!

. . .

For he remembered His holy
  promise,
And Abraham His servant.
He brought out His people with
  joy,
His chosen ones with gladness (Ps.
  105:1–6, 42, 43).

No other series of events stands out so vividly in the Old Testament. The Exodus and the miracles associated with it had an unparalleled impact on Israel's perception of God and their relationship with Him.

THE ROLE OF MOSES

The towering figure who served as both mediator of the miracles of this period and as Israel's law giver was Moses. He is one of history's most amazing characters. When Moses was born, the Pharaoh of Egypt had decreed death for every male child born to an Israelite. Yet Moses was brought up as a son in Egypt's royal family, where "he was learned in all the wisdom of the Egyptians, and was mighty in words and deeds" (Acts 7:22). In spite of his upbringing, Moses considered himself an Israelite and dreamed of freeing his people.

Moses' identification with the Israelite slaves was so great that, at age forty, he killed a taskmaster who was mistreating a Hebrew slave. When Moses realized the deed was known, he fled from Egypt. His next forty years were spent in the wilderness of the Sinai peninsula, where he herded his father-in-law's sheep. As the decades dragged on, Moses' dream died. But when Moses was eighty years old, God spoke to him from a burning bush, and everything changed.

Moses was called from herding sheep to become shepherd to God's people across the next forty critical years. Moses' first challenge was to win the freedom of his people. God used a series of ten devastating plagues, which struck at Moses' word, to bring Egypt's proud ruler to his knees and force the release of his slaves. God directed Moses and led the people into the Sinai Peninsula. On this journey the people faced a number of perils, each of which was overcome by God's personal, miraculous intervention. Again, Moses was the mediator of these miracles. When at last the people reached Mount Sinai, God Himself appeared atop the mountain, again in the guise of fire shrouded by clouds.

Moses, alone, climbed the mountain, where he was given the Ten Commandments and the rest of the Law which God intended to govern the life of His people. Thus Moses

gained his reputation as Israel's law giver as well as mediator of God's miracles. After Abraham, he was the most awesome and respected of sacred history's figures.

The book of Exodus leaves us at Sinai, as Moses established not only the moral code for Israel but also set out its religious practices.

The last three books of the Pentateuch continue the story of Moses' ministry as he—at last—brought Israel to the borders of Canaan. There Moses finally died.

MIRACLES IN THE BOOK OF EXODUS

The book of Exodus, which covers events of a one- to two-year period, relates the following extraordinary events caused by God which had religious significance.

Summary of Miracles in the Book of Exodus

Miracles of Preparation

THE MIRACLE OF THE BURNING BUSH　*Exodus 3:2–6*

This first miracle in the book involves the appearance of God to Moses as a "flame of fire" (see Mark 12:26; Luke 20:37). Moses saw the fire raging inside a bush, but the bush was not consumed. When Moses approached to see why the bush wasn't burned up, the Lord called to him. Moses was told to take off his sandals for he was standing on ground made holy by the presence of God. God then identified Himself as the God of Abraham and the patriarchs, and Moses hid his face in awe, unwilling to look at God.

Many people in discussing this miracle have focused on the failure of the fire to burn the bush; but far more significant miracles are involved.

MIRACLES OF THE BURNING BUSH　*(Exodus 3:2, 3)*

The miracle of the unburned bush. A flame which does not burn may seem to be a mira-

cle. In fact, the text emphasizes the flame no less than five times in verses 2 and 3. Moses was curious because there was a "flame of fire," the bush was "burning with fire" but "not burned up." It was certainly a "great [unusual] sight," and Moses wondered "why the bush does not burn." Moses was at first just curious, not frightened. He assumed there must be a natural cause, and he went closer to investigate it.

The description tells us much about Moses' state of mind. He was not superstitious, and he certainly didn't expect a miracle. Yet when Moses drew near, what he experienced was miraculous indeed.

The miracle of God's manifestation (Exodus 3:2). The Angel of the Lord (identified as God in 3:4) "appeared to him in a flame of fire."

Fire is frequently used in descriptions of manifestations of the divine presence (compare Gen. 15:17; Ex. 13:21f; 19:18; 24:17; Num. 9:15–16; 14:14; Deut. 1:33; 4:11–12; Ezek. 1:4, 13; 8:2; Ps. 78:14). Fire is formless, mysterious, nonmaterial. Humans draw back from raging fires, aware that fire is dangerous and destructive. Both the nature of God and His awesomeness are symbolized in His manifestations as fire.

At this appearance of the Lord to him, Moses hid his face in fear (Ex. 3:6). How striking that, as Moses came to know God more and more intimately, he lost his fear and begged to see more of God than he had been shown (see Ex. 33:18–23). It should be the same with us. It is right to be awed when we first sense God's presence. But as we grow in faith, it is appropriate to desire to draw closer and closer.

The miracle of God's conversation with Moses (3:7—4:17). The book of Genesis reports direct divine revelations to Abraham and others through dreams or in appearances as the Angel of the Lord. But this is the first report in the Bible of direct conversation with God. This appearance provided the context for a number of significant revelations. In this conversation with Moses, the Lord:

- identified Himself (3:6),
- announced His intent to free Israel (3:7–9),
- commissioned Moses as His agent (3:10–12),
- revealed His personal name to Moses (3:14–15),
- instructed Moses what to say to Israel's elders,
- described exactly what would happen when Moses confronted Pharaoh (3:18b–22),
- gave Moses three confirming signs, or miracles, and
- permitted Moses to have his brother Aaron as his spokesman (4:10–17)

Each element of this divine-human conversation authenticated the appearance of "Him who dwelt in the bush" as God (Deut. 33:16). Everything the Lord told Moses happened just as the Lord said, and Moses was able to do and to repeat the three signs he was given by the Lord.

THE RELIGIOUS SIGNIFICANCE OF THE MIRACLE APPEARANCE AND REVELATION OF GOD

This appearance of God is one of Scripture's pivotal events. It put sacred history on a different course. The appearance set in motion a series of events which led to the freeing of Israel from slavery, the giving of the Law on Sinai, the unifying of the people by a common religion and code of behavior, and their eventual settlement in the promised land. This miracle appearance of God to Moses was viewed from that point on as having the following religious significance.

The miracle appearance marked the revelation of God's personal name to Israel (Exodus 3:13–15). The title "God of your father . . ." was widely used in the ancient Near East. This was a title, not a name. In the biblical world, the "name" conveyed something of the essential nature of the person or thing named. When Moses asked the Lord how to respond if he were asked the name of the God he represented, Moses was seeking a deeper revelation of God's nature.

God responded by revealing the name *Yahweh,* or *Jehovah,* formed by the four consonants YHVH. Just what this name means, and what it reveals about God, has been discussed and debated. All agree that the name is constructed on the Hebrew verb "to be." Thus the translation in our text, "I AM." In Scripture, YHVH is associated with the Lord's personal involvement in the lives of his people and his intervention on their behalf. I AM emphasizes the ever-present nature of God, and it probably means something like "The God Who Is Always Present."

The Hebrews then enslaved in Egypt knew God as the One who had spoken in the past to their forefathers: Abraham, Isaac, and Jacob. They may have known God as the One who in the future would keep the covenant promises given to the patriarchs. But in all their decades of misery, they had never perceived God as present with them. In the next few months, they would come to know God as He *Who is Always Present,* as God made His presence known in miracle after miracle.

God told Moses, "This is my name forever, and this is my Memorial [how I am to be remembered] to all generations" (Ex. 3:15b). From this time onward, Israel was never to doubt the powerful presence of God, or His complete commitment to His people. From the Exodus onward, Israel was to remember that God would be with them always in His wonder-working power, meeting their needs as He had met the needs of His people long ago.

The miracle appearance marked God's commissioning of Moses (3:12). The appearance of God as fire within the bush launched Moses' career as God's agent. As the months passed, that commission would be unmistakably confirmed again and again. Yet an even more certain sign that Moses was God's man would follow.

God told Moses "this will be a sign ['ot, *miraculous confirmation*] that I have sent you:

When you have brought the people out of Egypt, you shall serve God on this mountain." The extraordinary event that would confirm for all time the divinely appointed nature of Moses' mission would be the assembly of Israel to serve God on Sinai—the very place where God was appearing to Moses in the burning bush.

The miracle appearance showed that the Lord is a covenant-keeping God (3:6–8). God announced Himself as the God of Abraham, then proceeded to state His intent to bring the Israelites into the land He had promised to Abraham's descendants. The series of events that brought about the redemption of Israel from slavery and led to the conquest of Canaan demonstrate how committed the Lord was to keeping His promises.

What reassurance this is for all believers. We can also rely on His promises to us.

The miracle appearance contained an implicit promise of life after death (Exodus 3:6; Matthew 22:30–32). Jesus pointed to God's first words to Moses when speaking with the Sadducees, who believed that death was the end. God told Moses, "I am the God of Abraham. . . ." God did not say, "I was the God of Abraham," as though Abraham were dead and gone. In saying "I am the God of Abraham," God indicated that Abraham existed even then, some 600 years after he had died.

In all these ways, God's appearance to Moses in the burning bush was one of history's most significant events.

THE MIRACLE OF MOSES' ROD
Exodus 4:2–5, 30–31; 7:9–13

When Moses expressed doubt that the elders of Israel would pay attention to a stranger from out of the Sinai, God gave Moses several miraculous signs to authenticate his mission.

The first sign was turning his rod into a serpent, and then back again into a rod. Later when Moses performed this sign for Pharaoh, the "magicians of Egypt" appeared to duplicate the feat.

THE TRANSFORMATION OF MOSES' ROD

Several features of this account make it clear that a real miracle was involved.

The use of Moses' own rod (4:2). God used the rod in Moses' hand. Moses knew this rod for what it was. It was no piece of specially prepared magic equipment designed to promote an illusion. Likewise, God will use what *we* have, transforming it as necessary to achieve his purposes.

Moses' reaction to the transformation (4:3, 4). God told Moses to throw the rod on the ground, where it became a serpent. The Hebrew language uses the general word for serpent but, since Moses "fled from it," it was probably a poisonous snake.

God then told Moses to take the serpent by the tail. The Hebrew word indicates that the still-fearful Moses "snatched at" or "grabbed" the serpent. It then became Moses' familiar rod once again.

The belief of the Israelites (4:30–31). When Moses performed the signs he had been given "in the sight of the people" of Israel, they believed. And when Moses indicated the Lord had promised to set them free from slavery, "they bowed their heads and worshiped."

Note that the miracle which confirmed the messenger also opened the hearts of the people to welcome his message. Like other miracles, this one had a deeper purpose than its surface appearance.

THE REACTION OF PHARAOH TO THE MIRACLE
(Exodus 7:9–13)

When Moses first spoke with Pharaoh, Egypt's ruler demanded he "show a miracle for yourselves." This was not a surprising demand.

Miracle stories in Egypt. The Egyptians enjoyed tales of magic and the supernatural. One popular work, known as *Tales of the Magicians,* tells of King Cheops (Khufu), who reigned about 2600 B.C., being entertained with tales of famous magicians by some of his sons. One story is about Waba-aner, whose wife was being unfaithful to him. Waba-aner molded a crocodile from wax and muttered a magic spell over the image. The next day, when his wife's lover left and stopped to wash nearby, Waba-aner's servant threw the wax figure into the water. It became a crocodile and killed the lover.

The Pharaoh of Moses' day would have known this and other tales of magic. It was natural for him to ask for magical proof of Moses' commission by God. And the story of Waba-aner would have prepared him for the specific sign that Moses was given!

The confrontation (7:10–13). When Pharaoh demanded Moses and Aaron "show a miracle [mophet] for yourselves," Aaron cast down his rod. The assumption is that as the spokesman for Moses, Aaron was bearing Moses' rod. Immediately it became a snake. But the feat was apparently duplicated by Egypt's magicians—until Aaron's rod "swallowed up" their rods. Several things are of note in this story.

The change of names (7:9–12). The Hebrew word for "serpent," *nahash*, is found in Exodus 4:2 and 7:15. In these verses, another word, *tannin*, is used. This word indicates *giant* reptiles, including crocodiles. The serpent Moses and Aaron produced was no garden snake!

Pharaoh's wise men (7:11). Pharaoh called for the very best Egypt could produce—its "wise men and the sorcerers" and its "magicians" with their enchantments. It took Egypt's best to compete with this stranger from the desert and his slave brother.

Trickery or magic? The wise men and magicians of Egypt duplicated Aaron's feat ("did in like manner," v. 11). Some have argued that the conflict was a pseudo-struggle between illusionists. By stroking the stomach of a reptile turned upside down, whether snake or crocodile, the creature can be placed in a listless trance. When thrown down, it becomes active again. So even if Aaron's staff-to-snake-to-staff transformation was a miracle, some scholars claim the Egyptians performed an illusion.

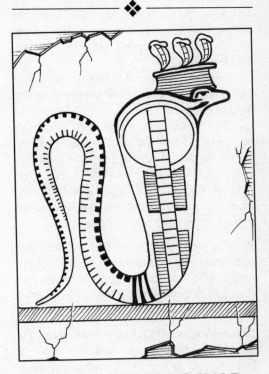

BIBLE BACKGROUND:

SNAKES IN EGYPTIAN RELIGION

In the ancient Near East, snakes were associated with wisdom, fertility, and healing. Not so in the Bible, where their association with temptation, sin, and Satan is established in the third chapter of Genesis. Nowhere in the Bible except during the Exodus period are snakes associated with miracles. Why did the Lord choose this miracle to give to Moses?

The answer lies in the role of snakes in Egyptian religion. While considered a source of evil and danger, the snake was the primary form of the god Apophis. The snake goddesses Renenutet and Meret-seger were worshiped so that snake-bite could be avoided or healed. The cobra-goddess Wadjyt was the patroness of lower Egypt, and the poised cobra was a symbol of Pharaoh's kingship and his title, *weret hekaw*, "great of magic."

When the serpent produced by Aaron's rod consumed the serpents produced by Egypt's magicians, it was a powerful sign of the impotence of the deities of Egypt before the God of Israel.

Others have pointed out that the serpent was worshiped as a God in Egypt, and that Scripture teaches that demons lie behind the pagan deities (compare Lev. 17:7; Deut. 32:17; Ps. 106:37).

Worship on Stele of Paneb, showing him worshiping the goddess Meret-seger in the form of a serpent

The events in Egypt represented a conflict between God and the dark powers that had bound his people. Perhaps we are to understand this initial confrontation as the beginning of a conflict of supernatural powers. Thus we can interpret the transformations performed by Egypt's sorcerers as real.

Proof of God's superiority (7:12). The magicians' triumph was temporary. Aaron's staff immediately consumed the great serpents produced by the magicians. God in his superior power was triumphant.

Pharaoh's response (7:13). Pharaoh refused to accept what his own eyes had seen. Since he had watched Aaron's rod devour the creatures produced by his own magicians and sorcerers, he had clearer evidence of God's presence with Moses than did the elders of Israel. A person who wills not to believe cannot be convinced, even by miracles.

It would take a series of devastating judgments to bring the proud ruler to his knees before the God of the Hebrew slaves.

THE MIRACLE OF MOSES' LEPROUS HAND   Exodus 4:6–8, 30–31

Moses had expressed concern that the elders of Israel might not accept him as God's messenger. God gave him a second authenticating sign, which he later showed to his people but not to Pharaoh.

THE SIGN EXPERIENCED BY MOSES   (4:6, 7)

The second authenticating sign given to Moses was a dual expression of the miracle-working power of God. Moses was to slip his hand inside his garment and touch his chest.

When he drew out the hand, it was leprous. Moses was then to touch his chest again, and when he drew the hand out it was restored. What can we say about this miracle?

It served as a "faith sign." Some have called it a faith sign, as it was intended to help relieve Moses' fears and resolve his doubts. As such, the miracle, called a "sign" in verse 8, was evidence to Moses of God's working in his life.

It was a traumatic experience for Moses. What horror Moses must have felt as he saw his hand covered with leprosy in its advanced stages. There was no known cure for this awful disease, which marked the victim as an outcast.

It was a test of faith for Moses. God told Moses to put his hand inside his clothing and hold the leprous hand next to his chest. The Hebrew word translated "leprosy" throughout the Old Testament means "infectious skin disease," and it is not limited to what we call leprosy today (Hansen's disease). Moses would have shuddered at the thought of placing his infected hand against his unprotected, healthy skin. Yet Moses obeyed, and when he drew out his hand it was fully restored.

It was a significant foreshadowing of God's saving power. In Scripture leprosy is often a mark of divine judgment (compare Lev. 13, 14; Num. 12; 2 Kings 5:1–14; 15:4–5; 2 Chron. 26:16–21). This sign may have suggested God's displeasure with Moses' hesitancy and his doubts. But the healing of the leprosy was far more significant than the discovery that the hand was infected. Whatever judgments God might inflict on His people, He would reverse them on evidence of repentance. In this miracle, the slaves would be able to see not only the power of God but the promise of the restoration of their freedom and the healing of their wounded hearts.

THE MIRACLE OF NILE WATER TURNED TO BLOOD   Exodus 4:9

God described a third miracle which Moses would be able to perform when he returned to Egypt. This was the ability to pour out clean water from the Nile River and see it turn into blood on the ground. The fascinating thing about this miracle is that it apparently was never performed!

An unperformed miracle. There is no evidence in the Exodus accounts that this miracle was needed to authenticate Moses and his mission. This miracle is similar to the turning of the waters of the Nile River into blood, which was the first of the ten plagues, but it is not the same—nor did it have the same purpose. This miracle, like the rod and the leprous hand, was intended to authenticate Moses as God's agent. The miracle of the Nile, along with the other nine, was intended to judge Egypt and its pagan gods (Ex. 12:12).

The significance of the unperformed miracle. It was apparently unnecessary for Moses to perform the third sign to convince Israel's leaders of his call from God. They were more ready to believe than Moses had feared. This provision of a third, unperformed miracle reminds us that God can do more than the necessary. His resources are endless. God has at hand whatever it takes to achieve His purposes.

THE TEN PLAGUES   *Exodus 7—11*

THE TEN AS "PROVING ACTS"

These chapters describe a series of ten devastating plagues that struck Egypt. The ten have rightly been called "proving acts." The book of Exodus lists three reasons why God imposed this series of judgments on Egypt. Through them:

God proved His superiority to the gods of Egypt. Exodus 12:12 declares, "And against all the gods of Egypt I will execute judgment: I am the Lord." Each plague demonstrated the futility of relying on the deities of the Egyptians.

God proved His presence to Israel. Exodus 6:7 says, "I will take you as My people. . . . Then you shall know that I am the Lord your God who brings you out from under the burdens of the Egyptians." Forever after, Israel looked back to this series of events as unmistakable proof of God's commitment to His people, the descendants of the patriarchs.

God proved His power to the Egyptians. Exodus 7:5 declares, "The Egyptians will know that I am the Lord, when I stretch out My hand on Egypt and bring out the children of Israel from among them." The Egyptians had worshiped idols. Through the ten great "proving acts" of God, they were forced to acknowledge the power of the one true God.

THE RELIGION AND GODS OF EGYPT

Egyptian theology was complex and, in many ways, confusing. Ancient Egypt was divided into forty petty states, called *nomes*. Each of these had local deities. As various *nomes* gained or lost political power, their prominence was reflected in the importance given the gods of the *nomes'* major cities. Over the centuries, attributes and roles ascribed to one deity were added to the attributes and roles of others. Thus, more than one deity might be worshiped as creator, or spoken of as supreme in the underworld, or viewed as the goddess of fertility or healing.

While the system of gods worshiped by the Egyptians was confusing, they looked to their gods to maintain the harmony of the natural universe. The gods governed the passage of night and day, controlled the seasonal flooding of the life-giving Nile River, and governed every other feature of life in the land.

It was stunning to the Egyptians when the God of the Hebrew slaves imposed on Egypt ten great proving acts which destroyed the harmony of their lives, shattering the illusion that they could rely on their gods.

In the ten plagues, the very foundation of Egyptian religion—the belief that their gods existed and were in fact able to maintain nature's harmony—was exposed. Egypt's gods were judged, and all power was shown to reside in a God the Egyptians had scorned—the one true God of their slaves.

BIBLE BACKGROUND:

HOW ANCIENT PEOPLES RATED DEITIES

In the ancient world and throughout Old Testament times, the power ascribed to deities was a reflection of the military might of their worshipers. The Babylonian warrior assumed that his gods were the most powerful during the era of Babylonian empire-building.

In the same way, the Egyptians—one of the most powerful nations on earth at the time of Moses—credited their gods with their dominant position in the world. It is no wonder that Egypt's young Pharaoh initially scoffed at the God worshiped by the Hebrew slaves. To Pharaoh, the powerlessness of the Israelites was proof of the feebleness of their God! It took the devastating series of plagues which God brought on the land to convince the proud Egyptians to submit to the God of their slaves. His acts revealed that *their* gods—not the God of Israel—were weak.

THE MIRACLE OF THE NILE TURNED TO BLOOD   *Exodus 7:14–24*

The Nile River was the source of Egypt's life. Each year its swelling waters deposited fresh soil in the fields along its shores, making the land fertile. Later in the year, its waters were channeled to irrigate the growing crops. The Nile also teemed with fish, which served as the basic source of protein for most Egyptians. It's no wonder that the Egyptians deified the Nile. The Nile god, known as Hopi, was portrayed as a vigorous but fat man. To strike at the Nile was to strike at Egypt's very life-source.

When Pharaoh scoffed at the signs Moses displayed (Ex. 7:9–13), Moses announced that God would strike the waters of the Nile and "they shall be turned to blood. And the fish that are in the river shall die, the river shall

stink, and the Egyptians will loathe to drink the water of the river" (Ex. 7:17–18).

Several things are significant about this first proving act.

It was clearly a miracle (Exodus 7:19–20). Some have tried to provide naturalistic explanations of the plagues of Exodus. To them, the "bloody Nile" was nothing more than a major outbreak of an algae which tinted the waters red. But the biblical text indicates that this curse included rivers, ponds, and pools of water throughout Egypt—and even water collected in buckets and cisterns (Ex. 7:19). This pre-announced event was a miracle indeed.

BIBLE BACKGROUND:

THE RELATIONSHIP OF EGYPTIAN MAGIC AND EGYPTIAN GODS

One standard title given the goddess Isis was *Weret Hekau,* "Great of Magic."

Egyptians had two names: a "real name" which was kept secret, and a public name. They believed that if an enemy learned the real name of a person, that enemy would have power over him. One Egyptian myth related how Isis created a serpent to sting the sun god, Ra. When its poison was killing this greatest of Egyptian deities, Isis promised to cure him if he would reveal to her his secret name. He did so, and she became "Great of Magic." By using Ra's name in incantations, she could force him to do whatever she demanded.

This story illustrates the link between Egyptian magic and the gods. To make any spell work, it was essential to call forth the spirit of deity *by name.* The Egyptians believed that the deity, when called upon by his or her real name, had to follow the desires of the magician who was casting the spell!

Since the magicians of Egypt turned water to blood "by their enchantments," they called on their gods to duplicate what God had done.

The miracle was "duplicated" by Egypt's magicians (7:22). The report that Egypt's sorcerers did the same thing "with their enchantments" reminds us that this was a conflict of supernatural powers. It was more than a demonstration of the power of the true God versus the figments of man's imagination. Behind the gods of Egypt lurked demons, exercising their powers to keep the peoples in spiritual bondage (Lev. 17:7; Ps. 106:37). Yet, how ironic the report that Egypt's magicians called on the powers of their deities to do by magic what God had done.

The miracle was duplicated, but not reversed! Here is the irony of the text. The demonic beings behind Egypt's deities could move only in the direction allowed by God! They could not reverse what he had done. And they didn't even *try!*

The gods of Egypt enabled the magicians to do on a tiny scale what God had done "throughout all Egypt." But this simply made matters worse!

Strikingly, this irony was not obvious to the Pharaoh. He took the work of his wise men, although it was tiny by comparison, as reassurance of the power of Egypt's gods. What empty comfort this must have been to the people of his land. They were forced to dig holes along the river bank so the sand could filter the water for drinking (Ex. 7:24).

The miracle was long remembered by the Egyptians. A catalog of catastrophes dating from 1350–1100 B.C. described terrible conditions in Egypt which occurred about a thousand years before. Among the listed disasters is one involving the Nile:

> Why really, the River is blood,
> If one drinks of it,
>   One rejects (it) as human
>   and thirsts for water.

It is fascinating to speculate about the source of this description, coming as it does so shortly after the Exodus events.

THE MIRACLE OF THE FROGS
Exodus 8:1–14

Egypt was familiar with frogs. Each year as the Nile began to recede from its flood stage, in September/October, frogs would breed in the pools of water left behind. In fact, one goddess of fertility, Heqt, was portrayed with the head of a frog. So there had always been frogs aplenty in Egypt. But before this

The Nile River and its water was the lifeblood of Egypt, and when it turned to blood they dug holes to let the sand filter the water for drinking.

miracle, there had never been frogs in such abundance.

The text tells us that frogs "covered the land," and Psalm 105:30 adds this detail: "Their land abounded with frogs, even in the chambers of their king."

There are several fascinating aspects to this second of the ten mighty acts that proved God's presence and power to both Israel and the Egyptians.

Heqt was goddess of fertility and childbirth. The fact that Heqt was linked with childbirth has led some to suppose that this plague was retribution for an earlier Pharaoh's demand that Egypt's midwives kill Hebrew male babies at birth (Ex. 1:15).

Egypt's magicians again made matters worse! (Exodus 8:7). Again Egypt's sorcerers duplicated Moses' miracle—and created more frogs! Perhaps these magicians intended to drive the frogs back into the river, but their magic was reversed by God. They actually multiplied rather than reduced the number of frogs.

Again, the irony is strong. "We can do that!" Egypt's sorcerers claimed. And in doing their best, they made the situation worse. With servants like these, Pharaoh didn't need any enemies!

Pharaoh at last asked Moses to entreat the Lord (8:8). For the first time, Pharaoh seemed to acknowledge the power of God. He begged Moses to entreat God to remove the frogs. But like many who call on God when in trouble, Pharaoh would quickly forget him when this trouble passed.

Moses permitted Pharaoh to say "when" (8:9–11). Moses gave Pharaoh the honor of saying when the frogs would go. In this way Moses, offered further proof of the power of Israel's God. There could be no trickery involved here. God would act on the timetable Pharaoh himself set.

It seems ironic that Pharaoh said "tomorrow." In effect, he asked for another night with frogs in his bedroom! How often we look to

the Lord and hope that perhaps he will act in our lives "tomorrow." Let's claim our privileges as God's children, and in faith call on the Lord to act in our *today!*

BIBLE BACKGROUND:
PHARAOH'S HARD HEART

Throughout the description of the plagues, reference is made to Pharaoh's hardened attitude [heart] toward Moses and God. The stubborn ruler refused to bow and submit to the Lord, no matter how great the evidence of his power.

Some Exodus verses describe Pharaoh's heart as hard (Ex. 7:13, 22), while others speak of God hardening Pharaoh's heart (Ex. 7:3), and still others—as in this case—speak of Pharaoh hardening his own heart (Ex. 8:15). How could God blame or punish an individual whose heart he had hardened?

In Old Testament thought, God was seen as involved in everything. This idiom in no way diminishes the Pharaoh's personal responsibility for his choices. We also need to ask what God *did* to harden Pharaoh's heart. What God did was to reveal gradually more and more of himself. When the elders of Israel saw the signs God gave to Moses, they believed and worshiped (Ex. 4:31). When Pharaoh saw the same authenticating signs, "Pharaoh's heart grew hard" (Ex. 7:13). God did not play with Pharaoh, forcing him to act against his will. Each succeeding revelation led to a reaction which further demonstrated Pharaoh's pride and arrogance.

We see similar responses today. As the gospel is shared, some welcome its good news while others reject it. Just as the sun melts wax and hardens clay, so the light of revelation melts open hearts while causing closed hearts to harden.

Even the removal of the frogs proved to be a plague (8:13, 14). Moses promised that, just as Pharaoh had asked, the frogs would "depart from you, from your houses, from your servants; and from your people" (Ex. 8:11). But Pharaoh had not specified "how" he expected the frogs to go. The frogs that infested the land simply died—"out of the houses, out of the courtyards, and out of the fields. The people gathered them together in heaps, and the land stank."

When God answers the prayers of sinners, it may not be what they expected!

The plague was more than a nuisance (Exodus 8:3; Psalm 78:45). When we read the description of the infestation, we're likely to laugh. The frogs would "come into your house, into your bedroom, on your bed, into the houses of your servants, on your people, into your ovens, and into your kneading bowls." But these frogs were more than a nuisance. Psalm 78:45 speaks of "frogs which destroyed [devastated] them." Apparently, none of the Egyptian people died, but the piles of rotting frogs polluted the land, and their stench permeated the air.

THE MIRACLE OF THE LICE   *Exodus 8:16–19*

Only a few verses are devoted to this third plague, but it is still significant. The meaning of the Hebrew word *kinnim*, translated as "lice," is difficult to determine. Among the suggested translation, along with "lice," have been "gnats," "mosquitoes," "maggots," and the more general term "vermin." The description of these vermin being "on man and beast" suggests "lice" is as likely a possibility as any other.

Note that:

The miracle was unannounced. Previous wonders had been pre-announced by God. This one struck without warning. It also apparently followed immediately after Pharaoh's hardened response to the divine relief from the plague of frogs (Ex. 8:15).

In a sense, this timing may be seen as evidence of God's grace. The longer the consequences of our wrong actions are delayed, the more likely we are to repeat them. A parent is wise to impose consequences for the wrong

actions of his or her children immediately, rather than to delay in hope that no discipline will be required. God struck immediately after Pharaoh hardened his heart as a clear indication that Pharaoh had done wrong.

The miracle could not be duplicated (Exodus 8:16–18). When Aaron struck the ground with his rod, the dust of the land "became lice on man and beast." This was an act of creation; of bringing life from inanimate matter. The magicians "worked with their enchantments to bring forth lice," but they could not. Only the Creator God can cause what is dead to live.

Newspaper headlines proclaimed in 1953 that Stanley Miller, a college science student, had created "life in a test tube." In fact, Miller had mixed chemicals and tried to duplicate conditions which evolutionists thought had once existed on earth. What he actually produced were some amino acids and other simple compounds found in living things—and ounces of sludge. While amino acids are building blocks in living creatures, they are not life. It was as though a person found three or four blocks in the back yard, and newspaper headlines trumpeted, "Local man builds 50-story skyscraper!"

In spite of the excitement in 1953, scientists in the years since have not come close to creating life—and they never will.

The miracle's source was acknowledged by Egypt's sorcerers (8:19). The magicians of Egypt were finally impressed. This was one feat they couldn't duplicate, and they reported to Pharaoh, "This is the finger of God."

The word for God here is the general term, *elohim*—not the personal name of Israel's God, Yahweh. This confession should not be understood as a testimony to the Lord. It was simply a confession by the magicians that they had been defeated by a supernatural power that far outdistanced the powers they represented. This confession is significant. Egypt's best admitted they fell short of these two representatives of the Lord whom Pharaoh still refused to take seriously!

Egypt's wise men were not heard from again. This is the last time the magicians or sorcerers of the Pharaoh confronted Moses and Aaron. They withdrew, defeated. But even more than a simple defeat may be involved.

The Egyptians made a fetish of personal cleanliness. Herodotus, the Greek historian, reported that no one was allowed to enter a temple in Egypt with vermin on his body and that priests were to shave their bodies every three days. And Egypt's wise men—drawn from the priestly class—were now lice-infested too. Not only were these opponents of the Lord defeated; they were cut off from the source of their powers. They had no doubt that in this plague a great supernatural power had been at work.

THE MIRACLE OF THE BITING FLIES
Exodus 8:20–32

Another miracle judgment struck immediately without any report of relief from the previous plague. Moses was told to "rise early" and wait for Pharaoh where he came down to the waters to bathe. Moses was to demand that the Israelites be permitted to go into the desert to worship the Lord. If Pharaoh refused, God would send "swarms of flies on you and your servants."

The Hebrew word translated "flies" is `arov. It is found only here in the entire Old Testament, making its meaning uncertain. It may be a general term for insects or—as the Septuagint renders it—it may refer specifically to the dog fly [stable fly], with a vicious bite which draws blood.

The prospect of Egypt filled with swarms of these insects "on you and your servants, on your people and into your houses" (Ex. 8:21) would be terrifying indeed. Pharaoh was told that this miraculous sign would be given "to-morrow." Then Moses and Aaron withdrew.

There are several distinctive elements in the account of this miracle.

The miracle plague was to strike the Egyptians only (Exodus 8:22–24). God's people were subject to the distress caused by earlier

plagues on Egypt. But from now on, only the Egyptians would suffer under the hand of God.

God declared, "I will make a difference between My people and your people." When we experience troubles, it may be hard for us to realize that the Lord still makes a distinction between his own and others. We have no idea how many troubles we have been spared. But we do know that in our trials, God provides a strength and peace which no others can know.

Pharaoh bore the brunt of this plague (8:21, 24). Both the announcement of this plague and its description focused on Pharaoh himself. "Thick swarms of flies came into the house of Pharaoh, into his servants' houses, and into all the land . . . ."

In Egyptian thought, the pharaoh of the land was the primary mediator between the people and Egypt's gods. It was his responsibility to maintain the harmony of the land. It is clear from the account of this plague that what motivated Pharaoh was not the welfare

After the lice came swarms of flies.

of his people but his own well-being! It was his personal suffering that moved him to call quickly for Moses and Aaron!

Pharaoh appeared willing to compromise (8:25–30). From the beginning, Moses had demanded that Israel be permitted to travel three days' journey into the wilderness to sacrifice to the Lord (Ex. 3:18; 5:3). This request was another evidence of God's grace. If Moses had demanded initially that Pharaoh free his slaves, resistance would have been intense. By asking for less than the Lord intended to do, God made it easier for Pharaoh to agree to Moses' request.

But this approach actually made no difference as far as the pharaoh was concerned. Intent on oppressing Israel, he was unresponsive to Moses' request.

Even while tormented by the biting insects, Pharaoh tried to negotiate. He told Moses that the Israelites could sacrifice "in the land" (Ex. 8:25). Moses replied that his people's sacrifices would be "an abomination" to the Egyptians, so Pharaoh's solution was impractical. The same word translated "abomination" or "objectionable" is used in Genesis 43:32 and 46:34. There it relates to the Egyptian's attitude toward eating with Hebrews and to the Hebrews' vocation as shepherds.

Pharaoh recognized the force of the argument and gave in. He promised to let the Hebrew people go, if only Moses will "intercede for me." Once again, we see Pharaoh's basic concern. He did not ask Moses to intercede for his people, but "for me."

Pharaoh again went back on his agreement (8:31–32). Moses promised to pray to the Lord, indicating that the flies will "depart tomorrow." As quickly as the swarms of flies had arrived they would disappear. And Moses warned Pharaoh not to "deal deceitfully any more" in regard to letting Israel go.

In spite of this warning, when the swarms were removed "Pharaoh hardened his heart at this time also; neither would he let the people go" (Ex. 8:32).

How clearly Pharaoh in these accounts represents the sinfulness of the human heart.

Called to represent his people and serve them, Pharaoh's first concern was always himself. When under intense pressure, Pharaoh seemed ready to submit to God, but as soon as the pressure was relieved, his arrogant and cruel attitude revived. In these reactions to God's self-revelation, we see mirrored the flaws of all humankind.

THE MIRACLE OF THE ANIMAL EPIDEMIC   *Exodus 9:1–7*

Anthrax has been suggested as the disease which caused this epidemic. It is clear from the text that it should be interpreted as a miracle, whatever the disease may have been. Its miraculous nature is seen in its prediction, its appearance at the designated time, and in the immunity of the Israelites' cattle.

The meaning of "all" in the text (Exodus 9:6). The text indicates that "all of the livestock of Egypt died" in the epidemic. How then could more cattle have been killed in hail storms, as described in Exodus 9:22f ? The answer is found in Exodus 9:3. The plague was limited to "your cattle in the field." So it was all the livestock of Egypt grazing on open range at the time of the plague that suffered in this epidemic. Those confined to stables or pens survived.

Pharaoh's skepticism displayed (9:7). Moses announced that the epidemic which killed the cattle of the Egyptians would not touch the cattle of the Israelites. This time Pharaoh sent servants to check, and he learned that not one head of Israelite livestock had died. Pharaoh ignored this evidence. Again, his heart "became hard, and he did not let the people go" (Ex. 9:7).

The plague had not harmed Pharaoh personally. He apparently didn't care that the wealth of his people was being destroyed.

THE MIRACLE OF THE BOILS
Exodus 9:8–11

In this sixth proving act, God caused boils to erupt on the Egyptian people and their animals. The Hebrew word *shehin,* translated as "boils," suggests deep, painful, ulcerous boils. Deuteronomy 28:27 warned Israel against disobeying the Lord lest God punish them with "the boils of Egypt." Clearly, the fiery eruptions were no normal inflammations.

The boils were on "all the Egyptians" (Exodus 9:11). Again Israel was exempt from the effect of God's judgment on the oppressors. The Egyptians were guilty corporately as well as individually for their nation's treatment of the Hebrew slaves.

The magicians were singled out for extreme affliction (9:11). The sorcerers to whom Pharaoh had turned to oppose Moses were so covered with boils that they "could not stand before Moses because of the boils." While all members of a sinful society bear some guilt, some individuals are more guilty than others. When God judges, his punishments are proportionate and fair.

Only now did God harden the heart of Pharaoh (9:13). After each of the preceding miracles, Scripture indicated either that "Pharaoh's heart grew hard" (Ex. 7:13; 7:22; 8:19; 8:32; 9:7) or that Pharaoh "hardened his heart" (Ex. 8:15). The natural inclination of Pharaoh's heart, without any intervention by God, had been clearly displayed. Some have taken God's hardening of Pharaoh's heart to be a judicial act. That is, Pharaoh had resisted God's will so stubbornly that part of God's punishment was to cause him to remain stubborn.

THE MIRACLE OF DEVASTATING HAILSTORMS   *Exodus 9:13–25*

This confrontation between Moses and Pharaoh was unique. Moses warned Pharaoh that if he had wished, God could have wiped out all the Egyptians. The land had been spared only to serve as an arena in which the Lord could display his power and prove his presence. In spite of the evidence of God's greatness in the preceding plagues, Pharaoh

continued to tyrannize God's people (Ex. 9:17, "exalt yourself against").

The downpour of "very heavy hail" (Exodus 9:18, 23). Some commentators have made much of the fact that Egypt does have infrequent and light hailstorms, arguing that the miracle involved intensifying and controlling the timing of a natural phenomenon. This misses the point, which is that each of the proving acts was unmistakably a supernatural event. The hailstones struck throughout Egypt, destroying the barley and flax crops which had just come up (Ex. 9:31) killing any humans caught in the fields, and felling livestock. The hailstones were of tremendous size, and "fire [lightning] mingled with the hail." The text specifically says that never had there been such a storm in all [any part of] Egypt "since it became a nation" thousands of years before!

There is no need to argue that this or any other plague which struck Egypt "really could have happened" by pointing to similar natural happenings. The biblical text emphasizes the fact that these were *miracles, not like* similar natural events.

❖

"Never had there been such a storm" as the hail and lightning God sent on Egypt.

The first death-dealing judgment (9:19). The earlier miracles were either nuisances or caused some suffering. It was a bother to have to dig along the Nile for water, and the biting flies and boils were a painful inconvenience. But now, suddenly, one of God's proving acts threatened to take the lives of Egyptians. There is a definite escalation in the seriousness of the actions caused by God.

Psalm 32:8, 9 states God's promise to instruct and teach his people in the way we should go, and warns, "Do not be like the horse or like the mule, which have no understanding, which must be harnessed with bit and bridle." The harder we, like Pharaoh, pull away from the will of God, the harder he must pull to bring us back to the path he wants us to take.

The first opportunity to exercise faith (9:19, 20). When God announced the coming hail storm, he warned the Egyptians through Moses to "gather your livestock and all that you have in the field" and take them inside.

The Bible says "he who feared the word of the Lord among the servants of Pharaoh" rushed to bring man and beast inside. The preceding plagues had led some of the Egyptians to some level of trust in the reliability of God's Word as spoken by Moses. This is what "faith" is—reliance on the trustworthiness of God's Word which leads us to act on it.

What disasters we too can avoid if we trust God's Word fully and make it our rule and guide each day.

Pharaoh at last acknowledged God by name (9:27, 28). When Moses first went to Pharaoh, he had scorned, "Who is the Lord, that I should obey his voice to let Israel go? I do not know the Lord . . ." But now, as terrifying lightning flashes illuminated the massive hail stones that pummeled his land, Pharaoh sent for Moses and Aaron and confessed, "I have sinned this time." He begged Moses to "entreat the Lord that there may be no more mighty thundering and hail." In his terror, Pharaoh promised, "I will let you go."

"Sinned this time" (9:27). Pharaoh had not just sinned "this time"; he had sinned continually. The admission forced from him by his fear fell far short of heartfelt repentance and far short of a genuine acknowledgment of the extent of his sins.

Let's not mistake fear-driven confession for a true change of heart. Under stress, many are ready to admit fault, even though they do not feel guilt.

"The Lord is righteous. . . . Entreat the Lord" (Ex. 9:27, 28). This was the first time that Pharaoh seemed to deal directly with the Lord by name. Pharaoh had asked Moses to intercede for him (Ex. 8:28), but now he began to see that the issue was not between Pharaoh and Moses, but between Pharaoh and the Lord.

"I will let you go" (Ex. 9:28). Moses warned Pharaoh not to go back on this promise. But as soon as the thunder, lightning, and hail stopped, both Pharaoh and his servants hardened their hearts and refused to release the Israelites.

True repentance and conversion are measured by behavior. Like Pharaoh, the person who bargains with God when under stress without an awareness of guilt and need for forgiveness will—when the stress is removed—quickly return to his or her old ways.

THE MIRACLE OF THE LOCUSTS
Exodus 10:1–20

Locusts were a devastating reality in the ancient East. They multiplied at an astounding rate. At times they gathered in swarms so thick that they literally blotted out the sun. One swarm of locusts that crossed the Red Sea in 1899 was estimated to cover 2,000 square miles! One square kilometer can contain fifty million insects, which can devour one hundred thousand tons of vegetation in a single night!

The miraculous nature of this locust invasion (Exodus 10:4, 6, 19). While this proving act again used a "natural" means, it was clearly an extraordinary event caused by God. It came when the Lord announced it would; it was more devastating and extensive than any locust plague in history (Ex. 10:14); and every single locust was removed in response to Moses' prayer.

The dialogue with Pharaoh (10:3–11). The text reports in unusual detail Moses' meeting with Pharaoh before this plague struck.

A clear warning was given (10:3–6). Moses clearly described the consequences to Egypt if Pharaoh should still refuse to let the Israelites go.

Pharaoh's servants urged him to free Israel (10:7). Pharaoh's "servants" were the high officials who ran Egypt's bureaucracy. They were aware of the devastation caused by the earlier plagues, which wiped out Egypt's cattle and early crops. They urged Pharaoh to get rid of Moses at any cost.

Pharaoh continued to bargain (10:8–11). At first Pharaoh told Moses to "go serve the Lord." But then he wanted to limit those who went into the wilderness for worship to adult men only. Moses refused, indicating that every Israelite and all their cattle would go out to worship.

At this, Pharaoh warned Moses. He declared that God had better be with them, because he was more determined than ever to persecute the Hebrew slaves (Ex. 10:11).

The escalation of the miracles was matched by the increasing hardness of Pharaoh's heart.

The life-threatening nature of the locust invasion (10:15). The hail had wiped out the early crops of flax and barley (Ex. 9:31). Now the wheat and spelt had sprouted, and these basic food crops would also be destroyed. Starvation for the Egyptian people was a significant possibility. It was this danger which led Pharaoh's officials to urge him to let the Israelites go.

Pharaoh had to understand the consequences. But the pressure the Lord placed upon him only hardened him further. We can-

not expect increased pressure to motivate anyone to change his or her attitude toward God. Only love can motivate a heart-response to the Lord.

Pharaoh again confessed he had sinned (10:16–17). When the fields of Egypt had been stripped of everything green, Pharaoh called for Moses "in haste." This confession of sin was as insincere as his earlier admission (9:27), and it was driven by the same motives.

God hardened Pharaoh's heart (10:20). Again, we have an example of what is probably a judicial hardening of Pharaoh's already stubborn heart. A person who travels too far along the road of arrogant rejection of God may find it impossible to turn, however compelling the reasons to do so.

THE MIRACLE OF THICK DARKNESS
Exodus 10:21–29

The ninth proving act struck Egypt without any warning. The Lord told Moses to

If locusts ate their basic food crops, the Egyptian people faced starvation.

stretch out his hand toward heaven, and for three days there was "thick darkness" which could "be felt" over all of Egypt.

The nature of the darkness (Exodus 10:21–23). Even Lockyer, who holds that the ten mighty acts which God performed against Egypt were true miracles, gives a naturalistic explanation for this miracle. He and others assume that the darkness was caused by sand from the desert carried by the *khamsin* winds that sometimes blow across Egypt.

But the darkness described in these verses is far different. It was a darkness which could "be felt"—so thick it caused people to grope their way about. It was an eerie darkness that no light from the sun or any lamp could penetrate. The darkness was so frightening that for the entire three days not one person dared to "rise from his place" (10:23).

A direct confrontation with Egypt's premier deity, Ra. We noted earlier that Exodus 12:12 states that one purpose of the miracles God performed was to execute judgment "against all the gods of Egypt." Some have tried to identify specific gods against whom each mighty act was directed. This may be possible in the case of a few of the miracles. For instance, a case can be made for seeing the miracle of the frogs as directed against the goddess Heqt (see page 67).

However, to strain to identify minor deities against whom this or that plague might be directed is to miss the point. Exodus 12:12 indicates that the *series* of miracles is a judgment against *all the gods* of Egypt—and there were hundreds!

The Egyptians assumed it was the duty of their entire pantheon of gods to maintain the harmony of nature and the peace of Egypt, the "blessed land." God's acts not only disrupted the harmony of nature, but also desolated Egypt and threatened the every existence of the nation and its people. *All the gods of Egypt* were shown to be powerless before the God of the people which Pharaoh and his nation had oppressed. And now the God of these slaves was exacting full payment for that oppression,

displaying the weakness of the gods on whom the Egyptians had relied.

At the same time, the plague of darkness may be interpreted as a judgment against the king of Egypt's deities—Ra, the sun. A hymn to Amen-Ra, dating from about the time of the Exodus, praised him as

The sole king, unique among the gods,
  with multitudinous names,
  whose number is not known,
Who arises on the eastern horizon,
  and sets on the western horizon,
Who is born early every day,
  and every day overthrows his enemies.

But suddenly, without warning and at Moses' signal, Amen-Ra did not arise. This king of Egypt's gods was overthrown, and darkness ruled. How utterly terrifying this must have been to the Egyptians—and what unmistakable evidence that all their gods were defeated.

Pharaoh continued to bargain (10:24). When the light returned, Pharaoh called Moses and told him to go and take all the Israelites into the desert. But again, Pharaoh demanded a concession. He insisted on keeping the livestock and herds of the Israelites, which had been exempt from the miracles that had destroyed the Egyptian cattle. Moses refused, demanding that all the Israelites' livestock go. The livestock were required for sacrifice, and "even we do not know with what [i.e., with how many] we must serve [sacrifice to] the Lord until we arrive there" (Ex. 10:26).

There's a principle here for us. We need to bring all to the Lord, for we never know ahead of time what the Lord may ask of us. Pharaoh's way was to hold back something; Moses' way was to give all.

Pharaoh threatened to kill Moses (10:27, 28). Again, the text confirms a judicial hardening of Pharaoh's heart. In frustration and fury, Pharaoh expelled Moses and Aaron from the palace and threatened them. He declared that the next time he saw either of them, he would have them killed.

Moses would never see Pharaoh again. Soon Pharaoh would send messengers begging the Israelites to leave.

The pattern in Pharaoh's hardening (compare Revelation 9:19, 20). It is tempting to read more into the phrase "the Lord hardened Pharaoh's heart" than we should. In view of the devastating judgments on Egypt, common sense suggests that Pharaoh simply *had* to give in to God. We may even go so far as to assume that God had to cause Pharaoh to act against his own better judgment. But this isn't true.

Revelation 9 describes a terrifying series of judgments that will strike the earth at history's end. These also bear the mark of miracles: they are extraordinary events caused by God for a religious purpose. Will these judgments bring about repentance and a change of heart? Revelation 9:20–21 relates,

But the rest of mankind, who were not killed by these plagues, did not repent of the works of their hands, that they should not worship demons, and idols of gold, silver, brass, stone, and wood, which can neither see nor hear nor walk. And they did not repent of their murders or their sorceries or their sexual immorality or their thefts.

Divine judgment tends to make a heart which has been hardened by sin and arrogance even more stubborn and resistant. Pharaoh's apparent repentances were never heartfelt or lasting. All the Lord needed to do to harden Pharaoh's heart was to nudge him in the direction he was already determined to go.

THE MIRACLE OF THE DEATH OF EGYPT'S FIRSTBORN   *Exodus 11:1–10; 12:29–36*

Pharaoh threatened Moses and expelled him from the palace (10:27–29). Before he left, Moses announced one last terrible judgment on Egypt. God would strike the firstborn "from the firstborn of Pharaoh who sits on his throne, even to the firstborn of the female servant who is behind the handmill" (Ex. 11:5). From highest to lowest, every Egyptian family would lose a loved one. Even the firstborn of any remaining animals would die.

The Ten Miracles

#	Miracle	Hebrew term	Distinctives	Special deity judged
1.	Nile to blood	*dam*	Water undrinkable, fish died Duplicated by magicians	Hopi
2.	Frogs	*tsefardea´*	Frogs infest land, died and rotted Duplicated by magicians	Heqt
3.	Lice	*kinnim*	All infested by vermin Magicians rendered unclean	
4.	Biting flies	*´arov*	All Egyptians bitten Israelites exempt—from now on	
5.	Animal epidemic	*dever*	Egyptian livestock in the fields died	Hathor
6.	Ulcerous boils	*shehin*	Painful boils incapacitated the Egyptians. For the first time God hardened Pharaoh's heart.	
7.	Hail storms	*barad*	Gigantic stones killed men and beasts. Early crops destroyed. First killing plague	
8.	Locusts	*´arbeh*	Locusts destroyed remaining crops. Egypt threatened with starvation.	
9.	Darkness	*hoshekh*	Supernatural darkness isolated, im- mobilized Egyptians	Amon-Ra
10.	Death of firstborn		The firstborn in every Egyptian family was killed at midnight.	

Moses' angry threat hung in the air as he left the stunned Pharaoh and his court.

"At midnight the Lord struck" (Exodus 12:29). Attempts to ascribe the deaths to a particular disease again miss the point. This was a miracle. The Lord struck all those who died at the same time—midnight. The deaths were selective—only the firstborn died. The miracle was inclusive—no Egyptian family was spared. Yet at the same time, the miracle was exclusive—not one Israelite or a single animal belonging to the Israelites died.

"Rise, go out . . . go" (12:31). Pharaoh's response was immediate and desperate. Just as Moses had predicted (Ex. 11:8), Pharaoh sent his officials to Moses and begged him to get out. The urgency of the Egyptian request was expressed in three active verbs in Exodus 12:31, which use three different words in the imperative, each of which can be rendered "go." We might express the rising desperation by rendering Pharaoh's message, "go, Go, GO!"

The final proving act at last won Pharaoh's unconditional surrender.

"None of the children of Israel" (11:7). The means God used to preserve Israel foreshadowed later revelation. God commanded the Hebrew families to kill a lamb and sprinkle its blood on the door frames of their dwellings. Those inside homes marked by the blood of the lamb were spared.

It was not that the Israelites were sinless, or even morally superior to their oppressors. The testimony of Scripture is that all have

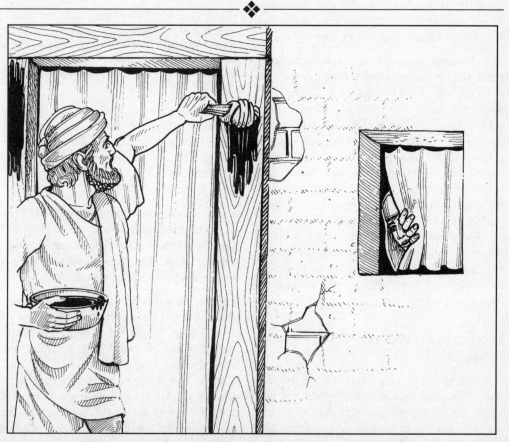

Blood on the doorpost was a sign for God to pass over an Israelite home.

sinned. It was the blood that God ordained should be shed which sheltered God's people from his wrath.

It is the same today and forever. Christ, the lamb of God, shed his blood that those who seek shelter in him might find forgiveness and be sheltered eternally from the wrath of God.

"They had asked . . . articles of silver, articles of gold" (12:35). Moses told the Israelites to ask [not "borrow"] the Egyptians for precious articles. The text suggests that the Egyptians were awed by Moses (cf. Ex. 11:3), and they readily gave their wealth away to any Hebrews who asked.

Much of this wealth would be freely given in later years by God's people to construct a portable worship center, which they carried with them in the wilderness. However great the accumulated wealth the Israelites gained, it was poor compensation for the years of harsh oppression they had endured.

The Passover recalled this tenth miracle (12:1–28). Between Moses' announcement of the tenth miracle in Exodus 11:1–10 and the description of its occurrence in 12:29–36, the book of Exodus established an annual celebration reenacting the experiences of that unforgettable night. Jewish families gathered and shared a meal featuring lamb and unleavened bread—bread made without yeast because there was no time for the bread to rise before the Israelites hurriedly left Egypt.

For all time, the Passover—Israel's festival of freedom—was to stand as a reminder of the ten proving acts by which God demonstrated his presence with the Israelites and his power over their enemies.

MIRACLES ALONG THE WAY
Exodus 13—17

The Israelites were freed from Egyptian slavery by ten miraculous "proving acts" which judged Egypt's gods and demonstrated the real presence of God to Egyptian and Israelite alike. Yet, release from Egypt was only the beginning of Israel's challenges—challenges which could be overcome only by the continual exercise of God's wonder-working power.

Taken together, this cluster of miracles speaks of God's complete provision for the needs of his people.

1. The miracle of the cloudy-fiery pillar.   P. 78
2. The miracle at the Reed Sea.   p. 79
3. The miracle of the healed waters.   p. 81
4. The miracle of the manna.   p. 82
5. The miracle of the quail.   p. 83
6. The miracle of the smitten rock.   p. 84
7. The miracle victory over Amalek.   p. 85

THE MIRACLE OF THE CLOUDY-FIERY PILLAR   *Exodus 13:21–22; 40:34–38*

Exodus 13 describes this miracle provision:

And the Lord went before them by day in a pillar of cloud to lead the way, and by night in a pillar of fire to give them light, so as to go by day and night. He did not take away the pillar of cloud by day or the pillar of fire by night from before the people (Ex. 13:21, 22).

The cloud has been described by some as a "luminous mist." Apparently, it changed, becoming a cloud by day and a source of light by night. This miraculous apparition had several functions during the travels of Israel from Egypt to Canaan.

It served as a visible reminder of God's presence with his people. There was no way that Israel in the wilderness could forget that God was with them. The majestic pillar in the sky was constant evidence of his nearness.

It served as a guide throughout Israel's travels (Exodus 13:21). Through the pillar of cloud, the Lord went before them "to lead the way." God did not stand back and tell Israel, "Go." Instead God went ahead, and said, "Come." It is the same in our experience today. The Lord never asks us to go on ahead of him or to travel alone. He stays with us. He who knows the way leads us to our personal promised land.

It served as a shield when Israel was endangered (14:19, 20). Egypt's Pharaoh did not remain content to let Israel go. His spies informed him that the Israelites were trapped on the shore of the "Red Sea." Pharaoh marshaled his army and set out to recapture the slaves. When the Egyptian forces approached, the cloudy-fiery pillar stood between Israel and the Egyptians, its dark side blinding the pursuers, and its bright side giving light to the escaping Israelites.

It marked Moses' conferences with God (33:9). This symbol of God's presence served to authenticate further Moses as God's confidant and the people's appointed leader by descending when God met with Moses.

It served as God's authoritative word of direction to Israel (40:36–38). The last chapter of Exodus sums up this aspect of the miracle cloud. When the cloud moved ahead, the people of Israel followed. And when the cloud hovered, the people did not move until the cloud led the way.

This also has a lesson for us. At times God leads us to wait—not to wait interminably, but to wait until he leads us on. Our times of waiting can be as significant as times for action.

Finally, Exodus 40:38 reminds us that the cloud was in sight of all the house of Israel "throughout all their journeys." In the same way, God remains close to us throughout our lives. All we need do is look to him.

THE MIRACLE AT THE REED SEA
Exodus 14:21–32

God led the Israelites away from the direct coastal route to Canaan, aware that this route would involve conflict with the inhabitants of that region (Ex. 13:17). Egyptian records use the same name for the route as this verse, "the way of the land of the Philistines," indicating that it was well fortified. Generations of slavery had not equipped the Israelites for warfare!

But God then proceeded to lead the Israelites into a trap, where they had no choice but to rely completely on him.

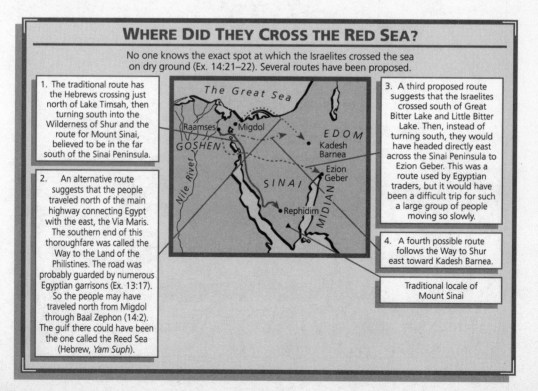

WHERE DID THEY CROSS THE RED SEA?

No one knows the exact spot at which the Israelites crossed the sea on dry ground (Ex. 14:21–22). Several routes have been proposed.

1. The traditional route has the Hebrews crossing just north of Lake Timsah, then turning south into the Wilderness of Shur and the route for Mount Sinai, believed to be in the far south of the Sinai Peninsula.

2. An alternative route suggests that the people traveled north of the main highway connecting Egypt with the east, the Via Maris. The southern end of this thoroughfare was called the Way to the Land of the Philistines. The road was probably guarded by numerous Egyptian garrisons (Ex. 13:17). So the people may have traveled north from Migdol through Baal Zephon (14:2). The gulf there could have been the one called the Reed Sea (Hebrew, *Yam Suph*).

3. A third proposed route suggests that the Israelites crossed south of Great Bitter Lake and Little Bitter Lake. Then, instead of turning south, they would have headed directly east across the Sinai Peninsula to Ezion Geber. This was a route used by Egyptian traders, but it would have been a difficult trip for such a large group of people moving so slowly.

4. A fourth possible route follows the Way to Shur east toward Kadesh Barnea.

Traditional locale of Mount Sinai

Map labels: The Great Sea · Raamses · Migdol · GOSHEN · Nile River · EDOM · Kadesh Barnea · Ezion Geber · SINAI · MIDIAN · Rephidim

The identity of the "Red Sea" (Exodus 14:2, 9). Scholars have known for some time that *yom suph* means "reed sea," not Red Sea. The Sinai peninsula has several lakes. God led the Israelites to the shore of one of these lakes. Its shallows were filled with papyrus reeds. The text of Exodus gives four reference points (Ex. 14:1–2). While they cannot be identified today, the names are suggestive. *Pi-hahiroth* means the "mouth of Hirot," a river or canal. Several fortified Egyptian towns were called "Migdol." The point of these identifications was to show that the Israelites were trapped, with no way to turn.

The Egyptians pursued (14:5–9). When Pharaoh heard that the Israelites were trapped on the seashore, he assembled his army to pursue. Their approach terrified the Israelites (Ex. 14:10), who cried out to the Lord but then complained bitterly to Moses (Ex. 14:11, 12).

Pharaoh seemed to have forgotten the terrible cost of conflict with Israel's God.

The waters of the Reed Sea divide (14:21). Lockyer makes much of the fact that the waters of the Red Sea are six thousand feet deep and miles broad at its narrowest point. But Israel crossed the Reed Sea, not the Red Sea. Yet it is clear from the text that the actual crossing was a miracle.

The wind which drove the waters back "divided the waters" (14:21, 22). The waters were not driven to one side of the sea, as with a normal wind, but formed "a wall to them on the right hand and on the left."

God divided the waters of the sea for the Israelites to cross.

The Israelites crossed "on dry ground" (14:22). Normally, the bed of such a sea would be thick mud. But the text specifically states the bed was dry ground for the Israelites' crossing.

The cloudy-fiery pillar spread darkness which held back the Egyptians (14:20). In contrast, the side of the pillar facing the Israelites provided light, so God's people could see to pass through the sea.

When the Egyptians pursued, they were "troubled" by God (14:24). Verse 25 seems to suggest that the seabed turned muddy again, bogging down the Egyptian chariots.

When the entire army had been committed, the waters returned (14:26–28). On God's command, Moses stretched his hand over the sea and the waters rushed back to drown the Egyptians. The text indicates that "not so much as one" soldier survived.

The "miracle at the Reed Sea" was actually a series of miracles, blended together to punish Egypt further and to demonstrate the unshaken commitment of God to his people Israel.

Messages in the Reed Sea miracles. What happened at the Reed Sea were undoubtedly extraordinary events caused by God for a religious purpose.

The miracles increased Israel's respect for the Lord (Exodus 14:30). Exodus indicates that Israel "saw the Egyptians dead on the seashore." The next verse again emphasizes the fact that Israel "saw the great work." Why this emphasis?

The most devastating of the plagues that struck Egypt *passed the Israelites by!* They were isolated in Goshen from the devastation which touched the rest of Egypt. They simply had not seen for themselves what the Lord could do.

At the Reed Sea, they *saw.* As the dead bodies of the army of their oppressors washed up on the shore, they could no longer question or doubt the power and presence of the Lord.

The miracles increased Israel's respect for Moses (14:31). This verse adds, "and [the Israelites] believed the Lord and his servant Moses." They had heard that plagues struck Egypt at Moses' command, but now they had seen Moses raise his hand and watched the waters recede and then return. For perhaps the first time, all Israel sensed the greatness of their leader, who had come to deliver them as their God's representative.

This cluster of miracles continued to instruct God's people. There are many lessons we can draw from the events described in Exodus 14.

- We're reminded that when God leads us into trouble, he will also provide a way out.
- We're reminded that God's presence provides protection from those who would harm us.
- We're reminded that God has devised ways to deal with every difficulty, however confusing or complex our present situation may be.
- We're reminded of the importance of complete reliance on the Lord. How many times Moses' word to Israel is God's word to us: "The Lord will fight for you, and you shall hold your peace."
- We're reminded that those who trouble God's people will suffer loss while those who serve him who will survive to rejoice and to praise.

THE MIRACLE OF THE HEALED WATERS   *Exodus 15:22–26*

Following God's victory over the Egyptian army at the Reed Sea, the Israelites traveled on into the wilderness. They traveled only three days before they ran out of water. The response of the Israelites was immediate and striking. They "complained against Moses." Moses prayed, and God met the need. He showed Moses a tree which could be thrown into the "bitter" waters to make it sweet (drinkable).

Israel's lack of faith revealed (Exodus 15:23, 24). The first thing this incident reveals is Israel's lack of faith. Just three days before, the people had witnessed the miraculous destruction of the Egyptian army. All they needed to do was look into the sky to be reminded of God's presence in the cloudy-fiery pillar. Yet when they discovered undrinkable waters, their first response was unbelief rather than faith.

The grumbling introduced here would characterize Israel's relationship with Moses and God on the journey both to and away from Sinai. No matter what God did, it would never be enough to satisfy his discontented people. And no provision of God would ever convince Israel that the Lord could be trusted in the next crisis.

God's gracious provision revealed (15:25). In spite of Israel's ungratefulness and lack of faith, God purified the waters so his people could drink. How graciously God provides, even when we don't deserve his gifts.

God's ability to meet every need further revealed (15:25). This miracle was not as spectacular as the miracles performed at the Reed Sea. Yet it was an *essential* miracle. Water for drinking is one of life's basic needs—essential for life itself.

"The Lord who heals you" (15:26). The miraculous provision of water served as an occasion for the Lord to present a "test" to Israel. The verse does not imply that God is about to test Israel. We might say that God proposed that Israel try out being obedient. If they obeyed, God would "put none of the diseases on you which I have brought on the Egyptians." God can do this, because he is Yahweh-the-Healer.

In essence, God suggested that his people had nothing to lose. The one who healed the waters of Marah had displayed his ability to heal. Why not then try obedience, and see how the Lord would be their personal healer as well as healer of the waters?

The message of the miracle. The test that God proposed suggests the primary message of the miracle to the Exodus generation. God has demonstrated his healing powers. If Israel would be obedient, God would commit himself to protect Israel from all the diseases of the Egyptians.

It's tempting to apply this verse as an open promise to all of God's people. Certainly God continues to be our healer, and often intervenes for us. But before assuming this verse states an unchangeable divine commitment, we need to look at Deuteronomy 28.

In Deuteronomy, the promise of healing is notable because it does not occur in the list of blessings God declared he would provide for an obedient Israel (Deut. 28:1–13)! On the other hand, if Israel was disobedient, God declared he would "strike you with the boils of Egypt, with tumors, with the scab, and with the itch, from which you cannot be healed" (Deut. 28:27).

God is gracious, and he meets our most basic needs. God is merciful, and he is our Healer. But even the most obedient believer, such as the apostle Paul, has no guarantee of physical healing by the Lord (cf. 2 Cor. 12:5–12).

THE MIRACLE OF THE MANNA
Exodus 16:1–5, 14–35

A month and a half into the wilderness, the Israelites' food supplies ran out. Again, the "whole congregation" responded with complaint rather than faith. The complaint motif recurs seven times in Exodus 16:2, 7, 8, 9, and 12. In spite of Israel's lack of faith, God told Moses he would "rain bread from heaven."

The nature of the miracle (Exodus 16:4). Some have provided naturalistic explanations of the manna to make the biblical account "credible." Honey-like gums and Arabian lichens have been put forward as candidates for the miraculous food. But the text makes it clear that God provided the food miraculously.

- Manna appeared six days, but not on the Sabbath (Ex. 16:4, 5).
- Manna met the daily need, whether much or little had been gathered (Ex. 16:16).
- Manna kept overnight spoiled, so it had to be gathered daily (Ex. 16:19–20).
- Manna preserved by Moses as a memorial never spoiled (Ex. 16:33–34).
- Manna was provided all the years Israel traveled in the Sinai, and it stopped the day the people entered Canaan 40 years later (Ex.16:35).
- Enough manna was provided each day to feed the Israelites who followed Moses— estimated at nearly two million (compare Ex. 12:37).

There is no doubt that what the Bible describes was a miracle.

The significance of the manna miracle. What is the religious significance of this extraordinary event caused by God?

Manna was continuing evidence of God's presence with Israel and his commitment to them. God met their every need.

Manna was rationed in a way that taught dependence on God for daily bread. The familiar phrase in the Lord's prayer reminds us that we need to learn this lesson as well.

Manna was intended to instruct Israel to depend on God's word, not to live by bread alone (Deut. 8:3). Jesus returned to this verse when challenged by Satan to turn stones into bread (Luke 4:4).

Manna was a symbol of divine provision of life itself (John 8:31–58). Jesus spoke of himself as the true bread from heaven, who provides eternal life to all who partake of him.

God's provision of manna had a significance far beyond its ability to sustain the life of the wilderness travelers. In this notable miracle, the Lord instructed Israel as well as modern believers.

THE MIRACLE OF THE QUAIL
Exodus 16:3–13

The Israelites complained of more than lack of bread. They also wanted meat! The overstatement of their condition in Egypt is laughable: "we sat by the pots of meat and . . . ate bread to the full" [i.e., "until we were stuffed!"]. Egyptian records of food supplied to hired workers on government projects show how faulty Israel's memory was. The

God's provision of manna underscored their dependence on Him.

typical worker's menu included bread, vegetables, and beer—and fish or meat occasionally.

God's miracle provision of quail. In response to Israel's complaint, God provided quail to supplement the manna. The text simply says that "quails came up at evening and covered the camp" (Ex. 16:13). The low-flying birds were easy prey for the hungry Israelites.

We are not told how God brought enough quail to feed the multitude. A parallel passage in Numbers 11 indicates that at that time a wind brought a great flock of quail, which settled around the Israelites' camp.

The episodic nature of the miracle. The miracle of the manna was a *sustained* miracle. Every week for 40 years God faithfully supplied the bread that preserved life. The miracle of the quail was episodic. The Old Testament records only two instances of this provision of a supplementary food.

This episodic miracle has a valuable message. The God who provides all we *need* will sometimes provide things that we *want* but do not need. When this happens, we should certainly be more grateful than the Israelites were.

THE MIRACLE OF THE SMITTEN ROCK   *Exodus 17:1–7*

As the Israelites traveled, they again camped where there was no water. They began to complain.

The intensity of the Israelites' complaints (Exodus 17:3, 4). This time when they grew thirsty, they accused Moses of trying to kill them and their children. The term "accuse" is appropriate, for the Hebrew word *rib,* is used. This word in the Old Testament relates primarily to formal court proceedings. The people were ready to take Moses to court and charge him with attempted murder!

Even worse, they had already determined the verdict. Moses cried, "They are almost ready to stone me!"

The underlying lack of faith (17:7). This incident is recalled in both the Old and New Testaments. In spite of the proof of God's presence provided by the pillar of cloud which led them, and the manna which daily fed them, the people "tempted [tested] the Lord, saying, 'Is the Lord among us, or not!'"

Later in Deuteronomy, Moses warned the next generation of Israelites, "You shall not tempt the Lord your God, as you tempted him in Massah" (Deut. 6:16). Jesus quoted this verse when challenged by Satan to leap from the pinnacle of the temple (Luke 4:9–12). The believer is to live by faith, confident that the God who has promised to be with us *is* with us, even when we don't see evidence of his presence.

Another proof-of-presence miracle (17:5–6). God provided further proof of his presence. He sent Moses, with some of the elders as witnesses, to strike a rock with his staff. When Moses did so, water flowed.

John I. Durham, in his commentary on Exodus, made this penetrating comment.

God provided water out of a rock.

Once more, when a need arises, the Israelites do not wait for it to be met; indeed they do not even assume that it can be met. Rather they attack Yahweh and put him on trial by attacking Moses to put *him* on trial. Their thirst, of course, was real. But infinitely more real was the powerful Presence of Yahweh in their midst. The lesser reality they embraced; the more important reality they ignored and doubted: so once more, God dealt with the lesser reality by a demonstration of the greater, underlying reality (p. 232).

All the miracles of Scripture, like this one, unveil God as the great underlying reality in our universe. How wonderful to have a personal relationship with him. How gently he frees us from doubts and fears by an inner evidence of his presence that is more wonderful than the miracles of old.

Paul's application of the miracle (1 Corinthians 10:4–6). In the New Testament, the apostle Paul identified Jesus with the "Rock that followed them." Paul's point was that throughout history Christ himself cared for the nation from which he sprang.

It was Jesus who met every need of Israel in ancient times. And this same Jesus will meet our needs as we journey with him in the walk of faith.

THE MIRACLE VICTORY OVER AMALEK   *Exodus 17:8–13*

For the first time, the traveling Israelites were forced to fight. Joshua led on the battlefield; but the key to victory was Moses, standing on a hill top. Whenever Moses' arms were upraised, Israel prevailed. When his arms drooped, the Amalekites won. Finally, Moses' two companions held up his arms, and the victory went to Israel.

The miracle victory reminded Israel that their success depended on the Lord rather than on their warriors and that Moses was God's chosen mediator.

THE MIRACLE PRESENCE AT SINAI
Exodus 19

Mount Sinai was a massive tower of rock thrust upward out of the surrounding plain. Known today as Jebel Musa, the 7,363-feet-high granite mountain dominates the surrounding countryside.

It was to this awe-inspiring mountain that God led Israel. There God would give Moses a law that spelled out the Lord's expectations of his people—a law which would regulate every detail of their lives and set Israel apart from surrounding peoples. At last, Israel would learn the lifestyle through which God's people could express their faith in Yahweh and through which succeeding generations could find blessing and peace.

The significance of the moment was underlined by further miraculous evidence of the divine presence.

More proofs of presence (Exodus 19:16–19). The evidence of God's miracle presence is described in these verses:

Then it came to pass on the third day, in the morning, that there were thunderings and lightnings, and a thick cloud on the mountain; and the sound

Lessons from the Miracles on the Way to Sinai

Miracle	Text	Lesson concerning God's presence
Pillar of cloud/fire	Ex. 13	God leads, guides, and protects his people.
Parting of Reed Sea	Ex. 14	God rescues from danger, protects his people from enemies.
Purifying bitter water	Ex. 15	God meets the basic life needs of his people.
Providing manna	Ex. 16	God continually meets the basic needs of his people on a daily basis.
Providing quail	Ex. 16	God may graciously provide what we want but do not need.
Bringing water from the rock	Ex. 17	God meets the needs even of the doubting and the ungrateful, but warns against testing him.
Victory over Amalek	Ex. 17	Success depends on God's presence and aid.

of the trumpet was very loud, so that all the people who were in the camp trembled. And Moses brought the people out of the camp to meet with God, and they stood at the foot of the mountain.

Now, Mount Sinai was completely in smoke, because the Lord descended upon it in fire. Its smoke ascended like the smoke of a furnace, and the whole mountain quaked greatly. And when the blast of the trumpet sounded long and became louder and louder, Moses spoke, and God answered him by voice.

Every sense of the Israelites was filled with evidence of God's presence. They saw the mountain shrouded in smoke and flame. They smelled and tasted the smoke. They felt the ground shake. They heard a loud trumpet-like

❖

Smoke and fire marked God's presence on Mount Sinai.

sound and actually heard God speak with Moses "by voice."

There could be no doubt. God was present on Mount Sinai. The evidence was overwhelming.

The purposes of the miracle (Exodus 20:18–20). These verses describe the reaction of the Israelites.

The people "trembled and stood afar off" (20:18). Both Psalms and Proverbs remind us that the fear of the Lord is the beginning of wisdom (Ps. 111:10; Prov. 9:10). The Israelites had doubted God, displaying a lack of faith and appreciation. As they stood before the mountain, the Israelites were at last awed and filled with a fearful respect for the One whose voice they now heard for themselves.

The people told Moses, "You speak with us, and we will hear" (20:19). The fear that God's miracle presence inspired created fresh respect for Moses. Israel accepted him as the authentic mediator of God's words to mankind. The conviction that God spoke to and through Moses has shaped Jewish as well as Christian thought from that moment.

Moses told the people that God intended the display to help them fear him (20:20). In the Old Testament, the "fear of God" does not indicate dread *of* God but rather awed respect *for* God. The reason that God wants us to fear him is explained in this verse: "so that you may not sin." A person filled with respect for God's power and his greatness will not doubt his presence or his ability to help. Rather than sin, as Israel had in doubting the Lord, the believer who respects God will follow him gladly.

❖

MIRACLES ALONG THE WAY

DISCIPLINE IN THE DESERT

Leviticus—Numbers

I t's dangerous to make God promises which aren't kept.

At Sinai the Israelites had sworn, "All that the Lord has said, we will do, and be obedient" (Exodus 24:7). But as the books of Leviticus through Deuteronomy trace Israel's journey toward the Promised Land, time and time again the Israelites disobey! And God intervenes with miracles—but now they are miracles of judgment.

Does God perform disciplinary miracles today? Certainly God did in times past!

Miracles of Discipline in Leviticus & Numbers

1.	The miracle judgment of Nadab and Abihu	p. 87
2.	The miracle judgment by fire	p. 88
3.	The miracle judgment by quail	p. 89
4.	The miracle judgment of Miriam's leprosy	p. 90
5.	The miracle judgment of Korah's followers	p. 91
6.	The miracle judgment by serpents	p. 93
7.	The miracle of Balaam's donkey	p. 94

THE MIRACLE JUDGMENT OF NADAB AND ABIHU   *Leviticus 10:1–7*

The book of Leviticus focuses attention on worship and holiness. The word "holy" is used 87 times, while words for "sacrifice" occur approximately 300 times in this 27-chap-ter book. And "priest" or "priests" are found 152 times.

It is clear that priests and their ministry are significant in this book on the worship and lifestyle of God's people. This is why the only miracle in Leviticus involves two priests—Nadab and Abihu, sons of Aaron.

The nature and cause of the miracle judgment (Leviticus 10:1). Nadab and Abihu "each took his censer, put fire in it, put incense on it, and offered profane fire before the Lord." The Hebrew word `esh zarah, means "alien fire." When the two approached the tabernacle worship center, fire flared from the Lord and killed them.

The text does not explain their sin. But the priestly prescriptions in Leviticus do. Leviticus 6:12, 13 instructed the priests to keep fire burning on Israel's altar. Leviticus 16:12 instructed the priests to use the altar fires to ignite incense offerings. The two young priests ignited their incense with alien fire, thus violating God's instructions for worship.

God's explanation (Leviticus 10:3). Moses offered this word of explanation to the bereaved father, Aaron. "By those who come near Me, I must be regarded as holy." It was especially important for the priests to pay close attention to God's instructions. In carrying out their duties, they came closer to the Lord than Israelites from any other tribe.

The priests, with the rest of the people, had committed themselves at Sinai by declaring, "All that the Lord has said we will do, and be obedient" (Ex. 24:7). Nadab and Abihu's disregard for God's worship instructions could not be tolerated if his people were to regard the Lord as holy and to obey him completely.

This miracle judgment established a pattern. While the people were on the way to Sinai, the Lord had overlooked their rebellion and disrespect. Now that the Law had been given and accepted, there would be no more divine indifference to sin. God would act to punish sin when it occurred in order to teach his people the necessity of trust and discipline.

God's miracle judgments may seem harsh. But his earlier leniency had failed to bring Israel to maturity or to deepen their faith. By the end of the journey from Sinai to Canaan, God's people had to learn to trust and obey the Lord. Then a disciplined and confident people would be ready to conquer Canaan and claim God's blessings.

THE MIRACLE JUDGMENT BY FIRE
Numbers 11:1–3

The book of Numbers describes the organization of the Israelite camp in preparation for the journey to Canaan. Beginning with Numbers 10:33, events on the journey to Canaan are described.

The first event (Numbers 11:1–3). The journey began in judgment. The first event was a familiar refrain: "the people complained." The Septuagint translates the Hebrew word for "complain" with the same term used to translate the many references to Israel's "murmuring" on the way to Sinai (see Ex. 16 and 17).

The Israelites still displayed the negative, untrusting, and hostile attitude they had shown earlier.

God was displeased, and acted. Now their behavior "displeased the Lord . . . and his anger was aroused."

The Law, which Israel had voluntarily accepted, provided a standard which the people had violated. Now a basis for judgment existed. God did not hesitate. "The fire of the Lord burned among them, and consumed some in the outskirts of the camp" (Num.

"The fire of the Lᴏʀᴅ burned among them, and consumed some in the outskirts."

1:3). The Lord would no longer put up with the rebellious behavior he had overlooked before.

The initial lesson taught by the miracle judgment. The nature of the miracle fire made it clear that God was the cause of this extraordinary event. It followed immediately upon the complaining of the people. Thus the link between cause and effect was clearly established, and Israel began to learn that obedience to the Lord meant blessing, while disobedience brought disaster.

This is a lesson each of us must learn. By God's grace, we are permitted to learn it from the experience of ancient Israel, recorded for us in God's book. If we will not learn this lesson from others, we may force God to teach us by our own personal experience.

How much better to take Scripture's lessons to heart, and to avoid so much suffering and pain.

THE MIRACLE JUDGMENT BY THE QUAIL   *Numbers 11:4–23, 31–34*

The next event on the journey immediately followed the first miracle judgment. The word for "mixed multitude," *asafsruf,* is best translated "rabble" or "riffraff." It should not be taken to refer to non-Israelites, as the root word means "to collect," indicating a gathering or group of people.

The cause of the judgment (Numbers 11:4–6). It was God's people—those who had been freed from slavery and given his Law—who surrendered to their craving for variety in their diet, rejecting God's provision of manna.

God's reaction (11:10). Again, the Lord's anger was "greatly aroused." Rather than be thankful for what God had provided, the Israelites wept and complained about what they didn't have.

The apostle Paul learned well the lesson Israel had not. In Philippians, Paul wrote, "In regard to need, I have learned in whatever state I am, to be content" (Phil. 4:11). Paul accepted what he received from the hand of God with thanksgiving, without focusing on what

he didn't have. When we understand that God is a loving Father who provides what is best for us, we will also be able to find contentment and peace.

Moses' frustration and despair (11:10–15). This complaining reaction of the people plunged Moses into despair. To him, leadership of Israel felt like an unbearable burden (Num. 11:11). Before we criticize Moses, let's remember that his emotions reflected the frustration and anger felt by God as well. There are times when others—even our own children—seem like an unbearable burden. Like Moses, we almost wish we could die (Num. 11:15).

In his frustration, even Moses forgot to trust in the Lord. He asked, "Where am I to get meat to give to all these people?" (Num. 11:13). When had Moses provided *anything* to meet Israel's needs? It had always been God, present with his people, who provided and preserved.

This is also an important truth to remember. When we are frustrated and we feel that we are at the end of our resources, we need to remember that God is the One who has provided. When we are full of ourselves, there is no room for God to store what he provides. When we are empty, there is space aplenty for him to fill us up.

God's gracious response to Moses (11:16–17). Before the Lord dealt with Israel, he promised to meet Moses' most pressing need. God would spread his spirit on the elders of Israel, enabling them to share some of the burden of leadership.

But why did God respond graciously when Moses complained while judging so severely the people who murmured against him? Moses had taken his complaint directly *to* God. But the people complained *about* God.

We honor the Lord when we acknowledge him as the cause of all things, expressing to him our fears and frustrations. The Israelites failed to honor God by recognizing his sovereignty in the situation. In fact, they "despised the Lord" by weeping and saying,

"Why did we ever come up out of Egypt" (11:20).

The miracle judgment (11:17–23; 31–34). As he had done on the journey to Sinai, the Lord provided quail to satisfy his people's craving for meat (see Ex. 16:11–13). But this time, "while the meat was still between their teeth, before it was chewed, the wrath of the Lord was aroused against the people, and the Lord struck the people with a very great plague" (Num. 11:33). And there they buried those who had yielded to their cravings.

Lessons in the miracle judgment of the quail. This experience was another lesson for Israel on how to live in relationship with the God who was present with them. Not only must Israel acknowledge his presence, but they must also accept his sovereignty in their lives relying on him to provide what was best for them.

This is the way that we must live if we are to be comfortable in our relationship with the Lord. God is sovereign, and he will supply what is best. May we learn to praise him for what we have, and may we find freedom from cravings for whatever he has not chosen to give.

THE MIRACLE JUDGMENT OF MIRIAM   Numbers 12:1–16

Aaron and Miriam, the brother and sister of Moses, "spoke against" Moses.

The brother's and sister's complaint (Numbers 12:1–2). The phrase "speak against" is used in Numbers 21:5, 7 and in other passages. It means "hostile speech." In this case, the two found fault with Moses for marrying an Ethiopian [a black]. Their complaint seemed to hinge on the notion of racial purity, so significant in ancient and rabbinic Judaism. God had spoken by Moses to Pharaoh, but through Aaron, and he had spoken by Miriam after the Reed Sea crossing (see Ex. 15). Their argument seems to have been that they—as "pure" Israelites—deserved more significant leadership roles.

Moses' reaction (12:3). The comment in this verse on Moses' humility is generally taken to have been added long after the original text was written. However, it has significance in context. The humbleness of Moses does not suggest that he didn't argue with his siblings. In fact, it suggests that Moses may have been swayed by their arguments! The truly humble person fails to recognize his or her unique gifts, and may be pushed aside by those less gifted who want the spotlight!

God intervened (12:4–8). God called the three together and confronted Aaron and Miriam. He affirmed the special relationship that Moses had with God, and asked "why then were you not afraid to speak against My servant Moses?"

The miracle judgment (12:9–13). When the Lord left, the three realized that Miriam had become leprous. Aaron pleaded with Moses to heal her, and Moses begged God to heal his sister.

The Lord condemned Miriam to seven days as a leper, during which she had to live outside the camp. Only after this public rebuke was Miriam healed.

Why not Aaron? Some have seen evidence of biblical chauvinism in the fact that only Miriam was stricken with leprosy. The reason why Aaron did not suffer the same fate is that he was Israel's high priest. And the Law specified that no person with a physical defect could come near the offerings made to the Lord (Lev. 21:21). If Aaron had been stricken with leprosy, he would not have been available to offer sacrifices for the sins of the Israelites.

The message of this miracle of judgment. It is tempting to suggest from this miracle that we are not to speak against our spiritual leaders. And this is probably an apt application. But it does not suggest the need for unquestioning agreement with all our leaders say. In Scripture, we have the standard by which all of us, leader and lay alike, are judged. We are to hew to that standard when any conflict between Scripture and leadership emerges.

What we can draw from this miracle is that leaders as well as the people whom they lead are accountable to God. No commission from God exempts us from the standards which Scripture holds up for all.

THE MIRACLE JUDGMENT OF KORAH'S FOLLOWERS *Numbers 16:1—17:12*

These chapters recount a rebellion against the authority of Moses and Aaron, led by a Levite named Korah and two others, Dathan and Abiram. The rebellion led to a series of miraculous events in which the rebels were judged and the authority of Moses and Aaron was confirmed by the Lord.

The rationale for the rebellion (16:1–3). Korah's rebellion grew out of an overemphasis on one facet of revealed truth. God had said that all of Israel was holy—that is, set apart to him (see Ex. 19:6). To Korah this meant that all God's people were equal, and so Moses' leadership was invalid. "Why," Korah asked Moses and Aaron, "do you exalt yourselves above the assembly of the Lord?"

Korah ignored unmistakable evidence that Moses was God's chosen leader for Israel. Moses was the one who had mediated the miracles that won Israel's freedom—the one who had trudged alone up Mount Sinai to meet with the Lord. By emphasizing one truth and ignoring another, Korah's reasoning led him into error and rebellion.

We must be careful lest we fall into the same error and fail to consider the whole counsel of God.

God's response to the rebellion (16:4–14). God through Moses commanded Korah and the two hundred and fifty leaders he had influenced to appear before the Tabernacle the next day, carrying censers. There they would see for themselves whom the Lord accepted, and whom he did not.

But Dathan and Abiram refused to appear. They would not dignify Moses by obeying *any* command of his. Instead they accused Moses of trying to exterminate the people and failing to bring Israel into the promised land.

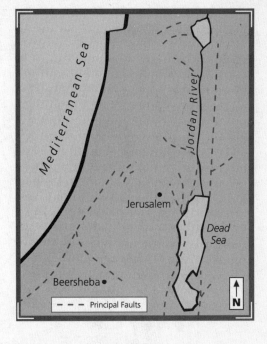

The miracle of the opened chasm (16:24–34). God dealt first with Dathan and Abiram. As they and their families stood at the door of their tents, the earth opened and swallowed them up.

The nature of this miracle of divine judgment was important to Moses. He announced beforehand that this specific miracle would confirm that all the miracles he was associated with had been done by the Lord, and not "of my own will."

It happened just as Moses said. The earth opened and "they and all those with them went down alive into the pit; the earth closed over them, and they perished from among the assembly" (v. 33).

The miracle of the consuming fire (16:35). At about the same time "a fire came out from the Lord and consumed the two hundred and fifty men [with Korah] who were offering incense."

Because of their rebellion, Dathan and Abiram and their families were swallowed up by a crack in the earth.

❖

The two miracle judgments made it clear that God had rejected the position taken by Korah and the more extreme position taken by Dathan and Abiram.

The miracle of the following plague (16:41–49). These judgments made it clear that it was God who had acted against the rebels. Yet the next day "all the congregation of the children of Israel" accused *Moses* of killing the Lord's people (Num. 16:41)! Clearly, Israel had not taken the judgments to heart or learned from them.

God reacted immediately with a plague which killed 14,700 people. Only Moses' hasty action in sending Aaron to stand between the dead and the living with a censer of incense kept the death toll this low.

Parallels with the plagues on Egypt. The trail of judgments that runs through Numbers has an interesting relationship to the plagues that struck Egypt.

In each case an increasing hardness was displayed. Pharaoh became more and more stubborn as judgment miracles followed one after the other. In the early chapters of Numbers, we see the Israelites become more and more stubborn as judgment miracle followed judgment miracle.

In each case the judgment miracles increased in severity. The miracles of Egypt show a gradual but definite escalation in severity. This same pattern is evident in Numbers.

In each case an ultimate resolution called for death. The miracles in Egypt culminated in the death of the firstborn. Even after this extreme judgment, Pharaoh marshaled his army to pursue Israel, and saw that force wiped out

(Ex. 14). The miracles in Numbers reveal such an intense stubbornness and unbelief that God's death sentence on the Exodus generation was fully justified.

For those who wouldn't respond to either grace (Exodus 16, 17) or discipline (Numbers), God exercised his option to set them aside, beginning anew with the next generation.

The miracle of Aaron's rod that budded (Num. 17:1–12). The final miracle in this sequence is not a miracle of judgment, but a miracle performed to *avoid* the necessity of future judgments.

Moses collected rods from the leaders of each of the twelve Israelite tribes and placed them in the tabernacle. The next morning, Aaron's rod had "sprouted, and put forth buds, had produced blossoms and yielded ripe almonds" (v. 8).

The miracle confirmed the role of the Aaronic priesthood, and the rod was preserved as a "sign against the rebels," to forestall future rebellions like that of Korah and the terrible judgments which must follow (Num. 17:10).

THE MIRACLE JUDGMENT BY SERPENTS   *Numbers 21:4–9*

Again, the people spoke "against God and Moses" (Num. 21:4). This faultfinding arose just after God had given Israel a victory over the Canaanites (Num. 21:1–3). Rather than be thankful, the Israelites reacted with hostility and complaints!

The miracle judgment itself (Numbers 21:6). Once again, God disciplined immediately, this time by sending "fiery [deadly] serpents" among the people. The Hebrew words in verse 6 say literally, "many biters and many bitten."

The Israelites responded (21:7). This time the Israelites quickly acknowledged their sin and begged Moses to ask God for relief. This was in stark contrast to their reaction the last time God disciplined them during Korah's rebellion. The people accepted responsibility for

their actions and confessed their sin—a sign of spiritual growth.

God provided an unusual remedy (21:8–9). God instructed Moses to mold a bronze model of a deadly serpent and to place it on a pole in the middle of the camp. God promised that any person who had been bitten by the deadly snakes could survive the ordeal by looking at the bronze serpent.

There is no medicinal value in looking at a bronze image. God's promised healing is clearly miraculous in nature. The bronze serpent saved lives in Moses' time, but it was later misused by Israel.

Israel's misuse of the bronze serpent (2 Kings 18:4). When Israel traveled beyond the area of the fiery serpents, they carried the bronze image with them. It may have served at first as a reminder of the cost of sin and of the saving grace of God. But in time it became an object of worship and veneration. Later generations

Looking to the bronze serpent for healing was a call to faith in God.

burned incense to it, calling it the "Bronze Thing" (*Nehushtan*). Finally, about 700 years later, King Hezekiah had it broken in pieces. It was destroyed along with other idols that Israel was worshiping in place of the Lord.

The true symbolic significance of the bronze serpent. Nearly 1,500 years later, Christ referred to this incident reported in Numbers when speaking with Nicodemus. Jesus said, "And as Moses lifted up the serpent in the wilderness, even so must the Son of Man be lifted up, that whoever believes in him should not perish but have everlasting life" (John 3:14, 15).

There are several points of comparison between the bronze serpent and the cross. These establish the serpent's true symbolic significance.

Each symbolize both the curse and its cure. The cross in Roman times was reserved to punish the most heinous of crimes. It served as a symbol of deadly sin as well as punishment. The fiery serpent was also linked with sin and its punishment. It was through Jesus' death on the cross that eternal life was provided for humankind, and it was through the image of a death-dealing serpent that people who were bitten could be healed.

Each addressed man's helplessness. The Israelites who had been bitten by serpents were doomed. The spiritual condition of every human being is equally desperate. Sinners have no hope of avoiding what Scripture calls the "second death," or hell (Rev. 20:14; 21:8).

Each promised life. The Israelites who looked on the bronze serpent were promised life rather than death. Each human being who looks to the cross of Christ is promised eternal life.

Each offered deliverance only to those who believe. The Israelites who believed the promise of healing hurried to look at the bronze serpent when bitten. The Israelites who did not believe failed to make that journey and died. In the same way, only the person who believes

God's promise of forgiveness wrought at Calvary will respond by trusting Christ and receiving eternal life.

The bronze serpent was a matter of life and death to those who had been bitten. For later generations, the bronze serpent served as a reminder that only God can preserve life. A faith-response to him is the key to salvation.

THE MIRACLE OF BALAAM'S DONKEY   *Numbers 22:1—25:10*

Balaam was a pagan seer or prophet. He was called by a worried ruler to curse Israel as God's people approached the borders of his land. Most Bible students know the story of Balaam's donkey, who miraculously spoke to the amazed prophet. But there are actually three miracles in the story of Balaam's brief association with the people of God.

The miracle of the speaking donkey (Numbers 22:22–30). Balaam was offered riches by the anxious king if he would curse Israel. Although God warned Balaam in a dream not to go, the lure of riches was too great, and Balaam won God's reluctant permission. On the journey, God's angel stood in the path of Balaam "as an adversary."

Sensing the angel's presence, the donkey avoided the danger three times. Finally, the donkey lay down and refused to go on, saving Balaam's life. Furious, Balaam beat the donkey. Then "the Lord opened the mouth of the donkey," who told Balaam what had *really* happened, and Balaam was enabled to see the angel.

It's beside the point to argue that a donkey can't talk, or that the dialogue between the donkey and Balaam displayed reasoning beyond the capacity of any animal. What we have is a miracle—an extraordinary event caused by God with a distinct religious purpose. Balaam's experience with the donkey forced him to realize that even though he had been employed to curse Israel, he should not utter a word other than those which God commanded (see Num. 22:38).

It took a message from a donkey for Balaam to see the error of his ways.

❖

The miraculous blessing of God's people (23:24). Three times Balaam ordered that sacrifices be made on heights from which he could see Israel's camp. Each time, rather than curse Israel, Balaam was commanded to bless them instead!

The wonder is not that God spoke through a pagan prophet. The significant thing is that in spite of Israel's constant rebellion, the Lord remained faithful in his commitment to them. That wonder is expressed in Balaam's first prophetic words:

God is not a man, that He should lie,
Nor a son of man, that He should
    repent.
Has He said, and will He not do?
Or has He spoken, and He will not
    make it good?
Behold, I have received a command
    to bless;
He has blessed, and I cannot reverse
    it.

He has not observed iniquity in
    Jacob,
Nor has He seen wickedness in Israel
    (Num. 23:19–21).

God's commitment to Israel remained unshakable. The Lord had chosen his people, and he would not change his mind ("repent"). In spite of their rebellion, God had not "observed" or "seen" it. This idiom means God has not taken Israel's iniquity into account in determining to remain faithful to his commitments. God's miracles of judgment were signs of his continuing love, not of rejection. As Scripture says,

My son, do not despise the
    chastening of the Lord,
Nor detest His correction;
For whom the Lord loves He
    corrects,
Just as a father the son in whom
    He delights (Prov. 3:11, 12).

What an important reminder to us. The discipline we experience is not an indication of divine rejection. It is a sign of God's loving commitment to us. God is determined to bless us, just as he was determined to bless ancient Israel. And God will do whatever is necessary to correct us and bring us to the place where he can truly bless.

The miracle plague on sinning Israel (Numbers 25:2–9). Balaam's blessings left the king who employed him angry and frustrated. But before leaving, Balaam suggested that the king employ young women to seduce Israelite men and draw them into idolatry (Num. 25:1, 2; compare Num. 31:16). Numbers 25:3 indicates, "So Israel was joined to Baal of Peor, and the anger of the Lord was aroused against Israel."

God again struck Israel with a plague, which killed twenty-four thousand (Num. 25:9). The plague was stopped only by the quick action of Moses. He told the leaders who served as judges within their clans to kill "every one of you his men who were joined to the Baal of Peor" (Num. 25:5).

Evidence of spiritual growth. As we review this sequence of judgment miracles, we find something lacking in the earlier miracle judgments against Israel. We find evidence of spiritual growth! God's program of discipline seemed to be working!

We noted some evidence of growth in Israel's reaction to the judgment involving fiery serpents. But in this judgment at Baal Peor—while God had to strike the people with a plague—*the people themselves took responsibility for punishing the guilty!*

In this episode, Phinehas was singled out. When he saw an Israelite man taking a Midianite woman into his tent, Phinehas entered the tent and drove his javelin through their joined bodies. For the first time, the Israelites expressed anger at the sinners who brought judgment on them. Their anger was not directed at God or Moses! What significant progress!

God had been wise in using miracles of judgment to discipline and purify his people. By the end of the 40 years of wandering, a new generation would be spiritually prepared to enter the promised land at God's command. There they would claim blessings which can be enjoyed only by those who are willing to walk hand in hand with the Lord.

MIRACLES IN DEUTERONOMY

The name *Deuteronomy* means "second law." In this great book, Moses speaks to the children of the Exodus generation, now matured and disciplined, and ready to conquer the promised land. Deuteronomy is an extended sermon, not a book of history, and it records no new miracles.

However, Deuteronomy does refer frequently to the miracles of the Exodus period. This shows how significant those miracles were in shaping Scripture's vivid picture of a God who acts on our behalf. The mighty acts God performed were stamped forever upon the memory of God's people.

For "did God ever try to go and take for himself a nation from the midst of another nation, by trials, by signs, by wonders, by war, by a mighty hand and an outstretched arm, and by great terrors, according to all that the Lord your God did for you in Egypt before your eyes? To you it was shown, that you might know that the Lord himself is God; there is none other besides him" (Deut. 4:34, 35).

CHAPTER 5

MIRACLES IN THE PROMISED LAND

DEMONSTRATIONS OF DIVINE PRESENCE

Joshua; 1 Samuel—2 Chronicles

When you are going through a dry spell spiritually, sometimes you would give anything to witness a miracle. Do we really need to see miracles to maintain our faith in God? Most of God's Old Testament people lived their entire lives without witnessing any miracles personally. Indeed, once the flurry of miracles associated with the Exodus subsided, miracles were rare.

But when the Bible hero Gideon asked an angel who visited him, "where are all His miracles which our fathers told us about," Gideon raised a question many of us want to ask.

In this chapter we check out the very few miracles which the Bible records from around 1390 B.C. to about 930 B.C. These miracles remind us that God is with His people, even when He seems silent or withdrawn.

MIRACLES IN THE BOOK OF JOSHUA

When Moses died, the Israelites were camped near the Jordan River, across from the territory that we know today as Israel. Joshua had been appointed as Moses' successor. He was to have the privilege of leading Israel in the conquest of that land promised by the Lord to Abraham and his descendants many years before (Gen. 12:7).

The main purpose of the miracles in the book of Joshua was to validate Joshua as God's new leader of Israel. They also fulfilled God's commitment to "fight for" his people (Deut. 1:30, 42; 20:4). The miracles described in Joshua are:

- The miracle crossing of the Jordan—p. 97
- The miracle fall of Jericho—p. 99
- The miracle hail—p. 100
- The miracle of the sun standing still—p. 101

THE MIRACLE CROSSING OF THE JORDAN Joshua 3, 4

This miracle is introduced with God's announcement to Joshua, "This day I will begin to exalt you in the sight of all Israel, that they may know that, as I was with Moses, so I will be with you" (Josh. 3:7). Joshua then called the people together, told them what was about to happen, and said "By this you shall know that the living God is among you, and that he will without fail drive out from before you the Canaanites . . . " (Josh. 3:10). The miracle crossing thus served to build the people's confidence in Joshua. But more importantly, it served notice of God's presence and his intention to assist in the conquest.

The nature of the miracle (Joshua 3:12–13). It was January, and the Jordan River was flooded by the early rains and snow melting from Mount Hermon to the north. The place where the Israelites had to cross was called the Zoar, a narrow depression about a mile wide, which was probably flourishing with plant life because of the annual floods. It would take a miracle for Israel to cross the swift river during this flood stage.

Joshua placed the priests carrying God's ark (see Ex. 25:10–33) about three thousand feet in front of the marching Israelites. When the priests' feet touched the waters, the flow from upstream stopped, while the downstream flow continued and drained the flooded river. The Israelites then safely crossed over into Canaan.

An unmistakable miracle. Some have sought a naturalistic explanation for the crossing. They have noted that several times in recorded history the Jordan's flow has been stopped when the river's high banks collapsed, damming its channel. For instance, in July 1927 a landslide near El-Damiyeh caused a stoppage of the Jordan's flow for about 21 hours. However, these stoppages did not oc-cur during flood stage, when the river had overflowed its banks.

The biblical account makes it clear that we are to understand this as an extraordinary event caused by God for the religious purposes noted above.

- The flow stopped the instant the priests' feet touched the water (3:15, 16).
- The text emphasizes twice that Israel crossed "on dry ground" (3:17). The same word is used to describe conditions when Israel crossed the Reed Sea (Ex. 14:21).
- The water resumed its flow as soon as the priests' feet touched land on the other side of the river (Josh. 4:18).
- The inhabitants of the land recognized the event as a miracle (Josh. 5:1).

Only a miracle could have allowed the Israelites to cross over the flooded Jordan River.

The memorial heap of stones (Joshua 4:2–7). An unusual but significant feature of this miracle was a monument which Joshua ordered built from 12 stones taken from the river. The stones were to "be for a memorial to the children of Israel" (v. 7). The word for "memorial"

With the priests and the ark of the covenant leading the way, God stopped the waters of the Jordan River so Israel could cross.

is *zikkaron,* a special word used of objects or actions designed to help Israel identify with a particular truth. The Passover feast, reenacting Israel's last meal in Egypt, was also called a *zikkaron,* translated "memorial" or "remembrance." This memorial beside the Jordan River was intended to help future generations of Israelites realize that when God acted for their forefathers, he had acted for *them.*

Christian communion as observed by believers today is a *zikkaron.* This is why Jesus said "do this in *remembrance* of Me" (Luke 22:19). When we take the bread and the cup, we stand at the foot of the cross. In our mind's eye we are there, as Christ's sacrifice is made for us. Calvary is more than a historical event; it is a historical reality which echoes through the centuries. Celebrating communion is just as significant for our generation today as it was for the first followers of our Lord.

This kind of echo is what Joshua intended future generations to hear through the heap of stones. God's miracle for that generation, through which Israel entered the promised land, was performed for each succeeding generation as well.

THE MIRACLE FALL OF JERICHO
Joshua 6—8

The story of the fall of Jericho ranks with David's defeat of Goliath as one of the most familiar stories in Scripture. Jericho was a fortified city which controlled the passes leading into Canaan's central highlands. Its strategic position made its destruction essential to the conquest of Canaan.

Archaeological investigations at Jericho. Jericho has been the focus of both archaeological investigation and heated debate. An early archaeologist, Garstang, described its destruction:

The main defenses of Jericho in the Late Bronze Age (c. 1500–1200 B.C.) followed the upper bank of the city mound, and comprised two parallel walls, the outer six feet thick and the inner twelve feet thick. Investigations along the west side show continuous signs of destruction and conflagration. The outer wall suffered most, its remains falling down the slope. The inner wall is preserved only where it abuts upon the citadel, or tower, to a height of eighteen feet; elsewhere it is found largely to have fallen, together with the remains of the buildings upon it, into the space between the walls which was filled with ruins and debris. Traces of intense fire are plain to see, including reddened masses of brick, cracked stones, charred timbers and ashes. Houses alongside the wall are found burned to the ground, their roofs fallen upon the domestic pottery within.

This destruction of Jericho's tumbled walls fits the account in Joshua. But the debate has focused on the pottery found at the site. Kathleen Kenyon, a later archaeologist, argued from pottery remains that Jericho fell in the 1200's B.C. Her view was accepted for decades, and the date of the Exodus was shifted from the traditional 1400 B.C., which corresponds with biblical references to dates, to the 1200's. Bimson in recent years has reviewed the pottery data, arguing convincingly that the archaeological evidence fits the earlier date rather than the late date.

The most interesting data from archaeology, however, was summed up by Unger:

The walls were of a type which made direct assault practically impossible. An approaching enemy first encountered a stone abutment, eleven feet height, back and up from which sloped a thirty-five degree plastered scarp reaching to the main wall some 35 vertical feet above. The steep smooth slope prohibited battering the wall by any effective device or building fires to break it. An army trying to storm the wall found difficulty in climbing the slope, and ladders to scale it could find no satisfactory footing (*Archaeology and the Old Testament,* 174).

It would take a miracle to take Jericho quickly. And this is exactly what God provided.

The peculiar conditions of the miracle (Joshua 6:3–5). The Israelites were instructed by the Lord to circle the city once for six consecutive days, in complete silence. The seventh day they were to circle the city seven times, and then when the priests blew their trumpets, to shout. And, Joshua was told, when the people shout, the wall "will fall down flat" (v. 5). The Hebrew wording says "sink down to the ground."

The Israelites obeyed the strange command of Joshua, and it happened just as God had said (Josh. 6:12–16). When the wall collapsed, the Israelites rushed the city and "utterly destroyed all that was in the city" (Josh. 6:21).

Some have suggested naturalistic explanations, such as an earthquake, for the collapse of the wall. Such attempts to make the biblical account credible are unnecessary. The fall of the wall was pre-announced; it happened at the moment the people shouted; the walls fell outward—all these facts emphasize the miraculous. Jericho's wall fell because God caused it to do so; no earthquake was necessary.

An associated miracle: Rahab's deliverance (Joshua 2; 6:22–25). Joshua had sent men earlier to scout the city. Two of them had been trapped in Jericho. Their lives had been saved by a prostitute innkeeper named Rahab. She hid them and then let them down over the city walls so they could make their escape. Rahab was convinced that God was with the Israelites, so she bargained with the two Israelites spies for her life. They promised that when Jericho fell, she and any family members found in her home would be spared.

When the walls fell, apparently that section against which Rahab's house was constructed (see Josh. 2:15) remained standing. The miracle was selective: God in his sovereignty spared Rahab's house, and she and her family were led safely out of the city (Josh. 6:22).

The book of Hebrews declares that "by faith the harlot Rahab did not perish with those who did not believe, when she had received the spies with peace" (Heb. 11:31). Even more striking is another New Testament reference to Rahab found in Matthew 3. Tracing the lineage of Jesus, Matthew reveals that "Salmon begot Boaz by Rahab, Boaz begot

Obed by Ruth, Obed begot Jesse, and Jesse begot David the king" (Matt. 1:5, 6). Rahab the prostitute, saved and transformed by her faith, was an ancestress of David, and thus of Jesus Christ.

Perhaps a greater miracle than the fall of city wall was the redemption and transformation of a human heart.

The meaning of the miracle at Jericho (Joshua 6–8). This miracle reflects a major theme in the book of Joshua: obedience brings victory, while disobedience brings defeat.

What is striking about the events at Jericho is that there was no apparent relationship between what God told the Israelites to do and the fall of the city. No army in history has ever attacked a city by walking around it for several days. Israel might have questioned the strange command. But instead Israel obeyed—and the city fell.

We are not given the choice of which commands of God to obey, depending on whether they are reasonable or sensible. The God we have been called to serve expects us to trust him and to follow him always.

The importance of obedience is underlined by the story of Achan. When Jericho fell, Achan violated God's command. He took some of the city's treasures and hid them. When the Israelites attacked the smaller city of Ai, Israel was defeated and 38 lives were lost. God revealed to Joshua that Achan's disobedience was responsible for the defeat, and Achan was executed. With the disobedient Achan purged, God again blessed Israel with victory.

The book of Joshua is a testimony to the victories to be won by those who trust God enough to obey his Word. Our success depends on our responsiveness to the will of our God.

THE MIRACLE HAIL
Joshua 10:10, 11

In a battle with a coalition of Canaanite kings "the Lord routed them . . . with a great slaughter." As the Israelites pursued, "the Lord cast down large hailstones from heaven on them as far as Azekah, and they died. There were more who died from the hailstones than the children of Israel killed with the sword."

No natural event. The Jewish sage Malbim, paraphrased by Rabbi Reuven Drucker in his commentary on the book of Joshua, observed:

The fact that hailstones descended from heaven and killed people could be construed as a natural event. In this case, however, it was clearly miraculous, because the hailstones killed only Emorites, not the Israelites who were following in close pursuit (p. 247).

An interesting Jewish Midrash [interpretation], noting that the text has the definite article—*"the* hailstones"—suggests that these were hailstones left over from the killing hail which fell on Egypt (Ex. 9:33). The event was clearly a miracle, fulfilling God's promise in Deuteronomy 20:4, "the LORD your God is He who goes with you, to fight for you against your enemies, to save you."

THE MIRACLE OF THE SUN STANDING STILL   *Joshua 10:12–14*

This brief miracle report is unique in Scripture. It seems to describe a major suspension of natural law. As the Israelites pursued the fleeing enemy, it appeared night would fall before final victory could be achieved. Joshua called on the sun and moon to stand still until the enemy army was wiped out. The text says,

So the sun stood still in the midst of heaven, and did not hasten to go down for about a whole day. And there has been no day like that, before it or after it, that the Lord heeded the voice of a man; for the Lord fought for Israel (Josh. 10:13, 14).

The nature of the miracle. Many commentators have debated the nature of this miracle. Is the description phenomenological? That is, does the text describe what Joshua and the Israelites *saw?* If so, God may have performed a *local* miracle, causing the sun's light to shine on Israel while the rest of the world experienced normal day and night. Or does the text make a *scientific* statement? If so, God may

have halted the earth's rotation, with all the adjustments this would have required. In either case, the prolongation of daylight was a miracle.

The real uniqueness of the miracle (10:14). In commenting on this miracle, the text says, "There has been no day like that, before it or after it." But what made the day unique was not the extension of daylight. The true wonder is "that the LORD heeded the voice of a man."

Normally God informs human beings that a miracle will take place. But Joshua himself "invented" and asked for this miracle! And God did as Joshua asked.

Some have assumed that it takes faith to believe in miracles. But whatever faith belief in miracles may require is overshadowed by the faith that Joshua exhibited. Of all the unchangeable things we know, the motion of the earth around the sun is perhaps the most regular. Day follows night without interruption. All our experience leads us to expect that this cycle will go on unchanged through our lifetime and beyond. Yet Joshua called on the Lord to halt the sun and moon until final victory could be won. And God did.

We're sometimes told that God has gone out of the miracle business. Certainly the kind of miracles that God performed in the Exodus age have not been repeated. But there are private as well as public miracles. The God who answered Joshua's prayer can and does answer our prayers. And if the request we make is for an extraordinary intervention by God on our behalf, we need to have the faith that Joshua demonstrated.

MIRACLES IN THE BOOK OF JUDGES

The book of Judges sketches critical events during the 400-year period between the conquest of Canaan and the emergence of the Hebrew monarchy. As story follows story, a common pattern emerges.

The Israelites turned away from God to worship pagan deities. God then permitted a neighboring people to oppress them. In desperation, the Israelites returned and appealed to the Lord. God then raised up a judge—a military-political-religious leader—who defeated the enemy and initiated a time of peace. After the judge died, the people again turned to idolatry—and the cycle begins all over again.

Many stories from the book of Judges are well known. We're familiar with Deborah, the first woman judge; and with Samson, Israel's strong man. Some extraordinary events took place during these years, such as Samson's pushing down the support pillars of the Philistine temple at Gath. But most do not fit our definition of a miracle.

In fact, the miracles that occur in the book of Judges are what we might call "private miracles." They were given to strengthen individuals rather than sent as a public witness of God's presence to Israel and its enemies. Aside from the angel appearance to the parents of Samson (Judg 13:9–23; see *Every Good and Evil Angel in the Bible*), the one report of unmistakable miracles involves Gideon.

Gideon the skeptic (Judges 6:12–16). An angel, apparently in the guise of an ordinary traveler, appeared to Gideon and announced, "The Lord is with you." Gideon was not impressed. "If the Lord is with us," he responded, "why then has all this happened to us? And where are all his miracles which our fathers told us about?"

The angel responded by informing Gideon that he was to be God's chosen instrument to defeat the Midianite raiders. These robbers or thieves appeared at harvest time, stripping the land of its crops. Although the angel promised Gideon "I will be with you, and you shall defeat the Midianites" (v. 16), Gideon remained skeptical.

Gideon asked for a "sign" (6:17). The Hebrew word used by Gideon is *'ot*. This word, found only here in the book of Judges, means a "miraculous sign"—something that is unmistakably the work of God. The text goes on to relate three signs that the Lord provided. The first authenticated the original message,

and the second and third strengthened Gideon's budding faith.

The rock-fire (6:19–21). In the tradition of hospitality, Gideon prepared a meal for his visitor. The angel asked Gideon to place the food on a rock. When the angel touched the food with the end of his staff, "fire rose out of the rock" and burned the offering. Then the angel disappeared.

Gideon was convinced. When the Lord told him to tear down the community's idolatrous worship center, Gideon did so, in spite of his fears (Judg. 6:25–27). When the Midianites approached, Gideon also sent messengers throughout the nearby tribes to assemble an army.

But Gideon was still hesitant and afraid.

Putting out the fleece (6:36–38). Gideon asked God to reassure him by another private miracle. Gideon put out a fleece, a piece of wool cut from a sheep. If the ground was dry in the morning and the fleece was wet with dew, Gideon would know God was with him. It happened just as Gideon asked.

Gideon used a fleece to gain reassurance.

Putting out the fleece again (6:39–40). Gideon approached the Lord and begged for further confirmation. This time he asked that the fleece be dry and the ground all around wet with dew. Again it happened as Gideon asked.

Reassured, Gideon set out to battle the Midianites.

Should we ask for confirming miracles today? Some have seen the experience of Gideon as a model for today. When faced with a significant decision, they think they should ask for a confirming "miracle," just to be sure that a specific choice is God's will. Typically the miracle requested is minor, and it's impossible to distinguish it from mere chance: "If I'm supposed to go, Lord, let my sister call me in the next ten minutes." While God can certainly influence one's sister, this "miracle" is hardly to be classed with the signs granted to Gideon. A phone call may be nothing but a coincidence; wet fleece on dry ground cannot.

Notice that Gideon's obedience to the will of God did not *depend on* the miracles of the fleece. As soon as Gideon realized that God was commanding him, he chose to obey. Long before setting out the fleece, Gideon tore down the local worship center and called for the men of Israel to assemble. He *acted before he was given the sign, not afterward.*

The miracle of the fleece was a gracious reassurance granted by God to a man who already trusted him enough to act on his word.

In living out our relationship with the Lord, we are not to try to find the will of God by "putting out the fleece." What we are to do is to seek God's will. Once we sense what his will is, we are to act on it. God has given us his Word, the Holy Spirit, and our fellow believers to help us find our way. We do not have to rely on "putting out the fleece" to determine what God wants us to do.

MIRACLES OF THE BOOKS OF 1, 2 SAMUEL; *1 Kings 1—13; 1 Chronicles; and 2 Chronicles 1—9*

These portions of the Old Testament tell the story of Israel's transformation from loosely associated tribes into a powerful and united monarchy under David and Solomon. The events reported in these books cover a period of about 120 years—between 1050 B.C. and 930 B.C. The chart below shows the relationship of the books to one another and to key figures.

Each miracle in these books is associated with worship. In the extraordinary events of this era, the Lord emphasized to Israel the importance of focusing on him.

It is perhaps no wonder then that Israel's greatest king, David—who forged the powerful and united nation that Israel became—was so deeply committed to worshiping the Lord. We see this reflected in the many stories which emphasize David's sensitivity to the Lord. This is also evident in the Psalms, Israel's prayer book. A total of 73 of the 150 psalms in this book bear the superscription, "a psalm of David."

c.1050	c.1010	970	930
1 Samuel	2 Samuel	1 Kings 1–13	
	1 Chronicles	2 Chronicles 1–9	
Samuel _____.			
Saul _____.			
David _____.			
		Solomon _____.	

Miracle reports (chapters)

1 Sam. 5, 6	2 Sam. 6	1 Kings 8; 12;
	1 Chron. 13	2 Chron. 7

A warrior and military strategist, David was also a consummate politician. He was an organizational genius who created a system for the administration of the new nation as well as a gifted musician and poet. But perhaps more than anything else, David was a man who loved and worshiped God. He related every experience of life to the God whom he knew was present with him.

The message of the miracles of this era—that we must put God first and do so on his own terms—was enfleshed in David. The heart of this shepherd boy who became a king remained focused on the Lord in spite of his personal flaws.

The miracles reported in these Scriptures are:

1. The miracle of Dagon's fall.—p. 104
2. The miracle of the tumors.—p. 105
3. The miracle return of the ark.—p. 106
4. The miracle judgment on Israel.—p. 106
5. The miracle on the ark's journey to Jerusalem.—p. 107
6. The miracle of the shekinah.—p. 109
7. The miracle judgment on Jeroboam.—p. 110

THE MIRACLE OF DAGON'S FALL
1 Samuel 5:1–5

Young Samuel had just been recognized as a prophet when the Israelites chose to rebel against the dominating Philistine army. On the first day of battle the Israelites were defeated. In desperation, the despondent Israelites sent two corrupt priests to bring the ark of the covenant to their camp (1 Sam. 4:1–10).

The significance of the holy ark. The ark of the covenant had been constructed in the time of Moses. Considered the most holy object in Israel's religion (Ex. 25), the ark was a portable chest which contained the Ten Commandments God had engraved in stone, a jar of manna, and Aaron's rod. The lid featured the figures of two angels, bending over a spot where once a year on the Day of Atonement sacrificial blood was poured by the High Priest (Lev. 16).

Most significantly, the ark was the place where God and man met in restored harmony on the great Day of Atonement. Thus the ark symbolized the presence of God with his people.

Why the Israelites sent for the ark (1 Samuel 4:3). The thinking of the Israelites is clear in this verse. They said, "Let us bring the ark . . . that when it comes among us *it may save us* from the hand of our enemies."

The verse displays a corruption of Israel's faith by pagan notions. The peoples surrounding the Israelites thought of their pagan idols as *real*. To them, an idol was a nexus at which the deity was present. The Egyptians even "fed" their idols, gave them baths, changed their clothes, and treated them as if the god which the idol represented were present in the image.

What the Israelites had fallen into believing, according to this verse, was that God would *have* to be present if they had the ark. With the ark, they could expect God to fight for Israel against the Philistines. Bringing the ark into the camp was an attempt to manipulate God!

The Philistines shared the Israelites' magical view, and they were terrified when they realized the ark of the God who had struck the Egyptians was in Israel's camp. They determined to fight the next day, fully expecting to lose (1 Sam. 4:7–9).

But the next day the Philistines won the battle—and the ark of God was captured. The

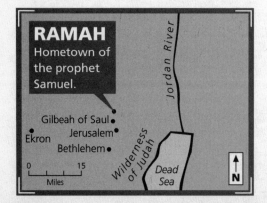

RAMAH
Hometown of the prophet Samuel.

Gilbeah of Saul
Ekron   Jerusalem
        Bethlehem

Jordan River

Wilderness of Judah

Dead Sea

0   15
Miles

N

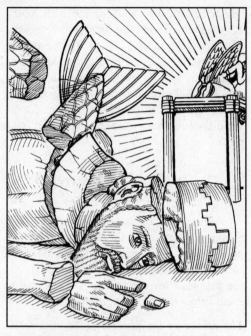

The Philistine statue of Dagon mysteriously fell down when the ark was placed beside it.

❖

capture was the first in a series of events which would shift the eyes of Israel from the ark to the invisible God whom it represented.

A dangerous trophy (1 Samuel 5:1–5). Following ancient custom, the Philistines placed the ark of the Lord as a trophy in the temple of their god, Dagon. There it would represent the "capture" of Israel's God by their own deity, testifying to Dagon's superiority.

The morning after the ark was placed in the temple, the Philistine priests were shocked to find that the statue of Dagon had fallen on its face before the ark of God (1 Sam. 5:3). The priests propped up their deity and braced it so the idol couldn't fall. But the next morning they found the statue of Dagon again on its face, with its head and hands broken off! (1 Sam. 5:4).

The event was recognized as a miracle, indicating that Israel's God was greater than the Philistine god Dagon.

How strange that those who acknowledge the greatness of the Lord would think he can be manipulated to serve human ends. God is no magic lamp that we rub when we want a need met, nor is he a talisman that we affix to the dashboard of our cars. Our God is the Creator of the universe, the miracle-working God who is free to act in any situation as he wills.

This first of the miracles associated with the ark began a healthy shift of focus from objects representing God to the one supreme Lord behind the objects. This was a concept Israel would need desperately if the Lord was to build a nation which would reflect his glory to all the world.

THE MIRACLE OF THE TUMORS
1 Samuel 5:6—6:6

The story of the captured ark continues with the report of an epidemic. The ark was carried to the Philistine city of Ashdod. While it was there, the Lord "ravaged them and struck them with tumors, both Ashdod and its territory."

The nature of the miracle (1 Samuel 5:6). The tumors were probably inflamed swellings of the lymph glands that are characteristic of bubonic plague. This view is supported by two facts. The tumors brought "very great destruction" (1 Sam. 5:9, 11), and the outbreak was associated with rats—carriers of the plague in ancient as well as medieval times (1 Sam. 6:4).

The response of the Philistines (5:7–12). The people of Ashdod realized that the plague was God's judgment on them and their God (1 Sam. 5:7). The leaders decided to send the ark to Gath, another of the five principle Philistine cities. But when the ark reached Gath, the plague broke out there as well. The ark was then taken to Ekron, and again the plague followed. At this point, the people no longer asked their leaders what to do. They demanded, "Send away the ark of the God of Israel, and let it go back to its own place, so that it does not kill us and our people" (1 Sam. 5:11).

The marks of a miracle. We have defined miracles in this study as extraordinary events caused by God with a religious purpose. While bubonic plague has natural causes, this outbreak was extraordinary. It occurred only where the ark of God rested. When the ark was moved, the plague followed. The Philistines concluded from the evidence that Israel's God was the cause of their distress.

The purpose of this miracle is also clear: God was judging Dagon as he had judged the gods of Egypt (Ex. 12:12). Through these plagues, God was forcing the Philistines to return the ark to Israel so it could continue its vital role in the religion of God's people.

What Israel had seen as a terrible defeat for the Lord—the capture of the ark of the covenant—had become an occasion for the Lord to display his power. What an important truth this is to remember when we experience defeats. God can use our setbacks and weaknesses to display his power and remind us of his loving presence.

THE MIRACLE RETURN OF THE ARK   *1 Samuel 6:7–16*

The Philistine leaders were willing to return the ark to Israel, along with golden tumors and golden rats that represented a "trespass offering." They remembered how Pharaoh had hardened his heart, causing the entire land of Egypt to be ravaged. So the Philistines determined not to resist Israel's God (1 Sam. 6:6). At the same time, they wanted to be sure the Lord had been the cause of the plague. The next miracle was God's response to a test devised by the Philistines.

The nature of the miracle (1 Samuel 6:7, 12). Every farmer knows about the patterning behavior of cows. When brought in at night, a cow will go to its own stall. If placed in a strange stall, it will show extreme distress. Cows will also stay close to their calves when their offspring are young and still suckling.

The Philistines also recognized these traits. They placed the ark on a cart, with their trespass offering, and hitched two milk cows which had young calves to the cart. Acting against their nature, and lowing in complaint all the way (1 Sam. 6:12), the cows left their calves and familiar territory and set out along the road to Beth Shemesh, in Israelite territory.

The Philistine leaders followed, watching as the ark was returned to Israelite hands. Then they returned home, no doubt in great relief.

THE MIRACLE JUDGMENT ON ISRAEL   *1 Samuel 6:19–21*

When the ark was returned to Beth-Shemesh, many of the curious Israelites peered at it and even looked inside. God struck the curious dead, creating terror among the people. They exclaimed, "Who is able to stand before this holy LORD God."

The nature of the miracle (1 Samuel 6:19). These sudden deaths were clearly caused by their gathering around the ark to look inside. The cause-and-effect link was so clearly established that the observers had no doubt the multiple deaths were a miracle—an extraordinary event caused by God himself.

The number of those who died was seventy—not 50,070, as translated by the King James Version. Hebrew numbers are difficult to read. Rather than use numbers, the Hebrews used letters of the alphabet. Thus *aleph* ["a"] was one, *bet* ["be"] was two, and so on. Tiny marks were then written above them to represent multiples of ten. As manuscripts aged or were copied, it was easy to mistake the original number. As the NKJV footnote indicates, it is best to understand the text to say that seventy men died because they looked into the ark of God.

Why God struck the Israelites dead. As the most holy object in Israel's religion, the ark represented the meeting of God with man. The cover of the ark was the place where sacrificial blood was poured on the annual Day of Atonement. The message was clear. Sinful man could meet with a holy God only through sacrifice. The ark may be interpreted as a symbol of the Cross of Christ, where Jesus shed his blood to make peace between mankind and God by offering himself as full payment for our sins.

Exodus 40:20–21 relates how the ark was placed in the tabernacle, concealed behind a curtain and partitioned off so that even the priests who ministered in the tabernacle would not be able to see it. When being carried by the Levites, the ark was to be covered by the veil that concealed it from the eyes of the priests (Num. 4:5). Numbers 4:20 warned that even the Levites, who carried the tabernacle and its contents during the wilderness journey, "shall not go in to watch while the holy things are being covered, lest they die."

What the Israelites did at Beth-Shemesh was to show a lack of respect or reverence for God by treating the ark as a common object.

The results of the miracle (6:20). The impact of the miracle was immediate. The Israelites were awed and impressed at the power of "this holy LORD God." The disrespect they had shown for the things of the Lord was replaced by an awed realization that God is holy and that he must be approached with deep respect.

The people of Beth-Shemesh were also uncomfortable in the presence of such a God, so the ark was moved about nine miles away. It was sheltered at Kirjah Jearim for the next 20 years.

1 Samuel 7:2 indicates that during this time all Israel "lamented after God." The Hebrew words read, "Went into mourning toward God." The idiom means that, at last, Israel wept in repentance. At last the Israelites realized they needed a revitalized relationship with the Lord.

Then Samuel challenged Israel to put away every idol promising that a return to the Lord would mean deliverance from Philistine domination. Israel did return. After a great revival meeting at which the people fasted and confessed their sins, Israel won a decisive victory over the Philistines at Mizpah (1 Sam. 7:4–14).

The significance of the miracles of the captured ark. The four miracles reported in 1 Samuel 5—6 were not isolated incidents. Each contributed to a vital message which Israel needed to hear. The miracles in Philistia revealed the power of Israel's God and his superiority to the deities of Israel's oppressors. The miracle at Beth-Shemesh reaffirmed the holiness of Israel's God, and the importance of treating the Lord with appropriate respect.

Once Israel grasped these two vital messages—that Yahweh, the God who is present with his people, was both powerful and holy—a radical change was gradually worked in their hearts. When at last confession and recommitment restored their relationship with the Lord, Yahweh again acted for them. The enemy was defeated, and the land had peace throughout Samuel's judgeship.

It's the same for us today. Our God is present with us. He is powerful and holy. When by confession and recommitment we live in intimate relationship with the Lord, he will act for us. And we will also know peace.

THE MIRACLE ON THE WAY TO JERUSALEM   *2 Samuel 6*

The next miracle recorded in the historical books occured during the reign of David. This miracle also involved the ark of God.

David unified the nation, establishing Jerusalem as his capital. Deeply aware of the role God must play in the life of his people, he intended to make Jerusalem a center for the worship of Yahweh as well as the political center of the nation. David in later years would revitalize worship by organizing the priests and Levites to serve God, by reviving the religious festivals ordained in the Pentateuch, and by writing many of the songs and hymns used in public worship.

David realized that his first step must be to bring the ark of God to Jerusalem. But as the ark was being transported to Jerusalem, a young man named Uzzah reached out to steady it. The moment he touched the ark, Uzzah was struck dead.

When Uzzah touched the ark to steady it on the cart, he was struck dead.

❖

Why did Uzzah die? (Exodus 25:10–14). According to instructions given to Moses, the ark was not to be touched by anyone. It was originally constructed with a ring at each of its four corners. Moses was told by the Lord that "you shall put the poles into the rings on the sides of the ark, that the ark may be *carried* by them" (Ex. 25:14).

But David had the ark placed on a cart for transport. When the cart tipped and Uzzah reached out to steady it, he accidentally touched the ark—and died.

David's initial reaction (2 Samuel 6:8, 9). The death of Uzzah both angered and terrified David. Why would the Lord do such a thing? Uzzah had only been trying to save the ark, and David's motives in transporting it to Jerusalem were pure.

But David had either ignored God's instructions for moving the ark, or he had failed to consult the Scriptures. In either case, the mode of transport conveyed a disrespect for the Lord that could not be tolerated if the new nation was to experience his blessing. The death of Uzzah again emphasized the holiness of Israel's God and the necessity of carefully seeking his will in every situation.

The ark arrived in Jerusalem at last (6:12–13). David left the ark at the house of a man named Obed-Edom, near the place where Uzzah had died. God uniquely blessed Obed-Edom during this period, so David concluded it was safe to bring the ark to Jerusalem as he had planned. This time David consulted Scripture to make sure he transported the ark according to its instructions (v. 13).

David and his people learned anew the lesson which Israel had experienced in Samuel's time. If we are to walk with God, we must treat him as holy and seek his will in every situation.

God was with David all the days of his life. In his 40-year reign, the territory controlled by Israel was multiplied ten times. For the first time, God's people possessed most of the land promised to Abraham's descendants (Gen. 12:7).

THE MIRACLE OF THE SHEKINAH   *1 Kings 6:19–21; 2 Chronicles 7:1–3*

David had dreamed of building a temple for the Lord in Jerusalem. But the Lord told David that his son Solomon would build the temple. David's last years were spend assembling materials for this great project, drawing plans and outlining the responsibilities of the priests and Levites who would serve at the temple (1 Chron. 22—29).

When David died and Solomon succeeded his father, the new king set about building the temple. It took seven years. Solomon himself led the service of dedication.

Solomon's dedicatory prayer (2 Chronicles 6:13). Pagan peoples viewed their temples as the "house" of their deities. This was where their gods lived. Solomon knew this would not be true of the Lord. He prayed,

But will God indeed dwell with men on the earth? Behold, heaven and the heaven of heavens cannot contain You. How much less this temple which I have built! (2 Chron. 6:18).

What Solomon asked was that God's "eyes may be open toward this temple," and that the Lord would answer prayers addressed to him by his people.

The miracle response (1 Kings 8:10, 11; 2 Chron. 7:1–3). Chronicles describes God's miracle response at the Temple's dedication.

When Solomon had finished praying, fire came down from heaven and consumed the burnt offering and the sacrifices; and the glory of the Lord filled the temple. And the priests could not enter the house of the Lord, because the glory of the Lord had filled the Lord's house (2 Chron. 7:1–3).

This "glory" of the Lord was the shekinah, a bright, visible expression of the very presence of God. This was an unmistakable miracle, an extraordinary event caused by God. But the appearance of the shekinah was not a unique event. It had happened before!

The glory of the Lord had appeared atop Mount Sinai in the time of Moses (Ex. 16:10; 24:16). It had filled the tabernacle when that worship center was dedicated (Ex. 40:34, 35). Ezekiel 43:4, 5 spoke of God's glory filling a yet-future Jerusalem temple. Both Isaiah 40:5 and Habakkuk 2:14 looked forward to history's end, when the whole world will be filled with his glory.

The meaning of this miracle was recognized immediately by all Israel. God was present with them. And he would answer their prayers.

The response of Israel to the miracle (2 Chronicles 7:3). Israel's response is described in this verse:

When all the children of Israel saw how the fire came down, and the glory of the Lord on the temple, they bowed their faces to the ground on the pavement, and worshiped and praised the LORD, saying:

"For He is good,
For His mercy endures forever."

Comparisons and contrasts with the miracles involving the ark of God. Like the other miracles in this sequence, this wonder drew attention to worship. When Solomon offered his prayer, the ark of the covenant rested in the temple, isolated in the Holy of Holies. Unlike the other miracles, which reflected Israel's failure to honor and respect the Lord, this miracle recognized Israel's commitment to him, demonstrated by construction of the temple. The earlier miracles, by which sins were judged and exposed, stimulated awe but also terror. This miracle, which recognized Israel's dedication to the Lord, also created awe. But now praise replaced fear, as all Israel realized that "He is good" and that "His mercy endures forever."

This is a good reminder for us. God intends to reveal himself to us. If we ignore him, his revelation may take the form of judgment. If we honor him and respond to his word as the ultimate reality, God will bless us and fill our lives with rejoicing.

THE MIRACLE JUDGMENT ON JEROBOAM   *1 Kings 12:25—13:6*

Solomon ruled Israel for forty years. Toward the end of his reign, he turned away from the Lord. The people had also begun to worship pagan deities (1 Kings 11:33). As a judgment, the united kingdom of David and Solomon was divided, into north and south.

The ruler of the new Northern Kingdom, which retained the name *Israel,* was Jeroboam. He was a competent man who had been one of Solomon's officials. God informed Jeroboam through the prophet Ahijah what he would do. He also promised Jeroboam that if he would be faithful to the Lord and keep his commandments, Jeroboam's dynasty would last (1 Kings 11:38).

But when Ahijah's prophecy came true, Jeroboam worried. He was afraid to let his people go up to Jerusalem each year to worship and celebrate the religious festivals which God had ordained. Jeroboam feared that shared worship would affirm the common bond between north and south, leading his people to demand reunification.

Jeroboam's sinful solution (1 Kings 12:25, 26). When he was confirmed as king, Jeroboam instituted a counterfeit religious system. This system was modeled on that revealed by Moses, but it was significantly different.

Jeroboam established two worship centers to serve as rivals to the temple in Jerusalem. He cast two metal bulls for these worship centers. The bulls did not represent Yahweh, but they replaced the ark. The bulls were intended to symbolize the presence of the Lord. The Israelites were to imagine God's presence as resting on the back of these idols.

Jeroboam also ordained ordinary men as priests rather than limit this office to the descendants of Aaron. He instituted a system of sacrifices. Jeroboam established religious festivals, but he directed that they be observed at different times than the Mosaic festivals.

We have already noted that God struck seventy men dead for peeking into the ark and struck Uzzah dead for touching it. This shows what a great sin Jeroboam's deliberate violation of God's Word truly was.

The miracle judgment (1 Kings 13:1–4). On the day Jeroboam dedicated his worship center at Bethel, God sent a young prophet to confront the king. The prophet cursed the altar and predicted its future destruction. The text indicates that the young prophet "gave a sign the same day."

The word for "sign" in this passage is *maasheh,* which is used to identify an unmistakable work of God (see p. 21). It might not have been miraculous for a newly constructed altar to split apart and for its ashes to pour out. But when this happened immediately following a prediction by a man who claimed to be speaking for God, it must be considered a miracle.

Jeroboam's reaction led to a further miracle (1 Kings 13:4). Furious, Jeroboam pointed at the young prophet and demanded, "Arrest him!" The text says, "Then his hand, which he stretched out toward him, withered, so that he could not pull it back to himself." Convinced now and frightened, Jeroboam begged the young prophet to pray that his hand be restored. In answer to this prayer, it was restored, "and became as before" (1 Kings 13:6). The humbled ruler offered to reward the prophet. But Jeroboam was not dissuaded from his intention to establish counterfeit worship in Israel.

The fate of the young prophet (1 Kings 13:11–30). The next event contributes to our understanding of the message of this miracle. God told the young prophet not to eat or drink while in the north. But an old prophet who lived nearby lied and said that the Lord had told *him* to give the younger man a meal. The young prophet took the older man's word and violated God's command. On leaving, he was met and killed by a lion.

When Jereboam set up an alternate worship center, God sent a prophet to confront him.

❖

The implications are profound. The young prophet died because he accepted man's word, which contradicted what he knew to be God's word. Jeroboam had done far worse. If the Israelites adopted the worship system established by the king, they would also be honoring man's word and rejecting the clear Word of God. If the young prophet did not escape the consequences of his failure to honor the Lord's word, how much more severe would Israel's punishment be for participating in counterfeit worship?

The message of the miracle was taken to heart by some. Second Chronicles 11:16 indicates that the priests and Levites in Israel moved to the south, and that "those from all the tribes of Israel, such as set their heart to seek the LORD God of Israel, came to Jerusalem to sacrifice to the LORD God of their fathers." This shift of population weakened Israel, and made "the son of Solomon strong" as long as he honored God as David had.

The miracle sequence. The miracles in the books of Samuel and the first half of 1 Kings and 2 Chronicles are clustered around the ark of the covenant. They served to rebuke God's peo-

ple for treating him lightly and to underline the twin themes of God's power and his holiness.

When Israel took these miracles to heart and honored God by obeying his Word, the nation prospered. It could be that the lessons learned in the time of Samuel and in David's early rule were the key to the rise of the united kingdom. Awareness of God's power and his holiness was also the foundation for Israel's prosperity during the early years of Solomon.

But God's people did not continue to live with an awareness of the Lord's power and holiness. In Solomon's later years, both king and people turned to idolatry. The united kingdom was torn in two, and the untrusting Jeroboam chose to ignore God's promise and to disobey his word. The last miracle in this sequence confirmed the message contained in the earlier miracles. God is both powerful and holy. And those who will not honor him will bear the consequences of their sins.

May we learn from the miracles of the ark to honor God in our own lives. And to act always in full awareness that our God is powerful. And that our God is holy. Such a God is to be held in awe. And to be obeyed.

❖

CHAPTER 6

THE MIRACLE MINISTRY OF ELIJAH

GOD'S CHAMPION AGAINST BAAL

1 Kings 17—2 Kings 2

Some marriages seem made in heaven. The union of King Ahab of Israel and Jezebel of Phoenicia seemed made in hell.

The two set out together to exterminate God's prophets and brought hundreds of pagan prophets of Baal and his consort Asherah into the northern Hebrew kingdom, Israel. They intended to replace Yahweh with Baal as the official god of the nation.

A single, bold figure stood up against the evil king and his pagan queen. At this critical moment in sacred history, God raised up the prophet Elijah, and through Elijah God performed a series of miracles which demonstrated conclusively that the Lord, not Baal, was the true and only God.

The Recorded Miracles of Elijah

1. Elijah stops the rains.—p. 112
2. Elijah multiplies a widow's food.—p. 113
3. Elijah restores the widow's son.—p. 114
4. Elijah calls down fire at Carmel.—p. 115
5. Elijah restores the rains.—p. 118
6. Elijah calls down fire on soldiers.—p. 119
7. Elijah divides the Jordan's waters.—p. 120

ELIJAH STOPS THE RAINS   1 Kings 17:1–8

King Ahab is introduced in 1 Kings 16. Verses 30–33 sum up his character and career.

Now Ahab the son of Omri did evil in the sight of the Lord, more than all who were before him. And it came to pass, as though it had been a trivial thing for him to walk in the sins of Jeroboam the son of Nebat, that he took as wife Jezebel the daughter of Ethbaal, king of the Sidonians; and he went and served Baal and worshiped him. Then he set up an altar for Baal in the temple of Baal, which he had built in Samaria. And Ahab made a wooden image. Ahab did more to provoke the Lord God of Israel to anger than all the kings of Israel who were before him.

Elijah the prophet. Elijah is one of the most striking figures in the Old Testament. Second Kings 1:8 describes him as a hairy man wearing a leather belt. The name *Elijah* means "Yahweh is God," so his name sums up his mission. Elijah was called to proclaim to Israel that Yahweh was the true God and to turn back the tide of Baalism that threatened to sweep the nation. All of Elijah's miracles demonstrated the truth that "Yahweh is God."

Elijah announced a drought (1 Kings 17:1). Elijah did not warn Ahab of the coming drought or give him a chance to repent. The king was committed to evil, and he was rapidly leading his people to a commitment to Baal. It would take a dramatic miracle to make Ahab pay attention to any prophet of the Lord.

So at God's leading Elijah sought out Ahab and announced, "As the Lord God of Israel lives, before whom I stand, there shall not be dew nor rain these years, except at my word."

"As the Lord God of Israel lives." To Ahab, the name *Yahweh* was an empty term, a word which he could safely ignore. It was "Baal" who seemed real to Ahab. Elijah announced the miracle as proof that "the Lord God of Israel lives." Only a God who was real could cause a drought at the word of one of his prophets—or bring rain at that prophet's word. Ahab and all Israel needed unmistakable evidence that Yahweh lived.

"Not be dew nor rain." This particular judgment was doubly significant. First, drought was to be one of the consequences of abandoning the Lord, a fact which Moses had spelled out for Israel in Deuteronomy 28. That passage warned, "Your heavens which are over your head shall be bronze, and the earth which is under you shall be iron. The Lord will change the rain of your land to powder and dust; from the heaven it shall come down on you until you are destroyed" (28:23–24).

Second, and more significantly, Baal was a nature god. He was viewed as god of the storm. One of his responsibilities was to provide rains and maintain the fertility of the land. The drought which would prove that God lives would also prove the impotence of Baal, challenging the king's claim that Baal was the deity on whom Israel could rely.

In New Testament times, Jesus revealed that this drought announced by Elijah lasted for three and a half years and that "there was a great famine throughout all the land" (Luke 4:25). God's power over the elements supposedly controlled by Baal was made plain.

"Except at my word." Droughts are natural happenings. But a drought that comes and goes at

the command of a man is not natural. Such a drought is an extraordinary event, and Elijah declared it was caused by God. Its purpose was to demonstrate the power and presence of Israel's living God.

Miracles and the miraculous (1 Kings 17:2–7). After making his announcement, Elijah hid. God directed him to a brook that flowed into the Jordan River. In this location, "ravens brought him bread and meat in the morning, and bread and meat in the evening" (1 Kings 17:6). This was not a miracle performed *by* Elijah—but God's miraculous intervention *for* Elijah.

The drought affected the whole land and brought terrible suffering. But God took care of his faithful prophet.

ELIJAH MULTIPLIES A WIDOW'S FOOD   *1 Kings 17:8–16*

As the drought worsened, the brook where Elijah was staying dried up. God then sent him to the home of a widow in Zarephath.

The irony of the location (1 Kings 17:9). The city of Zarephath was in Sidon, a territory ruled by the father of Ahab's wife Jezebel. This was the land from which the pagan missionaries intent on turning Israel to the worship of Baal had been recruited!

While Israel suffered from the drought, Elijah would be safe in the homeland of his persecutors. What an echo of Psalm 23:5, "You prepare a table before me in the presence of my enemies." God had thrown his protective mantle over Elijah; he was safe in the land of his enemies.

The widow and her situation (17:10–12). When Elijah arrived in Zarephath, he found a widow who was about to prepare the last remaining food in her house. The drought which struck Israel had also affected surrounding nations. There was no one to whom she could appeal for food when the little amount she had was gone (see 1 Kings 17:14). The widow was destitute and on the verge of starvation.

It is interesting that the widow recognized Elijah as a prophet. But her words, "As the LORD your God lives," are best understood as a polite greeting rather than an indication that she believed in Yahweh (see 1 Kings 17:24).

The woman's amazing faith (17:13–15). When the widow told Elijah of her desperate situation, the prophet directed her to feed *him* first, and only then feed herself and her son. The prophet also promised in the name of the Lord God of Israel that "the bin of flour shall not be used up, nor shall the jar of oil run dry until the day the Lord sends rain on the earth" (1 Kings 17:14).

In one way, it is amazing that the woman did as Elijah asked. On the other hand, she really had little choice. If she kept the last of the food for herself, she and her son would surely starve. If she did as Elijah said and God *did* maintain their food supply, they would live. Facing the options of certain death versus possible life, the widow made the wisest choice.

Elijah promised the widow's flour and oil supply would not run out.

It is strange how few people today show similar wisdom. Many who are introduced to the gospel, which promises eternal life, are unwilling to *listen.* How important in life-or-death issues to listen when someone speaks in the name of the Lord!

The widow made her choice, and "did according to the word of Elijah." Her risk of faith was rewarded, and "she and he and her household ate for many days."

Again, God demonstrated his power as well as his gracious provision for those who place their faith in him.

ELIJAH RESTORES THE WIDOW'S SON   *1 Kings 17:17–24*

While Elijah was staying with the widow, her son died. The widow confronted the prophet, who took him to the upper room where he was lodging and prayed for his restoration. The Lord answered Elijah's prayer, and the prophet took the living boy downstairs and presented him to his mother.

The widow's bitter words (1 Kings 17:17, 18). We can understand the widow's anguish. Had God preserved her family from the drought, only to take her son? Was God the kind of person who gives with one hand while taking away with the other?

But the widow also blamed herself as well as God. This is shown in her words, "Have you come to me to bring my sin to remembrance, and to kill my son?" The word "remember" has a distinct connotation in the Hebrew language. She implied that Elijah's presence drew God's attention to her as a sinner and that he remembered her sins and acted appropriately in taking her son.

People who do not know the Lord sometimes assume their tragedies are divine punishment. But the widow was about to learn that her tragedy would become an occasion for God to display his power and grace.

Elijah's prayer (17:19–21). Elijah questioned God's permitting the boy to die. But he also prayed that the child's life would be restored.

His prayer was answered and the child revived.

"Have You also brought tragedy?" Like the widow, Elijah struggled to understand the boy's death. Why would God do this? Did he intend to "bring tragedy"?

Elijah's reaction differed from that of the woman. She immediately concluded God was punishing her. But Elijah asked God about his intention. Did the Lord intend to bring tragedy, or was this event to be understood differently? In fact, the "tragedy" would soon become a cause for rejoicing, demonstrating that the widow needed to trust completely in the Lord and his spokesman (compare 1 Kings 17:24).

How often what we interpret as tragedy is intended by God as a blessing. How wise to adopt Elijah's stance—and look for the blessing that is hidden in the pain.

"He stretched himself out on the child three times." Elijah was truly a "man of God." An Israelite who touched a dead body was made unclean (Num. 19:11). Yet Elijah, out of his deep concern for the widow and her son, not only touched the child; he stretched out on his body. This was a symbolic act—an acted out way of praying, "Let this lifeless body be as my living body."

"Let this child's soul come back to him." The prayer, literally, was "let this child's life [*nephesh*] return."

Some people have called this miracle a "resurrection." It was not. History's only resurrection was that of Jesus. Raised, Jesus lives forever—his body transformed. The miracle described here, like the raising of Lazarus, was a resuscitation—a return to mortal life. The boy whose life was restored grew old and died again, just as Lazarus did. The restoration of mortal life is a miracle—but far less a miracle than the transformation we will experience in our resurrection when Jesus comes again.

God answered Elijah's prayer (17:22–23). The Lord answered Elijah's prayer and restored the child. Elijah brought the boy downstairs and presented him to his mother: "See, your son lives" (1 Kings 17:24).

The meaning of the miracle (17:24). The woman summed up the meaning of the miracle: "Now by this I know that you are a man of God, and that the word of the Lord in your mouth is the truth."

"You are a man of God." The miracle authenticated Elijah as God's spokesman. But the miracle did more. It also revealed Elijah as a caring, godly man. We need to keep this in mind as we read later accounts of what seem to be harsh acts of the prophet.

"The word of the LORD in your mouth." The miracle also authenticated the God whose word Elijah spoke. If there had been any doubt in her mind that the Lord is the living God, that doubt was erased. By giving life, Yahweh was revealed as living himself. There could be no doubt of his reality.

"The word of the LORD is truth." Truth as understood in the Bible has an unbreakable link to reality. What is true corresponds with what is real. What is false is unreal, and thus unreliable. The woman realized that the ultimate reality in our universe is God.

ELIJAH CALLS DOWN FIRE AT CARMEL   *1 Kings 18:1–46*

The most spectacular of Elijah's miracles was performed near the end of the three-and-one-half-year drought.

Ahab and Jezebel had massacred most of the prophets of the Lord (1 Kings 18:4). Yet the Lord told Elijah to go to Ahab, and that he would send rain. Before the return of the rains, however, Elijah proposed a contest with the prophets of Baal. The outcome would convince the people of Israel that the Lord is God.

Ahab's greeting (1 Kings 18:17–18). Ahab greeted Elijah as "troubler of Israel." The title was ironic, as Elijah pointed out. "I have not troubled Israel, but you and your father's house have, in that you have forsaken the commandments of the Lord and have fol-

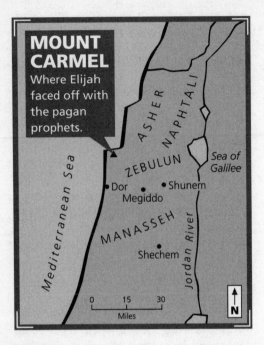

MOUNT CARMEL
Where Elijah faced off with the pagan prophets.

ASHER
NAPHTALI
ZEBULUN
Sea of Galilee
Mediterranean Sea
• Dor   • Shunem
Megiddo
MANASSEH
Jordan River
Shechem •

0   15   30
Miles

N

lowed the Baals." How often the guilty person blames others for the consequences of his own sins.

The gathering on Mount Carmel (18:19, 20). Throughout this story, Elijah took the initiative. He proposed gathering all Israel at Mount Carmel and calling the 450 prophets of Baal whom Ahab had imported. Ahab quickly agreed. This suggests that he fully expected Baal to defeat Yahweh. We might call Ahab a "true believer," who was completely wrong, in spite of his sincerity!

Elijah also called for the "four hundred prophets of Asherah, who eat at Jezebel's table" to join the contest. Asherah was the female counterpart of Baal who served as his consort. The prophets "who eat at Jezebel's table," were under the queen's direct authority. Jezebel chose *not* to send them to Carmel! This may imply that Jezebel was not convinced of the power of her gods. The conversion of Israel to Baal worship may have been motivated by politics rather than the queen's religious convictions!

Elijah's challenge to the people of Israel (18:21). The Israelites were vacillating be-

tween the claims of the two deities, Yahweh and Baal. Elijah called for commitment. The people must make a choice. A literal translation of the verse reads, "If Yahweh is God, go after Him; if Baal is, go after Him." The commitment Elijah sought was not belief alone but action as well. The Israelites must live out their commitment, "going after" [obeying, walking in the path laid out by] either Yahweh or Baal.

At this point, the people remained silent. They were unsure and indecisive. They wanted proof that one of the competing deities truly was God.

The test (18:22–24). When Elijah explained the test, he emphasized how unequal it appeared—a lone prophet of the Lord, facing 450 prophets of Baal. Surely they had the advantage!

Then Elijah proposed that each side build an altar, cut a bull in pieces, and place the sacrifice on wood laid out on the altar. But neither side would light the fire. This had to be provided in the form of fire from heaven. Only the true God would be able to perform this miracle: "The God who answers by fire, He is God" (1 Kings 18:24).

The failure of the prophets of Baal (18:25–29). Elijah let the prophets of Baal go first. Their futile efforts provoked a series of sarcastic remarks from Elijah. From morning until noon, the pagan prophets cried out "O Baal, hear us." Finally Elijah began to offer suggestions.

"Cry louder. After all, he's a god."
"Maybe he's meditating?"
"Maybe he's busy."
"Maybe he's off on a journey."
"Maybe he's sleeping, and you have
     to wake him up!"

Elijah's mockery stimulated Baal's prophets to greater efforts. The text indicates they "cut themselves . . . with knives and lances, until the blood gushed out on them." But at evening there was still "no voice; no one answered, no one paid attention."

BIBLE BACKGROUND:

WHY BAAL'S PROPHETS CUT THEMSELVES

The following is from one of six broken clay tablets called "Stories of Ba'al and Anat" from Ugarit. They reveal the bloodthirsty nature of these pagan deities. One tablet describes Anat destroying two armies and then, unsatisfied, building bleachers for massed warriors she engaged in deadly games. The text reads,

Once again Anat could fight with vigor,
  Slaughter everyone in sight.
Anat's body trembled with gladness,
  Her heart filled with joy
  Her soul gloated with triumph,
As, again, she waded knee deep in warrior's blood,
  Up to her thighs in their guts (I. Ii).

The prophets of Baal cut themselves because they believed their god was stimulated and excited by the scent of blood. And they were desperate to attract his attention!

Elijah's miracle victory (18:30–38). Elijah called the people to draw closer. He built his altar, made a trench around it, and prepared the wood and sacrifice. He also ordered that the offering and altar be saturated with water.

Some have ridiculed this account, arguing that if the drought was so severe, no water would be available. However, archaeologists have located wells below Mount Carmel which do not go dry even in droughts.

When all had been done, Elijah prayed aloud that God would "let it be known this day that You are God in Israel and I am your servant, and that I have done all these things at Your word" (1 Kings 18:36).

When Elijah prayed, fire fell. It consumed the sacrifice and burned up the altar stones and the pools of water in a trench Elijah had dug around the altar.

The people's response to the miracle (18:39–40). The people of Israel were con-

vinced. They shouted, "The Lord, he is God! The Lord, he is God."

Wherever the word *Lord* appears in the Old Testament, the Hebrew reads "Yahweh." This decisive event on Mount Carmel tipped the scales against the deities of Ahab and Jezebel, convincing the population that Israel's ancestral God, Yahweh, was the one true God.

Elijah commanded the people to seize the prophets of Baal. There was not one survivor among those who had conspired with the king to corrupt the faith of Israel. Deuteronomy 13:5 explains the execution. God had commanded,

That prophet or that dreamer of dreams shall be put to death, because he has spoken in order to turn you away from the Lord your God, who brought you out of the land of Egypt and redeemed you from the house of bondage, to entice you from the way in which the Lord your God commanded you to walk. So you shall put away the evil from your midst.

The religious purpose of the miracle (18:36–37). There are few miracles in Scripture performed with clearer intent. Elijah summed it up in his prayer. He called for fire to "let it be known this day that You are God in Israel." The miracle proved decisively that the Lord is the one true God.

But Elijah's prayer expressed another purpose as well. Elijah asked God to act "that this people may know that You are the Lord God, and that You have turned their hearts back to You again" (1 Kings 18:37). The miracle was intended to turn Israel's hearts away from Baal-Malquart, and back to the Lord. And for a time—through the ministry of Elijah and his successor Elisha—Israel's hearts were turned.

The king and queen remained stubborn. But the ordinary people no longer hesitated between deities. They chose the Lord.

God can perform the most wondrous miracles. Jesus performed many that were unmistakably God's work. Yet he was eventually rejected by Israel and crucified. There is no such thing as *compelling* proof. Individuals who are determined *not* to believe will not believe—no matter what God does to demon-

After three and one-half years, Elijah prayed for God to restore the rains.

❖

strate his power. For at least this moment in Israel's history—as a nation's destiny hung in the balance—the people of Israel were open and responsive to the Lord.

ELIJAH RESTORES THE RAINS
1 Kings 18:41–46

Three and one-half years earlier, Elijah had told King Ahab that there would be no rain in Israel "except at my word" (1 Kings 17:1). After the defeat and execution of the prophets of Baal, Elijah announced to Ahab "there is the sound of abundance of rain."

Elijah went to the top of Mount Carmel and prayed ["bowed down on the ground"]. At first only a tiny cloud appeared on the horizon over the Mediterranean. But soon the clouds filled the sky, and wind-driven rains

saturated the parched lands. Elijah warned Ahab to hurry home before the wheels of his chariot became bogged down in the mud!

Again, the miracle was in the timing, as well as in the abundance. God miraculously restored what he had miraculously taken away.

The extent of restoration. We can gauge how fully God restored the prosperity of the land from the biblical text and from history. First Kings 18:5 reports that Ahab had previously assigned one of his officials the task of identifying every spring and brook in the land which still had water that "perhaps we may find grass to keep the horses and mules alive." If the official was unsuccessful, the last of Ahab's livestock would have to be killed.

Why was Ahab so concerned about horses? Because these animal were needed to pull his military chariots, which might be described as the "tanks" of ancient warfare. How do we know the rains restored prosperity? We know because the records of Shalmanesser III of Assyria indicated that Ahab of Israel provided the most chariots—2,000—to the coalition of kings that defeated him in 853 B.C.

God sometimes uses his miracles to judge.

But God will also use his miracles to restore.

The miraculous in Elijah's life (1 Kings 19). The highest spiritual peaks sometimes lead directly to the darkest spiritual valleys. This was true for Elijah. When Ahab returned to his capital, he told Jezebel everything that had happened. Jezebel immediately sent a messenger to Elijah, threatening his life (1 Kings 19:2).

Jezebel's strategy. Jezebel could just as easily have sent soldiers to kill Elijah, but she didn't want to create a martyr. Her goal was to frighten the prophet and thus expose him to the charge of being a fraud. She could not fight God. But she might be able to discredit God's prophet.

Elijah's response to Jezebel's threat. Elijah fell into Jezebel's trap. Terrified, the prophet abandoned his ministry. The text indicates he "ran for his life" (1 Kings 19:3). Finally, after traveling for miles and growing exhausted, the prophet dropped to the ground and begged God to let him die.

God's response to Elijah's flight. Rather than speak harshly to Elijah, the Lord provided him with food that sustained him on a forty-day journey to Horeb [Mount Sinai]. There, where God had given Israel the Law accompanied by an awesome display of his presence (see Ex. 24:16–18), God spoke to Elijah in a whisper (1 Kings 19:11–12). The Lord reassured Elijah that other people in Israel also worshiped him. Elijah was not alone. The Lord also gave Elijah specific tasks to accomplish and provided him with a companion, Elisha.

The God who had judged the apostate King Ahab and his pagan prophets so harshly

was gentle with his depressed prophet. With a series of quiet miracles—strengthening for the journey, a gentle revelation—the Lord ministered compassionately to the man of God.

Encouragement from the incident. Elijah had abandoned his ministry and run away. Even more, his disappearance provided Jezebel with a propaganda advantage. But the Lord neither criticized nor condemned. Instead, he showed great compassion for Elijah and eventually restored his ministry.

What an encouragement to us. We are also vulnerable to those deep valleys that lie beyond the spiritual and emotional peaks in our lives. At times, we will also give God's enemies occasion to criticize him. How important to remember the quiet miracles that God performed for Elijah. Our Lord will strengthen and restore us in our "down" times, as he did his prophet of old.

ELIJAH CALLS DOWN FIRE ON SOLDIERS   *2 Kings 1:1–17*

After Ahab died, his successor Ahaziah was seriously injured in a fall. Ahaziah sent messengers to a pagan deity to ask if he would recover. God sent Elijah to confront the messengers. Since Ahaziah had showed contempt for the Lord by not seeking information from him, Ahaziah would die, Elijah declared. When his messengers reported this to the king, he sent fifty soldiers to bring Elijah to him.

"Man of God, the king has said" (2 Kings 1:9). These words alert us to the significance of the coming miracle. Jezebel still lived, and her son Ahaziah had adopted her religion and her policies.

Jezebel had earlier won a propaganda victory by forcing Elijah to flee. In that confrontation between the political and spiritual powers, Elijah had surrendered to the state. Confronted once more with the power of the state—expressed in the soldiers standing before him—would he surrender again, admitting the authority of the state over God? Or would this confrontation have a different outcome?

"Come down" (1:9). The army officer was confident. He commanded, "Man of God, the king has said, 'Come down.' He fully expected spiritual power, which he acknowledged by addressing Elijah as "Man of God," to bow to the secular power. To this officer, "the king has said" settled every matter.

"Let fire come down from heaven" (1:10). Elijah answered by announcing, "If I am a man of God, then let fire come down from heaven and consume you and your fifty men." In uttering the phrase "if I am a man of God," Elijah accepted his role as representative of the spiritual authority of God. When Elijah spoke, fire fell and consumed the soldiers.

The second fifty met the same fate (1:11–12). A second officer approached Elijah, arrogantly commanding him in the King's name, "Come down quickly." Again Elijah called down fire on the soldiers.

A third officer appealed for his life (1:13–14). A third officer approached Elijah with a totally different attitude. He never mentioned the king or his command. Instead, he appealed to Elijah as a man of God to "let my life and the life of these fifty servants of yours be precious in your sight."

"Let my life." The state is feared because it has the power of life or death. This officer had learned that the real power of life or death is God's, not the king's.

"These fifty servants of yours." The first two officers were committed to serve the state. But God requires our first allegiance. In any conflict between the two powers, the claims of the state must come last.

"Be precious in your sight." What a blessing that the Lord does have priority over the state. We can appeal to God because he *cares*. We cannot expect political powers to have any real concern for individuals.

This officer's appeal was heard, and his life was spared.

"Go down with him; do not be afraid" (1:15–17). It is unlikely that Elijah fully understood the issue involved in this confrontation. The angel's reassuring words, "Don't be afraid," suggested that Elijah himself feared the power of the king. But the angel's command, "Go down with him," reminds us of a vital truth. We live in a world in which believers must deal with the secular powers. We cannot and must not try to isolate ourselves from the society in which we live. Yet in our interaction with the powers of this world, we need not be afraid. God rules, and he is far greater than any secular power.

"Thus says the Lord" (1:16). When Elijah met the king, he spoke boldly. He announced God's judgment on the apostate ruler: "You shall surely die."

Elijah walked away unharmed.

And Ahaziah died.

The message of the miracle. A miracle is an extraordinary event caused by God for a religious purpose. It would be wrong to interpret the fire which killed a hundred soldiers as a petty act performed by a frightened prophet. God's purpose in performing this miracle was far more significant.

Because of this confrontation, all Israel would remember that in a direct conflict between the spiritual and political powers, the state was powerless. And we today are to take heart in this truth as well. As the palmist wrote in Psalm 56:11,

> In God I have put my trust,
> I will not be afraid;
> What can man do to me?

ELIJAH DIVIDES THE JORDAN'S WATERS   *2 Kings 2:1–11*

When Elijah's ministry was completed, God revealed that he and his companion Elisha would be carried to heaven without experiencing death. As the two walked together into the Jordan River valley, they were observed by a group of fifty prophets. When they got to the river, Elijah rolled up his cloak and struck the water. The river "was divided in this way and that, so that the two of them crossed over on dry ground."

BIBLE BACKGROUND:

THE "SONS OF THE PROPHETS"

The phrase "sons of the prophets" occurs only in 1 and 2 Kings, where it occurs 10 times in 11 different verses. Some take the phrase to mean "prophets in training," assuming that Elijah and Elisha set up a sort of seminary for prophets. Others interpret the phrase to mean "prophet," pointing out that "son of . . ." is idiomatic in Hebrew, indicating membership in a class or group. To say "sons of the prophets" indicates that the persons so identified are members of the group known as "prophets."

In either case, the fifty who witnessed the miracle performed by Elijah and later duplicated by Elisha were the future spiritual leaders of Israel.

The miracle by Elijah (2 Kings 2:8). The miracle of dividing the waters was clearly linked with two earlier miracles: the crossing of the Reed Sea and the dividing of the waters of the Jordan in the time of Joshua.

But why would Elijah perform this miracle now, at the end of his career? The answer was obvious when Elisha performed the same act a little later. This served as a sign that he had succeeded Elijah as Israel's premier prophet.

The miracle for Elijah (2:11–13). In earlier days, God had performed several miracles *for* Elijah. The Lord sent ravens to feed Elijah during the drought when he lived by the brook Cherith. God provided supernatural food that sustained Elijah for a forty-day jour-

ney to Mount Sinai. Now the Lord performed one other miracle for the prophet. As Elijah and Elisha walked in the Jordan valley, "suddenly a chariot of fire appeared with horses of fire, and separated the two of them; and Elijah went up by a whirlwind into heaven" (2 Kings 2:11). God took Elijah into heaven without sending him through the experience of death.

We often focus on the more spectacular miracles of Scripture: the crossing of the Reed Sea, the fall of Jericho's walls. But the more personal miracles God performed for his people are a rich source of encouragement and hope. God does the great things that a whole nation remembers. But the same God also does the small, compassionate things that we as individuals remember with wonder, thanksgiving, and praise.

God carried Elijah up into heaven.

THE MIRACLE MINISTRY OF ELISHA

SHOWING GOD'S COMPASSION

2 Kings 2—13

Miracles can tell us a lot about God. Elijah's miracles proved to Israel that God is real, and all-powerful. But we need to know much more. How does God feel about us? Can we ever feel comfortable in the presence of a miracle-working God? These questions suddenly became important to the population of the northern Hebrew kingdom, which had been convinced by Elijah's miracles that the LORD is God.

To answer such questions God sent Israel another prophet, Elisha. Elisha's miracle ministry revealed the compassion of a God who loves individuals, and who yearns to be gracious to all who trust in Him.

Elisha's deepest desire (2 Kings 2:9–10). Elisha had been Elijah's companion and apprentice during the final years of Elijah's ministry. Scripture's transition from the ministry of Elijah to that of Elisha is reported in 2 Kings 2. As the two men walked together in the Jordan valley on Elijah's last day on earth, Elijah asked his friend Elisha, "What may I do for you, before I am taken away from you?"

Elisha's request was, "Please, let a double portion of your spirit be upon me." In Israel the oldest son in a family was given a double portion of the family wealth as an inheritance (Deut. 21:17). Elisha asked to be Elijah's successor and to inherit his role as God's premier prophet in Israel.

The request was not for Elijah to grant. God himself calls his spokesmen. But Elijah promised that if Elisha witnessed Elijah's departure, God would grant what he desired. Elisha did see the angels who took Elijah to glory. (For a discussion of this angelic appearance, see the companion volume, *Every Good and Evil Angel in the Bible.*) Elisha did succeed Elijah. In fact, the recorded miracles of Elisha actually doubled those performed by Elijah himself. God granted even more than Elisha had asked.

Elisha the man. The earnest request of Elisha tells us much about the man. He had traveled with Elijah for some time, observing the kind of life Elijah lived. He was fully aware that the call to ministry was a summons to a life of challenge and difficulty, not a life of ease. But Elisha had a heart for God and a heart for God's people. Elisha was eager to serve.

How blessed we are when those in spiritual leadership are men and women who are

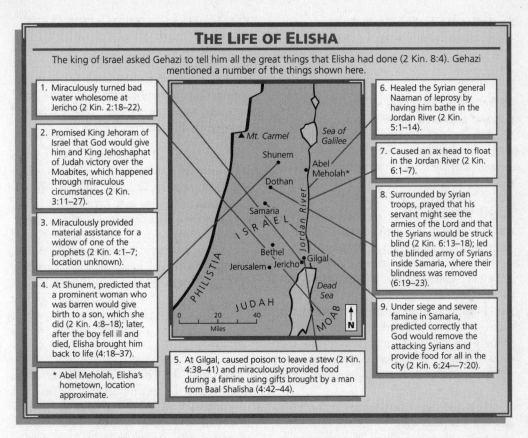

THE LIFE OF ELISHA

The king of Israel asked Gehazi to tell him all the great things that Elisha had done (2 Kin. 8:4). Gehazi mentioned a number of the things shown here.

1. Miraculously turned bad water wholesome at Jericho (2 Kin. 2:18–22).

2. Promised King Jehoram of Israel that God would give him and King Jehoshaphat of Judah victory over the Moabites, which happened through miraculous circumstances (2 Kin. 3:11–27).

3. Miraculously provided material assistance for a widow of one of the prophets (2 Kin. 4:1–7; location unknown).

4. At Shunem, predicted that a prominent woman who was barren would give birth to a son, which she did (2 Kin. 4:8–18); later, after the boy fell ill and died, Elisha brought him back to life (4:18–37).

* Abel Meholah, Elisha's hometown, location approximate.

5. At Gilgal, caused poison to leave a stew (2 Kin. 4:38–41) and miraculously provided food during a famine using gifts brought by a man from Baal Shalisha (4:42–44).

6. Healed the Syrian general Naaman of leprosy by having him bathe in the Jordan River (2 Kin. 5:1–14).

7. Caused an ax head to float in the Jordan River (2 Kin. 6:1–7).

8. Surrounded by Syrian troops, prayed that his servant might see the armies of the Lord and that the Syrians would be struck blind (2 Kin. 6:13–18); led the blinded army of Syrians inside Samaria, where their blindness was removed (6:19–23).

9. Under siege and severe famine in Samaria, predicted correctly that God would remove the attacking Syrians and provide food for all in the city (2 Kin. 6:24—7:20).

Map labels: Mt. Carmel, Sea of Galilee, Shunem, Abel Meholah*, Dothan, Samaria, ISRAEL, Jordan River, Bethel, Gilgal, Jerusalem, Jericho, PHILISTIA, Dead Sea, JUDAH, MOAB, N

0   20   40
Miles

---

eager to serve—not because they want the limelight, but because they love God and care about his people. How important it is that our hearts be like Elisha's, if we should receive a call to leadership.

Elisha's miracles (2 Kings 2—7). The recorded miracles of Elisha are double the seven performed by Elijah. There is another difference as well. While the major miracles of Elijah were miracles of judgment, the major miracles of Elisha were miracles which focused on life rather than death. The thirteen miracles performed by God through Elisha are:

ELISHA DIVIDES THE JORDAN'S WATERS   *2 Kings 2:13–15*

Elisha knew that he had been chosen as Elijah's successor. He had seen Elijah caught up into heaven. Now it was time to demonstrate his commission from God.

The miracle (2 Kings 2:14). When Elijah was carried into heaven, his cloak had fallen to the ground. Elisha had picked it up. Arriving at the Jordan River, Elisha used the cloak to du-plicate Elijah's earlier miracle (2 Kings 2:8). El-isha struck the water with the cloak, and the water divided so Elisha could cross over.

"Where is the Lord God of Elijah? This ques-tion was answered by the miracle. The God of Elijah was now with Elisha. Elisha's voice was raised in confidence, not doubt. Elisha had seen the miracle of Elijah's transformation, and this was confirmation enough for him. But there were others who needed to be con-vinced. Elisha raised his voice so the witnesses could hear and affirm the miracle of the di-vided water as the answer to his question.

"They . . . bowed to the ground before him" **(2:15).** The fifty prophets who had earlier seen Elijah divide the Jordan River recognized the significance of Elisha's act. They said, "The Spirit of Elijah rests on Elisha." And they showed Elisha the respect they had reserved earlier for Elijah as the recognized leader of God's prophets in Israel.

This was an authenticating miracle. Its purpose was made clear by the response of the witnesses. Elisha's position was now estab-lished.

ELISHA HEALS A SPRING'S WATERS
1 Kings 2:19–22

The men of Jericho appealed to Elisha to do something about the water in a nearby spring. They described the water as "bad," meaning toxic, or poison. Nothing would grow where these waters flowed.

"Put salt in it" (2 Kings 2:20). Elisha called for a new bowl filled with salt. Salt water is also toxic to man, animals, and land plants. Elisha was using a curse to cure a curse.

There is a fascinating foreshadowing here. The cure of the curse of sin was accomplished at Calvary, of which Deuteronomy 21:23 says, "He who is hanged [on a tree] is accursed of God." The curse that Jesus took upon himself became the cure for the curse that brought death to us, even as the salt which is toxic to humanity became a cure for the toxic waters of Jericho.

"Thus says the Lord" (2:21). Elisha spoke and acted in the name of the Lord. There was no suggestion that Elisha himself was special. It was the God represented by Elisha who was to be given the credit and glory for meeting the need of the people of Jericho.

When Elisha struck the water with Elijah's cloak, the Jordan divided.

Elisha's earlier miracle at the Jordan River had convinced the prophets that he had been commissioned by God. The people of Jericho had obviously heard of the event, for they begged Elisha to perform a miracle for them. This miracle performed in the name of the Lord reminded all Israel that the Lord is real and that he aids his people.

The miracle also set the tone for future miracles by Elisha. Most would be like this one—miracles of compassion in which God showed his willingness to meet his people's needs.

"The water remains healed to this day" (2:22). The comment added by the compiler of the history of the kings also reflects the situation today. Springs of pure water still bubble up near modern Jericho. The fruits and vegetables of the area are valued throughout the land.

ELISHA CURSES JEERING YOUNG MEN   *2 Kings 2:23–24*

As Elisha left Jericho and set out toward Bethel, a group of youths came from the city and mocked him. They repeatedly cried out, "Go up, you baldhead!" Elisha turned and cursed them in the name of the Lord. A few minutes later two female bears came out of the woods and mauled forty-two of the youths.

This miracle curse has troubled many, particularly as the original King James Version rendered this phrase, "There came forth *little children* out of the city." How could a compassionate prophet curse little children? And how could a compassionate God turn wild beasts upon them?

"Some youths" (2 Kings 2:23). The New King James Version corrects the impression that these were harmless children set on ridiculing a bald man. They were young adults, and their ridicule was not of Elisha's hairless state.

"Go up, you baldhead!" (2:23). The ridicule was directed against the report of Elisha that the Lord had caught Elijah up into heaven.

These young people mocked the very notion. How could anyone be caught up by angels? And how could anyone be foolish enough to credit any god with such an action? And so the cry "go up!" was a challenge to Elisha to duplicate the feat to prove his claims of what God had done.

This situation was similar to the Israelites who murmured against Moses in the wilderness. The mockery of Elisha by the youths was not directed against the prophet, but against God. These young people had heard of Elisha's miracle at the Jordan River. If they were from Jericho rather than Bethel, they had also witnessed his healing of the waters. Yet, they refused to believe.

He "pronounced a curse on them in the name of the Lord" (2:24). Some have suggested that Elisha overreacted. Perhaps he was sensitive about his baldness. Or just tired. But Elisha knew exactly what he was doing. He did not react irritably. He did not curse the youths because he was offended. He pronounced a curse on them *in the name of the Lord.*

Again, it is important to remember the significance of the "name" in Old Testament thought. The name expressed *the essence of the person or thing named.* To speak in the name of the Lord was more than a claim to be an authorized spokesman. It was an affirmation that the words spoken were in complete harmony with the character and will of the person named. Cursing these young men "in the name of the Lord" showed that Elisha was acting in full awareness of God's will and in complete harmony with God's character.

If this was the case, why did God punish these mocking young men? For the same reason that he had struck the curious who peeked at the ark at Beth-Shemesh (p. 106) and the same reason he had struck Uzzah when he reached out to steady the ark of God (p. 107). Elisha's encounter with these youths was a critical moment in Israel's history. It demonstrated clearly that God's people must hold him in utmost respect if they are to receive his blessing.

The curse was immediately fulfilled (2:24). Perhaps it was even as Elisha spoke that two female bears emerged from the woods and mauled forty-two of the youths. The consequences of showing disrespect for God were immediate and severe.

The lesson learned (2 Kings 3:1–3). Any reader of the Bible needs to be aware that the organization of scriptural material is significant. This is sometimes disguised by the artificial separation of passages by chapter and verse divisions. These were added many centuries after the text was originally written. This passage is a good example of this point.

Elisha traveled on, eventually returning to Samaria (2 Kings 2:25). Samaria was the capital city of the Northern Kingdom, Israel. So the geographical notation directs our attention to Israel's royal house. The opening verses of chapter three indicate that King Ahab was dead. But his legacy continued! Jehoram, a second son of Ahab, was now king, and "he did evil in the sight of the Lord." While his evil was not "like his father and mother," Jehoram maintained the counterfeit religious system instituted by Jeroboam (see page 110–111). Whatever respect the new king had for the Lord, it was not enough to bring obedience or radical change.

Respect for the Lord is the key to personal and national prosperity. Elisha fully understood this truth. When Elisha's God was mocked and jeered, the prophet responded appropriately. The fate of the young men was a warning to the entire nation—and especially to its ruler—that God must be treated with utmost respect.

ELISHA WINS A BATTLE FOR ISRAEL
2 Kings 3:1–26)

Moab had been subdued some years before by an earlier ruler. The Moabites rebelled and refused to pay tribute. The king of Israel recruited help from the kings of Judah and Edom and set out to punish the Moabites. The army took a roundabout route that left them stranded without water.

Jehoram's interpretation of the imminent disaster (2 Kings 3:10). Jehoram immediately assumed the Lord had brought the allied army to its present state in order to destroy it. He had experienced the Lord's judgments before, and he must have known that the official religion which he supported was an abomination to God.

Jehoshaphat of Judah sought a prophet's help (3:11–12). Jehoshaphat was one of Judah's more godly kings. He insisted that all the kings in this alliance consult a prophet of the Lord. The king of Israel was silent, but one of his officials knew about Elisha. Jehoshaphat was familiar with Elisha's reputation as a prophet of the Lord, so the kings went to consult him.

Elisha confronted Jehoram (3:13–19). When the kings arrived, Elisha dismissed Jehoram with contempt, telling him to go the gods of his parents.

Jehoram's sin. The king of Israel's response was, "No, for the LORD has called these three kings together to deliver them into the hand of Moab." This was not an expression of faith, but blame. Jehoram was declaring it was the Lord's fault that the kings were in such danger. Not only did Jehoram blame God; he even presumed to explain God's motive.

Elisha's contempt for Jehoram. The king's reaction deepened Elisha's contempt for Jehoram. But because the godly king of Judah was there, Elisha decided to tell them what God had to say. Elisha apparently used music to focus his mind on the Lord and become more open to divine revelation (2 Kings 3:15).

God's Word to Elisha. God told Elisha that he was about to show Israel that it was "a simple matter in the eyes of the Lord" to turn disaster into triumph. God commanded the kings to "make this valley full of ditches." The next morning God would fill the ditches with water, and this would be the key to a great victory by the coalition of kings.

Note that the kings were told to make the valley full of ditches. They had to have enough faith in God's words to act on them if they wanted to have God act for them.

The predicted victory over Moab (2 Kings 3:20–25). The next morning, as sacrifices were made to the Lord, "suddenly water came" and filled the ditches. The Moabites saw the morning sun reflecting blood red off the water, and they assumed the kings of Israel, Judah, and Edom had turned on each other. They rushed headlong to collect the expected spoils—and were attacked by the allied army. The Moabites fled after they crumbled under the assault. The Israelite-led coalition army pursued them and devastated the land of the Moabites.

The war ended without victory (3:26–27). The description of the end of the war has puzzled commentators. The typical interpretation of this text is that the king of Moab sacrificed his own son on the city wall. Some have suggested that this act horrified the Israelites, or that it had some unknown magical meaning which terrified them.

The explanation is much simpler. Verse 26 mentions that the Moabites tried to break through to the king of Edom. If the Edomites had been forced into an earlier treaty with Moab, a counter-attack to punish them would have made sense in the warfare patterns of the ancient world. And why had the Edomites joined the coalition? If Edom was threatened by a resurgent Moab, this would also make sense. It is likely that Edom had earlier been required by Moab to provide the heir to its throne as a hostage.

So the reference in verse 27 to "his eldest son" is not to the son of the king of Moab, but to the son of the king of Edom!

When the Moabites sacrificed the Edomite heir, "there was great indignation against Israel"—by the Edomites! The very thing that the Moabites had earlier assumed—that the allied kings fell to fighting among themselves—was now a very real danger. And so the Israelites "returned to their own land."

God won the battle, but Israel lost the war. The miracle God performed won the initial battle for the king of Israel and his allies. But Israel had set out to subdue Moab, forcing the king to begin paying the tribute exacted by an earlier ruler. This goal was not achieved.

An archaeological find known as the Moabite Stone celebrated the recovery of Moab's independence from Israel. The stone's inscription made it clear that the borders with Israel had been substantially strengthened. This explains why the coalition of kings took the long route to attack Moab: fortifications on the border with Israel were too strong.

This miracle demonstrated that when God fights for his people, they will be victorious. Israel's failure to reclaim dominion over the Moabites also revealed another truth: without the Lord, Israel could expect ultimate defeat.

The rest of Elisha's miracles were performed during the reign of Jehoram. This king never learned the lessons which the prophet's miracles clearly taught.

ELISHA MULTIPLIES A WIDOW'S OIL
2 Kings 4:1–7

The Old Testament shows a special compassion for widows and the fatherless (Deut. 24:20–21; Prov. 15:25). God has a special concern for the helpless. This miracle of Elisha reflects this concern.

The widow's need (2 Kings 4:1). The widow who appealed to Elijah had been married to one of the Lord's prophets. Her husband had died, leaving her and their two sons destitute and in debt. Her appeal was urgent, for the creditor was coming to take her two sons as slaves. The impending separation from her sons was almost more than she could bear.

"Nothing . . . but a jar of oil" (4:2). The oil was olive oil, used in cooking, burned in oil lamps, and eaten as a substance similar to butter.

The first question Elisha asked the widow was, "What do you have?" God is just as ready to perform miracles for us today as he was in the past. But when we ask for God's help, we must be willing to commit our own resources.

❖

BIBLE BACKGROUND:

SLAVERY IN THE OLD TESTAMENT

Children or adults could be sold into slavery to pay a debt. But a Hebrew slave could not be mistreated or held beyond seven years. At the end of seven years, the Hebrew slave was granted freedom and enough money and resources to launch an independent life. A man's motive in selling himself into slavery was sometimes to learn a trade or land management from his master. Young girls were often purchased as future brides for the buyer or his sons. Under Old Testament law, slavery thus had positive social intentions, unlike slavery as practiced in the pagan world or in modern nations. For a description of Old Testament laws governing slavery, see Exodus 21:1–10.

This does not mean that the law regarding slavery was always carried out. Even in the best of situations, a slave lost his right of self-determination. In the worst of situations, mistreatment occurred. At various times in Israel's history, the law's requirement that slaves be freed after seven years was ignored.

❖

"Go, borrow vessels" (4:3). Elisha told the woman to borrow several empty vessels. The limits to the miracle God would perform were not set by the Lord; they were determined by the widow's faith and obedience.

"Shut the door behind you and your sons" (4:4). Some miracles are meant to be public. Some are private, "family" miracles, whose workings aren't meant to be advertised. It is possible to confuse the two.

"Pour [the oil] into all those vessels" (4:4). The widow filled empty vessel after empty vessel until every one of the borrowed jars was full.

"Pay your debt; ... and ... live on the rest" (4:7). Preachers often make much of the fact that if the widow had had more faith, and borrowed more empty vessels, there would have been more oil. This is true. But let's remember that she had borrowed enough so that the oil paid her debt and she still had enough for her and her sons to live on.

There is no need to charge her with little faith. She had faith enough. And what God provided in this miracle was enough as well.

The message of the miracle. Again, this is an extraordinary event clearly caused by God. But what is the religious purpose of the miracle? On the one hand, it testifies to the compassionate love of God, and the concern of God's prophet. But more than that, it revealed clearly that faith was still a resource for the powerless. The God who could defeat armies could also meet the needs of the helpless who trusted in him.

❖

The miracle of the widow's oil demonstrated God's unlimited resources.

ELISHA PROMISES A PREGNANCY
2 Kings 4:8–17

Elisha wanted to do something for a woman who provided food and lodging for him when he visited her neighborhood. She herself had asked for nothing. But Elisha's servant Gehazi pointed out that her husband was old, and the woman had no son.

Elisha didn't hesitate. He called her and said "About this time next year you shall embrace a son" (v. 16).

The woman's reaction (2 Kings 4:16). The woman had become reconciled to her childlessness. It must have been a bitter process. Bearing children and especially sons was the dream of Hebrew women. Apparently, she had suppressed all hope of becoming a mother.

Elisha's announcement was painful, because the hope she had long since buried was aroused. The woman knew the anguish of hope disappointed again and again. Even hope offered by God's prophet seemed deceiving—a lie setting her up for another crushing disappointment.

The child's birth (4:17). The text indicates that "the woman conceived, and bore a son when the appointed time had come" (v. 17). In spite of the pain of disappointments, those who know God should never give up hope.

The meaning of the miracle. What marks this birth as a miracle is not the age of the husband but Elisha's pre-announcement. The miracle birth approaches the heart of the ministry of Elisha. He was called to demonstrate to Israel the life-giving and life-sustaining power of the God whom the royal family had abandoned.

ELISHA RAISES THE WIDOW'S SON
2 Kings 4:32–37

A few years later, this widow's son went into the fields with his father. He apparently suffered sun stroke and died. The unsolicited gift had been taken away!

The mother's reaction (2 Kings 4:21–25). Some have called the mother's reaction "cold."

She carried the boy to the room set aside for Elisha and closed the door. Then she politely asked for a donkey, brushed aside her husband's questions, and set out to find Elisha. Yet we can sense the urgency in her words, "Do not slacken the pace for me." She was trying to keep her boiling emotions under control.

The account also demonstrates her faith. She brought the body to Elisha's room, ready for his intervention. Rather than weep, she set out to reach the one person who could help.

"It is well" (4:25–27). As the woman approached, Elisha sent his servant to ask about her husband and son. Is something wrong? Her answer "It is well," may be taken as another expression of faith. Yet it seems more likely that the woman simply could not bear to speak of her son's death to Gehazi.

How often we respond the same way when someone asks, "How are you?" Although we may be aching inside, the answer we typically give, is "I'm fine. How are you?" There is a time for polite small talk. But when we truly hurt, we need someone with whom we can share our pain.

"Her soul is in deep distress" (4:27–28). When the woman saw Elisha, she fell down and grasped his feet. Elisha immediately sensed her deep distress and gave her his full attention.

How much we need a person like Elisha when we are in deep distress—a person who will be attuned to our emotions, willing to listen and to help.

The words "Did I ask a son?" spilled from the woman's lips. Before the prophet came, she had become reconciled to her life. There was no joy, but neither was there any deep pain. With the gift of the son, joy had been born. But with the deepening of her emotional life, there also came the potential for excruciating pain. Now the life she had lived before—suppressing her capacity for deep emotions—seemed so attractive. At least before, she had never known pain like this.

This truth speaks to us. Some are unwilling to take the risk of loving and being loved.

Some feel safer in the Christian community standing on the sidelines, not involved in the lives of fellow believers or needy people in the community. Such a life may feel empty. But at least there is no risk of being hurt.

The problem with this approach is that it doesn't allow us to see God working significantly in our lives, as the woman was about to experience.

"He arose and followed her" (4:29–32). Elisha sent Gehazi on ahead with his staff to try to restore the child. Then he hurried with the woman to cover the distance from Carmel to her home. When he arrived, he found the child "lying dead on his bed."

Elisha went into the room, shut the door, and prayed. Finally, Elisha stretched out on the child. [For a discussion of this act, see "Elijah Restores a Widow's Son," page 114–115.] And the boy's life was restored.

The mother's response (4:36–37). When Elisha called the woman into the room, he told her, "Pick up your son." At those words, she "fell at his feet, and bowed to the ground." The fall and the bowing should be separated. Suddenly all her suppressed emotions were released, and the woman collapsed. She then expressed her gratitude to Elisha and "picked up your son and went out."

The meaning of the miracle. This is the central miracle in the Bible's report of Elisha's ministry. [See the discussion of the literary form on page 106.] It is a miracle of the restoration of lost life. And this is the theme of Elisha's work. The God who punishes the wicked is the same God who can restore life to those who turn to him—just as the woman sought Elisha, his representative. How important it was that Israel turn to God, who alone can save.

ELISHA MAKES POISONED FOOD HARMLESS   *2 Kings 4:38–41*

During a time of famine, people ate wild seeds and plants to survive. At one gathering of prophets, poisonous wild gourds had been

added to a stew. Elisha added flour, miraculously neutralizing the poison.

ELISHA MULTIPLIES LOAVES OF BREAD   *2 Kings 4:42–44*

When there was not enough bread to feed the prophets who had gathered, Elisha announced in the name of the Lord that "they shall eat and have some left over."

"Twenty loaves of barley bread" (4:42). This miracle seems insignificant. Twenty loaves of bread? Surely that was enough to feed one hundred hungry men—but only if we assume that the loaves in this story were the same size as the bread we buy at the store. In fact, these barley loaves were no larger than small dinner rolls. There was hardly enough for three or four hungry men.

"Some left over" (4:44). This miracle foreshadows even greater miracles performed by Jesus. With fewer pieces of bread than this, Jesus fed thousands of people. The people who shared that meal probably recalled this wonder worked by Elisha in the name of the Lord. Perhaps they understood that in Jesus Christ, someone far greater than Elisha was among them.

ELISHA HEALS NAAMAN THE LEPER *2 Kings 5:1–19*

The healing of Naaman is a story most people know from their Sunday school days. Naaman was the commander of the Syrian army, and Syria was a traditional enemy of Israel. A young Israelite girl, undoubtedly captured in a raid on Israel, was a slave in Naaman's house. She told her mistress that there was a prophet in Samaria, Israel's capital, who could cure Naaman of his leprosy.

The report was passed from the wife to Naaman to the king of Syria, who wrote a letter to Jehoram, king of Israel.

The letter to Jehoram (2 Kings 5:6–7). The letter was brief and to the point. The Syrian ruler indicated he was sending Naaman to the king, "that you may heal him of his leprosy." Jehoram saw only one possible way to interpret the letter. Syria was looking for an excuse to launch a war against Israel. There was no way he could heal a leper. As a sign of his agitation and distress, the king tore his clothes.

In fact, the appeal to the king did not require *him* to do the healing. The Syrian ruler assumed that Jehoram would command the prophet to do the healing. But Jehoram did not even *think* of Elisha.

Elisha volunteers (2 Kings 5:8). Elisha sent a letter to Jehoram, asking him to send Naaman to him. The words "and he shall know that there is a prophet in Israel" are ironic. The Syrian, who worshiped a pagan god, would recognize Elisha as a prophet of God, even if the king of Israel did not!

Naaman's visit to Elisha (5:9–11). When Naaman arrived at Elisha's door, the prophet didn't even step outside. Elisha sent a messenger, who told Naaman to go wash seven times in the Jordan River. In this act, his flesh would be restored.

Naaman was insulted and "became furious." He was an important man! He had brought expensive gifts for the prophet (2 Kings 5:5). And besides, Elisha didn't act as Naaman thought a prophet should. A real prophet should be more like a magician: he should mutter an incantation in the name of his God, wave his hand, and heal the leprosy.

How like Naaman so many of us are. We have our own idea of how God should meet our needs. We assume that our needs are so important that the Lord himself should step outside to deal with us. Elisha's actions humbled and infuriated Naaman. But Naaman had to be humbled to the point where he would honor God and obey the prophet's command. How often humbling must occur before we are ready to receive God's help.

Naaman's healing (5:12–14). The angry Naaman left Elisha's home in a rage. The rivers of Damascus in Syria were cleaner and just as wet as the Jordan. If water would heal a leper,

he could have washed in them! But Naaman's servants respectfully suggested that if Elisha had asked him to do something really difficult, he would have done it. Why reject the prophet's prescription, they said, just because it is easy?

Again we have a reminder of the gospel message. "Only believe! Too easy." What a foolish reason to reject the good news of salvation in Christ.

Naaman's healing and his response (5:14–19). When Naaman did as the prophet said, "his flesh was restored like the flesh of a little child."

Naaman hurried back to Elisha and proclaimed his conversion: "Now I know that there is no God in all the earth, except in Israel." Naaman also asked for two mule loads of Israel's earth to take back to Syria with him.

He intended to spread it at the worship center where he sacrificed to symbolize that his worship was now directed to Israel's God. Namaan also asked for and was granted an exception to his promise to worship Yahweh.

Under protest, Naaman washed in the Jordan.

This was on state occasions, when he had to accompany the king of Syria to the temple of Rimmon, Syria's god.

The meaning of the miracle. God's grace calls for a faith response. The completeness of Naaman's conversion stands in sharp contrast to the reaction of Jehoram to Elisha's earlier miracle on his behalf (p. 126–127). The pagan general recognized God's hand and committed himself to worship the Lord only. The Israelite king failed to respond to God's gracious gift of victory. Ignoring the presence of God's prophet in Israel, he went his own way.

When we experience God's grace, it's important for us to recognize its source and to honor the Lord in our lives.

ELISHA CURSES GEHAZI WITH LEPROSY   2 Kings 5:20–27

When Naaman went to Israel, he took expensive gifts which he intended to give the prophet who healed him. After the leprosy was gone, Naaman tried to give Elisha a reward. Elisha refused. But after Naaman set out for home, Elisha's servant Gehazi hurried after him. Representing himself as a messenger of the prophet, Gehazi asked for a talent (about 75 pounds!) of silver and two sets of clothing. Naaman urged him to take 150 pounds of silver, which he did. Gehazi then hid the wealth in his home.

Elisha's judgment (2 Kings 5:25–27). When Elisha asked Gehazi where he had gone, Gehazi blandly said, "Nowhere." But Elisha knew exactly what had happened, and he described it for Gehazi. Elisha then announced the consequences: Gehazi and his descendants would be lepers "forever."

The meaning of the miracle. There are many lessons to be drawn from this miracle. The most important is that God's grace is free. We can never place a price tag on God's grace. We should not give others the impression that anything they can *do* or pay will bring God's gracious working in their lives.

In addition to this central message, there are others.

Ministry means putting others first (5:26). Elisha asked Gehazi if this was the time "to receive money . . . olive groves and vineyards. . . ." That is, is this the time to look out for ourselves and our material well-being? The answer, of course, is "No." Their mission was to look out for others and their spiritual well-being. Gehazi had been called to ministry. He had abandoned his calling for material gain.

"Your servant did not go anywhere" (5:25). How foolish to assume that we can hide our actions from God, or that what we do will never be found out by others. What we would not do if others were watching is something we should not do. Period.

"You and your descendants" (5:27). It is true that each person stands or falls before God on the basis of his or her own faith. But it is also true that what we do always affects others. Those most affected by our choices are our children and their children. We need to make choices that will bless future generations, not curse them.

ELISHA MAKES AN AX HEAD FLOAT
2 Kings 6:1–7

A dormitory occupied by a number of prophets needed to be expanded. One prophet who was working in the construction project lost an ax head in the Jordan River. The ax had been borrowed, and the young prophet was responsible for repaying what had been lost. Elisha met this need by cutting a stick and throwing it into the river, whereupon the ax head floated to the surface.

ELISHA BLINDS AND GIVES SIGHT
2 Kings 6:8—7:20

This passage contains an account of several miracles. Two of these are typically counted on lists of the fourteen miracles performed by Elisha. Because they have common features, these two miracles are treated together here.

The miracle context (2 Kings 6:8–12). The account begins with a report of Syrian raids on Israel. The Syrian high command would plan the attacks. But each time they raided, they were turned back by an Israelite force. The king of Syria concluded that one of his officers must be a spy, so he confronted them (2 Kings 6:11). One claimed the problem was the prophet Elisha, who "tells the king of Israel the words that you speak in your bedroom" (2 Kings 6:12). It was as if Elisha were present in the war room, watching and listening as the Syrians laid their plans.

The "first" miracle (6:13–17). When lists of Elisha's fourteen miracles are compiled, this next event is usually included. The king of Syria sent a force to capture Elisha, who was at Dothan. The Syrians arrived at night and surrounded the little cluster of homes.

Elisha's servant discovered the Syrian force and ran in terror to his master. Elisha told the servant not to worry, and asked God to open his eyes. The prayer was answered, and suddenly the servant saw a force of fiery angels deployed between Elisha and the Syrians. God had placed a hedge of protection around his prophet.

The "second" miracle (6:18–23). Elisha prayed that the Syrians would be struck with "blindness." The Hebrew word, found only here and in Genesis 19:11, doesn't indicate that the Syrians couldn't see. It means the Syrians were unable to *interpret* what they saw. They saw what God and the prophet intended them to see—a scene which didn't accord with reality.

Elisha boldly approached the Syrian commander and led his force inside the walls of Samaria, Israel's capital. Then the Lord "opened their eyes," and the Syrians realized where they were. The troops sent to take Elisha had been captured by Elisha!

The excited Jehoram wanted to kill the Syrians, but Elisha had a better plan. He would humiliate the Syrians by treating them as guests, then send them back to Syria. The strategy worked, and for a time no more raids were mounted against Israel.

The Syrians besiege Samaria (6:24—7:20). The Syrians later attacked Israel in force and besieged Samaria. Conditions inside the city became so desperate that some people resorted to cannibalism (2 Kings 6:26–31). The king blamed Elisha, God's representative, rather than acknowledging that it was a result of his own refusal to turn to the Lord.

In the name of the Lord, Elisha announced that food would be sold the next day at the gate of Samaria at bargain prices. One of the king's officers scoffed at Elisha's words. What Elisha announced was impossible, even for God (2 Kings 7:2). Elisha responded that the officer would see it, but he himself would never eat of the plenty provided by God.

That night the Syrian army heard noises that the soldiers interpreted as Hittite or Egyptian armies come to break their siege. Terrified, the entire Syrian force fled, leaving all its supplies behind. The next day, alerted by a few lepers who were crouched outside Samaria's walls, the people of the city poured out to gather the food the Syrians had left behind. The prophecy of Elisha came true. Food was sold to the hungry masses at bargain prices. And the officer who ridiculed God's ability to do as his prophet promised saw the food, but he was trampled to death in the peoples' rush to reach it.

The meaning of the miracles in this sequence. The common element in this section of 2 Kings is "revelation." God revealed the plans of the Syrians to Elisha. Elisha opened the eyes of his servant to reveal the angel army protecting them. Elisha confused the sight of the Syrian army so they completely lost touch with the reality of their situation; then he restored their ability to see and grasp reality. Finally, Elisha foresaw and predicted that the besieged and starving Israelites would be rescued and fed. This prophetic vision was rejected by Jehoram's officer, who died because of his doubts.

The message of these miracles is clear. God's revelation enables us to see the spiritual realities which must govern our actions in the material world.

THE LITERARY FORM OF THE ELISHA STORIES

The stories of Elisha's miracles are organized below in a literary form known as *chiasm*. Chiasm is the parallel arrangement of material, in which themes or thoughts are repeated in reverse order. That is,

A. Expresses idea #1
   B. Expresses idea #2
   B. Expresses idea #2
A. Expresses idea #1

When the chiasm has an odd number of elements, the single element standing at the center typically states the governing theme the author is developing.

If we review the recorded miracles of Elisha, we see that they have a chiasmic order. The single miracle standing at the center provides the key to understanding the underlying message not only of the whole, but also the unique contribution of each parallel pair.

The chart below so arranges fourteen miracles, counting miracles 13 and 14, which share the theme of blinding and restoring sight, as one.

Insights from the chiasmic organization of Elisha's miracles. There are many insights to gain from studying the order in which these miracle reports are organized.

Resurrection: life for the dead. This is the central theme of the miracle sequence expressed in G-7—Elisha's restoration of a child's life. Thus the miracles all express some vital truth about God's power to bring the spiritually dead to life and to restore what has been lost.

The message of these miracles is for Israel and for us. Israel abandoned the Lord and his word to follow a religion established by Jeroboam (see page 110–111). But if the nation would only turn back to the Lord, he would provide spiritual life and restore the nation's health.

God's good word to us is the same. However dead we have been to him in the past, however far we have strayed, his power has a resurrection quality that can revive and revitalize us.

Revelation (A-A): The first step toward new life. Miracles A-A are about revelation. In miracle A-1, prophets saw Elisha separate the Jordan's

---

A. Elisha divides the Jordan. (1)
   B. Elisha heals a spring of water. (2)
      C. Elisha curses jeering youths. (3)
         D. Elisha wins a battle. (4)
            E. Elisha multiplies a widow's oil. (5)
               F. Elisha predicts a child's birth. (6)
                  G. Elisha restores the child's life. (7)
H.   F. Elisha makes poison harmless. (8)
I.   E. Elisha multiplies loaves. (9)
J.   D. Elisha heals General Naaman. (10)
K.   C. Elisha curses Gehazi. (11)
L.   B. Elisha makes an ax head float. (12)
M. A. Elisha blinds and gives sight. (13, 14)

waters, and they recognized him as God's spokesman. They will hear his words.

In miracle A-13, 14, God enabled Elisha to see reality and opened the eyes of Elisha's servant so he would also know the truth. But the Syrian army wandered in a world of illusion, until Elisha opened their eyes as well. And the official who doubted God's word was trampled to death by the crowd rushing to get to the food he had said God couldn't provide.

If we would have what God alone can provide, we must rely on revelation, the Word of God, which guides us to life. To reject his Word means death.

Redemption (B-B): God's power redeems and saves. In B-2, Elisha healed a spring of water which destroyed all the vegetation it touched. What mankind needs is a new heart, from which the pure and refreshing will flow. God is not concerned with moral whitewashing. He requires that our hearts, from which our actions flow, be cleansed and purified.

B-2 and B-12 are linked by the water. In B-12, the ax head was lost in the Jordan River. Elisha miraculously made the ax head float so what had been lost could be recovered.

Those who accept revelation discover that in God's eyes, they are corrupt and lost. Yet God can purify the heart and save the lost.

Relationship (C-C): to live with God we must hold him in awe as God. C-3 and C-11 are linked by the word *curse.* The youths who jeered at God's power (C-3) suffered death. If we come to God, we must be prepared to treat him with utmost respect.

The attempt of Gehazi to deceive Elisha (C-11) showed how little he respected the Lord. As a leper, Gehazi lost the privilege of intimate relationship with God, expressed in Old Testament times by participation in the life of the community. The leper was forced to live outside the community (Lev. 13:45, 46).

Reconciliation (D-D): God's new life means peace with God. D-4 and D-10 are linked by warfare. God provided victory for the three allied kings in their battle with Moab (D-4). Yet subse-

quently the war was lost, and there was no lasting peace.

In D-10, the Lord brought healing and peace to Naaman, the leper (D-10).

It is important to note the role of obedience in each of these miracle accounts. The kings obeyed God and dug the ditches which were the key to the victory God provided. Yet Jehoash's heart was unchanged by God's blessing, and he returned home unwilling to submit to God's will. Naaman obeyed God; when he washed in the river Jordan, he was healed. Naaman then returned to Elisha to express his commitment to the Lord. Naaman, unlike Israel's king, had peace with God.

Provision (E-E): God supplies what we need to sustain the life he provides. The link between these two stories is the multiplication of necessities. In E-5, Elisha multiplied a widow's supply of olive oil. This not only saved her sons from slavery but also gave the family enough to live on.

In E-9, Elisha multiplied a tiny store of bread so that it fed one hundred men, with some left over.

In each case, God used what the needy had and multiplied it. In each case, there was more than enough. The God who gives us new life surely will supply what we need to sustain that life and us as well.

Preservation (F-F): God preserves the life he gives. In F-6, Elisha predicted a son's birth. The miracle speaks of the preservation of a family line in Israel.

In F-8, Elisha neutralized poison in the prophets' meal. This miracle preserved God's prophets from death.

We can perhaps see in the preservation of the family in F-6 a suggestion of the continuation of our lives beyond time into eternity. And F-8 contains a parable promising that nothing can take away the eternal life that God provides.

Additional insights from the chiasm. The arrangement of the miracle stories yields to further analysis as well. There is an additional relationship between the miracles. This relationship can be diagrammed as follows:

A-1
B-2
C-3
D-4
    E-5
    F-6
        G-7
    F-8
    E-9
D-10
C-11
B-12
A 13, 14

Arranged in this way, the key is God's miracle gift of resurrection life (G-7).

The miracle stories EF-FE are promises which can be claimed only by true believers. This is shown by the repeated reference to closed doors behind which the miracles E-5 and F-6 were performed, and the fact that miracles F-8 and E-9 were performed in a private gathering of God's prophets.

Only a person who has received new life from God can experience the wonder of his provision and preservation. The message of these miracles can be understood and appropriated only by those who have put their trust in him.

The miracles in ABCD and DCBA are miracles of gospel invitation. They are messages the lost need to hear: messages of revelation, redemption, relationship and reconciliation. Through them, we learn how to approach God and to receive the spiritual life he offers freely to all.

THE MIRACLE OF A LIFE RESTORED
2 Kings 13:20–21

One last miracle was associated with Elisha, but it was not a miracle which the prophet performed. A group was about to bury a dead man when raiders from Moab appeared. The funeral party placed the body in Elisha's tomb. When the body touched Elisha's bones, the man revived and stood up.

The message of the miracle is clear. Elisha was dead. But the God of Elisha lived! The promise implicit in Elisha's miracles still stood. God's offer of life was still open. Israel could turn to him—and live.

The cycle complete. This final miracle completes the cycle of the miracles of Elijah and Elisha. The focus now shifts from Israel to Judah, where the three final miracles contained in the books of history are found.

CHAPTER 8

MORE MIRACLES IN HISTORY, POETRY, AND PROPHECY

MAGNIFYING GOD'S PRESENCE

2 Kings—Daniel

Aggressive TV ads for the Psychic Hot Line promise to tell callers about themselves and their futures. But Old Testament prophets had to pass a far more rigorous test that any phone-line psychic. And pass the test they did!

God revealed the future to His prophets, instructed them to predict what would happen, and invariably their words came true. We see this phenomenon in miracle prophecies recorded in the Old Testament. And we see God celebrated for His miracle working power in Old Testament poetry.

THE MIRACLE OF UZZIAH'S LEPROSY *2 Kings 15:1–8; 2 Chronicles 26:1–21*

Uzziah (called Azariah in 2 Kings) was a man who "did what was right in the sight of the LORD" (2 Kings 15:3). Second Chronicles adds details. The king "sought God in the days of Zechariah. . . . And as long as he sought the Lord, God made him prosper" (2

Chron. 26:5). The same book reveals that Uzziah became "exceeding strong," developing a powerful military which won a wide reputation in the ancient world.

Uzziah's fall (2 Chronicles 26:16–19). When Uzziah became strong, "his heart was lifted up." The king arrogantly tried to usurp the privilege of burning incense in the temple, which God's Law reserved for priests alone. When the priests tried to stop him, Uzziah became furious. He was determined to offer that incense, no matter what the priests or God's Law said!

Uzziah's punishment (26:19–21). Before Uzziah could act, leprosy broke out on his forehead. The priests hurried him out of the temple, and indeed Uzziah was anxious to go! The Bible says that "Uzziah was a leper until the day of his death," and that he "dwelt in an isolated house, because he was a leper." The Hebrew phrase is "house of quarantine," and a similar phrase in Ugaritic suggests humiliation and disgrace. Uzziah's son, Jotham, became co-regent and ruled in Judah.

The message of the miracle. In Judah, the king was not an absolute monarch. He was to be responsive to God and to be guided by God's Law. As long as Uzziah was humble enough to seek God by submitting to God's revealed will, he and the nation prospered. But when Uzziah became too proud to submit to God's Law, the Lord struck him with leprosy and set him aside. What an important message for the people of Judah. If God would not stand for disrespect from a king, how much less will he tolerate disrespect from ordinary citizens! God is to be honored and held in awe.

THE MIRACLE OF THE ASSYRIAN SLAUGHTER   *2 Kings 18, 19; 2 Chronicles 32; Isaiah 37*

The fact that this story is repeated three times in Scripture underlines its importance. While the miracle itself is striking, its context provides clues to its lasting significance.

The setting (2 Kings 18:1–17). Some years before this account, an Assyrian army had taken Samaria and resettled the people of the Northern Kingdom in other lands. When Sennacherib of Assyria threatened Judah, King Hezekiah had stripped the land to pay a ransom. But the Assyrians were not satisfied. Some years later they returned, intent on subduing Judah and deporting its population. The Assyrians succeeded in destroying the fortified cities on Judah's borders and even threatened the capital city of Jerusalem.

But Hezekiah, one of Judah's most godly kings, had led a great revival in the land. When an Assyrian envoy called for Jerusalem's surrender, Hezekiah laid the envoy's insulting words before the Lord and begged for his intervention.

The Assyrian's insult to God (18:31–35). The Assyrian envoy stood outside the city walls and, speaking Hebrew, threatened and made promises, demanding the surrender of the city. In his diatribe, he warned, "Do not listen to Hezekiah, lest he persuade you, saying, 'The Lord will deliver us'" (1 Kings 18:32). The envoy then went on to compare Yahweh to the gods of the nations which Assyria had conquered. Had any of those gods delivered their people? Why then should they expect Yahweh to deliver them?

There was a direct challenge and an ironic one as well. At the founding of the nation Israel, God had done something no other god could do. He had taken for himself "a nation from the midst of another nation, by trials, by signs, by wonders, by war, by a mighty hand and an outstretched arm, and by great terrors" (Deut. 4:34). From the very beginning, God had set himself apart from all that others called "god!" Now the Assyrian envoy contemptuously lumped the Lord with the frivolous gods of the nations. What an insult to the one true God!

Hezekiah's prayer (19:14–19). When the Assyrian envoy later returned and again insulted the Lord, Hezekiah went to God in prayer. He affirmed his faith that "You are God, You alone," and asked the Lord to save Jerusalem that "all the kingdoms of the earth may know that You are the Lord God, You alone."

God answered Hezekiah's prayer (19:32–35). The prophet Isaiah conveyed God's answer to Hezekiah. The Lord would defend the city, and not even an arrow would fly over Jerusalem's walls.

A few nights later an angel killed 185,000 Assyrians, and Sennacherib returned to Nineveh, where he was assassinated by two of his sons. Because of the difficulty of translating numbers in Hebrew (see page 106), the number 185,000 has been challenged. But there is no doubt that a substantial number of the Assyrian force was devastated.

"That all the kingdoms of the earth may know" (19:19). There is a fascinating aspect to this request in Hezekiah's prayer. Herodotus, over two centuries later, told the story of Sennacherib's defeat after an unexplained military disaster. The memory of God's overthrow of

Thousands of Assyrians were killed by God's angel, without any fighting by Judah.

❖

the ruler who had ridiculed him was pre-served by this Greek historian, that the nations might know.

THE MIRACLE SIGN TO HEZEKIAH   *2 Kings 20:1–11; 2 Chronicles 32:24; Isaiah 38*

When Hezekiah became ill, Isaiah warned him that he would die. Hezekiah, who had been dedicated to the Lord, begged God for recovery. Isaiah returned with word that God would add fifteen years to Hezekiah's life. The king then asked for a sign [`ot] that he might be sure of God's intention.

The miraculous sign (2 Kings 20:8). In fact, a sign had already been given. Isaiah had told Hezekiah that in three days he would recover enough to go to the temple and worship (2 Kings 20:5). But Hezekiah could not wait for that sign. He had been facing death, and he wanted reassurance. This the Lord graciously provided. Isaiah asked whether Hezekiah wanted the shadow on some nearby stairs to move upward or downward ten "degrees."

The common notion that Hezekiah referred to a "sundial of Ahaz" (20:11) is not sup-ported by the Hebrew text. The original simply calls them "steps of Ahaz." It is most likely these were a set of stairs on which the passage of time was roughly estimated by where the sun's shadow fell. Hezekiah chose to ask that the shadow move *backward,* and it did.

It is not necessary to suppose that the position of the earth and sun were affected. It was the *shadow* that moved.

Hezekiah was then healed. A poultice of figs was laid on his boils, and Hezekiah recovered to live for fifteen more years.

The timing of the miracle. Hezekiah died in 686 B.C. If we subtract fifteen years, his illness and recovery took place in 701 B.C., about the time of Sennacherib's invasion. It is fascinating to speculate what might have happened in Judah if the godly King Hezekiah had not lived to pray for Jerusalem and his people.

Hezekiah had been a godly ruler, dedicated to the Lord. But the healing which God provided was not simply for Hezekiah. It was also for the nation. God may be gracious to us when we are ill. When we recover, it is only appropriate to ask ourselves how we may serve him in the additional years he has granted.

❖

SENNACHERIB'S OWN ACCOUNT

The military annals of Sennacherib have been recovered by archaeologists. Typically, the conqueror's report of this expedition into Judah failed to mention his defeat. For all Sennacherib's boasting, he failed to do to Judah what Shalmaneser had done to Israel a few decades before. He was unable to take Jerusalem and depopulate the Holy Land. Knowing the true story from Scripture, his boasting account sounds hollow indeed.

As for Hezekiah of Judah, he did not submit to my yoke, and I laid siege to forty-six of his strong cities, walled forts, and to the countless small villages in their vicinity, and conquered them using earth ramps and battering rams. These siege engines were aided by the use of foot soldiers who undermined the walls. I drove out of these places 200,150 people—young and old, male and female, horses, mules, donkeys, camels, large and small cattle beyond counting and considered them as booty. I made Hezekiah a prisoner in Jerusalem, like a bird in a cage. I erected siege works to prevent anyone escaping through the city gates. The towns in his territory which I captured I gave to Mitinti, King of Ashdod, Padi, King of Ekron, and Sillibel, King of Gaza. Thus I reduced his territory in this campaign, and I also increased Hezekiah's annual tribute payments.

Hezekiah, who was overwhelmed by my terror-inspiring splendor, was deserted by his elite troops, which he had brought into Jerusalem, and was forced to send me 30 talents of gold, eight hundred talents of silver, precious stones, couches and chairs inlaid with ivory, elephant hides, ebony wood, box wood, and all kinds of valuable treasures, his daughters, concubines, and male and female musicians. He sent his personal messenger to deliver this tribute and bow down to me.

❖

MIRACLES IN THE POST-CAPTIVITY BOOKS

In 586 B.C. the kingdom of Judah finally fell—to the Babylonians. Its people were de-ported to Babylon and settled there. Three Old Testament books of history take up the story of what happened later.

THE BOOK OF ESTHER

In time the Persians replaced the Babylonians as the dominant power in the Middle East. The book of Esther tells the fascinating story of how a young Jewish girl became queen of Persia, and saved her people from extinction.

The book is noted for a series of "coincidences" which led to the Jews' deliverance. While God is not mentioned in Esther, it is clear that the Lord was at work through a series of unlikely coincidences to preserve his people.

God no longer would perform miracles to deliver Israel. But God had not abandoned his people. The Lord was at work behind the scenes of history to preserve the people he had chosen as his own.

EZRA AND NEHEMIAH

These two books tell the story of the small parties of Jews which returned to Judah after decades of captivity in Babylon. There they rebuilt the temple and later the defensive wall of Jerusalem. Although Judah was only a tiny district in one of the 128 provinces in an empire dominated by Persia, Jews once again lived in their homeland. There they awaited God's next step in fulfilling his ancient promises to Abraham.

There are no accounts of miracles in these books, although the praise song in Nehemiah 9 affirms that the Lord is a miracle-working God (Neh. 9:10, 17). Yet it is clear that God was again at work—settling the Jews in their land and preparing them for a new age of miracles which would occur when the Messiah came.

MIRACLES OF THE POETICAL BOOKS

The books of the Old Testament classified as poetry are Job, Psalms, Proverbs, Ecclesiastes, and Song of Solomon.

JOB

Job is a work which tries to explain why bad things happen to good people. Job reported no miracles, but he did affirm the wonder-working power of God (Job 5:9). Job, the main character in the book, was challenged by God to consider his wondrous works (Job 37:14, 16).

PSALMS

Psalms is the hymn and praise book of Israel, filled with references to God's wonderful works, awesome deeds, signs, and wonders. While Psalms does not report any new miracles, the book sings a song of praise to God for his past wonders. The following passages in the Psalms refer to God's signs, miracles, and wonderful works.

PROVERBS

The book of Proverbs is a collection of sayings and practical advice intended to guide us to make wise choices in life. Because of the nature of this book, it contains no accounts of miracles.

ECCLESIASTES

The book of Ecclesiastes records one man's search for the meaning of life apart from God. Solomon, the traditional author of Ecclesiastes, limited himself to deductions he could make from personal experience and from observing life "under the sun." He refused to look to revelation or to consider miracles in his search. Solomon was forced to conclude that human life apart from God is meaningless.

The book stands as a powerful witness to the truth that humankind can find meaning only by establishing a personal relationship with God, who has revealed himself in his written Word and in miracle.

Bible Background: Verses in the Hebrew Psalms which Refer to Miracles

Psalm 9:1	Psalm 77:12	Psalm 104:25	Psalm 111:2
Psalm 28:5	Psalm 78:4	Psalm 105:1	Psalm 111:4
Psalm 40:5	Psalm 78:7	Psalm 105:2	Psalm 111:6
Psalm 44:1	Psalm 78:11	Psalm 105:5	Psalm 111:7
Psalm 46:8	Psalm 78:12	Psalm 105:27	Psalm 118:17
Psalm 65:5	Psalm 78:32	Psalm 106:2	Psalm 119:27
Psalm 65:8	Psalm 78:43	Psalm 106:7	Psalm 135:9
Psalm 66:3	Psalm 86:8	Psalm 106:22	Psalm 136:4
Psalm 66:5	Psalm 89:5	Psalm 107:8	Psalm 139:14
Psalm 71:17	Psalm 92:5	Psalm 107:15	Psalm 145:4
Psalm 73:28	Psalm 96:3	Psalm 107:21	Psalm 145:12
Psalm 75:1	Psalm 98:1	Psalm 107:24	Psalm 145:17
Psalm 77:11	Psalm 104:24	Psalm 107:31	Psalm 150:2

SONG OF SOLOMON

The Song is an extended love poem. Again, the author's subject matter means that he neither recounted nor referred to miracles.

MIRACLES IN THE BOOKS OF PROPHECY

PROPHECY AS MIRACLE

The *Revell Bible Dictionary* defines prophets and prophecy as follows. A prophet is

one who communicates or interprets messages from God. A prophet is a person authorized to speak for God. The prophet's message was called in Hebrew a *nebu'ah*, "prophecy;" sometimes it was also termed a vision, oracle, or burden, but most often it was identified as "the word of the Lord" (p. 822).

Recognizing the true prophet (Deuteronomy 13:1–5; 18:18–22). The Old Testament set up standards which a person who claimed to be a prophet had to meet. The tests are specific and clear:

- The prophet must be "from your midst, from your brethren" (Deut. 18:15). That is, the prophet must be a Hebrew, one of God's covenant people.
- The prophet must speak in the name of the Lord (Deut. 18:19). No true prophet will credit a pagan deity with his message.
- The prophet will be recognized by his ability to make accurate predictions about the future. "When a prophet speaks in the name of the Lord, if the thing does not happen or come to pass, that is the thing which the Lord has not spoken" (Deut. 18:22).
- Even if a prophet should make a prediction which comes true ["give a sign or a wonder"], but calls the hearer to abandon the Lord or his commandments, that "prophet" shall be put to death (Deut. 13:1–5).

Thus, a prophet of the Lord was determined by checking his message against God's revealed Word. He was also proven by his performance of miracles or by making predictions which came true.

The miracle of predictive prophecy. The Old Testament makes it clear that predictive prophecy is in itself a sign or a miracle. Isaiah, giving God's words to a rebellious people, spoke of the fact that only God knows and can reveal the future.

> Remember this, fix it in mind,
> take it to heart, you rebels.
> Remember the former things, those
> of long ago;
> I am God, and there is no other;
> I am God, and there is none like
> me.
> I make known the end from the
> beginning,
> from ancient times, what is still
> to come.
> I say: My purpose will stand,
> and I will do all that I please . . . .
> What I have said, that will I bring
> about;
> what I have planned, that will I do
> (Isa. 46:8–11, NIV).

In this great affirmation, the Lord claims not only to know but also to control the future. He can predict what will happen the next day or in a thousand years, because God is sovereign and will cause what he says to happen.

When a person speaking in the name of the Lord accurately predicts future events—precisely and without mistakes—his claim to be God's messenger is authenticated. In harmony with our definition of miracles, such prediction can be classified as an extraordinary event—one caused by God, with a religious purpose.

Since no person in his or her own strength can accurately predict the future, such events are extraordinary. Consistent accuracy in these predictions is evidence that God is the source of the prophet's prediction. And such predictions have religious purposes, not only to reveal information but also to authenticate the prophet as God's spokesman.

The extent of predictive prophecy in the Old Testament. Some have estimated that as much as a third of the Old Testament is predictive prophecy. The *Revell Bible Dictionary* observes that "predictive prophecy falls into one of two categories: near-term or far-term."

Near-term predictions tell what is about to be experienced by those in the prophet's own generation. Jeremiah's announcement that Hananiah would die within a year is a near-term prediction, and within two months Hananiah was dead. Habakkuk's prediction of a coming invasion of Judah by Babylon probably took place within two decades, even though its fulfillment called for the unexpected overthrow of Assyria by the Babylonians and the emergence of a new, vast empire. The fulfillment of near-term predictions served to authenticate the prophet as God's messenger (p. 826).

There are many examples in the Old Testament of far-term prophecy which has been fulfilled. About 700 years before Jesus' birth, prophets predicted he would come from David's line (Isa. 9:6, 7), be born of a virgin (Isa. 7:14) in Bethlehem (Micah 5:2), and spend his early years in Nazareth of Galilee (Isa. 9:1, 2). His death was described in detail, from his execution with criminals (Isa. 53:9, 12) and his burial with the rich (Isa. 53:9).

Several centuries before Jesus was born, psalmists described the offer of vinegar made while he hung on the cross (Ps. 69:21) as soldiers gambled for his clothing (Ps. 22:18). Even his dying words were recorded (Ps. 22:1; 31:5), as well as the fact that while his side would be pierced (Zech. 12:10), not a bone of his body would be broken (Ps. 34:20).

There are many more incidents of fulfilled far-term prophecy in Scripture, ranging from descriptions of coming world empires in Daniel to powerful images of the fate of cities and nations which oppressed God's people, Israel.

While near-term prophecy authenticated the prophet in the eyes of his generation, far-term prophecy which has been fulfilled authenticates the Bible itself as a miracle book. Such prophecies are powerful sources of objective data that support Scripture's claim to be the revealed Word of God.

In a sense, all predictive prophecy is miracle. But our study of all the prophecies of the Bible must await another book in this series. For the present, we can only note that the Bible is rich in prophetic miracles—and limit our examination of the writings of the prophets to their reports of other miracles.

MIRACLES IN THE WRITINGS OF THE PROPHETS

MIRACLES IN THE BOOK OF ISAIAH

Isaiah has been called the "evangelist of the Old Testament." His ministry extended over about 50 years, through the reigns of Uzziah, Jotham, Ahaz and Hezekiah of Judah, and into the reign of Manasseh. Throughout the 66 chapters of this towering work, condemnation of Judah's sins is balanced by promises of God's coming redemption though his servant, the Messiah.

While the book is filled with near-term and far-term prophecies, it contains no accounts of the kind of miracles we are studying here.

MIRACLES IN JEREMIAH AND LAMENTATIONS

Jeremiah has been called the "weeping prophet." He ministered during the last four decades of Judah's existence as a nation, constantly warning God's people to submit to the pagan nation Babylon. Condemned as unpatriotic for his warnings, Jeremiah and his message were rejected by a generation rushing toward God's judgment.

Jeremiah's prophetic words truly were from the Lord. He lived to see the city captured and its people deported to Babylon, just as he had predicted.

The book of Jeremiah doesn't report any miracles. The reason why is made clear in Jeremiah 21 and 32. King Zedekiah sent officials to Jeremiah to see if God would "deal with us according to all his wonderful works" (21:2) when the king of Babylon invaded. Jeremiah answered in God's name, "I Myself will fight against you with an outstretched hand and with a strong arm, even in anger and fury and great wrath" (Jer. 21:5). God would not perform miracles for his sinning people; indeed, he would work against them!

The same thought is expressed in Jeremiah 32:20–23. Jeremiah praised God for the signs and wonders he had done in Egypt, but expressed regret that Israel had "not obeyed Your voice or walked in Your law." In such a land, at such a time, God would work no miracles.

Jerusalem did fall, and Solomon's temple was destroyed.

The book of Lamentations, which tradition claims was written by Jeremiah from Babylon, captures the feelings of the captives as the people of Judah finally realized how much they had lost.

MIRACLES IN THE BOOK OF EZEKIEL

While Jeremiah prophesied in Judah during its last days, the prophet Ezekiel ministered to the Jewish community in Babylon. This community was made up of persons who had been captured in the Babylonian expeditions to Judah in 605 B.C. and in 598 B.C. Ezekiel warned the captives of the coming destruction of Jerusalem, even as Jeremiah warned the Jews still living in their homeland.

Many wonderful visions were given to Ezekiel (see especially Ezek. 1—3 and 40—48). But only one vision in Ezekiel fits our standard for a miracle—and this primarily because it is the reverse of a miracle experienced by Israel centuries before.

The shekinah entered the temple (1 Kings 8:10–12). When King Solomon dedicated the Jerusalem temple in 963 B.C., the visible glory of God filled the structure and awed the people. The shekinah's presence was a visible sign that the Lord would hear prayers directed toward his temple and would protect his people. (See the discussion of this miracle on page 109.)

Even as the Babylonian army marched toward Judah, the people took comfort in the fact that the temple stood in their Holy City. God had placed his presence there. Whatever sins Israel committed, God would never permit an enemy to overrun his temple. Then Ezekiel had a vision in which he served as the sole witness to a terrible event.

The shekinah left the temple (Ezekiel 8—11). Ezekiel was transported in a vision to Jerusalem. There he witnessed the people of Judah worshiping idols. Many of the elders of Judah had gathered in one of the rooms of the temple to worship images drawn on the walls! The vision made the extent of Judah's sin and idolatry clear, setting the scene for what Ezekiel witnessed next.

What Ezekiel saw was the shekinah glory of the Lord rising up from where it rested over the ark of the covenant in the innermost room of the temple. The shekinah slowly moved toward the door of the temple. It hovered for a moment as if reluctant to leave, then rose even higher. Finally, God's glory left the city and retreated over the eastern mountains.

The message of the miracle vision was clear. Judah's sins had caused God to withdraw his presence and protection. The city, guarded now by a temple which was nothing but a heap of stones, was no protection at all. Jerusalem and Judah were doomed.

Judgment—and hope (Ezekiel 11). As Ezekiel watched the shekinah withdraw, God gave him a message for the people of Judah. The city would surely fall, and his people would be scattered across the Babylonian Empire. But one day God would keep the promise he had made to Abraham. One day, God said, "I will gather you from the peoples, assemble you from the countries where you have been scattered, and I will give you the land of Israel" (Ezek. 11:17).

God's withdrawal was temporary, not permanent. His people must be punished. But they would not be abandoned. What a wonderful reassurance this is for us. Our sins may block our fellowship with the Lord, leading

God's shekinah glory rested over the ark of the covenant within the temple.

even to painful consequences. But our God stands ready to forgive and restore.

THE MIRACLES OF THE BOOK OF DANIEL

The first part of the book of Daniel reads like a book of history rather than a book of prophecy. But Daniel alone, of all the prophets, described a series of miracles. Several miracles are reported in the book's first six chapters. These miracles played a role in Daniel's advancement and ultimately influenced the conversion of Nebuchadnezzar himself.

The story of Daniel. Daniel was a young man who was deported along with Judah's leading families after the Babylonian invasion of 605 B.C. Along with three other promising Jewish youths, Daniel was enrolled in a school which King Nebuchadnezzar of Babylon had established to train officials to run his empire.

The miracle of Nebuchadnezzar's first dream (Daniel 2). The Babylonian king had a dream that disturbed his sleep, but when he awoke he couldn't remember the content of the dream. He called all his counselors and advisors, demanding that they tell him the dream and its meaning. The demand was unreasonable, but the king threatened to kill all his advisors if they failed. When the wise men were unable to help, Nebuchadnezzar began the slaughter (Dan. 2:1–13)! Those threatened included Daniel and his three Jewish friends, who were graduates of the king's school!

Daniel promised to tell the dream and its meaning (Daniel 2:14–18). When the soldiers came to take Daniel, he asked for time. Daniel then joined his three friends in prayer, asking God to reveal Nebuchadnezzar's dream, "so that Daniel and his companions might not perish with the rest of the wise men of Babylon" (v. 18).

God revealed the dream and its meaning (Daniel 2:19–23). That night God revealed the dream to Daniel. His prayer of praise serves as a model for us when our prayers are answered.

Daniel explained the dream to the king (Daniel 2:23–45). When Daniel was taken to the king, he was careful to give God the credit for the revelation. Daniel told the king that his dream concerned a great image, and he provided the interpretation.

Nebuchadnezzar was impressed by Daniel and Daniel's God (Daniel 2:46–49). Nebuchadnezzar honored and promoted Daniel and his three friends. This was the king's first encounter with the God of Israel, and he was impressed. He declared, "Truly your God is the God of gods, the Lord of kings, and a revealer of secrets" (Dan. 2:47).

The religious purpose of the miracle. There is no doubt that in the dream, and through Daniel's explanation of it, God addressed Nebuchadnezzar. As the sequence of miracles recorded in Daniel continued, it was clear that the Lord intended to be gracious to this world conqueror.

The miracle of the fiery furnace (Daniel 3). King Nebuchadnezzar was an arrogant man. He created a golden image, then commanded officials from throughout his empire to bow down and worship it. His reasoning may have been more political than religious: the worship of a ruler's gods was one way people in the ancient world expressed loyalty. But the three young Jewish men who came to Babylon with Daniel and who were at this great gathering refused to bow down. Some of the Babylonian officials were quick to accuse them!

The king's anger (3:13–15). Nebuchadnezzar was furious, and he confronted the three men. He gave them another chance to worship the idol, but they refused. The king couldn't understand their loyalty to their own God. He asked, "Who is the god who can deliver you from my hands?"

The faith of the young men (3:15–18). The three affirmed their belief that God, the supreme ruler of the universe, was able to deliver them. Yet they did not know that God would do so. No matter what God chooses to do, they declared, they would remain loyal.

This should be our attitude too. God can deliver us from cancer and any other illness or problem. But God may choose not to do so. Whatever God in his sovereignty chooses to do, we have the privilege of continuing to trust and honor him.

God delivered them (Daniel 3:19–27). Furious, Nebuchadnezzar ordered the three young men thrown into the firepit. Then the ruler

A burning fiery furnace.

and his officials saw four persons, walking unharmed in the flames.

Nebuchadnezzar's startled description of the fourth figure has caused confusion, leading some to believe the fourth figure was Christ. In Hebrew idiom the phrase "a son of God" simply means "a supernatural being" or "angel." Nebuchadnezzar realized immediately the fourth person was no mere human!

The king called the three out of the flames. To his amazement, not a hair on their heads was burned nor did their clothing smell of fire.

Nebuchadnezzar's confession (Daniel 3:28–30). This was the king's second experience with the God of Israel, and he realized the Lord was greater than he—a powerful king. Nebuchadnezzar issued a decree that no one should speak a word against the Lord, on penalty of death, "because there is no other God who can deliver like this" (v. 29).

The meaning of the miracle. On one hand, the miracle was a testimony to God's faithfulness toward those who are loyal to him. But again, the religious impact of the miracle was felt by Nebuchadnezzar. The arrogant ruler, who held the power of life and death over his subjects, was confronted by a power greater than him. Nebuchadnezzar decreed death, but God decreed life; and the earthly king's orders were set aside. God continued to show grace to Babylon's ruler by revealing more and more of himself. And Nebuchadnezzar, unlike Egypt's pharaoh in the time of the Exodus, acknowledged the powerful presence of the Lord.

Nebuchadnezzar's madness (Daniel 4).

Chapter 4 of Daniel is in the form of a confession of faith, sent by the king to everyone in his empire.

The king's dream and its interpretation (Daniel 4:1–27). The king told of a dream which only Daniel could interpret. The dream was a warning. Nebuchadnezzar was directed to set aside his pride and to honor God as the one who had given him his power. The ruler was also to "break off your sins by being righteous,

and your iniquities by showing mercy to the poor" (Dan. 4:27).

The dream came true (Daniel 4:28–36). A year after the dream, God struck the arrogant ruler. Nebuchadnezzar became mad and lived in the fields like an animal for "seven times" (v. 32). This term may refer to days or weeks, although in a later prophecy of Daniel a "time" [literally just a "seven"] represented a year (Dan. 9:24–27).

After this period, Nebuchadnezzar recovered his senses and returned to the throne. His concluding words have been interpreted by some as the confession of a sincere and saving faith in the Lord.

Now I, Nebuchadnezzar, praise and extol and honor the King of heaven, all of whose works are truth, and his ways justice. And those who walk in pride he is able to abase (Dan. 4:37).

One meaning of the miracle sequence. In each of the first three miracles recorded in Daniel, there was a single central figure: Nebuchadnezzar. Each miracle recounted an extraordinary event caused by God. And each miracle brought a positive response from the great ruler! Gradually, Nebuchadnezzar was brought to see more and more of the power of heaven's King, until at last this earthly king praised, extolled, and honored the Lord as the one true God.

The sequence reminds us of many wonderful truths. God is truly gracious. He even showed grace to the pagan ruler Nebuchadnezzar, who devastated Judah and destroyed the temple in Jerusalem. God's concern for human beings is universal. The Lord reveals himself to all people, and this happened even in Old Testament times. Any person who responds to God's revelation as Nebuchadnezzar did can and will be saved.

The miracle of the writing hand (Daniel 5).

After Nebuchadnezzar's death, Daniel continued to serve in the Babylonian Empire. When the event reported in chapter 5 of Daniel took place, a Persian force under Cyrus was assembled outside Babylon, a city considered impregnable because of its massive walls and defenses.

Inside the city, the current Babylonian ruler, Belshazzar, was giving a banquet. As the king and his guests partied, a hand appeared and wrote four words on the wall. Shaken by the supernatural event, the ruler called for an interpretation. But the king's wise men could neither read nor understand the message.

At last, someone suggested Daniel as an interpreter. The prophet, by this time an old man, reminded Belshazzar of Nebuchadnezzar's humbling by God many years before. Unlike Nebuchadnezzar, Belshazzar had shown contempt for God, even drinking from holy vessels taken from the Lord's temple in Jerusalem.

Daniel then explained that the words written on the wall represented descending values of currency. The meaning was that God had weighed Belshazzar and found him lacking. His kingdom would fall to the Persians.

That very night, the Persians diverted a river that flowed into Babylon to undermine

the city walls. They captured the city, killed Belshazzar, and took over Babylon's empire.

Once again, a ruler of Babylon was the focus of the miracle. But this ruler, unlike Nebuchadnezzar, had ignored the Lord's revelation of himself and arrogantly dishonored the Lord.

The message of this miracle is that the fate of all peoples and nations hinges on their response to the one true God.

Daniel is delivered from a lion's den (Daniel 6). When Daniel was an old man, jealous officials manipulated the Persian ruler of Babylon, Darius, into issuing a decree against prayers and petitions which they knew Daniel would violate. Because of a peculiarity in Persian law, even the ruler couldn't change a decree once it had been issued. So Daniel was condemned to be thrown to the lions.

Even though he could not take back his command, Darius expressed his hope to Daniel that "your God, whom you serve continually, He will deliver you" (Dan. 6:16). The anxious king stayed awake all night. The next morning he hurried to the lion's den. Daniel was alive! God had sent an angel, who shut the lions' mouths.

Both relieved and angry, Darius ordered that those who had plotted against Daniel should suffer the fate they had intended for him.

Darius later wrote a testimony honoring "the living God," ordering that every person in his kingdom should "tremble and fear before the God of Daniel" (Dan. 6:26).

Again, a ruler was the focus of this miracle. This ruler, like Nebuchadnezzar and unlike Belshazzar, knew about God and his wonder-working power (Dan. 6:16). Like Nebuchadnezzar, Darius both believed and openly witnessed to the power of God.

The larger message of the miracle sequence in Daniel. In Daniel's time, the Jewish people had been torn from the land which God promised to Abraham's descendants. As captives in Babylon, the Jews recognized their deportation from their homeland was punishment for their

Belshazzar was frightened when a hand appeared and wrote on the palace wall.

unfaithfulness to God. But the Jews must have wondered if their sins had been so terrible that God had permanently set them aside. Would he ever bring them home again?

The second half of the book of Daniel is filled with prophecy. Daniel's predictions describe in amazing detail a series of future world empires—Babylonian, Persian, Greek, and Roman—which would for centuries dominate the biblical world. Israel's questions about God's plans would remain unanswered for more than 400 years!

This helps us see the main message of the first half of the book of Daniel. *Daniel described miracles in which God displayed his sovereignty over the Gentile rulers of the ancient world!* Throughout the coming centuries Israel would remember that, although gentile powers dominated their homeland, God remained in control! Israel's God could bring a Nebuchadnezzar to his knees, punish a Belshazzar, and replace him with a Darius who honored the Lord and carried out his will.

And, until God moved again to keep his ancient promises to Abraham, through all the ups and downs of the ages, the Daniels of God—his faithful servants—would be protected and promoted to places of power and influence.

How clearly the miracles of Daniel prepared the way for the predictive prophecy which followed. How wonderfully those miracles remind us that, no matter what happens, our God is the Lord of history. He rules, even through those who don't know him.

THE MINOR PROPHETS

The last dozen writings of the prophets are shorter books. The name of this collection, "Minor Prophets," refers to their length rather than to the significance of the books. Unlike the book of Daniel, the Minor Prophets contain no narrative account of divine miracles. It is true that they contain miracle predictions about near and distant events. But we hope to explore this type of miracle thoroughly in a future book in this series.

The last book in the Old Testament, Malachi, was written about 400 years before the birth of Jesus. During those four centuries, God seemingly remained silent. We have no written record or documentation of any divine miracles during this long period. And so God's people waited for a new flurry of miracles. These would show clearly that God was about to reveal the next stage of his eternal plan.

CHAPTER 9

JESUS: A MAN MARKED BY MIRACLES

GOD WITH US

Matthew—John

No one in first century Judea thought of Jesus as an ordinary man. Some today attempt to cast Jesus as a simple visionary or a misunderstood but good man. But one phenomenon forced even contemporaries who were hostile to Jesus to hesitate. Jesus was a Man marked by miracles!

The people who witnessed the healings performed by Jesus had no doubt that they were seeing miracles. Some reacted with fear. Others responded with faith. The miracles made one thing perfectly clear. Jesus could not simply be dismissed as insignificant. Every person, now as then, must make a decision about the claims of this Man marked by miracles.

INTRODUCTION

For centuries Israel had experienced divine silence. After Malachi delivered his message around 450 B.C., no prophet spoke to Israel with God's voice for nearly five centuries. Israel lived in a great void, anchored to the past by the Scriptures, struggling to deal with changing conditions as sages and rabbis sought to determine how God's Law should be applied in an age when Gentiles ruled and ten times as many Jews lived outside the holy land as within it.

Yet Israel's hope was never extinguished. One day God *would* send the Messiah, the Anointed One promised by the prophets. Then the entire promised land would be occupied by a new Jewish state, and Israel rather than Rome would dominate the world. "The Lord will make you the head and not the tail; you shall be above only and not be beneath," Moses had promised (Deut. 28:13). In the coming messianic age, Israel would once again be obedient to the Lord, and the Lawgiver's ancient promise would be fulfilled.

GOD'S SILENCE IS BROKEN

Then the silence of God was broken. Rumors of angel annunciations kindled Jewish expectations, and these simmered for nearly thirty years. Then a prophet whose dress and lifestyle reminded Israel of Elijah appeared out of the desert. He preached repentance, called for public baptism as a sign of confession and recommitment, and warned Israel to get ready—the promised Messiah was about to appear.

For the first time in nearly 500 years, a prophet's voice was heard again in the Holy Land. John the Baptist had begun his ministry, preparing the way for Jesus, the Christ.

John's ministry reached its peak one day by the Jordan River. He had preached his fiery message of moral renewal, warning that judgment would follow hard on Messiah's heels. But that day John's cousin, Jesus, came to him for baptism.

John refused at first (Matt. 3:13–15). He knew his cousin Jesus well, and John's message was addressed to those who had strayed from the Law. "I need to be baptized by You, and are You coming to me?" John objected (v. 14). There was nothing in Jesus' life to confess—nothing that required the radical change of heart that John preached. Indeed, Jesus' life was more pure than John's!

Jesus came to be baptized by John.

Jesus insisted that he be baptized. "It is fitting for us to fulfill all righteousness," he said, meaning that it was only right for him to be baptized and take a stand with John to affirm the prophet's message. So John agreed. And on that day, John witnessed a miracle seen only by himself and Jesus (compare Matt. 3:16–17; John 1:29–34).

Earlier God had revealed to John that one day he would see the Spirit descend and rest on someone—and that this person would be the Messiah (John 1:33). "I didn't know him," John later confessed, perhaps distressed that he had not realized that his own cousin was the One. But as Jesus came up from the Jordan's waters, John saw the Spirit descending as a dove. He heard a voice from heaven announce, "This is My beloved Son, in whom I am well pleased" (Matt. 3:17). And John bore witness to what he had seen. "I have seen and testified that this is the Son of God" (John 1:34).

Then the truly unexpected jolted religious leaders and commoners alike. As Jesus began his public ministry, a new age of miracles came. Within the span of about three years, miracle after miracle was witnessed by thousands. Like Elijah and Elisha, Jesus multiplied resources. But while Elisha had fed a hundred with twenty loaves, Jesus fed thousands on far less! Like the two ancient prophets, Jesus raised a child who had just died. But then Jesus raised Lazarus, an adult who had been in the grave for three days!

Unlike any prophet in sacred history, Jesus even healed the sick. He restored withered limbs, gave sight to men born blind, and even expelled demons. The miracles of Jesus surpassed the miracles of the prophets of old. Even those most hostile to Christ and his message were forced to confess that he actually did work wonders.

MIRACLES MARK JESUS' BIRTH

The mark of miracles, which set Jesus apart, surrounded His birth as well as His public ministry. Both Matthew and Luke record several such wonders. Blending the two accounts, we can identify no less than thirteen miraculous signs associated with Jesus' birth and early years.

Gabriel appeared to Zacharias (Luke 1:11–22). While an aged priest named Zacharias was offering incense in the temple, the angel Gabriel appeared to him and announced that he and his wife would have a son. The son was to be named John, and the angel announced that he would be the forerunner of the promised Messiah. Many things about this incident bear the mark of the miraculous.

He was chosen to offer incense by lot (Luke 1:8). The ordinary priests who ministered in the temple were divided into twenty-four orders, or groups. Each order served for just two weeks a year in Jerusalem. There were so many priests in each order that only once in a man's lifetime might he have the privilege of offering incense at the time of morning or evening prayer. God saw to it that Zacharias was chosen by lot that one special time.

Elizabeth, his wife, was barren (Luke 1:7). The text emphasizes the fact that both Zacharias and his wife were old (Luke 1:7, 18). The implication is that both were too old to have children normally. As in the case of Abraham and Sarah, it took a special work of God to quicken Elizabeth's womb so that John could be born.

The birth would fulfill prophecy (Luke 1:17). The last words of Malachi, the final book of the Old Testament, predicted the coming of an "Elijah" who would turn the hearts of God's people to the Lord, in preparation for the coming of the Messiah. The angel announced that John, the child to be born to Zacharias and Elizabeth, would fulfill this promise-prediction.

Zacharias was struck temporarily dumb (Luke 1:20). Zacharias doubted the angel's promise, and as a consequence he was struck dumb until the child was born and named. When he

left the temple, observers realized that he had seen a vision which had literally left him speechless.

Gabriel appeared to Mary (Luke 1:26–38). Six months after Elizabeth conceived, Gabriel appeared to Mary. At the time Mary was probably a teenager, since in New Testament times most Jewish girls were married between ages 13 and 15.

The angel announced that Mary had been chosen by God to bear a son who would be the "son of the Highest" and the "Son of God." Mary was also told that her son would be the Messiah [the son of David] and that "of His kingdom there will be no end."

When Mary asked how this was possible, since she had never had sex with a man, Gabriel told her that God the Holy Spirit would overshadow her. The "father" of her son would be God Himself.

Unlike Zacharias, Mary expressed no doubt at this amazing announcement, but instead expressed her submission to God's will

"Do not be afraid, Mary."

(Luke 1:38). The touching faith of this Jewish teen-ager in response to the announcement of history's greatest miracle stands as an example for us today. As a woman of great and wonderful faith, Mary merits our appreciation and deepest respect.

Mary is "with child" by the Holy Spirit (Matthew 1:18). The announcement to Mary that she would become pregnant even though a virgin came true. Matthew looks back to the Old Testament prophet Isaiah and notes that God had promised that His Messiah would be virgin born. While some have noted that the Hebrew word *almah,* found in Isaiah 7:14, can be translated a "young unmarried woman," Matthew in translating the ancient prophecy into Greek uses the word *parthenos,* which can only mean a virgin. The "young unmarried woman" of the prophecy was always intended to be understood as an unmarried woman who was a virgin.

There can be no doubt that the virgin birth is one of the premier miracles of Scripture. If it were possible to create a viable fetus using only a woman's egg, that child would be a daughter, never a son. Only a male can provide the chromosome that, along with the woman's, makes possible the birth of a son. That chromosome, with the others that formed the theanthropic person Jesus (fully God as well as truly human), was provided by the Holy Spirit.

The virgin birth, predicted in the Old Testament and described in the New, marks Jesus as utterly unique. Like His miracles, as we will see, this beginning set Him apart from sacred history's prophets and clearly identified Him to Israel both as Messiah and as Son of God.

An angel appears to Joseph in a dream (Matthew 1:19–25). The text of Matthew describes Joseph both as "betrothed" to Mary (Matt. 1:18) and as her "husband" (Matt. 1:19). In New Testament times Jewish marriages were contracted in two stages. During the first stage a binding contract was entered into by the bride and groom. This was typically negotiated by the families, and executing it meant that the couple was fully committed to each other. The second stage was the wedding itself, in which the husband took the bride into his own home, to live with him as his wife. The phrase "before they came together" in Matthew 1:18 makes it clear that, while Joseph and Mary were contracted to each other, they were not yet living together.

In this case Joseph learned that Mary was pregnant and naturally assumed that she had been unfaithful to her commitment to him. Her pregnancy was grounds for public divorce and disgrace. Yet Joseph cared for Mary, and while he felt he could not go through with the marriage, he planned to protect her reputation by putting her away "secretly."

Before this could happen an angel came to Joseph in a dream and told him what Gabriel had told Mary. Mary was pregnant by the Holy Spirit. Joseph was to marry her, and when the son was born acknowledge him by naming him—a father's privilege in Israel. The name Joseph was to give Mary's child was Jesus, the Greek spelling of the Hebrew name Joshua, which in each language meant "Savior." This Jesus would "save His people from their sins."

The child in Elizabeth's womb recognized Mary (Luke 1:41). Mary was herself pregnant when she went to visit her relative Elizabeth, who was carrying the child who would grow up to become John the Baptist. When Mary greeted Elizabeth, the child in Elizabeth's womb leaped in recognition.

Elizabeth was filled with the Spirit and blessed Mary (Luke 1:41–44). Elizabeth, without hearing the story of Gabriel's appearance to Mary, blessed Mary and acknowledged her as "the mother of my Lord." This wonder must have comforted and encouraged Mary. She was not alone in understanding what God had done within her.

Zacharias predicts John's ministry (Luke 1:59–80). When Elizabeth's child was born, Zacharias spoke and confirmed that he was to be named John. The loosening of Zacharias' tongue was viewed as a miracle by onlookers. More significantly, Zacharias was then filled with the Spirit and prophesied concerning John's ministry. John was destined to "go before the face of the Lord" as one preparing the way for the Messiah.

Caesar called for a census that brought Mary and Joseph to Bethlehem (Luke 2:1–7; Matthew 2:6). On its surface, the Roman call for a census hardly seems to qualify as a miracle or wonder. The Emperor Augustus had instituted a policy of having citizens throughout the empire return to their home town to be counted, as a basis for assessing taxes. First century census documents from Egypt show that this policy was followed in lands besides Palestine and Syria.

Yet this census decree was instrumental in the fulfillment of a prophecy made by Micah some 700 years before Jesus' birth. The decree brought Joseph and Mary to Bethlehem just in time for the Christ-child to be born in the home town of King David! When events fall together in such a way that prophecy is fulfilled, we surely can call them miracles of Providence. God, behind the scenes, is ordering and timing what happens to fulfill His own purposes and plan.

Angels announced Jesus' birth to shepherds (Luke 2:8–20). The night Jesus was born angels announced His birth to shepherds in the fields near Jerusalem. The wonderful news was that "there is born to you this day in the city of David a Savior, who is Christ the Lord" (Luke 1:11).

This familiar part of the Christmas story is far more significant than we normally imagine. Today Christians tend to romanticize shepherds, seeing them as selfless individuals who are symbols of God's own care for His human flock. We do not realize that in the first century shepherds were viewed with suspicion and contempt. They were generally considered to be thieves, and in fact were not even allowed to testify in Jewish courts because their testimony could not be trusted! How appropri-

ate then that the angel appeared to shepherds, first century "sinners," with the good news that a Savior was born that very night.

What wonderful news that was, for them and for us, for like the shepherds we too need a Savior desperately.

Simeon identified baby Jesus as the Christ (Luke 2:21–35). Jewish ritual law called for the offering of a sacrifice by the mother after bearing a child. When Mary and Joseph traveled to the Jerusalem temple to offer the sacrifice, they were approached by an aged man named Simeon. God had told Simeon that he would not die until he had seen the Christ, the promised Messiah. Simeon was led to the temple by the Holy Spirit, who identified the infant Jesus as the Savior. Simeon held Jesus, and praised God for permitting him to see the one who would save God's people.

Anna the prophetess acknowledged Jesus as the Messiah (Luke 2:36–38). Anna joined Simeon in identifying Jesus as the promised redeemer.

A star brought wise men from the East to Judea to find Jesus (Matthew 2:1–12). When the wise men appeared in Jerusalem Jesus was probably about two years old (cf. Matt. 2:7, 16). Their familiar story is filled with wonders.

The wonder of the star (Matt. 2:2, 7). People today debate the nature of the star the wise men saw. Was it a super-nova, which appeared suddenly in the night sky? Was there a juxtaposition of planets, which gave the appearance of a bright and unexpected star in the heavens? Or was it simply a miracle-star, a bright new light shining above? We have no clear answer as to the nature of the star. But clearly there was an unusual light in the heavens, which the wise men not only recognized but which appeared to move and which in the end led them to the very home where Jesus lived (Matt. 2:9).

The wonder of the star's identification (Matt. 2:2). When the wise men entered Jerusalem they asked for the newborn king of the Jews, and stated that they had seen "his star" and had come to honor him. People have wondered what led the wise men to identify the new light in the sky with a Jewish ruler?

We know that Magi—the word rendered "wise men" in our English versions—were a special class of persons in the Persian Empire noted for their encyclopedic knowledge. We also know that a major center of Jewish learning existed from the sixth through first centuries in Babylon, where some of the Magi lived and worked. Most commentators suggest that the Magi of Matthew's Gospel linked the new star with a rather obscure prediction in Numbers 24:17, which reads "A Star shall come out of Jacob; a Scepter shall rise out of Israel."

While this theory is possible, we simply do not know how the Magi recognized the star as a symbol of the birth of the Messiah, the descendant of David, destined to rule Israel and the world. The appearance of the Magi is one of the wonders associated with the story of Jesus' birth and childhood.

Matthew makes it clear that they did come. They worshiped Jesus and gave him expensive gifts. And then, warned in a dream, they went home without telling Herod where Jesus could be found.

Joseph was warned in a dream to flee to Egypt (Matt. 2:13–15). This wonder too is associated with Jesus' birth and earliest years. King Herod the Great, noted for his fierce attacks on any who seemed to threaten his throne, determined to kill this "king of the Jews" the Magi had spoken of.

The dream warning is not the only wonder associated with the flight to Egypt. In addition there is the prophecy the flight fulfilled (Matt. 2:15), and God's provision for the journey.

Luke 2:24 tells us that when Mary came to the temple to offer the required sacrifice after childbirth, she offered "a pair of turtledoves or two young pigeons." According to Old Testament law, the normal offering was a lamb (Levitcus 12:6–8). Only if the family was too poor to afford a lamb could the woman offer a pair of birds. Joseph and Mary, then, were poor people. Yet it would be expensive to travel to Egypt and live there for any length of time.

Wise men from the east brought gifts to the young Jesus.

The answer, of course, is the gifts given Jesus by the Magi. Each of their expensive gifts could be, and undoubtedly were, sold and the proceeds used to finance the flight to Egypt that saved the Christ child from Herod's executioners. In this we clearly have yet another wonder of divine providence—striking evidence that God was personally involved in the birth and early life of our Lord.

Jesus was indeed marked by miracles, and His birth and early life were accompanied by wonders that set Him apart from all.

The underlying wonder of the Logos (John 1). We cannot understand Jesus if we simply treat the events surrounding His birth. The reason for this is simple. While conception and birth mark the beginning of existence for normal human beings, neither conception nor birth were a beginning for the Son of God.

John in his Gospel launches the story of Jesus where his story truly begins. In the first verses of the Gospel of John, Christ is called the "Word," our English rendering of the Greek word *logos*. That Greek term might also be rendered as the "expression" or "revelation." John takes us back into eternity, and asserts that in the beginning there was God. And that the Word was with God, and in fact was God. In fact the Word, the eternal expression of God, was the Creator of all, and the source of life and light. It was the Word, the One who has always expressed and revealed God, who came into our world as a human being. It was the Word, the One we know as the Son of God, the second Person of the Trinity, who bonded with humanity in Mary's womb, and who was born as a baby, grew into manhood, and began a miracle ministry in which He expressed God's compassion and love for humankind.

Ultimately it was the Word, the eternal Son of God, who in Jesus Christ found expression in the grand miracle of the Incarnation, who died on Calvary as a sacrifice for our sins, and who was raised again in the grand miracle of resurrection.

It is no wonder that Jesus' birth and early life were marked by miracles, for He Himself is the greatest miracle of all: God, come in the flesh; God, come to save us; God, calling us to find forgiveness and eternal life in Him.

THE MIRACLES OF JESUS FORCE US TO SAY YES OR NO TO HIM

Studies of Jesus' miracles often descend into debate about the credibility of individual wonders. The skeptic argues that the miracles weren't all that special. The sick were about to recover anyhow. The illnesses were psychosomatic—and moderns know how suggestion can bring about amazing cures in such cases. Jesus only seemed to be walking on water; really he was on the shore and the disciples were far enough away so that he *appeared* to walk on the surface of the sea. And besides, the critics claim, the miracle stories were written years later by disciples who were intent on making Jesus into someone he had never been—a deity rather than a Jewish rabbi whose teachings were within the traditions of Judaism.

Even believers sometimes argue the case for Jesus' miracles on the skeptic's grounds. The sicknesses described were serious. But no matter how responsive the victim was to suggestion, they reason, no cure of this malady could have been effected by such means. Many modern "faith healers" have been exposed as frauds because they pre-selected those they permitted on the stage and did not permit follow-up studies of their supposed "healings." Jesus' healings were different. The Gospel accounts were written so close to these miracle events that there were living witnesses who could have contradicted any lies or exaggerations. And so the debate rages on.

This kind of argument confuses the real issue. Miracle accounts are intrinsic to the message of the Gospels, growing out of the theology of the Old Testament. This theology affirms the existence of a Creator who lives and acts in the world he made on behalf of the people whom he has chosen. The miracles are consistent with the nature of the God of the Bible. A. Richardson states this position strongly:

The history which the Evangelists write is their good news, their gospel. They believed that in Jesus of Nazareth God had spoken his saving Word to the world. If we accept their gospel, we accept the history which they record, and we do not find it difficult to believe with them that the *form* of the revelation which God made in Christ included the working of the "signs" which proclaimed to opened eyes the fulfillment of the age-long hope of the prophets of Israel, the promise that God would visit and redeem his people. If we reject that gospel, we shall inevitably reject the view that Jesus performed miracles, or we shall seek to explain them away by means of the hypothesis of "faith healing" or other modern theories equally removed from the standpoint of the biblical theology. The truth is that, as we have all along maintained, the miracle-stories are a part of the gospel itself; Christ is to the New Testament writers the manifestation of the power of God in the world, and his mighty deeds are the signs of the effectual working of that power. But in this age the power of God is veiled; revelation is by the gift of faith. It is possible for us to fail to see Christ as the manifestation of the power and the purpose of God; then we shall be content with an explanation of the miracle-stories in terms of modern psychology or folk-mythology. The miracle-stories, as an essential part of the preaching of apostolic Christianity, confront us with the question whether the power of God was or was not revealed in the person and work of Jesus Christ. They compel us to say Yes or No (p. 126).

THE AUTHENTICATING FUNCTION OF MIRACLE CLUSTERS

As we examine each of the recorded miracles of Jesus, we will see that each had wonderful messages for those who observed it as well as for us today. But it would be a mistake to look at each miracle as an isolated event without considering the significance of the whole. In fact, the one unmistakable impression we gain from reading the Gospels is not that Jesus performed a miracle here and there, but that Jesus' whole ministry was marked by a concentrated cluster of miracles. And it is the significance of the several concentrated clusters of miracles recorded in Scripture that we must consider first.

The Exodus miracles. The first of these concentrated clusters occurred at the time of the Exodus. These miracles authenticated Moses as God's spokesman, essential because Moses was commissioned to introduce a new stage in God's eternal plan. Israel was to be formed into a nation. God's chosen people were to be governed by a Law revealed to Moses at Mount Sinai.

It was vital that Moses be firmly established as God's spokesman so the revelation he mediated would be accepted by all. This was accomplished by the ten proving acts—the ten plagues on Egypt.

Note that these ten establishing miracles were followed by a series of supportive miracles. These were performed on the journey to Sinai, and they continued on the journey to Caanan. The establishing miracles, acknowledged by Israel, were followed by supportive miracles which showed the Lord's presence with his people.

The miracles of Elijah/Elisha. The next cluster of miracles took place in the eighth century B.C. King Ahab had launched an intense campaign to make Baal worship the official religion of Israel. God's revelation was under attack.

At this critical stage in Israel's history, Elijah's miracles—especially the miracle at Mount Carmel—authenticated Elijah as God's spokesman and re-established the fact that "the Lord, He is God" (1 Kings 18:39). The earlier revelation given through Moses was reaffirmed, and the wavering population was called back to God.

The miracles performed by Elisha were supportive miracles. Like the miracles on the journey to Canaan, Elisha's miracles demonstrated the continuing presence of God with the people who would acknowledge him and his word.

The miracles of Jesus. The third concentrated cluster of biblical miracles occurred during Jesus' public ministry, which spanned only three years. Jesus, like Moses, was the mediator of a new revelation, which unveiled more elements of God's eternal plan. The miracles of Jesus also established him as God's spokesman, whose words were to be heard and whose teachings were to be accepted. His establishing miracles had to be significant; they authenticated a messenger whose revelation supplanted and superseded the Law given by Moses.

It was also essential that Jesus' establishing miracles authenticating the new revelation be followed by supporting miracles. These were necessary to demonstrate the presence of God with those who accepted the new revelation.

Just as the miracles of the journey served as supporting miracles for the establishing miracles of the ten plagues on Egypt; just as the miracles of Elisha served as supporting miracles for the establishing miracles of Elijah—so the miracles of the apostles recorded in the book of Acts served as supportive miracles for the establishing miracles of Jesus. The miracles of Acts demonstrated the presence of God with those who accepted Jesus and the revelation which came through him.

Miracle Clusters as Authenticating Acts

The Exodus Cluster
Establishing Miracles: The Ten Plagues
Moses is God's spokesman.
The revelation given by Moses is God's Word.
Supporting Miracles: The Journey Miracles
God is present with those who receive his revelation.

The Elijah/Elisha Cluster
Establishing Miracles: The Miracles of Elijah
Elijah is God's spokesman.
The revelation given by Moses is God's Word.
Supporting Miracles: The Miracles of Elisha
God is present with those who honor his revelation.

The Jesus Cluster
Establishing Miracles: The Miracles of Jesus
Jesus is God's spokesman.
The revelation given by Jesus is God's Word.
Supporting Miracles: The Apostles' Miracles
God is present with those who receive Jesus and his revelation.

MIRACLE CLUSTERS AND GOD'S SELF-REVELATION

The miracle clusters in Scripture vouch for God's messenger, authenticating the revelation they mediate. But there is another important function of the miracle clusters in Scripture. This function is seen clearly when we separate the miracles of Jesus and the apostles, and include a cluster of miracles which is the subject of unfulfilled prophecy.

The Exodus miracles. The Exodus miracles established Moses as God's spokesman. But they had an even more significant function. This function was stated by the Lord in Exodus, when he explained the purpose of the devastating plagues he brought on Egypt. On the one hand, the plagues were a judgment on Egypt's gods (Ex. 12:12). More importantly, the miracles were performed so the Egyptians might know that Yahweh is God (Ex. 7:5) and so Israel might realize that "I am the Lord your God, who brings you out from under the burdens of the Egyptians" (Ex. 6:7).

Israel had known God as the God of Abraham, Isaac, and Jacob. But the revelation of his personal name, Yahweh, "I AM," was given through Moses at this critical point in sacred history [see pages 176–178]. The Exodus miracles, both establishment and support, affirmed a central truth of Scripture: The Lord is God.

The Elijah/Elisha miracles. When the Elijah-Elisha miracles took place, the people of the Northern Kingdom, Israel, were wavering between Yahweh and Baal. Who was the real God? Whose ways should the Israelites follow?

Elijah the prophet was thrust into this gap. On Mount Carmel he performed a miracle which convinced Israel that "the Lord, he is God" (1 Kings 18:39). The establishing miracles of Elijah and the supporting miracles of Elisha served as a reaffirmation of the truth that the Lord truly is God and is present with his people.

The miracles of Jesus. The third cluster of miracles was concentrated in the three years that Jesus taught and healed in Judea and

Galilee. These miracles established Jesus as God's spokesman and authenticated his message. At the core of Christ's message was the stunning affirmation, "I and My Father are One" (John 10:30). Jesus had spelled out the meaning of this statement in a controversy with some Pharisees.

After being ridiculed for his claim of having seen Abraham, Jesus responded, "Most assuredly, I say to you, before Abraham was, I AM" (John 8:58).

Christ's listeners understood this claim, and they tried to stone him for blasphemy. Jesus was identifying himself with the Yahweh of the Old Testament! Christ was claiming to be God!

The apostolic miracles. If we treat Christ's miracles and the apostolic miracles as separate clusters, we make a fascinating discovery. The message of the apostles was that Jesus Christ is Lord (cf. Acts 2:36). Their miracles were performed in the name of Jesus Christ (cf. Acts 3:6; 16:18). The doctrine that Jesus Christ is Lord was supported by the miracles performed in his name—miracles which proved his continuing presence with his followers.

The end-time miracles. Old and New Testament writers foresaw a concentrated cluster of judgment miracles destined to take place at the end of history. Many of these awesome judgment miracles, which far overshadow the plagues on Egypt, are described in the book of Revelation. Second Thessalonians sums up the impact of this period of righteous retribution. It will be a time when "the Lord Jesus is revealed from heaven with his mighty angels, in flaming fire taking vengeance on those who do not know God, and on those who do not obey the gospel of our Lord Jesus Christ" (2 Thess. 1:7–9).

The self-revelatory aspect of miracle clusters. If we look at these miracle clusters as self-revealing acts of God, we find a fascinating pattern, shown in the chart above. Each cluster of miracles makes a decisive statement about who the God of Scripture is. These statements can be expressed in the form of a chiasm (see page 134).

Miracle Clusters and God's Self-revelation

A.	The Exodus Miracles:	The Lord is God.
	B. Elijah/Elisha Miracles:	The Lord is God.
	C. Jesus' Miracles:	Jesus is God.
	B. Apostolic Miracles:	Jesus is Lord.
A.	End-time Miracles:	Jesus is Lord.

In this arrangement, the central self-revelation is that of Jesus Christ as God. The other self-revelations support the central affirmation.

The first "A" miracle cluster introduces Yahweh to humankind as God. The second "A" miracle cluster forces all humankind to acknowledge Jesus as Lord and God. Each of the "A" miracles—the ten plagues and the end-time plagues—are miracles of judgment.

The first "B" miracle cluster resolves doubts by offering evidence that Yahweh truly is God, while the second "B" miracle cluster settles doubts by offering evidence that Jesus is Lord. The "B" miracles are miracles of provision.

The central "C" miracle cluster affirms the truth that the God of the Scriptures is Jesus—and that Jesus is the God of the Scriptures.

Viewed in these ways, as both authenticating and as self-revelatory acts, the miracle clusters of Scripture make important theological statements about the Bible's teaching about God. We cannot treat miracles apart from this theology. If we are to be biblical in our approach to the miracles of Scripture, we must accept them as they are described. If we are asked whether these miracles actually took place, we must answer a confident "Yes."

The miracles of the Bible are so tightly linked to what Scripture teaches about God that the only way to reject the miracles of the Bible is to reject the God of the Bible.

JEWISH RELIGIOUS LEADERS' RESPONSE TO JESUS' MIRACLES

The leaders' hostility. As we look at the Gospel accounts of Jesus' miracles, we are struck by the fact that the leaders of the Jews remained hostile to Christ in spite of his miracles. How could they be so blind? Were the miracles of Jesus nothing but rumors that an enlightened religious establishment could easily ignore? The answer to that question is evident throughout the Gospels. Christ's opponents could not and did not dispute that he performed miracles (John 3:2; 9:15–16). How then did they justify their rejection of Jesus as God's spokesman and his message as God's Word?

The leaders' strategy (Matthew 12:22–24). One day Jesus healed a man who was demon-possessed, blind, and mute. The healing was spectacular. Christ healed him "so that the blind and mute man both spoke and saw" (v. 22).

Many of the onlookers drew a logical conclusion from this event. The religious significance of this miracle might be that Jesus was the "Son of David," the promised Messiah!

But the Pharisees and other religious leaders responded by making this accusation: "This fellow does not cast out demons except by Beelzebub, the ruler of the demons" (Matt. 12:24). We see the logic of the strategy when we remember our working definition of a miracle. A miracle is an extraordinary event caused by God with religious purpose or significance.

An extraordinary event. The healing of this demon-possessed man was certainly extraordinary. Not one witness, whether leader or commoner, could challenge the fact of the miracle.

Pharisees and other Jewish leaders were hostile to Jesus and His ministry.

There were too many witnesses, undoubtedly including some leaders.

Caused by God. The people who witnessed this miracle naturally assumed that God was the source of Jesus' power. Who else but God could perform such miracles? Even the religious leaders had not challenged this assumption at first. When Nicodemus, a member of the ruling Jewish council, came to Jesus earlier, he confessed, "We know that You are a teacher come from God, for no one can do these signs that You do unless God is with him" (John 3:2). The "we" undoubtedly included Nicodemus' fellow leaders.

With religious significance. Nicodemus had spoken of Jesus' miracles as "signs." In the Old and New Testaments, this word indicates a miracle which authenticates the person who performed it as God's spokesman. The miracles were God's stamp of approval on Jesus and his message. God's people were bound by Scripture to listen and respond to such a person (compare Deut. 18:19).

From what Jesus taught and did, it was logical for the Jews to conclude that he was who he claimed to be—the promised Son of David, the Messiah, as well as the Son of God.

The leaders' problem and its solution. The leaders couldn't attack Jesus' miracles on the grounds that no miracles had taken place. Everyone agreed that Jesus performed miracles. The leaders could not attack the conviction that Jesus' miracles had religious significance. Such miracles required that the Jew who spoke in the name of the Lord must be heard (Deut. 18:19).

But the leaders could attack the assumption that the miracles of Jesus were caused by God! And this they did attack—both directly and through a campaign of rumors. They had to admit that Jesus performed miracles, but they charged the source of his miracles was Satan, not God!

If this notion were accepted, the religious implications were reversed. Rather than listen to Jesus, it would be the duty of the Jewish people to reject him and his teachings.

In the confrontation reported in Matthew 12, Jesus refuted this accusation. If Satan were casting out Satan, Jesus reasoned, he was fighting himself. No kingdom wracked by civil war—war against itself—could possibly stand. And besides, if Jesus were casting out demons by Satan's power, was it possible that Jewish exorcists were drawing on the demonic when *they* cast out demons?

The fact that the demons were subject to Jesus showed that even Satan was powerless before him. In reality, the miracles of Jesus demonstrated that God's kingdom was once again breaking into the world, as God's power was exercised for all to see.

The leaders did not hesitate. They had not launched their attack on Jesus' miracles to convince others, but to raise doubts and to give themselves an excuse for their hatred of the Lord. If Jesus were God, they would have to bow to him and surrender their privileged position as interpreters of God's will. And this they would not do.

As for the people, they hesitated too long. They were ready to exalt Jesus as a prophet as great as any Old Testament figure other than Moses. But they would not acknowledge Jesus as the Savior sent from God or entertain the possibility that he might be who he claimed.

And so the miracles of Jesus led not to acclamation but to a cross and a barren tomb. But that tomb witnessed the greatest miracle of all: the resurrection. This event proved without a doubt that Jesus was the Son of God with power (Rom. 1:4).

And since that moment the world has never been the same.

THE SOURCES WHICH REPORT JESUS' MIRACLES

How the Gospels differ from one another. The miracles of Jesus are reported in the four Gospels. Each of the Gospels draws a word portrait of Jesus, designed to present him to a different audience. The Gospel of Matthew was written for the Jews. It sought to prove that Jesus was indeed the Messiah prophesied in the Old Testament. The Gospel of Mark was written for the Romans, portraying Jesus as God's agent who carried out the Father's will. The Gospel of Luke was written for the Hellenistic [Greek] mind. It portrays Jesus as the fulfillment of the Greek ideal of excellence—as the perfect man. The Gospel of John was written to demonstrate to all that Jesus undoubtedly was the living Son of God.

Implications of the Gospel differences. Each of these authors arranged his material to fit his audience and theme. Each selected from among Jesus' miracles those which best advanced his Gospel's argument. Each shaped the emphasis of the miracle story to contribute to reaching his goal. Thus the sequence in which various miracle stories were recounted, as well as details emphasized by the Gospel writers, are sometimes different. When details differ, it doesn't mean the accounts *conflict*, but that the authors emphasized elements of the events that best suited his purpose.

This means that we need to be aware of how the same miracle story may be used in different Gospels to make different points. A sequence of miraculous events may be ordered differently to emphasize a particular author's point.

The Gospel writers selected from a range of miracles that Jesus performed. Some miracles are reported in all the Gospels, while others occur in only one. Such a selection process was natural, considering the different emphasis of each Gospel writer. This means a miracle reported in a single Gospel is no less true or important than a miracle reported in all four.

The miracles of Jesus. It is somewhat deceptive to speak of the miracles of Jesus. The biblical text often refers to miracles which are not described in any Gospel. These references make it clear that Jesus performed many more miracles than the 35 which the Gospels treat in some detail. Healing miracles in particular were performed by Jesus throughout his ministry, even during his last week in Jerusalem.

❖

GENERAL REFERENCES TO JESUS' MIRACLES IN THE GOSPELS

The following general references to miracles in Matthew alone make it clear that Christ performed many more miracles than are described in the Gospels.

Jesus went about all Galilee, teaching in their synagogues, preaching the gospel of the kingdom, and healing all kinds of sickness and all kinds of disease among the people. Then his fame went throughout all Syria; and they brought to him all sick people who were afflicted with various diseases and torments, and those who were demon-possessed, epileptics, and paralytics; and he healed them (Matt. 4:23, 24).

When evening had come, they brought to him many who were demon-possessed, and he cast out the spirits with a word, and healed all who were sick (Matt. 8:16).

Then Jesus went about all the cities and villages . . . healing every sickness and every disease among the people (Matt. 9:35).

Great multitudes followed him, and he healed them all (Matt. 12:15).

When Jesus went out he saw a great multitude; and he was moved with compassion for them, and healed their sick (Matt. 14:14).

They sent out into all that surrounding region, brought to him all who were sick, and begged him that they might only touch the hem of his garment. And as many as touched it were made perfectly well (Matt. 14:35).

And great multitudes followed him, and he healed them there (Matt. 19:2).

Then the blind and the lame came to him in the temple, and he healed them (Matt. 21:14).

Similar lists can be constructed from each of the other Gospels. In Mark: Mark 1:32–34, 39; 3:10,11; 6:2, 5; 6:55, 56. In Luke: Luke 4:40, 41; 6:17–19; 7:21, 22; 8:2; 9:11. In John: John 2:23; 6:2.

❖

Jesus' Miracles in the Gospels

Ch	Matthew	Mark	Luke	John
1		Catch of fish Synagogue demoniac Peter's mother-in-law Leper cleansed		
2		Paralytic healed		Water to wine
3		Withered hand		
4	Catch of fish	Stilling the storm	Synagogue demoniac Peter's mother-in-law	Nobleman's son
5		Demoniac of Gadara Woman healed Jairus' daughter	Catch of fish Leper cleansed Paralytic healed	
6		Feeding 5,000 Walking on water	Withered hand	Feeding 5,000 Walking on water
7		Syro-Phonecian woman's daughter Deaf/dumb man		Centurion's servant
8	Peter's mother-in-law Leper cleansed Centurion's servant Stilling the storm Demoniac of Gadara	Feeding 4,000 Blind man	Widow's son Stilling the storm Demoniac of Gadara Woman healed Jairus' daughter	
9	Paralytic healed Woman healed Jairus' daughter Two blind men healed Dumb demoniac healed	Demonized boy	Feeding 5,000 Demonized boy	Man born blind
10		Blind Bartimaeus		
11		Fig tree cursed		Raising Lazarus
12	Withered hand			
13			Infirm woman	
14	Feeding 5,000 Walking on water	Malchus's ear	Man with dropsy	
15	Syro-Phonecian woman's daughter Feeding 4,000			
16		END OF BOOK		
17	Demonized boy Coin in fish		Ten lepers	
18			Blind Bartimaeus	Malchus's ear
19				
20	Blind Bartimaeus			
21	Fig tree cursed			Catch of fish END OF BOOK
22			Malchus's ear	
23				
24			END OF BOOK	
25				
26	Malchus's ear			
27				
28	END OF BOOK			

The 35 described miracles. The Gospels describe in detail only 35 of Jesus' many miracles. The Gospel writers wove these miracles into their accounts in the order and with the details that best contributed to the distinct theme and purpose of their respective books.

The chart on page 163 lists the 35 described miracles of Jesus as they appear, chapter by chapter, in each Gospel. We can see quickly these important facts:

- No Gospel writer included all 35.
- Some miracles are included in all four Gospels and some in only one.
- The miracle accounts may occur in different order in different Gospels.
- In the Synoptics [Matthew, Mark, Luke], the writers tended to cluster miracles to establish something important about Jesus.

The framework of Jesus' miracles. Before we go on to look in detail at the miracles of Jesus, it's important to note that the entire ministry of Jesus was encompassed within a miracle framework. Matthew and Luke began with accounts of Jesus' virgin birth, and John began with an affirmation of Jesus' pre-existence. The grand miracle of Incarnation [page 8–14] set the stage for the signs and wonders Jesus' performed. Looking ahead, the miracles of Jesus were to be expected, for Jesus was God come among us in human flesh.

As Jesus' miracle-working days drew to a close, the grand miracle of Resurrection [page 15–17] marked their end as a new beginning. Again, looking back, the miracles of Jesus were to be expected, for in the resurrection Jesus was declared to be the Son of God with power (Rom. 1:4).

Viewed from either direction, looking ahead from the viewpoint of the Incarnation or looking back from the viewpoint of Resurrection, Jesus' miracles were in one sense not extraordinary at all, for the mighty works of Jesus were performed by history's most extraordinary personality.

Most of Jesus' ministry focused on individuals with special needs.

THE MIRACLES OF JESUS CHRIST

We are now ready to look at the 35 recorded miracles of Jesus. The order we will follow is the actual historical order—as best we can tell—in which these miracles took place, although they may be sequenced differently in the different Gospels.

1. Jesus turns water to wine.—p. 165
2. Jesus heals a nobleman's son.—p. 169
3. Jesus provides a great catch of fish.—p. 176
4. Jesus heals a demoniac in a synagogue—p. 171
5. Jesus heals Peter's wife's mother.—p. 174
6. Jesus cleanses a leper.—p. 181
7. Jesus heals a paralytic.—p. 183
8. Jesus heals a cripple at Bethesda.—p. 186
9. Jesus heals a withered hand.—p. 190
10. Jesus heals a centurion's servant.—p. 191
11. Jesus raises a widow's son.—p. 194
12. Jesus stills a storm.—p. 196
13. Jesus delivers a demoniac in Gedara.—p. 198

JESUS TURNS WATER TO WINE *John 2:1–11*

Jesus went to a wedding in Cana. When the supply of wine ran out, he turned more than 100 gallons of water into wine.

Weddings in New Testament times (John 2:1). Jewish marriages were two-stage affairs. Betrothal involved the signing of a binding agreement between two families. A couple who had been betrothed to each other was considered husband and wife. The actual union took place a year later, when the groom went to the home of the bride with his friends and brought her to their new home. Festivities might continue for a week, with the bride and groom treated as queen and king.

Jesus attended one such wedding in Cana of Galilee, a small town about four miles from Nazareth. His mother Mary was there, and we can assume that friends and relatives from all around gathered to rejoice with the newlyweds. The wedding was the site of Jesus' first recorded miracle.

Jesus and his disciples (John 2:2). Just three days before this wedding event, Jesus had been baptized by John and identified by the Holy Spirit as the Son of God (John 1:33–34). Four of the men who later became his disciples stayed with Jesus—Andrew, Peter, Philip, and Nathaniel. Quite possibly John was at the wedding too, although his name is not mentioned. Jesus and these disciples may have been passing through Cana on the way to Nazareth when all "were invited to the wedding."

Most commentators tend to see the wedding as a significant setting for Jesus' first miracle (John 2:11). They also see Christ's presence as blessing and confirming the institution of marriage. But Christ's presence at this event may have been more prophetic.

Weddings were joyous occasions. For perhaps the only time in what was a difficult life, the bride and groom were treated as queen and king. Married life in first-century Palestine began with joy, but for most couples it was marked by toil as the couple struggled just to survive.

What is fascinating is that Jesus' earthly ministry began with a wedding—and human history will end with a wedding. At history's end God's people will celebrate what Revelation 19:9 calls the "marriage supper of the Lamb." For Jesus, many trials lay between the beginning of his ministry at that wedding in Cana and the fulfillment of his ministry at the marriage supper of the Lamb.

Trials are also a reality for us between our discovery of Christ and the fulfillment of faith's promise. But for Jesus and for us, the beginning and the end are set aside for joy!

The hosts ran out of wine (John 2:3a). Wedding feasts often lasted a week. The hospitality shown to Jesus and his friends helps explain a possible reason for the shortage of wine. More people than were expected joined the festivities.

The shortage happened in spite of the fact that wine was generally diluted with water. Most rabbinic prescriptions called for three parts of water to one part wine; others called for seven parts water to one part wine. Wine in the Old Testament was viewed somewhat ambivalently. In its undiluted form wine was a "strong drink," and was condemned as a source of drunkenness (Prov. 20; 21:17; 23:20) and associated sins (Amos 2:8, 12; 5:11; 6:6). Yet wine was also a symbol of joy and feasting (Amos 9:13–14). Wine was given as gifts (1 Sam. 25:18; 2 Sam. 16:1), and was included among offerings made to the Lord (Ex. 29:40; Lev. 23:13; Num. 15:7).

To argue that Jesus would neither drink nor create a fermented beverage not only fails to fit the Scriptures; it is unnecessary to establish Scripture's position that drunkenness is a foolish sin.

The exhaustion of the supply of wine at the wedding in no way suggests the guests had drunk to excess.

Mary appealed to her son Jesus (John 2:3b–5). The exchange between Mary and her son Jesus is puzzling. Questions that have been raised include:

Why did Mary tell Jesus "they have no wine"? (John 2:3b). The implication is that Mary expected Jesus to do something about the shortage. But what did she expect? For some thirty years Jesus had lived a rather ordinary life in Nazareth. There was no reason for Mary to look to him for a miracle.

One possibility is that she hoped Jesus would contribute toward the purchase of additional wine. It was not unusual for guests to do so. Another possibility is suggested by the practice of mentioning a guest's name as a round of wine was poured. Mary may have been upset that the hosts ran out before Jesus could be honored.

Why did Jesus respond to Mary as he did? (John 2:4). Several things are puzzling about this verse. The NKJV reads, "Jesus said to her, 'Woman, what does your concern have to do with Me? My hour has not yet come.' "

1. "Woman," a polite form of address, was in no way harsh (compare John 19:26). Yet it was not the way grown sons generally addressed their mothers in the first century. It shows a distinct distancing of Jesus from his mother. Jesus was about to set out on the mission for which he came. One phase of his life on earth ended at his baptism—when the Spirit identified him as the Son of God—and another phase began. From now on his "family" would be composed of those who trust him as the Messiah (compare Matt. 12:48).

2. A literal translation of the Greek phrase is, "What to me and to you?" This was generally a harsh rather than polite phrase in the first century. It may have meant little more than "why involve Me?" Yet it further increases the distance between Mary and Jesus implied in his choice of the term *woman.*

3. The most difficult phrase is the last one Jesus uttered: "My hour has not yet come." If Mary was upset over a possible slight to Jesus by not mentioning his name when a round of wine was mixed and poured, Christ's remark may mean little more than "it isn't my turn [to be so honored] anyway."

However, most interpreters see far more implied. In the New Testament, Jesus' "hour" most often refers to his crucifixion (Matt. 26:45; John 7:30). What Jesus may have been saying was, "Once I act and reveal who I am, my course is fixed, and I have set out for the cross."

Jesus did act. A few minutes later he turned water into wine. This first miracle marked him: it revealed his glory and led his disciples to believe in him. With this miracle, performed to protect his hosts from the embarrassment of running out of wine, Jesus took the first step along a path which would bring healing to many, the agony of the cross for him, and salvation to us.

Why did Mary tell the servants to do whatever Jesus said? (John 2:5). Mary's words recall those of other saints who did not take "No" for an answer to their prayers (compare Gen. 32:26–30; 1 Kings 18:36–37; 2 Kings 4:14–28). Jewish readers would have taken her words as an expression of deep faith and confidence that Jesus would be able to do *something.*

Mary's confidence in Jesus was not misplaced. In spite of the fact that Jesus seemed to rebuke her, we must never lose sight of the fact that Mary was a woman of great faith.

❖

BIBLE BACKGROUND:

SUPPOSED EARLY MIRACLES OF JESUS

After the church was established, a number of pseudo-Gospels were written. Several of these described miracles supposedly performed by Jesus as a boy. Lockyer recounted a few. "When the holy family was threatened by a number of dragons emerging from a cave, Jesus leapt from his mother's lap and dispersed the dragons, saying, `Fear not, for although I am only an infant, it must needs be that all the wild beasts should grow tame in My presence.' Another miracle was that of the Child Jesus shortening a thirty-day journey into one day, and as the family entered Egypt 355 idols in a heathen temple there fell prostrate on the ground. Then there is the weird story about Jesus making twelve sparrows out of mud, clapping his hands and commanding them to fly."

These fables bear no resemblance to the miracles of Jesus recorded in the Gospels. And all are ruled out by the affirmation of John 2:11 that the changing of water into wine was the "beginning of" the miraculous signs which Jesus performed.

❖

Water changed into wine (John 2:6–11). The large stone jars contained water to be used for ceremonial washing of the hands, and perhaps to fill the ritual bath, the *mikva.* Rabbinic law specified the water for this bath had to be "living water"—i.e., running water. However, collected rain water would do in Galilee, which was far less rigid about such matters than Judea. Jesus' choice of these jars was an early indication of Christ's hostility to the constant

addition to God's written law made by the rabbis in New Testament times (see Matt. 15:9).

What occurred next was an unmistakable miracle. There was no way that the miracle Jesus performed could involve trickery. It was servants who followed Jesus' instructions and filled water pots from the larger jars. Servants followed Jesus' instructions and carried the filled pots to the master of the feast, who was responsible for mixing and distributing the wine. Jesus' future disciples stood by and observed all that happened. When the master of the feast pronounced the drink a far better wine than had been served earlier in the week, the servants knew. And the disciples knew. Jesus had turned the water into wine.

There are several things to note about this miracle.

The miracle was of the "old creation." There is a harmony between Jesus' miracle and what happens in nature. It is natural for water to fall from the heavens, to be absorbed by the roots of a grape vine, to be drawn up into the grapes, and then to be pressed out of the ripe grapes as "new wine." What Jesus did was not contrary to this natural process but in harmony with it.

The difference is that Jesus changed the water into wine without the agency of the vine—and that he did so immediately without the time required by the normal transformation.

We so easily take for granted the "natural processes" of this world that we fail to see the hand of God in what are actually wonders. Surely the God who designed nature to produce wine from water by such a complex process as we observe in the grape vine was not tested by producing wine that day in Cana.

The miracle was a sign (2:11). The Greek word used here for "sign" is *semeion,* which occurs 77 times in the New Testament. It is used to identify an act which calls for the exercise of supernatural power. Biblical signs are recognized as supernatural by observers. They au-

Jesus gave instructions for large jars to be filled with water, but what the servants drew from the jars was wine for the wedding.

❖

thenticate the person who performs the sign as someone sent by God.

The miracle was performed without incantations or spells. The people of the biblical world turned to magic to exercise some control over their environment. A "magician" would have made a great show of his attempt to turn water into wine. He would have uttered the names of angels and demons, and called them to do his will. In contrast, Jesus stood by quietly as the servants carried out his instructions, and then simply waited as the master of the feast took a first taste. Jesus' power to perform miracles did not lie in his mastery of magic but within his own person.

The miracle manifested Jesus' glory (2:11). In Scripture, God's "glory" is associated with his self-revelation. And the display of God's glory throughout Scripture is linked closely to God's acts in our universe.

John, in the introduction to his Gospel, wrote that "the Word became flesh and dwelt among us, and we beheld His glory, the glory as of the only begotten of the Father, full of grace and truth" (John 1:14). The miracles of Jesus made it clear that God was again acting in this world. The reality of who Jesus was began to shine through in this very first miracle. With each succeeding wonder, Christ's deity beamed brighter and brighter, until the resurrection set to rest any shadow of doubt. Jesus is God incarnate as a human being.

The miracle developed the disciples' trust in Jesus (2:11). Two disciples had heard John identify Jesus as the Son of God (John 1:34). They found the others and excitedly reported, "We have found the Messiah [the Christ]!" (John 1:41). Another, Nathaniel, had been convinced by speaking to Jesus himself (John 1:47–51). These men *already* believed in Jesus, at least to the extent to which they knew him. What the miracle at Cana did for them was to deepen their existing faith rather than create a non-existent faith.

Personal applications of the miracle at Cana.

Mary, Jesus' mother, seemed certain that Jesus could do something about the failure of the wine supply. She didn't know what he might do, but she appealed to him anyway. Even his strange response did not quench her confidence. Mary surely did not expect the solution that Jesus provided. Christ solved the problem in his own way, by performing the first of a number of miracles recorded in the Gospels.

It's important for us, when we're faced with a situation that seems hopeless, to follow Mary's lead and turn to Jesus. We may not receive an immediate reply; we may even feel put off. But like Mary, we need to have confidence in his ability to come to our aid.

We can never predict what Jesus will do to help us. But we can know that our God is a miracle-working God and that his solution to our problem will be far better than our own. As Christ answers our prayers, he continues to display his glory. And our faith in him continues to grow.

JESUS HEALS A NOBLEMAN'S SON
John 4:46–54

An anxious father traveled twenty miles to beg Jesus to heal his dying son.

The background of the miracle. This miracle, like Jesus' first, also occurred at Cana of Galilee. But time has passed. In the interim, Jesus had performed miracles in Jerusalem during Passover week (John 2:23) which impressed the religious leaders so much that they concluded at first that God must be with him (John 3:2). When Jesus returned home, he was welcomed by his fellow citizens of Galilee. Many had witnessed the miracles He had performed in Jerusalem.

Stories about Jesus had spread rapidly. When "a certain nobleman whose son was sick at Capernaum" heard that Jesus was in Galilee, he immediately went to him (John 4:46, 47).

The parties to the miracle. More people were involved in this miracle than is generally true of Jesus' miracles. The participants or parties to the miracle were Jesus, the anxious father, the dying son, bystanders, and the nobleman's household. Significantly, Jesus' disciples are not mentioned by John. The text says "Jesus came again to . . . Galilee," not when *they* came. Jesus was apparently traveling alone.

Jesus. Jesus had now performed miracles which had set him apart. Tales of his wonders spread rapidly. The Passover was a religious festival which every Jewish man in Judah and Galilee was supposed to attend. Many other Jews came from across Eastern and Western worlds. But at this point in his ministry, the people were unclear just who Jesus was. They knew only that God had worked wonders through him, indicating that he must at least be a prophet.

The nobleman. The word translated "nobleman" means "royal official." The fact that he lived in Capernaum indicates he was an officer in the service of Herod Antipas, tetrarch of Galilee and Perea. Herod was addressed by the courtesy title of "king."

When we meet the royal official, however, we don't see an important man; we see an anxious father. All the externals such as social position meant nothing; all he could think of was the son who appeared to be dying. When he heard that Jesus was in Cana, he didn't hesitate. He set out immediately and in person to beg Christ to heal his son.

The dying son. Twice the text emphasizes the fact that the son was "at the point of death" and dying (John 4:47, 49). A true emergency existed. The fear that drove the father was well-founded.

The bystanders. The reference to bystanders is almost an aside in the text, but it is clear that many people witnessed the exchange between Jesus and the anxious father. We see this in John 4:48. Jesus addressed the crowd and said, "Unless you *people* see signs and wonders, you will by no means believe." The word *people* was supplied by the translators of this text, because the "you" is plural. Jesus was not rebuking the father. He was commenting on the attitude of the crowd. They trailed after Jesus not because they were eager to hear and believe what he might say, but because they wanted to see a miracle!

The nobleman's "whole household." In biblical times, the household of an important man included not only his wife and children and other relatives but also his servants and, in many cases, others who depended on his generosity (known in Rome as "clients").

The servants clearly shared the official's concern for his son. When the child suddenly recovered, several set out from Capernaum to report the wonderful news.

It is significant that as a result of the miracle, "he himself believed, and his whole household (John 4:53). Each person made his or her own choice of faith. Yet they had seen proof of Jesus' power and his compassion. It was natural for them to join their master, placing their trust in Jesus Christ as well.

How the story unfolds. The official heard that Jesus was in Cana and immediately set out to reach him. When he found Jesus, he implored Christ to "come down and heal his son" (John 4:47).

We can imagine the onlookers drawing closer, waiting to see what Jesus would do. Will they get to see another miracle? This was when Jesus looked at them and rebuked them. All they were concerned about was seeing "signs and wonders."

At this, the father burst out, "Sir, come down before my child dies" (John 4:49). The royal official could care less about witnessing a miracle. It was his desperate need, not curiosity, that drove him to Jesus.

How important to distinguish the curious from the needy today. God has not called us to debate theology or pander to the interests of those who love to speculate about religion. There are men and women all around us who hurt and for whom only a relationship with Jesus can heal. These are the people to whom we are to give our time and show Christ's compassion. These are the people whose hearts God is preparing to open.

Jesus then spoke to the father who had begged him to go to Capernaum. "Go your way; your son lives" (John 4:50). We might paraphrase this, "Go on home. Your son is all right." This comment from anyone else might have been considered a cold, heartless remark. But the official did not see it as such. He took it as a binding promise. Believing, he started back to Capernaum.

On the way "down"—Cana lies in the highlands well above Capernaum—servants met him and told him the boy was all right. Apparently the father had expected a gradual recovery, for the Greek wording is better translated, "He asked them the hour when he *began to get better*" (John 4:51). The servants' answer revealed that at the very moment Jesus had said "Your son lives," the boy had recovered completely and instantly!

The text indicates that the father and his whole household—including no doubt the son—put their trust in Jesus.

And so John concluded, "This again is the second sign Jesus did when He had come out of Judea into Galilee" (v. 54). This was Jesus' second sign in Galilee.

Jesus' unbounded power. This miracle of Jesus did more than authenticate him as God's spokesman. It demonstrated that Jesus' power is unbounded. The space of twenty miles between Jesus and the dying boy was no barrier to our Lord. He spoke, "He lives," and the son's recovery was instantaneous and complete.

In the same way, no boundaries exist for Jesus today. Christ is in heaven, but he is also here with us. Any word he speaks will be obeyed, to the outer limits of the universe. No matter what our emergency, we can reach him instantly as well. He hears our prayers today, just as he heard the pleadings of the anxious father so long ago. As Christ in compassion reached across the miles to meet that father's need, so he will reach out today to meet ours.

Faith that grows. It is always important in looking at a miracle story to be alert for repeated words and themes. In this story "faith" is a repeated theme. The word *believe* occurs in John 4:48, 50, 53. Faith is also implicit in the anxious father's efforts to reach Jesus. He would not have set out unless he had some hope, some budding belief that Jesus could help.

In the account, faith was contrasted with curiosity. The crowds that observed the miracles were there because they wanted to see a miracle. There is no indication in the text that the miracle, to which only the father and his household were actually witnesses, had any impact on the curious. The cry, "Show us a miracle," was not an indication of faith, but unbelief.

In the account, faith was interpreted as growing. The theme of faith is clearly developed in the miracle account.

1. The father had some faith initially, as demonstrated by the fact that he set out to find Jesus. It may have been little faith, fanned by desperation. But faith it was.
2. His faith was then tested by Jesus' command and promise. It is significant that the command, "Go your way," was uttered first. But the promise *accompanied* the command: "Your child lives."

How often we delay obeying God, hoping that he will act or that he will at least give us more faith. But the only way our faith can grow is by exercising it. To exercise our faith, we must obey the commands of God, however strange they may seem.

This miracle reminds us that with every command there is a promise. With every step of obedience, we move further into the circle of God's richest blessings.

3. Faith that is exercised grows and spreads. The official's faith not only matured; it was reflected in his "whole household" (John 4:53). It is not that the household believed *because of* the father's faith. The father's faith—focused as it was on Jesus and his word—*directed the attention* of the members of his household to the Lord.

They believed because they saw Jesus for themselves. But they looked to Jesus in the first place because the official directed their gaze toward him.

Faith in John's Gospel. One of the main themes of John's Gospel is trust, or faith. Near the end of his Gospel, John wrote, "Truly Jesus did many other signs in the presence of his disciples, which are not written in this book; but these are written that you may believe that Jesus is the Christ, the Son of God, and that believing you may have life in His name" (John 20:30, 31). How clearly the healing of the nobleman's son illustrated John's theme.

In the face of death, a hopeful faith drove the anxious father to Jesus. Christ gave him a command and a promise. In faith the father obeyed and claimed the promise. And the result was life. The son recovered, and new faith was born in the hearts of all in that household who witnessed the healing.

Today, looking into the Scriptures, we also place our trust and faith in Jesus. As we do, we are given eternal life in his name.

JESUS HEALS A DEMONIAC IN A SYNAGOGUE   Mark 1:21–28; Luke 4:31–37

When a demon-possessed man interrupted a synagogue service where Jesus was teaching, Christ commanded the demon to leave.

Background of the miracle. Jesus was already established as a wonder-worker when he went to the synagogue outside Capernaum one Sabbath. After performing notable signs in Jerusalem during Passover, Jesus had moved his primary residence from Nazareth to Capernaum (Matt. 17:24), where he stayed with a successful fisherman named Peter (Mark 1:2–31).

That morning in the synagogue, Jesus was teaching the Scriptures. His exposition of the Old Testament was different from what the worshipers expected. The text indicates they were astonished "for he taught them as one having authority, and not as the scribes" (Mark 1:22).

By Jesus' time, what is known as rabbinic Judaism was already well established. A long oral tradition regarding their faith and beliefs had been built up, consisting of the rulings of earlier rabbis. This body of interpretations would continue to build during the first century. Thus, those who taught in the synagogues usually cited the words and sayings of earlier sages or contemporaries like Hillel or Shammai. But when Jesus spoke, he did not cite the rabbis. He taught as if he himself was Scripture's interpreter—as "one having authority."

It was in the context of Jesus' authoritative exposition of the Word of God that a striking miracle took place.

Parties to the miracle. The parties to this miracle were Jesus, the demonized man, the demon, and the assembled congregation.

Jesus. This miracle was placed early in Jesus' ministry by both Mark and Luke. It is interesting that immediately before relating this story, Luke described in some detail what Jesus taught in his home synagogue in Nazareth.

It was traditional during synagogue services to honor an important visitor by inviting him to read and comment on the Scriptures. In Nazareth, Jesus was handed the scroll containing the prophecies of Isaiah. He turned to a messianic passage, Isaiah 61:1, 2, read it, and then announced, "Today this Scripture is fulfilled in your hearing" (Luke 4:21).

The demon-possessed man. The text describes this man as one "who had a spirit of an unclean demon" (Luke 4:33). Demons are just as real as angels. Like angels, they are personal beings created holy by God, who chose to fol-

low Satan in a great rebellion which occurred before the creation of Adam and Eve. (See the companion volume, *Every Good and Evil Angel in the Bible.*)

Typically, the people who are described as demon-possessed in the Gospels display various symptoms, ranging from apparent madness and unusual strength to a variety of physical infirmities. But this man appeared normal. He attended synagogue with his neighbors, acting no differently than they. He apparently lived according to Moses' laws and was outwardly "clean," while within he was in the grip of corruption.

This demon-possessed man is a healthy reminder to us. We judge by appearances. The well-dressed man or woman sitting beside us in the pew may seem completely respectable. But it is not appearance that counts with God. God considers what is in the heart.

The demon. What a commentary on the spiritual state of Israel—the demon felt comfortable in the synagogue! The people had gathered to worship God. Yet there was no sense of the reality of God to make the demon uncomfortable—until Jesus joined that company.

There are spiritually powerless churches today. And there are spiritually powerful churches. The difference is Jesus. Where Christ is loved and honored—where hearts are lifted in praise and his Word is lived—no unclean person or demon can be comfortable.

The congregation. The congregation gathered that Sabbath heard Jesus teach. They witnessed the deliverance of the demonized man. They were not passive witnesses. But neither were they convinced, for they did not understand what they saw that day.

How the story unfolds. The accounts in Mark and Luke agree in every detail about this miracle. Jesus was teaching in the synagogue. The congregation was amazed because he taught as a person having authority, not as a person relying on established rabbinic authorities.

As Jesus was teaching, one man in the congregation interrupted with an anguished shout. It was a man with an unclean spirit, a demon. It was the demon and not the man who shouted, "Let us alone! What have we to do with You, Jesus of Nazareth? Did You come to destroy us? I know who You are—the Holy One of God!" (Luke 4:34).

Jesus immediately rebuked the evil spirit, commanding it to be quiet and to come out of the man.

At Jesus' command, the demon uttered a shriek, convulsed the man he possessed, and left. The congregation witnessed the whole thing in amazement. They couldn't grasp what was happening. They knew that Jesus commanded the unclean spirit and that it obeyed him. But what did it all mean?

The story was told "throughout all the region around Galilee," and Jesus' fame spread (Mark 1:28).

In the story, the event unfolded rapidly—the confrontation with the demon took place in moments. Yet so much of what happened in those moments is significant.

The demon's reaction to Jesus (Mark 1:24). The Greek verb used to describe Jesus' teaching suggests that he expounded the Scriptures for some time. The congregation quickly realized that Jesus' teaching was different.

But while the congregation wondered, one man in the synagogue had been growing more and more agitated. He was responding to the emotions that surged in an evil being who had taken up residence in his life—a demon.

The demon was not concerned with Jesus' teaching but was reacting to Christ himself. Finally the demon could stand it no longer. Gripped by terror and revulsion, the demon forced his host to stand and shouted at Jesus.

Let us alone! This first cry shows how painful it was for the demon to be in Jesus' presence. To demons, who conceal themselves in darkness, it is agonizing to be in the presence of light. And Jesus was and is the Light of the World (John 8:12).

What have we to do with You, Jesus of Nazareth? The phrase means "What have we in common?" In the first century it was typically spoken by an inferior to a superior. The demon recognized the authority of Jesus and that Christ would be responsible for whatever would follow.

There is perhaps more here for us. The cry reminds us that demons have nothing in common with Christ. When Satan rebelled, he and his followers turned their back on God. They became the enemies of their Creator, hostile to all whom he loves. Whatever means the demon used to gain access to the man he possessed, his intent was to do harm—while Jesus came to help and to redeem.

Did You come to destroy us? The demon was aware that God had decreed punishment for the devil and his angels (Matt. 25:41). What troubled the demon was "when?" The query torn from the demon was, "Are you here to judge us *now*?"

Likewise, there is no uncertainty about the fate of human beings. The only question is, "How soon will the day of judgment dawn?" How important it is to respond to the gospel today, while the door of salvation remains open.

I know who You are—the Holy One of God! While Jesus' humanity concealed his essential deity from human beings, his identity was known to demons. His shining essence was evident to the demon, who was not limited to physical sight. Mark frequently described encounters with demons who identified Jesus as the Son of God (see Mark 3:11; 5:7).

The demon's reaction to Jesus displayed both terror and doubt. The demon was afraid of what Jesus might do to him, but at the same time he was forced to acknowledge Jesus' authority over him.

Jesus' response to the demon (Mark 1:25). The Greek word translated "rebuked" has a technical meaning. It refers to a commanding word spoken by God or his spokesman. By this word, evil powers are forced to submit.

Jesus' first command: "Be quiet." The literal meaning of the word is "be muzzled." While the demon was able to shriek, he did not utter another word.

Why was Jesus unwilling to receive the testimony of this and other demons (see Mark 1:34)? Some suggest Jesus had not yet laid a foundation in teaching and wonder-working to be ready to state his claim. Others wonder if Jesus was guarding himself against the charge made later by the Pharisees that he derived his power from Satan (see Matt. 12:24). A better explanation may be the general conviction in first-century Judaism that any testimony from certain sources was suspect.

For instance, in Jesus' time a shepherd was not allowed to give testimony in court. The reputation of first-century shepherds as vagabonds and thieves made whatever they might say suspect in the eyes of the rabbis! If the testimony of a shepherd was automatically discounted, how much more the testimony of a demon?

Jesus needed no such testimony to establish his deity. His words and his miracles spoke for themselves.

Jesus' next command: "Come out of him." The demon had no choice but to obey. He uttered a shriek, threw his host into a convulsion, and left the man.

The reaction of the congregation (Mark 1:22, 27). This story appears to focus on the confrontation between Jesus and the demon. Certainly this is its most dramatic element. Yet the greater significance of the miracle is seen in two words which bracket the miracle—words which describe the reaction of the congregation to Jesus.

"They were astonished at his teaching" (Mark 1:22). The Greek word used here is *ekplesso.* It is usually used to describe the reaction of uncommitted listeners to Jesus' teaching. It suggests an amazement which so stunned the listener that he was unable to grasp the meaning of what has happened. Jesus taught as a person having authority, but the congregation

could not imagine what this implied about him.

"Then they were all amazed" (Mark 1:27). This describes the congregations' reaction to the miracle. The word used is *thambeo,* which emphasizes the fright caused by an amazing event.

The *Expository Dictionary of Bible Words* notes, "This family of words helps to remind us that Jesus' acts and words were 'amazing' primarily to those who did not believe in him" (p. 38). The phrase, "So that they questioned among themselves" further describes the congregation's reaction. It implies their intense argument and dispute. Jesus was clearly special. His teaching was unique. But what did it mean? Even demons obeyed him. But who was he?

Today, looking back from the perspective of the Cross and the Resurrection, we have no doubts about Jesus' identity or his authority. Yet even in his own day this miracle, and others recorded in the Gospels, began to forge a chain of evidence that left those who ultimately rejected him without excuse.

JESUS HEALS PETER'S WIFE'S MOTHER   *Luke 4:38, 39; Matthew 8:14–15; Mark 1:29–31*

Jesus returned to Peter's house from the synagogue and healed Peter's mother-in-law of a fever.

Background of the miracle. Jesus had just cast out a demon from a man in the synagogue at Capernaum (p. 171). He and four fishermen friends went to Peter's house, where Jesus probably stayed while in Capernaum. There Jesus was told that Peter's mother-in-law was suffering from a severe fever. What follows is recounted in each of the synoptic Gospels, but it is the briefest account of any miracle recorded there.

Parties to the miracle. The central figures were Jesus and Peter's mother-in-law. Mark made an oblique reference to members of the household, simply saying that "they" told Jesus about the sick woman, while Luke indicated "they" made request of him concerning her.

Jesus. The picture of Jesus in this miracle contrasts with that in the miracle account which immediately preceded it. There, Jesus was described as a figure with immense authority, displayed both in his teaching and in his casting out of a demon. In this miracle, Jesus seems more of an ordinary man. He walked home from the synagogue with his friends. He went into the house where he was staying, ready to eat a meal. When Jesus learned that Peter's mother-in-law was sick, he went in to see her.

These are all ordinary acts—the acts of a common man. And they remind us that while Jesus was truly God, he was also fully human.

The mother-in-law. None of the evangelists do more than identify the sick woman by her relationship to Peter. She lived in Peter's house (Luke 4:38), which suggests she was a widow. She was sick with what Luke—a physician interested in medical details—described as a "high" fever.

The household. No one in the household was named. The ruins of a larger home in Capernaum have been excavated and tentatively identified as Peter's residence. The "they" in this text probably included Peter's wife, any children, and perhaps servants.

How the story unfolds. Returning from the synagogue, Jesus found Peter's mother-in-law was sick. He went into the sick room. Each Gospel writer adds a detail to what happened in that room. Jesus rebuked the fever, and it left immediately. Jesus also touched the woman, then took her hand to help her up from the bed. Completely restored, Peter's mother-in-law then served the men the meal which she had prepared the previous day, before the Sabbath.

Jesus "rebuked" the fever (Luke 4:39). The Greek word for "rebuked"—*epetimesen*—is the same word Jesus used when he cast out the

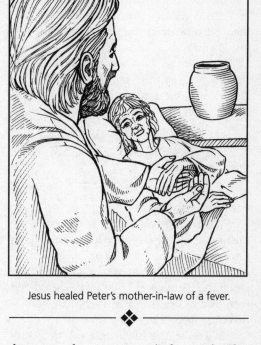

Jesus healed Peter's mother-in-law of a fever.

demon in the synagogue (Luke 4:35). This word had a technical meaning. It indicated a commanding word spoken by God or his spokesman, by which evil powers were forced to submit.

Just as the demon was an evil power bent on harming humankind, so sickness was an evil power. Christ came to break the grip of every evil that holds down humanity. This mission will ultimately be fulfilled at our resurrection. In the meantime, Jesus' ability to heal was clearly demonstrated in this and many other miracles described in the Gospels.

The outcome of the miracle (Luke 4:39). Each Gospel's account of this miracle relates that "she arose and served *them*."

How neatly we could apply this miracle if only the text read, "She arose and served *him*." Then we could point out the symmetry of salvation. Jesus served us by making us spiritually whole, and in response we commit our lives to serving him. But each of the three accounts agrees—that she got up and served *them*. It was as though nothing out of the ordinary had happened. The men returned home. The mother-in-law, who had laid out the table and the food the previous afternoon, had them sit down and then she served them— just like any other Sabbath.

It is almost as if the miracle were too small a thing to interrupt the pattern of the family's life. We can almost imagine a later conversation:

"Anything special happen after synagogue?"
"No, nothing much. Oh, wait. Jesus healed Peter's mother-in-law."
"That was nice. What did she serve for Sabbath dinner?"

What a difference there had been in the synagogue after Jesus expelled a demon. In the synagogue there had been anxiety, uncertainty, and confusion as the congregation pondered the meaning of what it had heard and seen. But in Peter's house, everything continued on in its ordinary way.

In a sense, this "unexceptional" miracle of Jesus at Peter's house reflects something of our own experience with the Lord. His miracles for us are often quiet and ordinary. Yet it is his presence in our home that averts so many tragedies, maintaining the peace that we enjoy. Perhaps the little miracles of Jesus, performed behind closed doors so that ordinary people can continue on in their ordinary ways, are the most significant miracles of all.

JESUS PROVIDES A GREAT CATCH OF FISH   *Luke 5:1–11*

Jesus' miracle at the Sea of Galilee illustrated the mission to which he called his disciples.

Background of the miracle. Each of the synoptic Gospels gives an account of Jesus' call of a closely knit group of fishermen to become his disciples. Each writer portrayed a few fisherman on the shore of the Sea of Galilee [called Lake Gennesaret by Luke]. Some were mending drag nets, while others listlessly threw cast nets (Matt. 5:18–21). Only Luke's

Gospel went into detail about what happened there that day, and only Luke described the miracle of the great catch of fish.

According to Luke and Mark, the call of the disciples followed miracles Jesus performed in the synagogue at Capernaum in the home of Peter. It's important to remember this. Otherwise, we might get the impression that Jesus just happened to be at the seaside, where he invited four strangers to become his disciples. It wasn't like that at all.

Jesus' relationship with the fishermen. The four fishermen were Peter, Andrew, James, and John; and Jesus knew each of them well. Peter and Andrew had met Jesus the day he was baptized by John the Baptist several weeks or months before (John 1:35–42). James and John were partners with Peter in a successful fishing business. Several of these fishermen, perhaps all four, had been with Jesus in Cana of Galilee, where they witnessed his first miracle (John 2:2).

The four had undoubtedly been witnesses to miracles Jesus performed in Jerusalem before returning to Galilee. They had been together in the Capernaum synagogue when Jesus cast a demon out of a man in the congregation. It is clear that the four were already very close to Jesus. After this miracle,

they went with Jesus to eat together at Peter's house (Mark 1:29).

So Jesus' call to discipleship was no spontaneous invitation issued to strangers. Jesus had invested significant time in their relationship before calling these four to become his disciples.

It's good to remember this. At times we try to rush others into a decision about Jesus. We need to invest time as Jesus did, building a relationship in which others can come to know and trust us. Then through us, they can come to know and trust Christ.

The call to become disciples. Sometimes the word *disciple* is used in the Gospels to describe the curious who became loose adherents of his movement. But when *disciple* is applied to the Twelve, it has a different, more technical meaning.

In the first century, those intent on becoming religious leaders attached themselves to a man who was already recognized as a rabbi, an expert in written and oral Law. They became "disciples" and lived with their teacher for a period of years, intent on mastering all that the teacher knew and becoming as much like him as possible (see Luke 6:40). This training, a rigorous spiritual apprenticeship, was the only way a person could gain a position of religious authority in Judaism.

It was to this rigorous spiritual apprenticeship that Jesus called the four fishermen that day. They would have to leave their business behind, abandoning all to be with Jesus night and day. In coming years, Jesus' disciples would gradually learn from his example and from his public and private teaching, until they were fully equipped to become leaders in the movement Jesus founded. It was no light thing to be a teacher's disciple in New Testament times. Discipleship called for informed commitment.

This is why Jesus spent so much time with these men who formed the core group of the Twelve, whom he ultimately assembled. They had to know and trust him, so that when he called them to discipleship, they would make the choice with eyes wide open.

The parties to the miracle. Luke 5 provides the sharpest and most detailed description of the setting of the miracle. The central parties to the miracle were Jesus and Peter, a great crowd, and Peter's fishing partners.

Jesus. Jesus was teaching crowds that had gathered in response to his spreading fame. Yet he paid primary attention not to the multitudes but to individuals—and particularly Simon Peter.

Peter. In spite of his closeness to Jesus, Peter was still busy working as a fisherman. Every hint in Scripture indicates that he was a very successful fisherman. Although originally from the small town of Bethsaida (John 1:44), Peter had purchased a large home in Capernaum, the political center of the district, and he and his partners fished and marketed their catch from there. He was clearly the most influential in the partnership, as he continued to be after becoming a disciple of Jesus.

In almost every dialogue between Jesus and the disciples, Peter's is the first voice we hear, opinionated but not always right (see Matt. 16:22–23; 26:33–34). In this account, Peter expressed not only his own feelings, but the unspoken feelings of his partners.

The multitudes. Aside from providing the occasion for the miracle and the call of Jesus' first disciples, the crowds that had come to Capernaum to see Jesus had no role in the miracle report.

Andrew, James, and John. These three of the four who were called by Jesus to be his disciples that day are almost ignored. We are told of their reaction to the miracle (they were astonished), and of their response to Jesus (they "forsook all and followed him"; Luke 5:11). But otherwise, they stood outside the spotlight, letting Peter speak what they may have been feeling as well.

How the story unfolds (Luke 5:1–11). The crowds that had gathered to hear Jesus pressed so close that Christ, standing on the shore of Galilee, was almost pushed into the water. So Jesus got into Peter's boat and asked his friend to push him out from the shore. There, isolated from the crowd, Jesus taught from the boat.

When he finished teaching, Jesus told Peter to row out to deeper water and let down his nets. Peter, an experienced fisherman, knew there were no fish. Most fishing on Galilee was done at night, and the schools of fish the fisherman pursued were never found where Jesus told Peter to let down his nets.

Peter, complaining a bit ("We have toiled all night and caught nothing"), did as Jesus said. But Peter let down only one net rather than the "nets" Jesus had called for (compare Luke 5:4 and 5:5). Even this partial obedience was rewarded overwhelmingly. So many fish were caught in the net that it began to break!

It took all the partners working in two boats to bring in the catch. The two boats were so full of fish that they began to take on water.

The miracle had a peculiar effect on Peter. He fell on his knees and begged Jesus, "Depart from me, for I am a sinful man, O Lord!" (Luke 5:8). Instead of leaving, Jesus reassured

Peter. He was not to fear, for God had something more important for Peter to do than catch fish: "From now on you will catch men."

The story ended with the partners pulling their boats on the shore, leaving everything behind—boats and fish as well—to set out after Jesus.

Reluctant obedience (Luke 5:5). Peter was clearly reluctant to launch out into deeper water and let down a net. After all, Peter was an experienced fishermen. He knew the ways of fish, and where they could be found. Peter knew there was no way any fish would be in the spot where Jesus told him to let down the net. In spite of all this, Peter respected Jesus. He obeyed not because he expected a miracle, but out of respect.

But respect only carried Peter so far. Peter couldn't see the sense in letting down "nets." Reluctantly, Peter did push out and let down one net.

Jesus had told Peter to let down his nets *"for a catch"* (Luke 5:4). But Peter was unprepared when suddenly the net bulged with fish. When Jesus tells us to obey and get ready for results, it's best that we be prepared!

Jesus told Peter, "Let down your nets for a catch."

Peter's use of "master" and "Lord" (Luke 5:5; 5:8). At the beginning of the story, the reluctant Peter addressed Jesus as *epistata.* The word is typically translated "master," even though "boss" perhaps better captures its flavor. Although it was a blue-collar word, no disrespect was implied. The use of *epistata* still implied recognition of Jesus' authority.

Even so, *epistata* was not as significant a word as the one Peter chose after the great catch of fish. Stunned as only an experienced fisherman would be, Peter fell on his knees before Jesus and cried out, *Kurie,* which has the force of "supreme Lord" (Luke 5:8). Peter was overwhelmed with the realization that God was present in this Jesus, whom he had been treating only as a respected friend!

It is good for us to be on familiar terms with Jesus. We can go to him as *epistata,* or even as a brother and friend. But we can never forget that Jesus is at the same time the supreme Lord of the universe, whom we are to view with respect and awe.

Peter's request (Luke 5:8). At first, Peter's response to the miracle amazes us. Why did Peter ask Jesus to go away, using the excuse that he was a sinful human being? Why wasn't Peter excited about the miraculous catch? Why wasn't he thankful?

Not the miracle, but the miracle worker. Peter's reaction is rooted in the fact that he was no longer concerned with the miracle. The miracle had forced Peter to look at Jesus in a new way. It was one thing to see Jesus perform miracles for others. But it was another thing entirely for Peter to experience the miracle *personally.* This time he felt the net's ropes ripped out of his hand. He struggled to lift the surging net. He hurriedly transferred fish from the net to the boats. He saw the loaded boats sink deeper into the water until the waves began to sweep over their sides. Peter had felt and smelled and tasted this miracle for himself. And suddenly he was forced to look at Jesus with fresh eyes and to see him for the awesome person he was.

In that moment of personal discovery, Peter fell to his knees and cried out, *Kurie,* "O Supreme Lord."

Not the fisherman, but the sinner (Luke 5:8). Just as the miracle forced Peter to look at Jesus with fresh eyes, the sudden realization of who Jesus was triggered self-discovery. Peter had thought of himself primarily as a master of his trade. Now he was overwhelmed by the realization that "I am a sinful man."

We cannot stand in the presence of Jesus and see him clearly as the Holy One of God without becoming sensitive to the fact that we are sinners. A person who compares himself to other people can take some comfort in the fact that many are worse than he. But if we compare ourselves to Jesus Christ, we take no comfort at all. We know how far short we fall.

When this happens, our first reaction may be that of Peter, who felt both guilt and shame. Peter's impulsive solution was to beg Jesus to withdraw. But if Jesus were to withdraw from us, we would be left with our problem of guilt and shame unresolved.

"He and all who were with him were astonished" (Luke 5:9). The word translated "astonished" is *thambeo,* which is also used in Luke 4:36. In each case, it depicted fright caused by an amazing event. Peter and the others were uncertain of the meaning of the great catch of fish. They knew it was a miracle. They felt a sudden awe of Jesus. But what did this demonstration of Jesus' power *mean?*

Their initial reaction of fear was only natural. Like Peter, the others had experienced Jesus in a new way. Their recognition of his deity and their own sinfulness made them anxious. This holds a lesson for us. God may seem a frightening specter as long as his intentions remain a mystery. But when Jesus speaks, he makes his intentions clear.

"Do not be afraid" (Luke 5:9). Jesus' first words reassured the fishermen. In making himself known to Peter and his friends, Jesus intended no harm. There is no need to be afraid of Jesus Christ.

"From now on you will catch men" (Luke 5:10). Jesus knew that Peter and his partners were sinners. But Jesus wanted them as his own nonetheless. By choosing to follow Jesus, their lives would be reoriented. The partners who had once invested their lives in catching fish would soon invest their lives in a far more significant task. They would share in Jesus' ministry, investing their lives in capturing human hearts and turning them to the Lord.

"They forsook all and followed him" (Luke 5:11). The miracle had its desired effect. Peter and his partners looked not at what Jesus had done, but at Jesus himself. They bowed to the ground, confessing Jesus as supreme Lord.

Now when their supreme Lord commanded them to follow him, they were ready. What a stunning discovery. In coming to earth, the Son of God had not come to punish or to condemn, but to recruit followers who would make his mission their own. Captured by this vision, the four fishermen left everything behind and with joy and wonder set out to follow him.

May we make the same discovery, as his miracles refocus our attention, challenging us to follow Jesus as well.

CHAPTER 10

JESUS: MIRACLES OF THE MESSIAH

GOD'S SAVIOR HAS COME

Matthew—John

What do Jesus' miracles tell us about Him? What did the miracles Jesus performed tell the people of His own day?

Centuries before Christ's birth the prophet Isaiah described the kind of miraculous healings that would mark the introduction of the messianic age. The recorded miracles of Jesus fulfilled this 700-year-old prophecy exactly!

The kind of miracles that Jesus performed—miracles done by no prophet before His appearance—were proof positive that Christ was the promised Messiah, the Savior of Israel!

JESUS CLEANSES A LEPER   *Mark 1:40–45; Luke 5:12–15*

Jesus touched and healed a leper who appealed to him for help.

Background of the miracle. The leprosy of the Old and New Testament was any infectious skin disease. The social impact of the disease was even greater than its physical problems. While suffering from such a disease, a person was to be isolated from the community. To touch a leper made a person ritually unclean. Leviticus 13:45 says, "His clothes shall be torn and his head bare, and he shall cover his mustache, and cry, 'Unclean! Unclean!'" Other people were to be warned of the leper's unclean state so they could avoid contact.

Because this disease made a person ritually unclean, priests were given the duty of examining rashes to see if they should be classified as leprosy. Detailed instructions for making this diagnosis are included in the book of Leviticus. A person who recovered from leprosy was to go to a priest, who would examine him and pronounce him ritually clean again.

Parties to the miracle. In each report of this incident, the text mentions only Jesus and the leper. This was apparently a private miracle. Mark notes that it was the leper rather than others who "went out and began to proclaim" his cure freely (v. 45).

Jesus. Mark emphasized Jesus' compassion for the leper who appealed to him for healing (Mark 1:41). Jesus healed the leper, not as a sign, but simply because he cared.

The leper. Luke described the man as "full of leprosy" (Luke 5:12). His case was severe, and he had probably been a leper for a long time. Yet this leper expressed confidence that Jesus could heal his disease if he chose to do so. The leper was right. Jesus could heal him—and he did.

How the story unfolds. The story is told abruptly, with only Matthew providing anything like a transition statement (Matt. 8:1). The leper saw Jesus, and fell down before him, begging for healing. Jesus responded by reaching out to touch the leper while saying "be cleansed." Instantly the leprosy was gone.

Jesus told the man to go to a priest, as the Old Testament required, so he could be certified as ritually clean. And, although Jesus warned the leper to tell no one, the leper was so excited by his cure that he couldn't help telling everyone he met what Jesus had done for him.

"Lord, if you are willing" (Luke 5:12). The leper had no doubt about Jesus' ability to cure him. But he was uncertain as to whether Jesus would be willing to do so. The rabbis thought leprosy was God's punishment for slander, one of the most wicked sins in rabbinic eyes. The leper's hesitant request may reflect his question, "Will Jesus help so great a sinner?"

Many people are burdened by guilt, and they wonder if God could possibly care for them. But Jesus' response to the leper offers wonderful assurance and relief.

"Moved with compassion" (Mark 1:41). Mark takes us into the heart of Jesus and reveals what moved him to act. The Greek word for "compassion" is *splanchnizomai*, which depicts the emotions of pity, compassion, and love. Jesus *did* care, no matter what the leper's past sins.

This word is not used often in the New Testament. But when the Gospels portray Jesus as being moved by compassion, his subsequent action usually marks the turning point in a person's life. This was the case with the leper. And it can be true for us.

Whatever our past, whatever our failings or needs, Jesus does have compassion for us. And when we come to him for help, he will change our lives.

"He put out His hand and touched him" (Luke 5:13). The act was doubly significant.

It was a true expression of compassion. As much as the leper needed healing, his heart must have ached for the touch of another human hand. How terrible it must have been to see everyone draw back as he approached, lest they be contaminated by brushing against him. Jesus responded to the man's heartache, giving him not only what he asked for—healing—but what he longed for as well—a human touch.

It was a stunning demonstration of spiritual power. According to the law, anything which touched an object or person who was ritually unclean became unclean itself. But Jesus' touch had the opposite effect! It removed the disease which had made the man unclean.

"Go and show yourself to the priest" (5:14). Jesus instructed the cleansed leper to do what God's Law required. Jesus' conflicts with the Pharisees and others over "the law" was over their additions to the Old Testament, not over the Law itself.

"He charged him to tell no one" (5:14). It would be easy to criticize the healed leper for disobeying Jesus. Yet we can understand how he couldn't keep silent. The joy he felt simply overflowed.

How strange it is—when Scripture urges us to tell others of the cleansing we have experienced through Jesus—that so many Christians keep silent. The leper was healed of a disease which cut him off from fellowship with other human beings. Christians have been cleansed from sins which once cut us off from personal relationship with God. How powerfully the joy of that cleansing should move us to share Christ's love with others.

JESUS HEALS A PARALYTIC   *Luke 5:18–26; Matthew 9:2–7; Mark 2:3–12*

Four friends carried a paralyzed man to Jesus. Jesus shocked onlookers by forgiving the man's sins and then curing the paralysis.

Background of the miracle. Luke noted that as more and more people heard about Jesus, multitudes gathered to hear him and be healed (Luke 5:15). The furor apparently brought to Capernaum a delegation of "Pharisees and teachers of the Law," made up of rabbis from Galilee, Judea, and Jerusalem. Their mission was to evaluate Jesus' teaching.

On this particular day great crowds had gathered, and the delegation had seen Jesus heal many people (Luke 5:17). The delegation later met with Jesus inside a home, most likely Peter's (Luke 4:38). These men represented the spiritual leaders of Judaism, and they were listening critically. They needed to decide how to deal with this young preacher who was working miracles and drawing such great crowds.

It was while Jesus was dealing with them that this interruption described in three of the Gospels took place.

The parties to the miracle. This miracle account carefully described the interaction between several parties. There was Jesus, who was presenting his teaching to the delegation sent to examine him. There was the delegation made up of Pharisees and teachers of the law. There was a paralyzed man and the friends who carried him to Jesus.

Jesus. Jesus was clearly the focus of attention. Crowds had come to hear him, and he had healed many. In all this, he had been carefully observed by the delegation of religious leaders. When this miracle happened, he was in a room with his examiners. There is no hint that Jesus was making a defense of his teaching. Rather, he was actively instructing those who assumed they had the authority to evaluate him!

The Pharisees and teachers of the law. These were men who had undergone the rigorous training required of anyone in Judaism who wanted to become a spiritual leader. The term *Pharisee* was used to describe a small, dedicated core of people, mostly laymen, who were totally committed to keeping God's law as interpreted by the rabbis.

These men honored what was called the oral law—memorized interpretations of the written Law of Moses and legal rulings of earlier rabbis—as if it were the very word of God. Later they would become the enemies of Jesus. He ignored the oral Law and criticized the Pharisees for following precepts which canceled out the written Word of God.

At this point, these influential men had not made up their minds. Yet, like the teachers of the Law who were there with them, the Pharisees had come to judge Jesus by their standards. It had never occured to them that their standards might be judged by Jesus' teachings!

The paralyzed man and his friends. These men are portrayed as individuals of persistent faith. They were determined to reach Jesus, because they firmly believed he could heal their friend.

There is a powerful contrast here. The Pharisees and law teachers came to Jesus to evaluate him. The paralytic and his friends came to Jesus for help. Faith recognizes its need for the things that only Jesus can provide. Unbelief assumes the right to judge God himself.

How the story unfolds. Jesus was inside a home teaching the investigating committee. The crowd had pressed around the house outside, hoping to overhear. When the paralytic was brought by his friends, there was no way to get through the crowds packed around the door and windows.

But the paralytic's friends were not about to give up. They climbed the outside staircase that led to the flat roof. These were typical features of Palestinian homes. They broke through the roof, letting the paralyzed man down into the room where Jesus was teaching. Mark pictured this graphically: they "dug through" (*apestgasan*) the layers of plaster, sticks, and mud used to construct the roof.

Jesus recognized their faith and responded to it. He declared, "Man, your sins are forgiven" (Luke 5:20). This shocked the delegation of religious leaders. Only God could forgive sins! Sensing their thoughts, Jesus challenged them. Was it easier to say, "your sins are forgiven" or to say "rise up and walk?" Then, to show that his words were authoritative, Jesus told the paralyzed man to get up, pick up the pallet on which he had been carried to the house, and walk home.

The man got up and carried his bed home. No one who comes to Jesus with faith goes away the same.

Luke concluded, "They were all amazed, and they glorified God and were filled with fear, saying, "We have seen strange things today" (5:26).

"When He saw their faith" (Luke 5:20). This is the first direct reference to faith in Luke's Gospel, although the issue of belief versus unbelief has already been raised (compare Luke 1:20, 45). But what does Luke mean by "faith"? In his Gospel and in Acts, faith is ascribed to persons who act decisively on the conviction that God's help is to be found in Jesus.

The persistence of the paralytic's friends demonstrated the reality of their faith. Biblical faith is more than wishful thinking. It is a confidence that Jesus can help which moves us to act according to his Word.

"Man, your sins are forgiven you" (5:20). The paralytic came for physical healing. Jesus first provided spiritual healing. Jesus would give the man what he wanted—but first he would give him what he *needed*. We can live with physical infirmities. But we cannot survive without God's forgiveness.

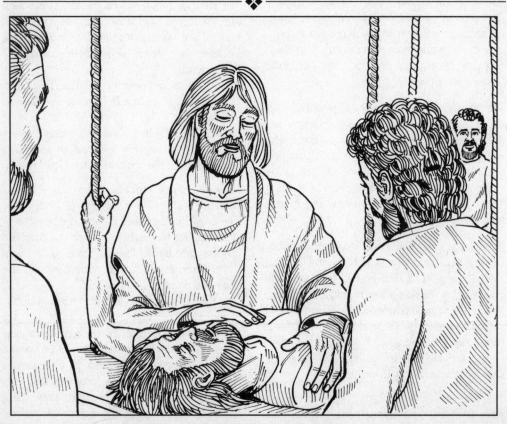

A man lowered through a roof received healing from Jesus.

"Who is this who speaks blasphemies?" *(5:21).* We can almost hear the investigating committee breathe a sigh of astonishment. Now they could categorize Jesus!

"Who is this?" This was the question they had been sent to answer. Was Jesus really a messenger sent by God? Might he even be the Messiah? Or was he another of those fraudulent figures who often appeared on the religious scene, gained a few moments of notoriety, and then disappeared? How should the religious establishment react to him?

The wonder is that they needed to raise the question at all. All that day the delegation had seen Jesus heal. Later a man who had been given sight by Jesus would state the obvious: "Why, this is a marvelous thing, that you do not know where he is from. . . . If this man were not from God, he could do nothing" (John 9:30, 33).

The teachers of the law and Pharisees who were so reluctant to acknowledge Jesus' authority simply *had to know* that the miracle worker had come from God.

"Who speaks blasphemies." Unwilling to accept the testimony of Jesus' miracles about his identity, the delegation was quick to fasten on his words. Jesus had pronounced the paralytic's sins forgiven.

In first-century Judaism, the forgiveness of sins was thought to be something God would announce only in the final day. Jesus spoke as if he had divine authority to forgive sins, although the scribes and Pharisees observed, "Who can forgive sins but God alone?" (Luke 5:21; compare Ps. 103:3; Isa. 45:25). What's more, Jesus' pronouncement also brought forgiveness into the realm of the present. To the Jewish leaders, this was blasphemy indeed.

Although the leaders did not announce then that Jesus was a blasphemer, this conclusion had been fixed in their mind. Although Jesus went on to prove that he had the authority to make such a pronouncement, the investigating commission had made up their minds. By their standards, what Jesus had said

was blasphemous. This was enough to settle their attitude toward him.

Many people think it presumptuous for human beings to claim they know their sins are forgiven, and that they are assured of heaven. They consider this pride, as though we had confidence in our own goodness. But those who realize that Christ died for our sins so we might be forgiven do know the joy of redemption. Our forgiveness rests entirely on what Jesus did for us—not on what we do for ourselves.

"Which is easier, to say?" *(5:23)* Jesus was not asking whether it is easier to forgive sins or to heal paralysis. He was asking about *words*.

Do Jesus' words have meaning? Jesus asked which is easier *to say*. The obvious answer is that it is easier to say sins are forgiven. It is easier because there is no way to tell whether such words have meaning. Forgiveness is a transaction that takes place between an individual and God. No one can peer into the heart to witness that inner transaction.

But if a person says to a paralytic, "Get up, pick up your pallet and go home," there is an immediate and sure way to tell whether his words are empty. If the paralytic gets up and goes home, the words of the speaker are authoritative indeed. If the paralytic continues to lie there, the words of the speaker are meaningless.

"That you may know" *(Luke 5:24).* Jesus healed the paralytic as a witness to the investigating committee. Are the words of Jesus authoritative? Does he have the right *(exousia)* to forgive sins? To show how powerful his words were, Christ turned to the paralytic and told him to get up and go home.

"And they were all amazed" *(5:26).* An unusual Greek word is translated "amazed" in this passage. The word is *ekstasis,* from which our word *ecstasy* comes. In classical Greek, the word implied an intense but passing excitement. Here it conveyed a sense of astonishment. Luke filled in the portrait of the delega-

tion's reaction, for the "all" is best to be taken as referring primarily to the delegation in the room where Jesus taught.

"They were all amazed." The miracle astonished the onlookers. What irony this is. These men, who claimed spiritual authority in Judaism because they had mastered the words of the written and oral law, had come to pass judgment on Jesus. But with a few brief statements, Jesus proved that the words he spoke were infused with an authority and power they could not match, or imagine.

The religious leaders spent their lives arguing about words. But not one of them could heal a paralytic. Yet they dared to assume they had the right to judge the teaching of a man whose words had miracle-working power!

"They glorified God." Some take this statement as a positive assessment of the investigating committee's reaction to Jesus' miracle. It is not. The phrase more likely reflects the delegation's unwillingness to give Jesus any credit at all!

Later the religious leaders of Judaism would tell a blind man Jesus had healed, "Give God the glory! We know that this man [Jesus] is a sinner" (John 9:24). No miracle ever changed a closed heart. And this miracle didn't change the conviction of the Pharisees or teachers of the Law that Jesus had committed blasphemy.

"They were filled with fear" (v. 26). The Greek word used here is the most common term for fear—*phobos.* Frequently in the Gospels, when the religious leaders are described as being afraid, the fear makes them resist an impulse to attack Jesus (compare Matt. 21:46; Mark 12:12). In the face of such a notable miracle, the delegation was afraid to take a stand against Jesus.

"We have seen strange things today" (v. 26). We cannot imagine a more noncommittal expression. The delegation walked away, its members shaking their heads.

The healing of the paralytic proved that Jesus' words rang with God's authority, but the Pharisees withheld their stamp of approval.

They were convinced that a teacher whose words did not agree with their understanding of God's plan must be wrong. But not one had the courage to pronounce *anathema* on those who listened to what Jesus said. They would not risk exercising the religious authority they claimed, because the miracle had filled them with uncertainty and fear.

And so they shook their heads and went away. All anyone heard them say was, "Strange. Really strange."

And strange indeed it is—strange not that Jesus should forgive or heal, but that human beings still tend to cling to wrong ideas about God in spite of the authoritative words spoken by Jesus. As we study miracle after miracle in the Gospels, may we have the faith to recognize Jesus for who he is and—like the paralytic—come to him.

JESUS HEALS AN INVALID AT BETHESDA   *John 5:1–18*

Jesus healed a man who had been an invalid for 38 years.

Background of the miracle. Jesus walked through a crowd of disabled people gathered around an open-air pool. Verse 4, which is not found in the more reliable Greek manuscripts, explains that they gathered there because they believed an angel stirred the waters occasionally. After this stirring, the first person into the pool would be healed.

This miracle took place on the Sabbath. The Old Testament decreed that a person should do no work on the Sabbath (Ex. 20:8–10). By Jesus' time, the rabbis had expanded this simple command by going into great detail about what constituted "work."

For instance, it was permissible to have a fire which kept water hot if the fire was built before the Sabbath. But cold water could not be added to the hot water, lest the cold be warmed. Heating water would constitute work. However, it was permissible to add hot water to cold water in a cup, on the theory that the cold would cool off the hot, and this would not be work (*Mishna,* Shabbat 3:5). It is not surprising that the religious leaders with such a mindset were shocked and angered at what Jesus did on the Sabbath.

Parties to the miracle. The text focuses on Jesus, the invalid, and "the Jews." When John uses the phrase "the Jews," he is referring to the religious leaders, not to the general population and certainly not to the Jewish people as a race.

Jesus. Jesus initiated a conversation with the invalid. People generally approached Jesus for healing, and they usually began the conversation. In this case, Jesus selected one from the many in need and initiated the conversation. It is also striking that Jesus walked through the crowd of the infirm unrecognized. While most would have heard of Jesus, there was nothing out of the ordinary about his appearance.

The invalid. The man had been bedridden for 38 years, and he was without hope of being cured. He had no idea who Jesus was. Even after his healing, when questioned by the religious leaders, the text says "the one who was healed did not know who it was" (John 5:13). There is no question about one thing: faith was not a condition of this healing.

The Jews. The Jewish leaders were scandalized that the man, after being healed, was carrying his bed (a cloth pallet). When they learned the miracle had been performed by Jesus, all they could think of was making an accusation against him "because he had done these things on the Sabbath" (John 5:16).

How the story unfolds. John organized his report of this miracle story into five vivid scenes.

Scene 1. John sketched the setting, telling about the crowds of "sick people, blind, lame, paralyzed" lying near the pool. These were people we would classify as "incurable." Their only hope was for a miracle. John then drew attention to a single individual: a man who had been an invalid for nearly four decades.

Scene 2. Jesus entered, walking through the crowd. He stopped before the invalid and asked him a question. The man's answer revealed his hopelessness. After 38 years, he had lost not only the ability to move but also all hope. Without further comment, Jesus told the man to get up, pick up his bed, and walk. The invalid must have felt the strength flow back into his limbs, for he immediately got up

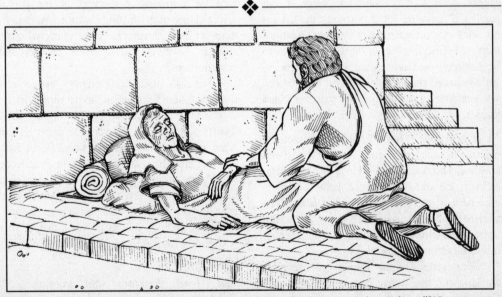

"When Jesus saw him lying there, He said to him, 'Do you want to be made well?'"

and did as Jesus said. Jesus walked away and was lost in the crowds (John 5:13).

Scene 3. The man was spotted by "the Jews," members of the religious establishment. They confronted him for carrying his pallet on the Sabbath. When the healed invalid told what had happened, the religious leaders interrogated him about who had instructed him to violate the Sabbath. The man replied that he didn't know who he was.

Scene 4. Jesus found the man he had healed in the temple. He identified himself and warned the man to "sin no more, lest a worse thing come upon you" (v. 14). The man then hurried to the religious leaders and reported that it was Jesus who had made him well.

John commented on the leaders' reaction: "The Jews persecuted Jesus" because he had done these things on the Sabbath (John 5:16). The phrase "and sought to kill him" is not in the best Greek texts, but it accurately reflects the intent of the religious leaders as described in other passages.

Scene 5. Later, the incident led to an open confrontation between Jesus and the religious leaders, which featured an extended teaching by Jesus. This is a basic pattern in the Gospel of John—a miracle precedes a message. In this particular message, Jesus pointed out that his miracles demonstrated his intimate relationship with God the Father, and that he was to be honored as God. If the religious leaders truly believed the Old Testament, they would acknowledge Jesus, for the Scriptures testified to him.

"A certain man" (John 5:5). The characteristics of this man are significant. He had been an invalid for a long time. He didn't expect to recover. He didn't recognize Jesus or know who he was; thus, he was without faith. Even after being healed, he didn't know Jesus. But later, when Christ found him, the man recognized the One who healed him.

This gives insight into God's gracious working for the unsaved of every age. Are God's miracles reserved only for the believer who knows the Lord and exercises faith in him? No, because Jesus showed his grace to an invalid who neither knew nor believed in him. God is free in his sovereignty to show grace to any human being, as he often does in unexplained healings and in other ways. How often an anonymous providence raises up those who do not know or acknowledge God.

Yet it is significant that the healing prepared the beneficiary in this story for a later meeting with Jesus. Jesus Christ was ultimately recognized as the source of blessing.

"Do you want to be made well?" (John 5:6). Jesus' question was penetrating. It's true that the invalid had lost much because of his illness. His limbs atrophied, and he lost the ability to move. He declared, "I have no man" to help. He lost the network of friends which those with a normal life typically build.

Yet for nearly four decades, the invalid had looked to others for alms. If he were healed, he would have to become responsible for himself. He would have to find work, to reenter a social world to which he is a stranger. "Do you want to be made well" is a valid question indeed.

How many today don't really want to be well! How many who live on welfare fear the idea of assuming responsibility for themselves? How many invalids want to be dependent on their caregivers? How many who are spiritual invalids fear spiritual growth and commitment?

The sick man didn't answer Jesus' question. He offered an excuse, explaining why he couldn't be made well. But note that Jesus didn't wait for his answer. He said to him "Rise, take up your bed and walk" (John 5:8).

Perhaps the question, "Do you want to be well?" was raised to force us to face our own inner hesitancy. Maybe the command, "Rise, take up your bed and walk," was uttered to remind us that we *are* to be responsible; that with God's help we can walk—and carry our own load.

"The Jews therefore said to him . . ." (5:10–12). When the invalid told them about his cure, the religious leaders gave not a single thought to the man or what the cure must have meant to him. They didn't rejoice with him or seem to care. All they wanted was to find the person who had violated their rules on Sabbath behavior so they could confront him!

When in the name of religion we lose our capacity to care about others, there is something wrong with our religion.

"The one who was healed did not know" (5:13). The healing of the invalid was an act of sovereign grace. There was no appeal by the invalid to Jesus; he exercised no faith—he didn't even know who Jesus was.

"Jesus found him in the temple" (John 5:14). The healed man didn't go looking for Jesus. Perhaps this would have been an impossible task, because Jerusalem was crowded during religious festivals (compare John 5:1). But Jesus did go looking for the man.

It's significant that Jesus found the man in the temple. He may have gone there to thank God for his healing. Or perhaps the religious leaders had taken him there to be questioned about the incident.

In any case, Jesus found him—and warned him. "You have been made well. Sin no more" (John 5:14). A literal translation of the Greek is "don't keep on sinning." Some interpreters point out that the phrase suggests that when Jesus healed the man's body, he also forgave his sins. Others emphasize the connection between sickness and sin in the Bible. But it is more likely that when Jesus warned "lest a worse thing come upon you," he was speaking of the spiritual consequences of sin.

"The man departed and told the Jews that it was Jesus" (5:15). The man has been criticized for "betraying" Jesus. Yet Christ didn't try to hide his miracles, nor is there any indication that Jesus told the healed invalid not to tell anyone what had happened. In fact, when the leaders hurried to accuse Jesus, he used the occasion to state his true identity and to press his claim for Israel's allegiance.

While we as believers are commissioned to tell others about Jesus, we are not responsible for their response. Perhaps we should grant this man who was healed the same consideration.

"Because he had done these things on the Sabbath" (5:16). We have already noted the extreme emphasis on Sabbath-keeping that characterized the Pharisees and experts in biblical Law. The Gospels record seven Sabbath healings. Several of them led to serious confrontations with the religious establishment. The seven are:

1. Jesus healed the demoniac in the synagogue at Capernaum. See page 171.
2. Jesus healed Peter's mother-in-law. See page 174.
3. Jesus healed the cripple at Bethesda. See page 186.
4. Jesus healed a man with a withered hand. See page 190.
5. Jesus healed a man born blind. See page 222.
6. Jesus healed a woman bound by Satan. See page 225.
7. Jesus healed a man with dropsy. See page 227.

"But Jesus answered them" (5:17). The incident gave Jesus an opportunity to confront the assumptions of the religious leaders and to state his claims openly. The text indicates that Christ's claims were clearly understood. "The Jews sought all the more to kill him, because he not only broke the Sabbath, but also said that God was his Father, making himself equal with God" (v. 18).

The religious leaders didn't reject Christ out of some misunderstanding of who he claimed to be. They understood his claims perfectly, and they rejected him *because of these claims.*

The larger meaning of the miracle. The miracle displayed the power of God to act in sovereign grace on behalf of anyone whom he chooses. Miracles don't depend on our faith: God is free to work with or without our cooperation.

The miracle also showed that God is willing to touch the lives of those who do not know him. His compassion is not limited to members of his spiritual family.

More significantly, the miracle Jesus performed on the Sabbath supported his claim to be One with the Father. He acted as sovereign Lord, choosing to show grace to whomever he wished. He acted on the Sabbath, asserting his Lordship over that holy day. And the nature of his miracle—restoring a hopeless invalid—suggests what Christ's power can do if we heed the gospel call to arise and walk with him throughout life.

JESUS HEALS A MAN WITH A WITHERED HAND   *Luke 6:6–10; Matthew 12:9–14; Mark 3:1–6*

Jesus healed a man with a withered hand on the Sabbath, infuriating the Pharisees and scribes [experts in Mosaic Law].

Background of the miracle. This is another of Jesus' Sabbath miracles (see the list on page 189). Jesus' performance of miracles on the Sabbath angered the religious establishment, which had defined in minute fashion every action a person could perform on the holy day. They had gone far beyond the simple Old Testament prescription for observance of the Sabbath. The charge that Jesus was a Sabbath-breaker was one of the most serious the Jewish leaders lodged against Jesus.

Parties to the miracle. The individuals who interacted in this miracle account were Jesus, the man with the withered hand, and "the scribes and Pharisees."

Jesus. In this account Jesus was the central figure, confronting the religious leaders whose efforts to discredit him were constantly frustrated. Jesus is also portrayed as a truly godly person who, unlike the leaders, had a deep concern for disabled man.

The man with the withered hand. He was the silent beneficiary of Jesus' compassion and

power. We know little about this man except that he was there and Jesus healed him.

The scribes and Pharisees. The Pharisees were committed to strict observance of Israel's Law. The "scribes" were men whose status was based on a knowledge of the Old Testament and what was known as the oral law—the rulings of earlier and contemporary rabbis. In the Gospels they are also called "lawyers," and "experts in the Law."

This passage shows these men in a bad light. They gathered in the synagogue not to worship but to find some charge against Jesus. They watched intently to see what Jesus would do for the man with the withered hand, not because they cared about his suffering, but so they could criticize and condemn if Jesus healed him. They are displayed as vindictive and heartless, more concerned about themselves and their privileged position than the people they led.

How the story unfolds. Jesus was teaching in a synagogue. In the congregation was a man with a withered hand. Scribes and Pharisees were also there, hoping Jesus would heal the man so they could accuse him of Sabbath-breaking.

Jesus interrupted his teaching and told the man with the withered hand to stand. As all eyes shifted toward the disabled man, Jesus challenged the religious leaders. He asked them "Is it lawful on the Sabbath to do good or to do evil, to save life or destroy?"

Jesus glared angrily at each scribe and Pharisee (Mark 3:5), but they remained silent. Jesus then told the man to stretch out his withered hand, and Christ restored it. The scribes and Pharisees remained silent, but they seethed with internal anger at this healing. Later they discussed "what they might do to Jesus" (Luke 6:11).

"A man was there" (Luke 6:6). Many have suggested that the scribes and Pharisees *arranged* for the man to be in the synagogue that morning. Their own presence—and the intentness with which they watched—does seem to suggest a trap!

"That they might find an accusation against him" **(6:7).** These men were completely closed to what Jesus was teaching. Their only concern was finding evidence on which they might accuse him of lawbreaking.

"Is it lawful on the Sabbath to do good or to do evil, to save life or to destroy?" **(6:9).** The rabbis did make exceptions to the Sabbath laws on work in order to "do good." For instance, giving alms was considered a major good work in Judaism. Yet, to give alms required carrying a coin or some food and transferring it from one person to another. On the Sabbath, it was unlawful to put something in the beggar's bowl, or to carry something outside the house to give to him. But the Mishna said,

> [If] the beggar stuck his hand inside,
>   and the
> householder [took something] from
>   it,
> or if [the householder] put
>   something in it and he [the
>   beggar] removed it,
> both of them are exempt (SHABBAT,
>   III. J-L).

Again, the Mishna dealt with exceptions to putting out an oil lamp. If this were done to save the wick, it would be work—because to put out a wick was considered an action which turned it into charcoal. However,

> he who puts out a lamp because he
>   is afraid of
> gentiles, thugs, a bad spirit,
> or if it is so that a sick person might
>   sleep,
> is exempt [from punishment]
>   (SHABBAT V 2:5 A-C).

It is clear, then, that even the scribes and Pharisees recognized in principle that it was lawful to do good on the Sabbath. In the synagogue that morning, Jesus' unanswered question showed up these scribes and Pharisees as hypocritical and heartless.

No wonder they raged inside (Luke 6:11). With a few words and a miracle of compassion, Jesus exposed their wickedness. They had no sense of guilt, but they were very sensitive to shame. And Jesus shamed them in front of everyone.

"He . . . looked around at them with anger" **(Mark 3:4).** Jesus felt compassion for the man with the withered hand. But he was angered by the heartlessness of the scribes and Pharisees. By having such disregard for another human being in need, these men who claimed to set the standard of piety in Israel had actually betrayed the God they claimed to honor.

Orthodoxy of the head without orthodoxy of the heart is an insult to God.

The meaning of the miracle. In addition to revealing the power of Jesus, this miracle contrasted the attitude of Jesus and the religious leaders of his time toward human beings. To Jesus, people were precious and their needs were paramount. To the Pharisees, ordinary people were nothing but *am ha-eretz,* "people of the land," commoners whose lack of dedication to the details of the law made them contemptible.

How amazing that to God each of us is of immeasurable worth, no matter what others may think of us. Those who dismiss any person with contempt reveal how far they are from the heart of God.

JESUS HEALS A CENTURION'S SERVANT   *Matthew 8:5–13; Luke 7:1–10*

A Roman army officer appealed to Jesus to heal his servant, displaying an amazing faith in Christ's power.

Background of the miracle. Centurions were the working officers of the Roman army. The title comes from the fact that they originally led one hundred men [from a term for a "century"]. They were intelligent and well-paid, typically staying in the military beyond the normal twenty-year enlistment. When discharged, centurions received a large bonus and generally became influential citizens of the cities in which they settled. In every mention of centurions in the New Testament, they are presented in a positive light (see also Mark 15:39; Acts 10:2; 27:43).

We do not know whether this centurion was retired or on active duty in Capernaum. We do know that the elders of the Jews interceded on his behalf—an unusual thing for a Jew to do for a Gentile. But their description of the centurion was also unusual. Most people in the Roman forces occupying Palestine were antagonistic toward the Jews. But this centurion was described by Jews as one who "loves our nation, and has built us a synagogue" (Luke 7:5).

The story appears in both Matthew and Luke. The details differ in the two accounts, but these are easily reconciled. The heart of the story is the same in each Gospel.

Parties to the miracle. Combining the two accounts, we see the following persons interacting in this miracle account: Jesus, the Jewish elders of Capernaum, the centurion, the sick servant, and friends whom the centurion sent to meet Jesus.

Jesus. In this story, Jesus is portrayed as the reliable object of an unusual faith. The centurion counted on Jesus far more than did the Jews to whom Jesus was sent. This is perhaps a foreshadowing of the church. In the book of Acts, far more Gentiles than Jews responded in faith to the message of the gospel.

The centurion. Several things about the centurion are attractive. He had a deep concern for a servant. The Greek word is *doulos,* "slave." In the hellenistic world, slaves were property. It was unusual for an important person to be concerned over a slave's well-being. In addition, the centurion had made an effort to understand the people among whom he was assigned. Rather than hold the Jews and their religion in contempt, this army officer had come to love the people and to honor their God. He was apparently a person of faith as well.

The centurion's slave. The only thing we know about this slave is that he was "lying at home paralyzed, dreadfully tormented" (Matt. 8:6). This is all we need to know about another person. If someone is hurting and we can help, it is our duty to respond.

The Jewish elders. These were the leading men or civil rulers of Capernaum rather than the scribes and Pharisees who made up the religious establishment. They interceded for the centurion to let Jesus know they considered him worthy of help, even though he was a Gentile who had no real claim to mercy from a Jewish prophet.

The centurion's friends. Luke 7:6 indicates that at one point the centurion sent friends to meet Jesus and to express the centurion's awareness that he was unworthy of welcoming Jesus into his home. This showed the centurion's sensitivity, for a strict Jew would consider himself defiled if he entered the house of a Gentile.

How the story unfolds. A centurion who lived in Capernaum, where Jesus had performed many miracles, had a sick slave about whom he was deeply worried. When the centurion heard that Jesus had returned to the city, he asked the Jewish elders of the city to intercede for his servant (Luke 7:3–5). Jesus heard them and started off with them toward the centurion's house.

The group was not far from the centurion's home when several of his friends meet Jesus with a message: the centurion realized he was "not worthy that You should enter under my roof." The centurion did not feel worthy to approach Christ in person (Luke 7:6, 7). But the centurion, as an army officer, understood how authority worked. So if Jesus would just say the word, he knew that his slave would be healed.

But the centurion was so concerned about the torment experienced by his slave that he couldn't wait. A few moments later, he himself arrived to plead for his slave (Matt. 8:6), personally expressing his confidence that Jesus need only say the word and his slave would be healed.

"Say the word, and my servant will be healed."

❖

Both Gospel writers indicate that Jesus "marveled," and told the crowds that "I have not found such great faith, not even in Israel" (Luke 7:9; Matt. 8:10).

Matthew followed up by quoting Jesus' warning to Israel. People from all over the world would respond with faith to Jesus as the centurion has and have a share in the kingdom promised to Abraham. But the "sons of the kingdom" would be cast into outer darkness (Matt. 8:11, 12).

Then Jesus dismissed the centurion. "As you have believed, so let it be done for you." And the slave was healed "that same hour" (Matt. 8:13).

The two accounts. Many interpreters have seen "errors" in these two Gospel accounts, arguing that the discrepancies disprove the doctrine of inspiration. But are the differences really errors? The narrative above integrates the two accounts easily, showing how the details in one Gospel supplement rather than contradict the details in the other.

But why the differences? Each Gospel writer had his own theme and audience in mind as he selected details to include in his account. Matthew's account doesn't mention the centurion's relationship with Jews. Matthew's account contrasts the faith-response of this Gentile with the lack of faith exhibited by Jesus' own people. The story is not only a miracle account but also an acted-out parable. Israel must respond with a faith like this Gentile's, or it will lose any privileges it counted on through physical descent from Abraham.

Luke, on the other hand, emphasizes the human dimension of Jesus' ministry. He, the elders, and the centurion are all part of a community. The Gentile centurion respects the Jews and their religion; the Jewish elders intercede for this Gentile with Jesus; Jesus willingly goes with them to the centurion's home. In Luke the thing that binds all the parties to the miracle together is a common faith in Jesus.

The elders appeal to Jesus for healing; the centurion exhibits an even greater faith than theirs. There is no warning to Israel in Luke, because Luke is intent on showing that through a common faith in Jesus the barriers that separate people can be broken down.

Luke, writing to the Hellenistic world that idealized harmony between peoples, shows that such harmony is possible when people have a common faith in Jesus Christ. Matthew, writing to Jews, is intent on showing his Jewish brothers and sisters that faith in Jesus is a matter of life and death.

In each Gospel, the focus is on faith in Jesus and an understanding of the source of his authority. But the details selected by each writer explore the implications of faith in a way that is appropriate to his audience.

"I also am a man placed under authority" (Luke 7:8; Matthew 8:9). The centurion explained what he meant with an illustration. He has soldiers under him. When he says "go," they go. As one "under authority," his right to command is rooted in his connection with the Roman emperor—the source of all authority in the Roman Empire. The soldiers

did not obey him as a person but as a representative of the emperor.

Under whose authority then was Jesus? The answer is that Jesus' connection was with God—the source of all authority in his universe. It follows that Jesus need not come to see the slave to heal him. Jesus only had to speak the word. Because Christ spoke with God's authority, the centurion knew that if Jesus commanded it, his servant would be healed. This is faith indeed.

While the Jewish people witnessed Jesus' miracles and wondered, the centurion saw them and believed. How ironic. The meaning of Christ's miracles was clear to a Gentile military man, while God's chosen people hesitated and held back.

"The sons of the kingdom will be cast out" (Matthew 8:12). The Jews of the first century believed that in addition to any personal merit they might gain from keeping the Law and from good works, they also accrued merit from the patriarchs Abraham, Isaac, and Jacob. Thus, not only was the nation God's chosen people; individuals were also given a boost in their efforts to earn salvation by their descent from Abraham.

Jesus' warning cut against this belief which was entrenched in rabbinic Judaism. What won the centurion Jesus' commendation was not his ancestry but his "great faith." Jesus went on to say that many people outside the Jewish nation [the meaning of "from east and west"] would have a place in the kingdom of heaven. Ancestry has nothing to do with salvation. The kingdom of heaven is for those who, like Abraham (Gen. 15:7) and the centurion, have faith in Christ.

This is true for us today. It's not what we do for God that wins us a place in his kingdom. It is faith in what God through Jesus has done for us.

JESUS RAISES A WIDOW'S SON   Luke 7:11–17

Jesus stopped a funeral procession and raised the only son of a widow.

Background of the miracle. Jesus had an itinerant ministry, traveling especially throughout the province of Galilee (compare Matt. 4:23). Luke places one of these journeys the day after the healing of the centurion's slave (see p. 191). Jesus came to the city of Nain, which was not far from Nazareth. As Jesus arrived, a large crowd was following a funeral procession.

Jewish custom required that a person be buried the day he or she died. The body was carried not in a coffin, as our text suggests, but in an open wicker bier. It was considered important for people to join a funeral procession as it passed by, so the mourners could be accompanied as a loved one was laid to rest. Thus, the raising of the widow's son was witnessed by many.

Parties to the miracle. The central figures in the drama were Jesus, the widow, her son, and the crowd accompanying the bier.

Jesus. Although Luke emphasizes the human side of Jesus, this is the only miracle report in which Luke mentions Jesus' compassion. In contrast, Christ's compassion for the hurting is mentioned three times in Matthew (14:14; 15:32; 20:34) and three times in Mark (1:41; 6:34; 8:2). No one in this report either asked for or expected the miracle which Jesus performed.

The widow. Luke indicates that Jesus had compassion "on her" (Luke 7:13). While Luke portrays her tears, he also introduces two special reasons for Jesus' emotional response. First, the dead man was her only son. And second, the woman was a widow.

The plight of a widow in biblical times is expressed in this saying of Rabbi Eliezer, "A slave gains when he acquires freedom from his master, but for a woman it is a liability, for she becomes disqualified from receiving *terumah* and loses her maintenance" (bGitt. 12:b). A wife was vulnerable in the ancient world. While her husband lived, he assumed the responsibility of her support. When he died, she was left on her own.

The problem was complicated in this case by the fact that in first-century Judaism, women could not inherit property from their husbands. Family property passed to the sons or, in exceptional cases, to a daughter. While there were systems by which wealthy husbands could provide support for their wives after death, the typical Galilean family had little. So it fell to the oldest son to care for his mother, in accord with the commandment, "Honor your father and your mother" (Ex. 20:12).

But the widow of Nain was truly a tragic figure. She had lost her husband, and now their only son, so that she herself was left destitute. No wonder Jesus had compassion on her!

The dead son. When Jesus raised the widow's son, he addressed him as "young man" (v. 14). The term suggests he was unmarried and had no children.

The crowd. The reaction of this crowd to Jesus' miracle contrasted starkly with the healing of a paralyzed man (Luke 5:26). In that healing, the religious leaders glorified God *instead of* giving Jesus any credit. In this case, the crowd glorified God because "a great prophet has risen up among us" (Luke 5:16).

How the story unfolds. Jesus "happened" to reach Nain just as a funeral procession was leaving. Jesus felt compassion on the widow. He told the widow not to weep and placed his hand on the bier to stop the procession. He then addressed the young man, commanding him, "Arise." Restored to life, the young man sat up, began to speak, and was presented by Jesus to the widowed mother. The crowd was awed, and they glorified God for raising up a prophet in Israel once again.

"Young man, I say to you, arise" (Luke 7:14). Several of the miracles of Jesus have been compared to those performed by Elijah and Elisha in the eighth century B.C. Like these two prophets, each of whom restored a dead person to life, Jesus also raised the dead. But there is a significant difference in the description of the process. Elijah and Elisha prayed, waited, and even stretched themselves out on the dead bodies before their return to life. Jesus did not appeal to God. He simply spoke to the dead, and the young man revived.

Christ had power *in himself* to raise the dead, for he *was* God.

The comparison between Jesus and the earlier prophets was not lost on the witnesses. Their happy cry, "A great prophet has risen up among us," reflects their immediate association of Jesus with Elijah and Elisha.

"God has visited his people" (7:16). The phrase is idiomatic, meaning "God is again acting for us!" The miracles that had marked God's intervention for Israel in the past were now being performed by Jesus. Surely history had again reached a major turning point!

"When the Lord saw her" (Luke 7:13). Luke earlier reported conversations in which others called Jesus "Lord" (Luke 5:8, 12; 7:6). But this is the first time Luke referred to Jesus as "the Lord." With this miracle, Luke expected his readers to recognize who Jesus was.

The meaning of the miracle. The miracle at Nain had great religious significance. First, it revealed Jesus' compassion. Second, it established the unlimited extent of Jesus' power. He exercised control over demons (Luke 4:33–36, 41), disease (Luke 5:12–15; 5:17–26), and now even death (Luke 7:11–17). Third, its correspondence to miracles performed by Elijah and Elisha marked Jesus unmistakably as a prophet in the eyes of the people.

But there is perhaps an even more important message. In this miracle of restored life, Jesus took the initiative. He saw the need, felt compassion, reached out to touch the dead man, and restored him to life. What a clear picture this is of our salvation. We did not seek God. As lost sinners, we were hostile to God and counted among his enemies because of our wicked works (Col. 1:21). But God had compassion on us. God took the initiative. He sent his Son to earth, and in his death on Calvary Jesus reached out to touch us. In this act, he did more than restore physical life. The crucified and risen Christ provided forgiveness and eternal life.

Jesus took the initiative. All we can do is to accept by faith the wonderful gift of life that he alone can give.

JESUS STILLS A STORM   *Mark 4:35–41; Luke 8:22–25; Matthew 8:23–27*

Jesus was asleep in a small boat when a sudden squall threatened to sink it. The terrified disciples awoke Jesus, who calmed the storm and used the incident to teach them about faith.

Background to the miracle. The Sea of Galilee lies between high hills. Sudden winds funneled between these hills can whip up the waters and create waves that endanger small boats. However, even the fishermen who were in the boat with Jesus were terrified by this storm, convinced they were about to die.

This miracle account is a favorite of most believers. Nearly every sentence in the brief story has immediate application to our lives.

Parties to the miracle. This is one of several "private miracles" performed for the benefit of Jesus' disciples. This miracle not only saved them but instructed them as well. The parties to this miracle were Jesus and an unspecified number of his disciples.

Jesus. Jesus was exhausted after a full day of ministry, and was asleep in the boat. The image of Jesus asleep while the storm raged around them is a vivid portrait of his calm confidence in God.

When Jesus was awakened by his terrified disciples, he immediately took charge, commanding the churning waters to "be still" (Mark 4:39). Jesus then used the experience to teach the disciples about faith by challenging them to evaluate their reaction during the storm.

The disciples. When the storm struck, the disciples were navigating the boat while Jesus slept. As the storm grew worse, they became terrified. Finally they woke Jesus up. When Christ commanded the storm to stop and the waters immediately become calm, the disciples were fearful and amazed. They asked each other, "Who can this be, that even the wind and the sea obey him?" (Mark 4:41).

How the story unfolds. Jesus slept as the disciples sailed a fishing boat toward the opposite

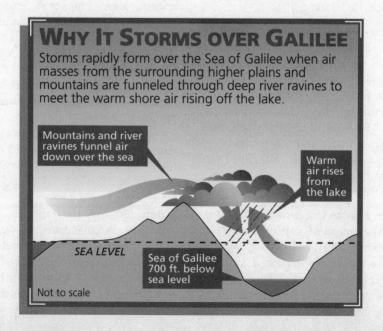

WHY IT STORMS OVER GALILEE

Storms rapidly form over the Sea of Galilee when air masses from the surrounding higher plains and mountains are funneled through deep river ravines to meet the warm shore air rising off the lake.

Mountains and river ravines funnel air down over the sea

Warm air rises from the lake

SEA LEVEL

Sea of Galilee 700 ft. below sea level

Not to scale

In the midst of a storm, Jesus rebuked the wind and sea—and they became calm.

❖

shore of the Sea of Galilee. A terrible storm struck suddenly. The terrified fisherman, certain the boat was about to sink, awakened Jesus. He stopped the storm and rebuked the disciples for their lack of faith. The amazed disciples voiced the question Mark wanted his readers to consider: "Who can this be?"

"He . . . rebuked the wind" (Mark 4:39). We have seen this term *rebuked* used by Jesus when casting out a demon (page 174) and when healing sickness (page 171). It is a word which indicates the subduing of an evil power. Some have taken its use here to indicate that Satan was behind the strong storm that struck while Jesus slept. In this view, Jesus' "rebuke" was of the demonic beings behind the storm.

This suggestion is unlikely. Ever since the Fall, nature itself has been turned against hu-

manity (Gen. 3:17, 18) and mankind has become vulnerable to all sorts of natural disasters. The miracle is intended to show Jesus' power over nature itself, and so to suggest his deity. The Creator alone can control material creation. Jesus' action that day recalled the words of Psalm 89:8, 9.

> O Lord God of hosts,
>   Who is mighty like You, O Lord?
>   Your faithfulness also surrounds You.
>   You rule the raging of the sea;
>   When its waves rise, You still them.

The answer to the disciples' question, "Who can this be?" had been provided long ago in the Word of God.

Personal application of the miracle account. This miracle account is a favorite of believers perhaps because it speaks so clearly and directly to each of us in our own lives.

- The great windstorm represents the storms we face in our lives.
- The boat represents our security, which is threatened by the waves beating into it.
- Jesus asleep in the boat represents the apparent silence of God when we are overcome by stress or fear.
- The cry "do You not care that we are perishing" (Mark 4:38) expresses our own deep feelings of abandonment by God when life overwhelms us.
- Jesus' rebuke of the wind and sea remind us of Christ's sovereign control over every circumstance in our lives.
- The calm that followed immediately after the storm symbolizes the inner calm we can experience when we rely on Jesus' love and his Word.
- Jesus' rebuke, "Why are you so fearful?" (Mark 4:40), reminds us that when Jesus is in our lives, we must trust him, even when life's storms intensify.
- Jesus' question, "How is it that you have no faith?" invites us to remember all that Christ has done for us in the past. Remembering yesterday's goodness strengthens the faith we need to face today and tomorrow.
- The disciples' fear reminds us always to hold Jesus in awe, remembering that he truly is God.
- The question, "Who can this be?" is answered by the miracle and the Scriptures. We are to concentrate on him, and not let life's circumstances confuse or distract us.

JESUS DELIVERS A DEMONIAC IN GEDARA   *Luke 8:27–39; Matthew 8:28–34; Mark 5:1–20*

Jesus met a violent man who terrorized the region of Gedara, and cast many demons out of him.

Background of the miracle. Demon possession was a reality in New Testament times, as it is in our own day. For a fascinating exploration of this subject, see *Every Good and Evil Angel in the Bible.*

Mark and Luke give lengthy reports of this miracle, and each writer mentions only one demonized man. Matthew mentions two men and identifies the area where the miracle took place as Gergesa rather than Gerasa (Mark; see the NKJV footnote to Luke 8:26). The variants in the names are not a major problem, because one refers to a town and the other to a district in the general area of Decapolis [the "ten cities"], which was Gentile territory.

The discrepancy between the number of demonized men has led some interpreters to argue that one of the Gospel accounts must be in error. But one authority makes this point:

Suppose you told a friend, "Jim was at the party but came late," while another person told the same friend, "Jim and Carl came late to the party." Should you be charged with an error because you failed to mention Carl when telling about Jim? Of course not. Why then should the New Testament be charged with an error because Matthew mentions two demon-possessed men while Mark and Luke tell about only one? (*Bible Difficulties Solved,* Baker, 237).

The fact is that the basic elements in each Gospel are the same, and there is no major conflict among these three different accounts. For the sake of simplicity, our discussion will draw from the accounts in Mark and Luke. They are longer and more detailed than Matthew's version.

Parties to the miracle. The interaction in the story focuses our attention on Jesus, the demonized man, the demon, and the people of the region.

Jesus. Again, Jesus is shown to be in complete control in a confrontation with a demon. Although the many demons exercised control of an individual, Jesus' power over the demons was undiminished.

The demonized man. The contrast between the condition of the man while dominated by demons and after Jesus expelled them is sharply drawn.

The symptoms of extreme demon possession seen in this man include the following:

- Disregard for personal dignity (nakedness, Luke 8:27).
- Withdrawal from society (Luke 8:27).
- Disregard for normal comforts (lived in the tombs, Luke 8:27).
- Affinity for unclean, isolated locations (lived in tombs, Luke 8:27).
- Violence against others (Luke 8:29).
- Unusual physical strength (Luke 8:29).
- Inarticulate speech (Mark 5:5).
- Self mutilation (Mark 5:5).

Perhaps the decisive demonstration of possession was the recognition by the demon of Jesus (Luke 8:30) and forced submission to him (Luke 8:31).

What a contrast we see in Luke 8:35, which describes the man who had been freed from the control of demons as "sitting at the feet of Jesus, clothed and in his right mind." The evil powers which had dominated him were gone, and the transformation was evident to all.

The demon. The demon had complete control of the man, and spoke through his voice. The name "Legion" was descriptive rather than personal. The name was appropriate because many demons had taken up residence in the victim's personality. But it is also clear from each account that the demons had to acknowledge the sovereignty of Jesus and to do whatever Christ commanded.

The people of the region. The people of the region reacted strangely to the miracle. Rather than see the possibilities for healing of their own sick by Jesus, they felt only a terror of the unknown, and they begged Jesus to leave the region.

How the story unfolds. Jesus sailed with his disciples across the Sea of Galilee to Gentile territory. As soon as he landed, he was met by a demon-possessed man. The demon was forced to his knees before Jesus, for he recognized Christ as the "Son of the Most High God," and begged Jesus not to "torment me." The demon confessed that his name was Legion, "because many demons had entered him."

The demons, fully exposed, begged Jesus to let them enter a nearby herd of pigs. Jesus permitted them to do so, but the pigs ran into the sea and drowned.

The demonized man was fully restored and listening to Jesus when people from the area hurried to this location to find out what had happened. They were so terrified by the supernatural events that they begged Jesus to leave their territory.

When the restored man asked permission to go with Jesus, Christ sent him home, encouraging him to "tell what great things God had done for you."

"He lived in the tombs" (Luke 8:27). Tombs as the resting place of the dead were ritually unclean for Jews. It is fascinating to note that the demons in this man begged to enter pigs,

"There met Him a certain man who had demons for a long time."

who were also ritually unclean. The account is thus bracketed by references to the unclean places preferred by demons. This underlines their own corrupt and corrupting nature (see Luke 8:29, which calls the demon an "unclean spirit").

"What have I to do with you" (8:28). The Greek saying, "What to me and to you," is both an admission of Jesus' superiority and an expression of the demon's desire to distance himself from Christ.

"I beg You, do not torment me" (8:28). The demon's cry may sound pitiful. But that demon had no pity on the man whom he tormented. Although Jesus had commanded the demon to leave the man, and the demon had to obey, he begged Jesus for a concession.

"Legion, because many demons had entered him" (8:30). There were 6,000 men in a fully staffed Roman legion. This name doesn't necessarily mean there were 6,000 demons infecting this victim. It does indicate what the text states: that "many demons had entered him."

We know little about how a demon settles into the personality and gains control over a person. This passage reminds us that more than one demon can express itself through individuals who become vulnerable to possession. Satanism and demon possession are often depicted by movie producers who know nothing of the terrible reality. This encourages the foolish to seek out such experiences.

"Into the abyss" (8:31). The "abyss" is a place in which some of the angels who fell with Satan are currently confined, awaiting God's final judgment (see 2 Pet. 2:4; Jude 6).

"He permitted them" (8:32). Christ's control over the demons was so complete that they could not act of their own volition. They could do only what Jesus permitted them to do. It is ironic that the demons begged to be permitted to enter other living beings, even animals. Yet as soon as they entered the pigs, they dashed into the sea and were drowned.

What God permits the evil spirits to do always proves to be their undoing.

"The whole multitude . . . asked him to depart" (8:37). The interesting thing about this request is that it was made after the people of the region had carefully examined what had happened. They "heard" reports of what had happened (Luke 8:34), and then "went out to see what had happened" (Luke 8:35). When they saw the demonized man fully restored, they inquired and learned "by what means he who had been demon possessed was healed" (Luke 8:36). Yet, after going through this process and learning the facts, the "whole multitude" asked Jesus to leave.

How amazing! Were they afraid Jesus' powers would be turned against them? Were they worried about the possible fate of other herds of pigs? Couldn't they see what Jesus' powerful, healing presence might mean to them and their loved ones?

We can't understand how these people, after such careful examination, could turn Jesus away! This is a powerful reminder to us that while the facts call for full commitment to Jesus, commitment remains a matter of faith.

"Jesus sent him" (8:38, 39). The man Jesus had restored wanted to go with Jesus. Instead, Jesus sent him to his "own house" to "tell what great things God has done for you." Christ still has a mission for those who make the commitment of faith to him. And it is the same mission on which the man freed from demons was sent. We are to go to our "own house"—our own family, our own coworkers, our own neighborhood—and tell what God has done for us.

The message of the miracle. The miracle accounts emphasize the total control the demons had gained over their victim. Yet that control was easily broken by Jesus. He easily expelled not one but many demons. The response of the Gerasenes and the freed victim portray the two possible responses we can make to Jesus. The miracle itself emphasizes the absolute and total authority of Jesus over all in the spiritual realm that might harm us.

JESUS HEALS A HEMORRHAGING WOMAN   *Luke 8:43–48; Matthew 9:20–22; Mark 5:25-34*

While Jesus was on his way to respond to a father's desperate appeal for help, he was touched by a woman with an unstoppable menstrual flow. She touched the hem of his clothing and was healed.

Background to the miracle. The condition of the woman with the flow of blood is far more serious than we might imagine. The medical complications are significant enough, for the constant loss of blood drains the victim of iron and other vital minerals. But in Judaism, such a flow of blood also made the woman ritually unclean.

The menstruant was *niddah,* and prohibited from having sexual relations. Rabbi Yoshaayah taught that a man should separate from his wife when she even *neared* her period. Rabbi Shimeon bar Yohai, in commenting on Leviticus 15:31, announced that "he who does not separate from his wife near her period, even if he has sons like the sons of Aaron, they will die."

The problem for the woman who sought out Jesus was even more acute. Menstruant women transferred their impurity to whatever they touched, including household implements and their contents. The rabbis decreed that even the corpse of a woman who died during her period had to undergo a special purification with water *(tNidd.9.16).* Thus the woman in this miracle account was not only cut off from her husband but also disqualified from the contribution she would normally have made to the family. And this had been the woman's experience for twelve long years (Luke 8:43)!

It is no wonder that, as Luke relates, she had "spent all her livelihood on physicians" (Luke 8:43). The tragedy was that although she had spent all she had, she "could not be healed by any."

Parties to the miracle. There seem to be only two parties to this miracle—Jesus, and the woman—although Peter has a small speaking part. Yet there is one other person who is not mentioned in this story of a miracle within a miracle. And that is Jairus, the anxious father of a dying daughter who had asked Jesus to treat her.

Jesus. Jesus had set out on an urgent mission, but he stopped when he felt "power going out from Me" (Luke 8:46). Christ was so filled with healing power that it was unnecessary for him to direct it. The miracle emphasizes the intrinsic power that resides in Christ.

The woman. Mark makes a point of this woman's reaction when Jesus stopped in the middle of the crowd and asked who touched him. She was "fearing and trembling, knowing what had happened to her" (Mark 5:33). The fear and trembling she felt may have been anxiety over Christ's reaction to being touched by an "unclean" woman. Any of the religious leaders of the time would have been horrified and angry, for her touch would have made *them* unclean. What the woman did not yet realize was that Christ had such a vitalizing holiness that a simple touch from him cleansed the unclean.

Peter. Mark describes "the disciples" reaction to Jesus' question about who touched him, while Luke casts Peter as the spokesman. Peter couldn't understand why Jesus would ask this question. How could anyone possibly identify a single touch while pushing his way through a crowd of people?

Peter failed to understand that Jesus was speaking of a special kind of touch—a touch which tapped into Jesus' unlimited source of power.

Jairus. This anxious father is not mentioned in this account, but his presence can be sensed. He had urged Jesus to come to his home because his only daughter was dying. It must have been hard enough for Jairus as the multitudes that thronged Jesus slowed their progress. But when Jesus actually stopped—to listen closely to this woman's story and then to encourage her—Jairus must have been frantic.

Didn't Jesus realize that his mission was *urgent?* How could the Lord dawdle when Jairus's little girl was dying?

And then as soon as Jesus finished speaking with the woman, word arrived that the daughter had died. We can only imagine the father's emotions, but from Jesus' words to him, fear seemed to predominate (Luke 8:50).

How the story unfolds. As Jesus followed Jairus to his home, a woman who had suffered from a continual menstrual flow for a dozen years came up behind him. Convinced that she would be made whole if only she could touch Jesus, she reached out and made contact with the hem of his garment. And her flow of blood miraculously stopped!

Jesus stopped too and asked who had touched him. The disciples did not realize that Jesus was speaking of a special touch. They expressed surprise that Jesus should ask such a question.

Finally the woman came forward, trembling. She fell down in the position of a supplicant and told her story, relating that she was healed the moment she touched Jesus. Christ not only showed no anger over being touched by a woman who was *niddah,* but explained,

"Your faith has made you well." Then he dismissed her with a blessing, "Go in peace" (Luke 8:48).

"Somebody touched Me" (Luke 8:46). What was so special about the touch of the woman?

It was intentional. The woman did not simply brush against Jesus accidentally. She intended to touch him.

It was purposeful. The woman was intent on being healed from the flow of blood that had made her an outcast for so many years.

It was faith-driven. The woman believed that Jesus had power in himself to heal her. It was this faith that drove her to find Jesus and to touch him.

It was efficacious. When the woman touched Jesus, she was healed immediately, and she felt the difference. She did not have to wait to see if the bleeding had really stopped. She knew immediately.

"Your faith has made you well" (Luke 8:48). The Greek word translated "made you well" is *sesoken,* from *sozo,* "to save." The primary focus is on deliverance from her medical condi-

A woman came up behind Jesus and touched His garment to receive healing.

tion. But in view of the implications of this woman's conditions in rabbinic Judaism, a broader meaning is implied.

- *The flow of blood* drained her physically.
- *The flow of blood* made her socially unclean and isolated her from others in the community.
- *The flow of blood* made her religiously unclean, and cut her off from worship at the temple.

Jesus' touch, however, *saved her physically* by restoring her health; saved her socially by restoring her fellowship with others in the community; and *saved her spiritually* by enabling her to join again those who worshiped God at the temple and on Israel's religious holidays.

What a picture this is of our salvation. When we approach Jesus with this woman's kind of faith, he saves us physically (a promise to be fulfilled completely in our resurrection). He saves us socially, as the Holy Spirit bonds us to others in the body of Christ to form a new and loving community. He saves us spiritually, forgiving us and making us children of God with access to the Father.

The tense of the Greek verb translated as "healed" in verse 48 emphasizes that the woman's healing had taken place, and that her deliverance would continue to affect her life. It is the same for us. We are saved once for all when we trust Jesus as Savior. And the saving impact of Jesus in our lives will continue to affect us for time and eternity.

"Your faith has made you well" (Luke 8:48). When the woman had told her story to Jesus, Jesus announced it was her faith that had made her well.

This statement is significant, for it is another clear expression of the gospel principle of grace. The woman was healed not because of any merit of hers, but because she exercised faith in Jesus. In the same way, people today can reach out to touch Jesus. How? Our approach to Jesus must be:

- *Intentional*. We consciously choose to come to Jesus Christ.
- *Purposeful*. We come to Jesus with the awareness that we are spiritually sick and need healing.
- *Faith-driven*. We come to Jesus because we believe that he and he alone can save.
- *Efficacious*. We sense within ourselves the Holy Spirit's testimony that we have been truly saved and made well.

"Go in peace" (Luke 8:48). The blessing with which Jesus dismissed the woman is also ours to claim. Christ had met her need on every level, bringing peace. When we come to Jesus with this woman's kind of faith, he meets our every need, and we also find peace.

JESUS RAISES JAIRUS'S DAUGHTER
Luke 8:41–56; Matthew 9:18–26; Mark 5:22–43

Jesus responded to the pleas of Jairus to help his daughter. The girl died while Jesus was on the way to her home, but Christ restored her to life.

Background of the miracle. The man who came to Jesus for help, Jairus, is identified in Luke 8:41 as a "ruler of the synagogue" (*archon tes synagoges*). This was an important position in Judaism. Three men represented the synagogue in local government. The president of this group of three was the "ruler of the synagogue." He was also was considered an archon of the local community ("rulers" in Matt. 9:18).

The head of the synagogue was not necessarily a rabbi, but he was an educated man who could evaluate the competence of those invited to read the Scriptures and address the people. He also ran the financial affairs of the synagogue and was responsible for ensuring correct behavior at worship. *This position* was unpaid, and it was held by those who were greatly respected in the community. Such a person was aided by a paid assistant who took care of the many practical details of maintaining the synagogue and its services (the "attendant" of Luke 4:20).

We know then that Jairus was an important man who held a respected religious and governmental post. It is significant that at least some persons of high standing—as well as the disadvantaged and the oppressed—had a real faith in Jesus.

Parties to the miracle. The central figures are Jesus, Jairus, and Jairus's daughter. We are also given glimpses of some people gathered at Jairus's home.

Jesus. Jesus was responsive to the synagogue president's request to come and heal his dying daughter. But on the way, Christ stopped to deal with a woman who had an unstoppable menstrual flow (see page 201). Given the urgency of Jairus's request, it may seem strange that Jesus paused for so long. His delay is explained when he went to the home and brought the girl, who had died, back to life. By waiting for the worst to happen, Jesus brought even greater joy to Jairus and offered proof of his power.

Jairus. Although he was an important man, he did not hesitate to hurry to Jesus to plead for help for his dying daughter. Jairus clearly was a man with faith in Jesus, for he believed that if Jesus would come and lay hands on his little girl, she would live.

We can only guess at Jairus's agony when Jesus delayed to speak with the woman whose flow of blood had been healed. Likewise, we can only imagine his joy when Jesus later delivered his daughter to him, alive and restored.

Jairus's daughter. Luke noted that the girl was twelve years old. This was just before the marriageable age of 13. Her death just before the experience of becoming a wife and mother adds to the sense of tragedy that Luke conveys.

The people gathered at Jairus's house. These are described as "those who wept and wailed loudly" (Mark 5:40). The implication is that they were professional mourners—women hired to accompany a funeral procession and loudly bewail the loss. When Jesus announced that the little girl inside was not dead but sleeping, those making the commotion ridiculed him. Their attitude may reflect their preference for a day's pay over the life of the young girl. Selfish self-interest is sometimes stronger than concern for the suffering.

How the story unfolds. Jesus responded to the urgent request of Jairus to go with him to save his young daughter's life. As they pushed through the crowds, a desperate woman touched Jesus and was cured of a chronic flow of blood that had ruined her life. Jesus then stopped and talked with her!

By the time Christ was ready to move on, messengers reported the child's death. But Jesus told Jairus not to fear but "only believe, and she will be made well."

When they arrived, they discovered that professional mourners had already filled Jairus's house and were making a great commotion. Jesus was ridiculed when he told them the girl was not dead but "sleeping." Jesus then removed the mourners, went into a room with the body of the girl, and called her back to life. The parents were amazed when he opened the door and told them to get her something to eat.

"He fell down at Jesus' feet and begged Him" (**Luke 8:41**). No matter how important we may be, there are times when our need is so desperate that there is no room for pride. It was this kind of situation which Jairus faced that day. How wonderful that we can go to Jesus with our needs, as Jairus did.

"Your daughter is dead. Do not trouble the teacher" (**8:49**). The messengers who came from Jairus's house were wrong on two counts.

They assumed that death limited Jesus' power. Soon they would see Jairus's daughter alive and well again. Even death submits to the word of Jesus Christ.

They assumed that Jesus would not want to be bothered with Jairus's suffering. Even when God does not intervene to help, Christ does care for us and feels with us in our pain.

"Only believe, and she will be made well" **(8:50).** It would be easy to misunderstand this sentence. Jesus did not say, "Only believe *in order that* she may be made well." Jairus's belief was not a condition of the girl's healing. Jesus said, "Only believe *and* she will be made well."

Belief in Jesus would calm the father's fears and give him hope until Jesus actually made her well. Then the father would not need faith; he would possess what faith had led him to expect.

It was Jesus, and not Jairus's faith, that performed the miracle. Jesus' ability to exercise his power doesn't depend on human faith. Faith in Jesus will carry *us* through our dark times, until God acts to meet our needs. Then faith's expectation will be rewarded with the thing for which we had hoped.

"She is not dead, but sleeping" **(8:52).** This seems a strange saying, because the girl *was* dead. But the key to understanding these words is to realize what they and he meant by "dead."

To the parents and the mourners, "dead" meant gone—cut off from the realm of the living, forever lost to loved ones. To Jesus, biological death was as temporary as that peaceful unconsciousness into which we slip each night. Jesus knew there will be an awakening for the dead, just as there is an awakening each morning for the sleeping. Paul captured the glory of this truth in 1 Thessalonians 4:13, 14, where he encouraged believers not to

sorrow as others who have no hope. For if we believe that Jesus died and rose again, even so God will bring with him those who sleep in Jesus.

Our dead sleep now. But when Jesus returns, there will be a grand awakening!

The meaning of the miracle. This miracle reminds us that Jesus controls both death and life. As with Jairus's daughter, the death of our loved ones brings grief and fear. Yet this miracle account reminds us that while we wait for

the great reunion that will come when the dead in Christ are raised, we wait in faith. We will be "made well" in that glorious time.

JESUS HEALS TWO BLIND MEN
Matthew 9:27–31

Jesus healed two blind men who cried out to Him as "Son of David."

Background of the miracle. Blindness has been common in the Middle East since before biblical times. Yet the Old Testament records no such miracle of restoring sight as Jesus performed (see Matt. 4:23; 8:16–17; 9:35). Each of the Gospels reports several incidents of him restoring sight to the blind. Why such an emphasis on these events and on other healing miracles?

Isaiah 35:5, 6 associated such healings with the messianic age. Isaiah predicted for Israel that when God "comes to save you,"

Then the eyes of the blind shall be
    opened,
And the ears of the deaf shall be
    unstopped.
Then the lame shall leap like a deer,
And the tongue of the dumb sing.

The miracles that Jesus performed fulfilled this prophecy. They should have been recognized by the Jewish people and their teachers as proof of who Jesus was. We learn in this miracle story, however, that the first people to clearly see the significance of what Jesus did were two blind men!

Parties to the miracle. The miracle account, told in just three verses and recorded only in Matthew, mentions only Jesus and the two blind men.

Jesus. Jesus is given two titles in these verses: Son of David and Lord. Both are significant for understanding the implications of the event.

The two blind men. They are the first persons in Matthew's Gospel to address Jesus as "Son of David." This was a Messianic title, for the promised deliverer was to be a descendant of

David and thus one qualified to inherit Israel's throne.

How the story unfolds. Just after Jesus left Jairus's house (see p. 203), he heard two blind men calling to him as "Son of David," asking for mercy. Jesus took the blind men inside the house [where he was staying?] and questioned them about their faith. Each professed faith in him, addressing him as Lord. Christ then touched their eyes and restored their sight.

Although Jesus "sternly warned them" not to tell anyone, they "spread the news about him in all that country."

"Do you believe that I am able?" (Matthew 9:28). Why the emphasis on faith in this miracle account? There are several reasons.

Faith, not desperation. When people are desperate, they often cry out to God without any conviction that he can help—or even that he exists. Jesus' questioning revealed that the blind men came to him not out of desperation but in faith.

Focused, not general. Christ asked in pointed fashion, "Do you believe *that I am able to do this?*" The power of God is made available to us in Jesus. Our faith is not to be in some abstract being "out there," but in the person of Jesus Christ, God the Son incarnate, our Savior. Jesus' questioning revealed that the blind men truly trusted him and his ability to save.

Effective, not futile. Some interpreters make a serious error with these words. They assume that when Jesus said "according to your faith," he meant that if they had *enough* faith their sight would be restored. Not at all. The healing was according to the object of their faith. They were healed because their trust was in Jesus.

Faith in Jesus still opens the channel through which God's love and power will flow.

"Son of David . . . Lord" (Matthew 9:27, 28). Christ's questioning of the two blind men established that their faith was truly in him. It also established that they understood who he was. Their cry "Son of David" is the first public acknowledgment recorded in Matthew that Jesus was the promised Messiah. During their questioning by Jesus, they also acknowledged Jesus as Lord.

The word *Lord* in the first century was sometimes used in addressing a superior as a sign of respect. But its use in this context is far more significant. Jesus was not only Israel's Messiah; he is history's sovereign Lord.

To have real faith in Jesus, we must recognize and acknowledge him for who he truly is.

Jesus "warned them sternly" (Matthew 9:30). The Greek word used here is *embrimaomai,* which occurs only five times in the New Testament (Mark 1:43; 14:55; John 11:33, 38). Always it is connected with deep emotion. Why the emotion here, and why the stern warning?

When this miracle took place, Jesus had been teaching and working miracles in Judea and Galilee for some time. Now, at last, the message of his miracles to Israel had been recognized by the two blind men. No wonder Jesus felt strong emotion at that moment. And no wonder Jesus questioned them so closely about their faith. Had they *really* understood? They had!

But Jesus knew that the rest of the people would *not* understand. Neither would they respond with a faith like that of these two men. It was best that this miracle, so briefly stated but so meaningful to Jesus, not be reported to the doubting crowds.

But the blind men, excited by their healing, couldn't keep quiet. They spread the news everywhere. They couldn't sense what the miracle healing had meant to Jesus. They only knew what it had meant to them.

How important it is to realize that the miracles God performs may be as significant a blessing to him as they are to us.

JESUS CASTS OUT A MUTE SPIRIT
Matthew 9:32–35

Jesus cast out an evil spirit that had blocked a man's ability to speak.

Background of the miracle. Matthew indicates this miracle took place as two blind men whose sight had been restored (see page 205) were leaving Jesus' house (Matt. 9:32). The two miracles are linked also by Matthew's intent to contrast the responses to Jesus by the blind men, the crowds, and the Pharisees. The two miracle accounts should thus be examined and taught together.

Parties to the miracle. The three brief verses that contain this account focus our attention on the interaction of Jesus, the mute man, the multitudes, and the Pharisees.

Jesus. Jesus had just been recognized by two blind men as Israel's Messiah and sovereign Lord. His miracles, performed in fulfillment of prophecy, offered proof of his identity (see *"Background of the miracle,"* above).

The mute man. The Greek word used of his disability is *kophos,* which generally has the meaning of "deaf mute." The text makes it clear that the cause of his malady was not organic, but oppression by an evil spirit.

The multitudes. Matthew emphasizes the astonishment of the crowds which witnessed this miracle and their awareness that "it was never seen like this in Israel" (9:33). No Old Testament prophet worked miracles like those which Jesus was performing.

The Pharisees. These influential men had a reputation for piety because of their strict observance of Mosaic Law. They had decided that Jesus' power must come from Satan, not God.

How the story unfolds. As the blind men whose sight Jesus had restored left, a mute man was brought to Jesus. Jesus cast out the evil spirit who had blocked the man's powers of speech, and the mute began to speak. The crowd was amazed, because in all of sacred history nothing like Jesus' miracles had been witnessed. The Pharisees, confirmed in their hostility toward Jesus, muttered and accused him of being part of a satanic conspiracy.

Three responses to the two miracles. This miracle must be examined with the healing of the two blind men which immediately preceded it. Matthew's point in linking the two was to demonstrate the differing responses to those who observed Jesus' performing miracles.

The two blind men. The two blind men realized that Jesus' miracles marked him as the Messiah, and they put their trust in him (Matt. 9:27, 28).

The crowd. The crowd acknowledged that "it was never seen like this in Israel." No healings such as these had been performed by Israel's prophets. But the phrase "seen like this" is significant. While such miracles had never been *seen,* they had been *predicted by Isaiah* (see p. 205)! And that prediction associated the miracles Jesus performed with the coming of the Messiah. In fact, the first two miracles mentioned In Isaiah 35:5 are:

> Then the eyes of the blind shall be
>   opened,
> And the ears of the deaf shall be
>   unstopped.

If we understand *kophos* to mean "deaf mute," these are the very miracles Matthew recorded in this passage!

The crowds, like the two blind men, had all the proof they needed that Jesus was the Messiah! But unlike the blind men, they simply could not "see."

The Pharisees. The judgment of the Pharisees is harsher and more revealing. These men who took such pride in their knowledge of the Law should have noticed immediately the relationship between the miracles Jesus performed and the messianic promises. Unlike the crowds, they were *willfully* blind. In ascribing Christ's miracles to Satan, they rejected the testimony of the Scriptures which they claimed to honor.

No wonder John reported Christ saying at another time, "You search the Scriptures, for in them you think you have eternal life; and these are they which testify of Me. But you are not willing to come to Me that you may have life" (John 5:39, 40).

The meaning of the miracles. These miracles have a unique function. Note that these two miracles are found only in Matthew's Gospel and that his Gospel was directed primarily to a Jewish audience.

In selecting these two miracles and focusing attention on the response of various groups to Jesus, Matthew presents a strong argument for Jesus' Messiahship. These miracles are linked in prophecy with the messianic age to be instituted by God.

But do people respond when Jesus offers his miracles as proof of his messiahship? A few recognized him and respond with faith (the two blind men). Most were confused and unable to grasp the meaning of what they had witnessed (the crowds). And the religious leaders, who knew most about the Scriptures and should have understood the significance of Jesus' wonders, were simply "not willing" to submit to him. They not only rejected him; they turned others against him by charging that he was part of a satanic conspiracy.

Jesus presents himself today as the wonder-working Savior, and we must also decide for or against placing faith in him.

JESUS FEEDS 5,000 PEOPLE *John 6:1–14; Matthew 14:13–21; Mark 6:30–44; Luke 9:10–17*

Jesus fed a large crowd which followed him into the wilderness, using only a few small loaves and fishes.

Background to the miracle. It was the responsibility of the head of each Jewish family at mealtime to look up to heaven while thanking God, and then to break and distribute bread for the meal. One of the most common of such mealtime prayers was, "Blessed art Thou, O Lord our God, King of the Universe, who brings forth bread from the earth."

In performing this miracle, Jesus assumed the role of head of the family as well as the role of God, bringing forth bread to meet the needs of his people.

The Gospel writers followed Jewish custom in counting only the men when reckoning the crowd. While the ideal woman of rabbinic lore stayed at home, it is clear from the Gospels and from various references in early rabbinic literature that women went to the market and worked in the fields with their husbands at harvest time. Some have estimated that the crowd Jesus fed, if the women and children were added, might have been fifteen or twenty thousand.

This is an especially significant miracle, for it is reported in all four of the Gospels.

Parties to the miracle. The significant figures in this miracle account are Jesus, the disciples, the thousands who had followed Jesus into a wilderness area, and a boy who shared his lunch.

Jesus. Jesus' revealed his deity by creating bread, as if in answer to the usual mealtime prayer.

Jesus' disciples. The disciples showed sensitivity to the needs of the crowd for food and shelter (Matt. 14:15). But their solution, to "send them away, so they can buy bread," was not acceptable to Jesus. The disciples were stunned when Jesus ordered, "*You* give them something to eat" (Mark 6:37).

The crowds. Great crowds had followed Jesus into a "deserted" (uninhabited) area. They had come hastily, without bringing food to eat on the way. Jesus saw them as sheep, wandering aimlessly, helpless without a shepherd.

The boy. The boy who provided the food Jesus multiplied is mentioned only by John (6:9). How strange that in many Sunday school lessons, he is made the focus of this story rather than Jesus.

How the story unfolds. Jesus had been surrounded and harried by crowds of people coming and going. He told his disciples it was time to rest, so they set out by boat to find a deserted place.

But other people recognized him as the boat passed. By the time the boat landed, a new multitude had gathered to greet him. Jesus couldn't escape, even for a moment. Rather than being irritated, Jesus was deeply moved; these ordinary people to him were like sheep without a shepherd. So he began to teach them.

When evening drew near, the disciples reminded Jesus that it was late, and they were in an uninhabited area. Jesus needed to send the people away soon, so they could "buy themselves bread." Jesus shocked the disciples by his reply: "*You* give them something to eat" (Mark 6:37).

Confused, the disciples objected. It would take at least eight month's wages to buy enough bread for such a crowd, even if that much bread were available. Jesus asked, "How many loaves do you have?"

The disciples reported they could come up with five loaves (each about the size of a modern dinner roll) and two small fish. Jesus told the disciples to have the crowd sit down in groups, as they would at mealtime. Christ then blessed the bread [i.e., said the prayer used before eating] and began to break the bread and fish into smaller pieces. The food was miraculously multiplied. After everyone had eaten, twelve flat wicker baskets of food were left over.

Jesus then sent the crowds away. While he went up into the mountains to pray, the disciples set out by boat to cross the sea.

Sheep not having a shepherd (Mark 6:34). Jesus' imagery has deep Old Testament roots. Moses prayed that God would provide a successor who "may lead them [Israel] out and bring them in, that the congregation of the Lord may not be like sheep which have no shepherd" (Num. 27:17). God's answer in that situation was to set apart Joshua—which is the Hebrew version of the name "Jesus."

Even more significant is the use of the image in Ezekiel 34. In that passage, the prophet condemned the false shepherds who mistreated God's flock and who led them astray. God promised,

"Indeed I Myself will search for My sheep and seek them out. As a shepherd seeks out his flock on the

Jesus blessed the bread and fish and gave it to the disciples to distribute.

day he is among his scattered sheep, so will I seek out My sheep and deliver them. . . . I will feed My flock, and I will make them lie down," says the Lord God. "I will seek what was lost and bring back what was driven away, bind up the broken and strengthen what was sick" (Ezek. 34:11–12, 15–16).

What happened that day by the Sea of Galilee identified Jesus with the Lord God of the Old Testament, whose concern was for the well-being of the flock. In Christ, God was seeking out and feeding Israel not only with bread but with truth as well.

"You give them something to eat" (Mark 6:37).

Jesus didn't expect the disciples to perform a miracle. But the command, with its emphatic "you" in the Greek, is significant.

Jesus challenged the disciple's solution. The disciples had been concerned for the crowd. But their solution was to send them away so they could "buy themselves bread" (Mark 6:36). But Jesus did not come to send people away. He came to draw them to him. He came because the people could not "buy themselves" what they required to meet their deepest need. Only Jesus could meet that need, and he did so supremely on Calvary.

Jesus challenged the disciple's vision. Jesus was training his disciples so they would be able to meet the needs of the shepherdless. "*You* give them" was a challenge to help them catch a vision of the mission for which they were being prepared.

Jesus challenged the disciple's understanding. The answer to their confusion on how to fulfill Jesus' command was not to buy bread but to look to Jesus. Christ never asks us to do anything without providing the needed resources to complete the task.

The miracle that followed illustrates this principle. Jesus took what the disciples had and multiplied it. No matter how limited our resources, God's ability to multiply them is as unlimited as they were on that day in the wilderness.

Twelve baskets of fragments (Mark 6:43).

The Gospel writers report that everyone in the crowd ate and were filled, after which they took up 12 baskets of fragments. Some have seen significance in the number 12. There were 12 tribes of Israel. Messiah's provision was so generous that even his scraps can supply the needs of Israel, as represented by the 12 surplus baskets.

"Take him by force to make him king" (John 6:15).

John adds a detail not mentioned in the other Gospels. After the meal, the enthusiastic crowd decided that Jesus must be the prophet promised by Moses (Deut. 18:18). Why not then acclaim Jesus king?

Jesus later commented on their motive. "You seek me, not because you saw the signs, but because you ate of the loaves and were filled" (John 6:26). The people had not seen the meaning of the miraculous sign which identified Jesus as the Lord God, their Shepherd. All they knew was that he was someone who could feed them. Self-interest, not faith, lay at the root of their enthusiasm. No wonder they were ready to proclaim Jesus king.

How ironic are the phrases "take him by force" and "make him" king. Those who acclaim a person king will be willing to submit to his will. The crowd intended to make Jesus submit to their will, thus robbing him of his royal authority. Let's be careful not to do the same. When we come to God in Jesus' name, may our prayers be for that which is in his will. As true followers of Christ, we should not attempt to cajole him into doing our will.

Miracle and message (John 6:26–66).

John's Gospel follows a pattern noted before (p. 186). He describes a miracle, then records a lengthy teaching of Jesus which is related to it. That lengthy teaching in John 6 has been called Jesus' "Sermon on the Bread of Life."

In this sermon, Jesus pointed out the selfish motives of the crowds who followed him. But Christ himself is the true bread, the source and sustainer of life. He is the true bread of heaven, who has been sent by the Father to give eternal life to everyone who believes in him. The ancestors of his hearers who had eaten manna in the wilderness were all dead, but those who would appropriate Christ—figuratively eating his flesh and drinking his blood—would live forever.

John notes that after this sermon "many of his disciples [used here in the sense of loose adherents] went back and walked with him no more" (John 6:66). They had eagerly received the bread that sustained physical life, but they rejected the Word that promised eternal life.

Some people today preach a false gospel, which promises material prosperity to those with enough faith. How eagerly the crowds in Jesus' day would have welcomed such a gospel. And how quickly we turn away from the true gospel as well. The authentic gospel promises us new life, but then it calls us to live this new life not for ourselves but for the Lord.

The meaning of the miracle. Commentators tend to follow many side trails in discussing the feeding of the 5,000, but we must not forget this miracle's central message. In each Gospel, this miracle is an acted-out parable. Jesus declared himself to be the Lord God, come to shepherd his people, as he had promised through the prophet Ezekiel.

JESUS WALKS ON WATER   *Matthew 14:22–33; Mark 6:45–52; John 6:15–21*

Jesus walked on a stormy sea and joined his disciples in their small boat.

Background of the miracle. After Jesus fed the 5,000, he "made" his disciples get in their boat and go on ahead of him (Matt. 14:22). The strong Greek verb in this passage is often translated "compelled."

What was the urgency?

- Jesus may have sent the disciples ahead to help diffuse the crowd that wanted to make him king (compare John 6:15).
- Jesus wanted to escape both the crowd and the disciples, to get some rest (Mark 6:31–32).

- Jesus definitely wanted to spend some time alone with his Father in prayer (Matt. 14:23).

The separation of Jesus from his disciples provided the occasion for this miracle.

When the disciples first saw Jesus approaching them on the lake, they mistook him for a ghost. Their fear reflected the common first-century belief that ghosts were hostile beings, the shades of malevolent men who had died, and who would harm human beings.

Parties to the miracle. Jesus is the central figure. The others involved are the twelve disciples, with the emphasis on Peter.

Jesus. After resting and praying Jesus was walking on the surface of the Sea of Galilee, apparently crossing it to join the disciples who had gone on ahead by boat. The miracle displayed Christ's control of the forces of nature.

The disciples. The disciples' initial reaction of fear was transformed to worship as the miracle impressed them with the fresh realization that Jesus was "the Son of God" (Matt. 14:33).

Peter. Peter is both a good example and a bad example in this miracle account. He alone had faith enough in Jesus to step out of the boat into the stormy sea. But once on the waters, his gaze was torn from Jesus and fixed on his surroundings. We are also asked to risk in response to Jesus' call. Peter's experience reminds us not to take our eyes off Jesus in difficult situations.

How the story unfolds. Jesus hurried his disciples into a boat and away from the crowds. It is likely that he told them to wait for him until a fixed time and if he had not arrived by then, they should set out to cross the lake. But the sea was stormy and the wind was in their face. By four o'clock in the morning, the disciples were only halfway across the lake.

When they noticed a figure walking on the water, the disciples were terrified, assum-

Jesus approached the disciples, walking on the water in the midst of a storm.

❖

ing it must be a ghost. But Jesus called out and identified himself. Peter then asked the Lord to tell him to join him on the waters. Jesus did, and Peter stepped out into the stormy waters. He walked a few steps toward Jesus but was distracted by the raging winds and began to sink.

Jesus caught Peter's hand and lifted him up, calling him a "little-faith" person and asking, "Why did you doubt?" (Matt. 14:31). When Jesus and Peter got into the boat, the winds and the sea calmed down.

Amazed, the disciples worshiped Jesus. For the first time in Matthew's Gospel, they expressed the belief that Jesus was "the Son of God" (Matt. 14:33; see also Matt. 16:16; 26:63; 27:40, 43, 54).

"The fourth watch of the night" (Matt. 14:25). The Romans divided the night into four watches, the Hebrews into three. The Roman system was adopted by all the Gospel writers. Thus, Jesus approached the boat between 3:00 A.M and 6:00 A.M

"It is I" (14:27). The Greek phrase is *ego eimi,* and it may reflect the Old Testament name *Yahweh,* meaning "I AM." No wonder Jesus could encourage his disciples to "take courage" [rendered "be of good cheer" in our text], and "do not be afraid." Since God was with them, they had no reason to fear.

"Command me to come to You" (14:28). The incident with Peter offers an interesting commentary on Jesus' words of encouragement.

"Lord, if it is You" (14:28). The conditional here has the meaning, "*Since* it is You." Jesus had announced, *ego eimi* ("it is I"). Peter had confidence that Jesus truly was Lord.

"When Peter had come down out of the boat" (14:29). Jesus said, "Take courage." Peter showed his courage by stepping out boldly into the surging waters.

"He was afraid, and beginning to sink" (14:30). Jesus had said, "Do not be afraid." Out on the waves alone, Peter did fear. And he began to sink. Fear may overcome us also when we take our eyes off Jesus and concentrate on our circumstances.

"O you of little faith" (14:31). It is far better to be a "little faith" person than a "no faith" person. But best of all is to be a person of "great faith."

"Why did you doubt" (14:31)? At first, the answer seems obvious. Peter doubted because the circumstances were fraught with danger. But the question encouraged Peter and the disciples to look deeper. Jesus had announced "It is I." No matter how hazardous the circumstances may be, there was no reason to doubt when Jesus was present.

This is one of the most important messages of this miracle for us today. We can become so obsessed with difficulties and dangers that our doubts overwhelm us. Yet if Jesus, the Son of God, is with us, he is in control of every circumstance. We need to be as bold as

Peter in walking through our stormy waters, yet wiser than Peter by never forgetting Jesus' presence in our lives.

"They had not understood" (Mark 6:52). Mark's account of this miracle displays a slightly different emphasis than Matthew's. Mark draws our attention to the disciples' hardened hearts. The phrase indicates an underlying attitude which accounts for their amazement at Jesus' ability to walk on water and at the immediate calming of the waters when Jesus entered the boat. They had just seen Jesus feed 5,000 people. They should have recognized his claim to be the Lord, come to offer himself as Shepherd to his people (see p. 208f.).

While this emphasis is different from Matthew's, the two accounts are actually in complete harmony. The private miracle performed on the Sea of Galilee taught the disciples what the feeding of the 5,000 had not—

that "truly, You are the Son of God" (Matt. 14:33).

The meaning of the miracle. With this miracle, we have evidence that the true identity of Jesus was beginning to dawn on his disciples. They would grasp the full meaning of that confession—"You are the Son of God" (Matt. 14:33)—only later, after the Cross and the Resurrection.

Looking back from that perspective today, we can see in this miracle more evidence that Jesus was who he claimed to be. We can see something of what it means to live in relationship with the Son of God.

The life of faith calls for a boldness like Peter's. He was willing to risk leaving the security of the boat to walk alone on the stormy lake. Faith also calls for a continual awareness that Jesus is with us. This will dispel our doubts, no matter how difficult our circumstances may be.

CHAPTER 11

JESUS: MIRACLES OF THE SON OF GOD

ASSURANCE OF THE RESURRECTION
Matthew—John

Miracles accompanied Jesus throughout His public ministry. Even as Jesus hung on Calvary's cross, wonders took place around Him.

The miracles of Jesus mark Christ as God's messenger. And Jesus' own words mark Him as the Son of God. As we read the accounts of the wonders this Man performed we are confronted with evidence that supports His claims about Himself.

But all Jesus' miracles, as wonderful as they were, pale before the grand miracle of the Resurrection (see pages [15–17]). In the words of the apostle Paul, by His resurrection from the dead Jesus was "declared to be the Son of God" (Romans 1:4).

JESUS HEALS A SYRO-PHOENICIAN GIRL Matthew 15:21–28; Mark 7:24–30

Jesus first ignored and then responded to the plea of a Gentile woman who begged him to cast a demon from her daughter.

Background of the miracle. This miracle took place in the region once controlled by the cities of Tyre and Sidon, which lay on the Mediterranean coast about thirty and fifty miles, respectively, from Galilee. While Jesus often "withdrew" from the crowds to rest (Matt. 4:12; 12:15; 14:13) this is his only recorded retreat to Gentile territory. His search for solitude was thwarted, however, as "he could not be hidden" (Mark 7:24). He was apparently recognized by some people who had come from this region earlier to hear him (Mark 3:8; Luke 6:17).

The woman from this region who appealed to Jesus was called a "Greek" by Mark. He used the term as a synonym for "non-Jew." Matthew identified her as a Canaanite, one of the ancient pagan peoples who were Israel's traditional enemies. While the Bible reports healings by Jesus of non-Jews in Jewish territory, this is the only miracle he performed for a pagan in Gentile lands.

Parties to the miracle. The persons in this miracle story are Jesus, the Canaanite woman, and the disciples.

Jesus. Jesus left Jewish territory to escape the crowds so he could rest. But even here, he was recognized. The most striking feature of this account is Jesus' apparent coldness to and initial rejection of a desperate woman. It seems so out of character for Christ, normally so compassionate, to fail to respond to anyone who requested his help. Especially troubling to some interpreters is Jesus' comparison of the Jews to "children" and Gentiles to "dogs."

The Canaanite woman. Following Jesus in spite of his apparent indifference, the woman begged him to help her "severely demon-possessed" daughter (Matt. 15:22). When Jesus finally spoke to her, her reply showed her wisdom and faith.

The disciples. The disciples were puzzled observers. They were irritated when the woman trailed after them, constantly crying out for Jesus' help. They suggested that Jesus help her in order to get rid of her. This shows they misunderstood the critical issues involved.

How the story unfolds. Jesus' attempt to get some rest was frustrated when he was recognized even in gentile territory. One persistent woman annoyed the disciples by following Jesus around, crying out loudly for help. When they urged Jesus to heal her and get rid of her, Christ explained that he was "not sent except to the lost sheep of the house of Israel" (Matt. 15:24).

The woman fell at his feet and begged him to help. Jesus refused, saying it wasn't good to throw the children's bread to dogs. The analogy was clear: the Jews were the children; she and other Gentiles were dogs! The woman agreed, but pointed out that dogs do eat the crumbs that fall from the table as the children eat. Christ commended her faith and indicated her request had been granted. At that moment, her daughter was healed.

"Son of David" (Matthew 15:22). This title is reserved for Israel's Messiah, the promised King from David's line. In using this title, the Canaanite woman acknowledged Jesus as the Jewish Messiah. Later she worshiped him as "Lord" (Matt. 15:25), a term which emphasized Jesus' rule over humankind. Christ was

"Son of David" for Israel; "Lord" for all mankind.

"Send her away, for she cries out after us" (15:23). Jesus' reply (Matt. 15:23) made it clear that the disciples were urging Jesus to send her away with her request granted. But note their motive. The disciples were moved by annoyance, not compassion.

"Not sent except to the lost sheep of the house of Israel" (15:24). Jesus at an earlier time had sent his disciples on a preaching mission with the warning, "Do not go into the way of the Gentiles, and do not enter a city of the Samaritans. But go rather to the lost sheep of the house of Israel" (Matt. 10:5, 6). Christ was Israel's Messiah. His mission required him to concentrate his initial efforts on recalling straying Israel to relationship with God.

Mark, writing to the Gentiles, included a detail that Matthew left out. He quoted Jesus as saying to the woman, "Let the children be filled *first*" (7:27). God always intended that the gospel message have a universal impact. Yet it was only right that Jesus should first present himself to Israel as the fulfillment of the prophets' hopes and dreams.

"Throw it to the little dogs" (15:26). It is true that first-century Jews dismissed Gentiles as dogs. But Christ's analogy in this verse is not a condemnation of the Gentiles. He pictured a familiar household scene. When the family gathered for a meal, the parents didn't take food prepared for the children and put it on plates to feed puppies. Mom and dad may have a real affection for the puppies, but they don't give them the meal prepared for their children.

God had prepared the meal of miracles and wonders for Israel, the covenant family, who like lost sheep had strayed far from God. Miracles and wonders were not to be "thrown away" on Gentiles. Most of them would not be tuned in to spiritual matters.

"Crumbs" (15:27). The woman didn't argue or plead. In saying "Yes, Lord," she acknowledged the validity of Jesus' position. But she used Christ's own analogy. While it was true that the meal is prepared for the children, the puppies do get any crumbs that fall from the table. All she was asking for was one of those crumbs.

What a faith this Canaanite woman displayed. The miraculous healing she asked for would not be a problem for Jesus. She knew his power was so great that such a miracle would be a mere crumb from a table laden with goodness. And she was right.

"Great is your faith" (15:28). Jesus acknowledged and praised the faith in the woman's statement, then healed her daughter. While the woman had no right to a miracle healing—for these were intended as signs and witnesses to God's chosen people—her faith caused a crumb to fall into her life.

What a lesson for us. The healing we need—whether inner spiritual healing or physical restoration—is no great challenge for God. Our healing is only a crumb that falls from a table that groans under the weight of the wonders God has prepared. How can we fail to have faith in a God so great, whose miracle-working powers know no limits.

JESUS HEALS A DEAF AND DUMB MAN   Mark 7:31–37

Jesus healed a man who was deaf and dumb.

Background of the miracle. Mark places this miracle immediately after the healing of the Syro-Phoenician woman's daughter (see p. 214). In her case, Jesus had emphasized the fact that his miracles and wonders were intended especially for Israel. This miracle, performed along the shore of the Sea of Galilee, emphasizes this fact as well. It is just the kind of miracle which the prophets said would mark the ministry of the Messiah (see Isa. 35:5). The healing miracles of Jesus unmistakably marked him as the promised Saviour-King.

Parties to the miracle. The parties mentioned in this miracle account are Jesus, the deaf and dumb man, and an undefined "they."

Jesus. Jesus was back in Jewish territory, where he responded without hesitation to those who sought healing.

The afflicted man. We are told nothing about this disabled individual.

"They." Unnamed persons play a significant role in this miracle account. "They" brought the deaf and dumb man to Jesus. "They" were cautioned by Jesus to tell no one about the miracle. And "they" were astonished by what Jesus did.

How the story unfolds. Jesus left the Gentile region where he had healed a Syro-Phoenician woman's daughter. Back in familiar territory along the Sea of Galilee, he encountered a deaf and dumb man brought to him by some of the man's friends. He healed the man so he could both hear and speak. Jesus cautioned the witnesses to tell no one about the healing, but they spread the report everywhere. Everyone reacted with astonishment and approval.

"Departing from the region of Tyre and Sidon, he came ... to the Sea of Galilee" (Mark 7:31). The geographical reference connects this miracle with the healing of the Syro-Phoenician woman's daughter. We need to read the account of the two miracles together and interpret the second in view of Jesus' remarks to the woman.

"They begged Him to put His hand on him" (7:32). This may simply be Mark's way of describing a request that Jesus heal the man. Or it may imply that they expected Jesus to heal *their way*. When we come to the Lord with our requests, we do well if we come without any expectation of the precise way in which Jesus will meet our needs.

"He took him aside from the multitude" (7:33). This is one of only two times that Jesus took someone aside for private healing (compare Mark 8:23). At the same time, it fits Mark's emphasis on Christ's desire to have closer personal contact with those whom he healed. The special touching of ears and

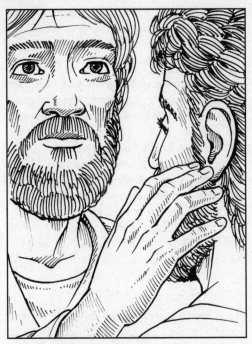

In healing a deaf-mute, Jesus touched his ears and tongue and said, "Be opened."

—————— ❖ ——————

tongue may have been a response to the "conditions" implied in the request of those who brought the victim that Christ might "put his hand on him."

Christ will often touch those who are weak in faith in ways that strengthen the faith they have.

"Ephphatha." It was not Jesus' touch that healed. The healing took place "immediately" when Jesus pronounced, "Be opened." He who created the universe with a spoken word (Gen. 1:3, etc.) needed no more than a word to perform this miracle.

"They were astonished beyond measure" **(7:37).** Mark reports this as a delayed reaction from the crowd. Jesus had told the people crowded around to tell no one, but they proclaimed it "widely." Even after they had time to consider what had happened, they were overwhelmed. They understood *what* Jesus had done: "He makes both the deaf to hear and the mute to speak." Although they felt

positively about Jesus ("he has done all things well."), they did not catch the significance of the miracle.

Yet a Gentile woman had recognized Christ as the Son of David, Israel's Messiah (Matt 15:22). She had even agreed when he explained that his miracles were "bread" provided for God's "lost sheep," Israel (Matt. 15:27). They were more than acts of kindness, in spite of the compassion that moved Jesus for those whom he healed. Jesus' miracles were signs which identified him to Israel as the Messiah predicted by the Old Testament prophets.

A pagan woman had understood the meaning of Jesus' miracles, but his own people—for whose instruction the miracles were intended—were astonished. All they could say was, "Good job!"

JESUS FEEDS FOUR THOUSAND PEOPLE   *Matthew 15:30–38; Mark 8:1–9*

Jesus miraculously provided food for another crowd, which had been with him for three days.

Background of the miracle. Some interpreters have assumed this account is not a separate miracle but a doublet—a repetition of the earlier story of the feeding of five thousand people (Matt. 14:21; Mark 6:44). There are similarities between these accounts:

- Both happened in the country.
- Both featured bread and fish.
- Both portrayed Jesus giving thanks and breaking bread.
- Both portrayed the disciples distributing the food.
- Both ended in a boat trip.

At the same time, there are significant differences which indicate the two feedings were separate events.

- The numbers fed differ: five thousand and four thousand.
- The locales differ: northeast and southeast shores of the Sea of Galilee.

- The seasons differ: green grass is emphasized in the story of the five thousand.
- The initial amounts of food differ.
- The number of baskets of food left over differ.
- Different baskets are specified: in the story of the five thousand they are shallow woven trays; in the story of the four thousand the baskets are giant, hamper-sized containers.
- The length of time the people were with Jesus differs.

The two accounts not only report different events; they intentionally parallel the works of two of the Old Testament's premier prophets, each of whom miraculously fed God's people twice (Moses—Ex. 16; Num. 11; Elisha—2 Kings 4:1–7, 38–44).

See pages 208–211 for a discussion of parallel elements in the two miracle accounts.

Parties to the miracle. The miracle report featured Jesus, his disciples, and a hungry crowd.

Jesus. Jesus expressed his concern for the crowds that had been with him for some time. He took what little food the disciples could find and multiplied it to feed about four thousand men.

The disciples. Although they had witnessed the earlier feeding of five thousand people, the disciples again expressed confusion about how this crowd could be fed. Again they said "Where could *we* get enough bread" (Matt. 15:33). We often forget what Jesus has done for us before, never thinking of turning to him for help when faced by a new need.

The crowd. "Great multitudes" followed Jesus into the wilderness to receive and witness his healing miracles (Matt. 15:30). According to how the Jews reckoned time, the "three days" the crowd was without food doesn't imply they hadn't eaten for 72 hours. An evening, the following day, and the next morning—as little as 30 hours—would be considered "three days."

The four thousand counted were the men only. If women and children are added, the crowd may have been as large as twelve thousand to fifteen thousand.

How the story unfolds. Jesus had been performing healing miracles for a great crowd. On the third day, Jesus expressed compassion and concern. If sent away without being fed, some people might "faint on the way" (Matt. 15:32). Jesus' disciples were frustrated. Where could they find enough food in such an isolated spot to feed such a great crowd?

Jesus sent them to find out how much food was available. Then he seated the crowd, gave thanks for the bread and fish, and had the disciples distribute them to the crowd. After everyone had eaten, the disciples filled seven large baskets with leftover food.

"How many loaves do you have?" (Matthew 15:34). In each account, Jesus took the little food his disciples had and multiplied it to supply thousands. If we give Jesus what we have, however small, he will use it to supply the deeper needs of many.

"Seven large baskets full" (15:37). The "large baskets" in this account were *spuridas,* large woven baskets about the size of a large laundry hamper. The apostle Paul was let down over the walls of Damascus in this kind of basket (Acts 9:25)!

These baskets were much larger than those used (*kophinoi*) after collecting leftovers following the feeding of the five thousand. What a reminder to the disciples, and to us, of the superabundance of Christ's ability to satisfy our needs.

JESUS HEALS A BLIND MAN   *Mark 8:22–26*

Jesus used an unusual method to heal a blind man.

Background of the miracle. Typically, Jesus' healings took place instantaneously, and they were implemented by a verbal command from him. This incident is distinctive in that the restoration of a blind man's sight was gradual, and the text doesn't mention a spoken command. It is also unusual in that Christ touched the blind man not once, but twice.

We can understand the reason for Christ touching some people whom he healed. Jesus touched a leper he restored out of compassion: he knew how much this man, isolated as he was from others, needed to feel a human touch (p. 181). Jesus also touched a deaf and dumb man whom he made well, possibly to increase his faith (see page 216). But there is no suggestion in Mark's account of the reason why Jesus took this man aside and twice touched his eyes to implement the healing.

Parties to the miracle. The text focuses on Jesus and the blind man, who was taken aside from the crowd for healing.

Jesus. Jesus responded to a request that he put his hands on a blind man (i.e., heal him).

The blind man. All we know about this blind man is that he had lost his sight as a youth or adult. When his sight began to return, he reported that "I see men like trees, walking" (Mark 8:24). He recognized the blurred, wavering images of trees, so he must have known what trees looked like before losing his sight.

How the story unfolds. In Bethsaida, a fishing village beside the Sea of Galilee, a blind man was brought to Jesus for healing. Christ took him aside, spat in his eyes, and laid hands on him. The man's sight was only partially restored, and he told Jesus what he could make out. Jesus then "put His hands on his eyes again." This time the man's sight was fully restored. Then Jesus sent the man away with orders not to tell anyone what had happened.

"Put His hands on his eyes again" (Mark 8:25). Commentators have wondered why Jesus abandoned his usual method of instantaneous healing by command. Some have seen a symbolic meaning: the spiritual sight of his disciples also grew gradually.

A better suggestion was made by John Calvin: "He did so most probably for the purpose of proving, in the case of this man, that he had full liberty as to his method of proceeding, and was not restricted to a fixed rule. . . . And so the grace of Christ, which had formerly been poured out suddenly on others, flowed by drops, as it were, on this man."

Calvin's comment is helpful. We often yearn for instantaneous grace; yet God's grace may be best measured out drop by drop, that we may savor it day by day. Both grace that is poured out and grace which is measured out drop by drop bring healing.

JESUS DELIVERS A DEMONIZED BOY
Mark 9:14–29; Matthew 17:14–21; Luke 9:37–43

A desperate father brought his demon-possessed son to Jesus after Christ's disciples were unable to exorcise the demon.

Background of the miracle. Mark gives the most complete account of this miracle and of the conversation of Jesus with the father and his disciples. There is one significant difference among the three reports of the event.

Matthew identified the son's malady as epilepsy. Both Mark and Luke identified it as demon possession. This is not a contradiction. Matthew spoke of the symptoms, while Mark and Luke identified the underlying "disease." The symptoms as reported in Mark were clearly like those of epilepsy: Mark reported that whenever the demon seized the boy "it throws him down; he foams at the mouth, gnashes his teeth, and becomes rigid" (9:18).

In many ancient cultures, all diseases were assumed to be caused by evil spirits. In Egypt two medical traditions developed: one in which diseases were treated medically, and the other in which illnesses were treated by incantations and invocation of the gods. In later Egypt these traditions merged and the magical approach became dominant.

The New Testament writers distinguished between illnesses which had natural causes and maladies caused by demons. Many of the afflicted are spoken of as cripples, blind, or deaf while others—often with the same problems—are identified as afflicted by demons.

The activity of the demons portrayed in the New Testament makes it clear that these spiritual beings are *hostile* to humankind. When demons dominate an individual, they don't use their powers to bring that person health and happiness. Persons who seek contact with the demonic under the naïve assumption that they will gain some sort of power or privilege are deceived indeed.

Parties to the miracle. This miracle account reports on Jesus' lengthy interaction with the father and his disciples. It also contains significant information about the demon who tormented the son.

Jesus. Jesus was again shown to have power over Satan's hosts. We also sense Christ's frustration with the father as well as his disciples. In spite of all that Jesus had done to demonstrate who he was, none seemed to understand or to respond with appropriate faith.

The father. The father came looking for Jesus. When he arrived, Christ was on the Mount of Transfiguration with three of his disciples (Mark 9:1–13). Since Jesus was not around, the father looked up some of his disciples and asked them to perform the healing.

Jesus' remark about a "faithless generation" (Mark 9:19) was made immediately after the father told of the disciples' inability to help (Mark 9:18). The implication is that Jesus was frustrated by the father's failure to realize that he was the source of the healing power which marked him as the Messiah. We can never substitute reliance on "faith healers" for faith in Christ, even though the healers may claim to be Jesus' representatives. We should bring our needs to Jesus.

The disciples. After the miracle healing, the disciples asked Jesus why they couldn't cast out the demon. This was a relevant question, since Matthew 10:1 reports that Jesus had earlier sent his disciples out to preach and had given them "power over unclean spirits." Yet the disciples were not able to help the son. Why? Jesus gave two reasons.

First, the disciples had "little faith" (Matt. 17:20, see footnote). Jesus immediately went on to explain that he didn't mean a "little *amount of* faith." If faith were to be measured by its size, the tiniest amount [a "mustard seed"-sized faith] could move mountains (Matt. 17:20). No, faith's effectiveness depends on its *object,* not its amount.

The disciples had assumed *they* could cast out the demon. After all, hadn't they done it before when Jesus sent them out by two (cf. Matt. 10:8)? The implication is that they had slipped into the error of relying on *their* authority rather than Jesus' authority in trying to cast out the demon.

Second, Jesus commented that "this kind [of demon] does not go out except by prayer and fasting" (Matt. 17:21; Mark 9:29). This reflects the teaching of Daniel 10 that Satan's angels, the demons of the Old and New Testament, are of different ranks and powers. The demon which had entered this man's son was no ordinary demon, but one of unusual rank. He had resisted every effort of the disciples to cast him out. "Prayer and fasting" represent the need for total dependence on the Lord's power.

In spite of the strength of this particular demon, it also recognized and reacted to Jesus (Mark 9:20). When Jesus rebuked [commanded] the evil spirit, it convulsed the child—then left him (Mark 9:28). Even the strongest demons cannot resist Jesus or believers who command them in Jesus' name. (For more on demon possession and exorcism, see *Every Good and Evil Angel in the Bible.*)

The demon. Mark's Gospel gives us much information about the demon. It was of unusually high rank and power (Mark 9:29). It had taken possession of the son when he was a child (Mark 9:21). It showed its intense hostility toward human beings by throwing the boy into fire and water, as if intent on destroying its host (Mark 9:22). This account of demon possession, along with Luke 8, provides vivid images of the evil intent of demons and clear descriptions of their major characteristics.

How the story unfolds. Jesus returned from the Mount of Transfiguration and found scribes and Pharisees debating a recent event with his disciples, while a crowd looked on. As Jesus approached, a man cried out, begging Jesus to look at his son. The son was demon-possessed, and the demon regularly threw the boy down, injuring him. The man told Jesus he had asked his disciples to heal the boy, but they couldn't.

Jesus expressed his frustration at this fresh evidence of unbelief, but he told the father to bring the son to him. When the demon saw Jesus, it threw the boy into a seizure. As the child writhed, Jesus asked how long this had been happening to him, learning he had been afflicted since childhood. The demon had often tried to kill his host!

"If you can do anything," the father pleaded, "have compassion on us and help us" (Mark 9:22).

Jesus told the father that all things are possible to the person who believes. The father, torn by hope and doubt, declared, "I believe, help my unbelief."

Jesus then rebuked the unclean spirit, commanding it to leave the child. The boy was racked with a last great convulsion, and then fell down as if dead. The demon was gone!

Later the disciples asked Jesus why they were unable to cast out the demon. Jesus replied that the reasons were complex. They lacked the necessary faith, and the demon was unusually powerful. After this, Jesus and his disciples moved on through Galilee.

"If You can do anything" (9:22). The father in this story stands in contrast with others who came to Jesus in the assurance that he could help. Even a Roman centurion had so much confidence in Jesus that he didn't even ask Jesus to visit his sick servant—only to speak the word. This father, however, came to Jesus not with confidence but with a last, desperate hope.

This demonstrates that whatever motivates a person to turn to Jesus, it is coming to Jesus that counts.

"Lord, I believe; help my unbelief" (9:24). The key word in this verse is "Lord." When our faith wavers, we are to reflect on who Jesus is, and remember that he is Lord.

"Lord" (9:24). This single word sums up the message of this miracle. Jesus is Lord. This truth was disputed by the religious leaders of Jesus' day. It was doubted by those who most needed his help. Even the disciples did not fully realize it. But Jesus demonstrated his authority by casting out the unusually powerful demon that had taken possession of the young victim. Jesus is Lord of all. Even a little faith, as long as it's centered on Jesus, can change our lives.

JESUS PRODUCES TAXES FROM A FISH'S MOUTH   Matthew 17:24–27

Jesus told Peter to catch a fish and take the temple tax from its mouth.

Background of the miracle. Exodus 30:13–16 specified that every Israelite male age 20 and older should pay a half-shekel into the temple treasury annually. This religious tax was used with other funds to support the temple ministry. The collection of this tax was the occasion for one of Jesus' most unusual miracles.

Parties to the miracle. The parties to the miracle were the collectors of the religious tax, Peter, and Jesus.

The tax collectors. The collectors of this tax were temple officials. Their behavior seems strange. Rather than asking for the tax, they asked Peter if Jesus paid it.

Peter. Peter hastily answered the tax collectors' question with a "Yes." Edersheim suggested that Peter sensed a trap in the officials' question, and said "Yes" in order to avoid the trouble that a different answer might have made for Jesus.

Jesus. Jesus' gentle questioning of Peter made it clear that Peter had spoken before he thought. Jesus resolved the issue by providing the tax money in an unusual way.

How the story unfolds. Peter was questioned by collectors of the temple tax. Did Jesus intend to pay it? Peter answered "Yes." When Jesus next saw Peter he asked, "From whom do the kings of the earth take customs or taxes, from their sons or from strangers?" Peter answered correctly, and Jesus summed up: "Then the sons are free."

Without explaining further, Jesus sent Peter to cast a line into the nearby waters. The fish Peter caught had in its mouth a coin that would pay both Peter's and Christ's annual temple tax.

"From whom do the kings of the earth take customs or taxes" (Matthew 17:25). In Christ's day Rome ruled the world, collecting taxes from all over the Mediterranean world. But taxes were not collected in Rome. Much of the foreign tax money was used to provide free grain and entertainment for the Romans. This was well known in Judea and Galilee, which groaned under taxes imposed not only by the Romans but also by the Herods.

Thus when Jesus asked Peter this question, Peter rightly answered that earthly rulers collected taxes from strangers.

"Then the sons are free" (17:26). Jesus' conclusion is significant. Because he was the Son of God, he was not obligated to pay the temple tax! Peter had given the wrong answer, whatever his motive had been.

There was, of course, another implication. If God required Israel to pay the temple tax, then the Jewish people could not be "sons." The common first-century assumption that physical descent from Abraham guaranteed a place in God's family was wrong! Faith in Jesus the Messiah, not physical descent from Abraham, makes a person a child of God.

"Lest we offend" (17:27). Jesus instructed Peter to pay the temple tax with money provided

miraculously. There was no need to make an issue of the symbolic meaning of the temple tax. The real issue then as now was Jesus himself, and nothing should be allowed to distract the people's attention from the question of who he was.

JESUS HEALS A MAN BORN BLIND
John 9

Jesus set off an intense controversy when he gave sight to a man who had been blind since birth.

Background of the miracle. John 8:12 records Jesus' affirmation to the Pharisees that "I am the light of the world. He who follows Me shall not walk in darkness, but have the light of life." The event reported in John 9 is an acted-out parable, demonstrating the truth of Jesus' statement and applying it both physically and spiritually.

Physically, Jesus gave sight to a man who was born blind. This was no restoration of lost sight. It was a creative act; bringing something into being that had not existed before. In the same way, God's creative act is involved when a person is given spiritual sight.

Spiritually, there's a difference between light and darkness, seeing and being blind. The man to whom Jesus gave sight gradually came to realize who Jesus was. This was indicated by his descriptions of the One who healed him. Note the sequence: the Healer was "a Man called Jesus" (John 9:11); "a prophet" (John 9:17); "from God" (John 9:33); and, "Lord" (John 9:38).

In contrast, the religious leaders who were finally forced to acknowledge that Christ had performed a notable miracle insisted that "this Man is a sinner" (John 9:24). The blind man saw, while the sighted men were blind to "the light of the world" (John 9:5).

Parties to the miracle. The entire chapter is devoted to this miracle and its effects. While Jesus performed the miracle and later spoke again with the man who had been healed, the man himself was the focus of the account. The chapter reports a series of intense conversations—between Jesus and his disciples, between the man and the Pharisees, between the parents and the Pharisees, and between the man Jesus. The chapter contains seven scenes:

1. The miracle—John 9:1–7
2. The man is questioned by neighbors—John 9:8–12
3. The man is cross-examined by Pharisees—John 9:13–17
4. The parents are cross-examined—John 9:18–23
5. The man is cross-examined again—John 9:24–34
6. Jesus seeks out the man—John 9:35–38
7. Significance of the miracle—John 9:39–41

How the story unfolds. One Sabbath as Jesus and his disciples passed by, they asked him about a man born blind. "Who sinned?" Jesus replied that sin was not the cause of his blindness. Acting as the "light of the world" (John 9:5), Jesus restored the blind man's sight.

The miracle set off a furor. Even the man's neighbors couldn't believe he was the same person. The man explained what happened and how Jesus gave him sight.

The neighbors brought the man to the Pharisees, who cross-examined him. The miracle caused a debate among these religious leaders. Some argued that a person who would "work" on the Sabbath couldn't possibly be from God. Others objected, "How can a . . . sinner do such signs?" When the man himself was asked, he replied, "He is a prophet."

The Jews [a term John used of the religious leaders] refused to believe the man was born blind until they questioned his parents. The parents insisted that this was their son, and that he had been blind since birth. But they were afraid to say any more, because they knew the leaders had agreed to expel from the synagogue anyone who declared that Jesus was the Christ.

Frustrated and angry, the Jews again called for the man whose sight had been restored. Under their hostile probing, the man asked, perhaps tongue in cheek, if "you also want to become his disciples." The "also" re-

vealed this man's commitment to his Healer. When the leaders reacted angrily, the man expressed amazement. "Since the world began," no one had opened the eyes of one born blind. "If this Man were not from God, He could do nothing" (John 9:33). This obvious conclusion was scornfully rejected by the religious leaders, and the man was ejected.

Jesus then found him and asked if he believed in the Son of God. As soon as the man learned that Jesus was the Son, he believed and worshiped. Christ then explained the significance of the miracle. He had come to differentiate between the blind and the sighted. His presence showed that those in Israel who claimed to have spiritual insight were actually blind, while those considered spiritually blind recognized Christ, and were given sight. The remark insulted the Pharisees, who challenged him: "Are we blind also?"

Christ's answer underlined the truth that a deliberate rejection of the One who is the light had condemned them to God's judgment.

Scene one: the miracle (John 9:1–7). Jesus restored the sight of a man born blind.

"Who sinned" (9:2). It was commonly believed by the Jews that serious disabilities were punishment for sin. The question of whether the man or his parents had sinned reflected a misunderstanding of Exodus 34:7. This verse stated that punishment of the guilty extended to the third and fourth generations. Sin corrupts our relationships so deeply that several generations of any family will be affected by serious sin.

"That the works of God should be revealed in him" (9:3). Tragedies give God an opportunity to reveal himself in unique ways. It was a tragedy that robbed Joni Erickson Tada of her ability to move. But through Joni, the Lord has encouraged thousands, and he continues to display his glory.

We cannot choose how God will glorify himself in us. But we can seek to glorify him whatever our situation.

"Spat on the ground and made clay" (9:6). Commentators have linked the mode of healing used by Jesus in this situation to the original creation of man from the earth. Irenaeus, an early church father, wrote "That which the artificer—the Word—had omitted to form in the womb he supplied in public, that the works of God might be manifested in him" (Adv. Haer. 15:2).

Scene two: the man was questioned by neighbors (9:8–12). The stunned neighbors could hardly believe the now-sighted man was the one who had sat and begged. The man explained what happened, giving credit to "a man called Jesus."

Scene three: the man was cross-examined by Pharisees (9:13–7). The neighbors brought the man to the Pharisees, who were confused and upset by the reported healing.

Pharisees. Members of this influential group were committed to keeping every detail of God's Law as interpreted by the rabbis.

"Does not keep the Sabbath" (9:16). By the Pharisee's definition, Jesus' healing of this blind man was "work," for he had "made clay" (John 9:6). The Pharisees' legalistic interpretation of Sabbath-keeping was more important to them than a stunning act of God. Let's be careful not to let our theology keep us from recognition of a true work of God.

"How can a . . . sinner do such signs?" (9:16). There were only two possible answers. Either Jesus was not a sinner or Jesus did not perform the miracle. The "Jews" [the religious leaders] chose not to believe in the miracle—until they questioned the parents and found they couldn't deny it. They were not willing to admit the only other reasonable possibility—that Jesus was not a sinner but a man of God.

Scene four: the parents were cross-examined by the Pharisees (9:18–23). The Pharisees were finally convinced that the man had been blind since birth. But the parents refused to say any more out of fear that they would be "put out of the synagogue" (John 9:22). A person put out of the synagogue would be cut off from assistance if he fell into poverty or dire need. A person with a business would not be able to trade with people in the community. Many who had been friends would no longer speak to the ostracized person. To confess Christ in the face of the threat of being "put out of the synagogue" took a courage that the parents lacked.

Scene five: the Pharisees cross-examined the man again (9:24–34). The Jews refused to consider that their interpretation of Sabbath Law might be wrong. Instead, they rejected a sign which, like so many others, had identified Jesus as God's spokesman. The key word in these verses is "know."

The Pharisees claimed to know based on rabbinical interpretations of the biblical command not to work on the Sabbath. They concluded:

- We know this man is a sinner (9:24).
- We know God spoke through Moses (9:29).
- We do not know where this man came from (9:29).

The man claimed to know based on the miracle and the obvious:

- I know that while I was blind, now I see (9:25).
- We know that God does not hear sinners (9:31).
- We know that God hears anyone who worships him and does his will (9:31).
- If this man were not from God, he could do nothing (9:33).

The once-blind man saw the issues clearly and held fast to his convictions in spite of pressure from the religious leaders. What moved the man was not fear of these powerful leaders but wonder at their claim not to know where Jesus was from. There was no question in his mind—Jesus was a man sent from God.

The leaders followed through on their threat and "cast out" the man. The implication is that he was put out of the synagogue, not just their presence (John 9:34). We suspect that the man cared little for their punishment. He could see! Nothing Christ's enemies could take away was a loss—compared with the wonderful gift Christ had given him.

Scene six: Jesus sought out the man (9:35–38). When Jesus found the man, he led him to the full commitment of faith. Christ identified himself as the Son of God, and the man immediately affirmed, "Lord, I believe! And he worshiped Him" (John 9:38).

How often a gracious work in our lives gently leads us to faith's full commitment.

Scene seven: the significance of the miracle (9:39–41). Christ's own comment brought the miracle's meaning into focus. Jesus himself is the pivot on which every person's eternal destiny turns.

Only those who admit they are lost and blind, then look to Christ for spiritual sight, will find the salvation he offers. Any who claim they can see—like the Pharisees—will remain blind to the gospel offer. And their sin will remain.

Deliberate rejection of Jesus, the light of the world, leaves a person in eternal darkness. How good it is to see the light, and come to know God in his Son.

JESUS HEALS A WOMAN BOUND BY SATAN   *Luke 13:10–17*

Jesus healed a woman with a chronic back problem on the Sabbath.

Background of the miracle. This is another Sabbath healing. Like other healings on this holy day, it offended the religious leaders. Their rules for what was proper on the Sabbath went far beyond the simple biblical proscription against work (Ex. 20:8–11).

The rabbis' rulings made allowance for a physician to attend a person with a life-threatening emergency on the Sabbath. But in their eyes, it was not lawful to help a person with a chronic illness. Such an illness could wait for treatment on some other day!

Jesus as God had created the Sabbath. He was not bound by their human regulations.

This particular healing also revealed the fatal flaw in rabbinic Judaism. Rules had become the ultimate reality, and the true message of God's Word had been missed.

Centuries before, the prophet Isaiah had predicted this misuse of Scripture and described its consequences. In chapter 28 of his book, the inspired prophet characterized the message of God's Word as "the rest with which you may cause the weary to rest," and as "the refreshing." Yet Israel refused to listen. And so to Israel the Word of God was to become

> Precept . . . upon precept, precept
>   upon precept,
> Line upon line, line upon line,
> Here a little, there a little (Isa.
>   28:10).

What was the result of this focus on the details of the divine Law to the exclusion of its meaning? The divine judgment was,

> That they might go and fall
>   backward, and be broken
> And snared and caught (Isa. 28:13).

By turning God's Word into lists of rules to keep, the grace of God had been overlooked. By piling up precept upon precept, Israel committed itself to a religion of works which so hardened the religious leaders that they would not acknowledge the Messiah. The irony is that his coming was intended to free God's people from everything that bound them.

Both the grace of God and the blindness of legalism are shown clearly in this Sabbath miracle.

Parties to the miracle. In relating this miracle, Luke draws our attention to Jesus, the infirm woman, and the reactions of the ruler of the synagogue and "all the multitude."

Jesus. Jesus initiated the healing, without being asked.

The woman. The woman was referred to as "a daughter of Abraham" (Luke 13:16). The reference was not to her physical descent from Abraham, although the people in the synagogue may have understood it this way. The reference was to her faith: she had a faith like Abraham's. He believed God and was declared righteous (Gen. 15:7).

The ruler of the synagogue. One of the responsibilities of the *archesynagogos* or ruler of the synagogue was to maintain order in the Sabbath services. This man was committed to the strict interpretations of the Law which characterized the Pharisees. His indignant reaction was typical of those described in Isaiah 28. He missed the refreshing intent of the law, transforming it into precepts which blinded him to God's grace.

The "multitude." This was Luke's term for the ordinary people, who saw what Jesus did and responded openly without the blindness of the religious leaders.

How the story unfolds. As Jesus was teaching, he saw a woman with a bent back. She had not been able to stand upright for 18 years. Je-

sus called to her and announced that she was loosed from her infirmity. Then he touched her and she straightened up. This scandalized the ruler of the synagogue, who rebuked Jesus for healing on the Sabbath.

Christ called him a hypocrite, pointing out that even the legalistic Pharisees untied their animals on the Sabbath to give them a drink. How much more precious was the daughter of Abraham whom he had loosed, after she had been tied in knots by Satan all these years!

The response shamed Jesus' opponents, but the common people rejoiced over the wonderful things he was doing.

"He called her to Him" *(Luke 13:12)*. This was no response to prayer or faith by the woman. Jesus initiated the encounter and acted to heal the woman. Christ showed compassion. His action showed the dramatic contrast between God's attitude toward the hurting and the attitude of the nation's religious leaders.

"Loosed from your infirmity" *(13:12)*. The terms Luke used in describing this event were common among physicians of that time. He also provided a careful description of the stages of the healing. First the woman's cramped muscles were relaxed [loosed]. Then Jesus touched the woman to strengthen her spine so she could stand upright.

"Glorified God" *(13:13)*. The woman was thrilled by what God had done. What a contrast with the indignant reaction of the ruler of the synagogue. Would the *archesynagogos* have been upset if *he* were the person healed? The capacity to rejoice with others who are blessed by God is one indication of God's work in our own lives.

"Hypocrite!" This word described Greek actors who held masks over their faces to represent the person whom they portrayed. It came to mean play-acting or inconsistency—pretending to be someone you are not or behaving differently in public than in private.

"Woman, you are loosed from your infirmity."

Jesus' charge was leveled at the inconsistent behavior of the Pharisees. Their rules allowed for the needs of farm animals on the Sabbath, while refusing to give consideration to the needs of people. And they claimed to represent God!

Christ's concern for a woman who had suffered for 18 years revealed the heart of God while exposing the grudging attitudes of the Pharisees. No wonder Jesus' adversaries were "put to shame" (Luke 13:17)!

"Loose his ox" (13:15). Note the play on words in the story. Jesus loosed the woman (Luke 13:12) and was criticized by a man who would never hesitate to loose a farm animal.

"Satan has bound" (13:16). This was not a case of demon possession but of demonic *oppression*. Satan was identified as the cause of this woman's physical disability, but Jesus did not indicate that he dominated her personality. The apostle Paul's "thorn in the flesh" was another example of this phenomenon (2 Cor. 12:7). (See *Every Good and Evil Angel in the Bible*.)

"All His adversaries were put to shame" (13:17). This phrase does not mean that Jesus' adversaries *felt* ashamed. "Put to shame" means that the emptiness of their claim to represent God was exposed for everyone to see.

This miracle of Jesus revealed clearly the heart of God. Other hearts were revealed that day as well: the woman's, the synagogue ruler's—and even the hearts of the onlookers, who praised God for Jesus' good works.

JESUS HEALS A MAN WITH DROPSY
Luke 14:1–6

While eating Sabbath dinner at a Pharisee's house Jesus healed a man with dropsy.

Background of the miracle. This is the fourth Sabbath miracle reported by Luke (6:6–11; 13:10–17). It reminds us that healing on the Sabbath was a major cause of conflict between Jesus and the Pharisees. See pages 186 and 225 for background.

Parties to the miracle. Luke focuses on the interaction between Jesus and a hostile group of "lawyers and Pharisees" who were observing Jesus closely. The parties to this miracle are:

Jesus. Jesus was dining at the home of a "ruler of the Pharisees." The phrase suggests that the man (an *archon*, ruler) was a member of the Sanhedrin and belonged to the Pharisee party.

Lawyers and Pharisees. A "lawyer" was a person versed in the written Law [Old Testament] and the oral Law [traditional interpretations]. The Pharisees were members of a small but influential group that argued for the strictest interpretation of written and oral Law.

The man with dropsy. Dropsy was an illness caused by a "serious abnormal accumulation of fluid in the body's tissues."

How the story unfolds. Jesus was eating at the home of a leading Pharisee, where he was being watched closely by the other guests. These guests were also members of the religious elite. A man with dropsy was also at the meal.

Jesus took the initiative and asked whether it was "lawful" to heal on the Sabbath. When no one was willing to risk an answer, Jesus healed the man with dropsy.

Jesus then asked which of them would not "immediately" help one of their farm animals which had fallen into a pit on the Sabbath. They couldn't answer! They couldn't rebut Christ's actions or his argument.

"A certain man who had dropsy" (Luke 14:2). Many commentators have suggested the man with the dropsy had been planted at this gathering by Jesus' enemies. There is good reason for this theory. In the first century, serious diseases were thought to be God's punishment for sin. The host was a "leading Pharisee," and his guests were members of the religious elite. These men normally would have been unwilling to sit down to a meal with any "sinner."

The man was seated directly "before him," so Jesus could hardly fail to notice him (Luke 14:2). Finally, when the man was healed, Jesus "let him go" (Luke 14:4).

How like the Pharisees to use others in an effort to trap or discredit Jesus.

"They kept silent" (Luke 14:4). No one was willing to risk answering Jesus' question about whether it was lawful to heal on the Sabbath.

"Which of you?" (14:5). After healing the man with dropsy, Jesus asked another question. Which of them wouldn't pull from a pit an animal which had fallen in on the Sabbath? Members of the Qumram sect held that an animal which fell into a pit should not be lifted out on the Sabbath. But the dominant view in Jesus' time was that an ox or donkey which had fallen into a pit could be helped out "immediately" (*Shabbat 128b*).

To this they "could not" reply. There was no answer they could give without condemning themselves.

The significance of the miracle. Jesus' miracles had several vital functions. On one level, they served to reveal God and demonstrate his compassion. On another level, they served as signs which marked Jesus as the promised Messiah. On yet another level, they exposed human hearts, showing some to be filled with faith and others to be hypocritical and far from the attitudes of the Lord. In this miracle report, God's compassionate heart and the hypocrisy of Jesus' antagonists are clearly revealed. The Pharisees would rush to save one of their valuable animals, but they cared nothing for a person in need.

The miracles of Jesus show not only who he was, but who we are apart from God's transforming grace.

JESUS RAISES LAZARUS   *John 11*

Jesus restored life to Lazarus three days after his death.

Background of the miracle. Jesus had already restored the life of a widow's son (Luke 7) and Jairus's daughter (Luke 8; Mark 5). Each of these restorations occurred immediately after the person had died.

The custom in first-century Judaism was to bury an individual on the day of his death. But the Jews were aware of the possibility of a coma, so they would check a tomb for three days after the burial to see if the victim had revived. After three days, all hope of awakening from a coma was gone, and the body would have begun to decay.

The raising of Lazarus was significant because it took place the full three days after he had died, plus one extra day (John 11:39)! There could be no doubt in anyone's mind that Christ had restored a person who was truly dead.

It is no wonder that this most spectacular of Jesus' miracles troubled the chief priests and Pharisees. After this, they were certain that "if we let him alone like this, everyone will believe in him, and the Romans will come and take away both our place and nation" (John 11:48). Thus the greatest proof of who Jesus was became the critical event that drove the Jewish hierarchy to seek Jesus' death (John 11:53).

There can be no vacillation for modern believers. We must accept Jesus for who he is, acknowledging him as Lord. If we fail to do this, we take sides with the rulers of first-century Israel and choose to force him out of our lives.

Parties to the miracle. The entire chapter is devoted to this miracle account and Jesus' interaction with the people involved. These include: Mary and Martha, the sisters of Lazarus; the disciples, and especially Thomas. John also reports the reaction of those who had come to comfort the sisters as well as the response of the Jewish leaders.

Jesus. Jesus is portrayed in this account as one who dearly loved Lazarus and his sisters. Yet he failed to respond to an urgent plea to come and heal his friend. The delay seems out of character. But when Jesus finally did arrive, Mary—perhaps with some hint of rebuke—declared, "If You had been here, my brother would not have died" (John 11:32).

Jesus called on the sisters to believe that he had power over death in the present as well as at history's end. Then Jesus called to Lazarus, who stumbled out of his tomb—still wrapped in the strips of linen that served as burial clothes.

The disciples. Jesus and his disciples were across the Jordan River in Perea when word of Lazarus's illness arrived (John 10:40). They had retreated in part because the hostility of the leaders had become so intense that Christ was in danger of being stoned (John 11:8).

After the messenger's arrival, Jesus stayed in Perea for two more days. Then he told his disciples, "Let us go to Judea again" (John 11:7). The disciples were afraid. They objected when Christ told them that "Lazarus is asleep," assuming that Jesus meant that Lazarus was resting after the crisis had passed. But Jesus meant that Lazarus was dead. He stated his intention to wake him. The disciples' fears were reflected by Thomas, who declared, "Let us also go, that we may die with Him" (John 11:16).

Thomas. This disciple is commonly known as "doubting" Thomas because of his refusal to believe in Christ's resurrection until he could touch the wounds in Jesus' hands and side. But here we see Thomas in a different light, as "loyal" Thomas.

Thomas was certain that danger awaited all of them in Judea. But he encouraged the disciples to stay with Christ. Thomas had no hope; he did not expect to die *for* Jesus, or to be able to turn the danger aside. The best Thomas and the others could expect was to die *with* Jesus. And this Thomas was ready to do. Nothing could separate loyal Thomas from his Lord.

We are blessed because God has said, "I will never leave you nor forsake you" (Heb. 13:5). Courageous Thomas reminds us that we are to be as committed to God as he is to us—whatever the danger, whatever the cost.

Martha. She and her sister Mary were close to Jesus. They often sheltered him in their Bethany home when he visited Jerusalem. Bethany, about twenty miles from Perea, was only two miles outside Jerusalem. Christ stayed at Bethany when Jerusalem was crowded with pilgrims during the annual festivals.

When Martha saw Jesus, she expressed faith in him: "if you had been here, my brother would not have died." But Martha went on to say that "even now" (11:28) she believed God would give Jesus whatever he asked.

This statement was one of great faith, but even Martha's faith couldn't grasp Jesus' meaning when he told her, "Your brother will rise again" (John 11:23). She assumed that Jesus was speaking of the final resurrection at history's end. Jesus then affirmed that he was the resurrection and the life. The eschatological hope was present in his person. God's plans and promises were fulfilled *in him.*

Martha, still unaware of what Jesus intended, confessed her belief that Jesus truly was the Christ, the Son of God.

How often Martha is remembered only for her attention to dinner preparations and her criticism of Mary, who chose instead to listen to Jesus' teachings (Luke 10:40, 41). Here we see Martha in a far more flattering light, as one whose faith in Jesus burned bright and true—and one whose faith was about to be rewarded!

Mary. Mary, the second sister, then came out to greet Jesus. Like Martha, she expressed her faith: "If You had been here, my brother would not have died." But unlike her sister, Mary sobbed as she spoke. Even if she shared her sister's hope, she must not have felt it in her moment of loss.

Lazarus. We know little about Lazarus. He is not mentioned elsewhere in the Bible, although we are told that Jesus had developed a deep affection for him. Even after Lazarus was raised, John's account mentions nothing of what Lazarus felt or said or did. But he was a silent and powerful witness to the power of Jesus.

There are many unknown people whose actual words have not been passed on to future generations, but whose restored lives serve as powerful witnesses to Jesus Christ. Many times a believer does not need to say anything: the difference Jesus makes in his or her life will shine through brightly. May our lives, renewed and transformed by Jesus, be the witness to our neighbors that Lazarus was to his.

The mourners. The mourners who had come to comfort Mary and Martha were stunned by Jesus' miracle. Many "believed in him" (John 11:45). But others rushed to report to the Pharisees what Jesus had done. By this time, the entire city of Jerusalem was aware of the attitude of the Pharisees toward Jesus. Those who hurried to them certainly didn't go with an intent to witness!

The chief priests and Pharisees. These men had to admit that "this man works many signs" (11:47). But they didn't intend to submit to him. Instead, their hostile attitude toward Jesus became even more fixed, and they determined to kill him—one way or another.

Caiaphas. As the Jewish high priest, Caiaphas served as president of the Sanhedrin. He summed up the fears of the religious leaders and passed judgment. Jesus must die.

In saying "it is expedient . . . that one man should die for the people" (11:50), Caiaphas was representing the leaders' concern. As the founder of a messianic movement, Jesus' teaching might stimulate a rebellion, bringing Roman armies against Judea. Some interpreters have argued that Caiaphas' reference to the Romans' taking away "both our place and nation" expressed fear for the temple ("our place"). It is far more likely he was referring to the privileges enjoyed by his own priestly class.

While Caiaphas had one thing in mind, his words were prophetic. Christ would die for the nation—not to keep the Roman armies away, but to defeat sin and Satan and make eternal life available to all.

How the story unfolds. Jesus and his disciples were about twenty miles from Bethany when a messenger arrived with word that Lazarus was sick. For two days Jesus did nothing. Then he told his disciples it was time to return to Judea, explaining that Lazarus was "asleep" (has died). The fearful disciples accompanied Jesus on the day-long walk back to Bethany.

Martha hurried out to meet Jesus, expressing her belief that if Jesus had been there her brother would not have died. Jesus announced that he was the resurrection and the life, leading her to confess her belief that he was the Christ, the Son of God.

Martha then brought out Mary, who also expressed her belief that if Jesus had been with them her brother would not have died. Mary was weeping, heartbroken; and as Jesus followed her to Lazarus's tomb, he also wept.

At the tomb, Jesus told the onlookers to roll away the stone that closed the burial place. Martha objected. Lazarus had been dead and buried for four days: there would be a stench. But Jesus reminded her of their earlier conversation, and the stone was rolled away.

Jesus then thanked the Father aloud for always hearing him. He offered this prayer for the sake of the bystanders, that they might believe God had sent him. Jesus then shouted, "Lazarus, come forth!" (John 11:43). And the dead man, restored to life, stumbled out into the light, still wrapped in his grave clothes and his face covered with a cloth.

On Jesus' command, the tight wrappings were removed, and many of the stunned onlookers believed in Jesus.

Other witnesses to the miracle hurried into Jerusalem to carry word to the religious leaders. These men gathered almost in despair. What could they do? Jesus was performing such amazing miracles that soon everyone would believe in him!

There was no thought in their minds that *they* should consider his claims. Jesus was too great a threat to their own position and to the *status quo!* They concluded that Jesus must die. From that day forward, they set about get-

Jesus called to Lazarus and he came out of the tomb, still in graveclothes.

ting rid of this "Christ." John revealed in his Gospel that they even plotted to kill Lazarus, whose existence was a convincing witness to Jesus' power (John 12:10, 11).

Jesus, knowing their intent, withdrew with his disciples to a remote town (John 11:54), where he stayed quietly until the next Passover arrived (John 12:1).

"He whom you love is sick" (John 11:3). The sisters had no doubt of Jesus' love for their brother. How they must have anguished as the messenger hurried to Jesus. But before he could cover the 20 miles to tell Jesus, Lazarus died.

"For the glory of God" (11:4). Although Lazarus was dead when the messenger arrived, Christ said that the sickness would not *end in death.* The end would be life restored, and Christ glorified.

Our sicknesses too—even our last sickness—will not end in death. History is rushing even now toward God's intended end— resurrection and life eternal for Christ's own. For the glory of God!

"Jesus loved Martha and her sister and Lazarus" (11:5). It is often harder for those left behind to sense God's love for them than to be-

lieve that God loved the person who has died. John through his Gospel wanted us to know that Jesus does care, deeply, for the grieving.

"Our friend Lazarus sleeps" (11:11). The Bible appropriately speaks of death as sleep (1 Cor. 15:51; 1 Thess. 4:14). We can be confident as we lie down at the end of our earthly existence that we will awaken, and rise again.

"He groaned in the spirit and was troubled" (11:33). This—and the shortest verse in Scripture, "Jesus wept" (John 11:35)—reminds us that even as God permits our suffering, he feels with us.

Christ knew that he was about to bring Lazarus back to life. But he did not discount the pain of his dear friends. Instead, he entered into their pain, felt it deeply, and wept with them.

It is good for us to remember that God is committed to bringing good out of all the things that happen to us (Rom. 8:28). Yet it is important to remember that God takes our hand in the meantime and does not abandon us in our sorrow. He feels our pain. And he weeps with us as we grieve. And then, when the time is right, God will wipe away all tears from our eyes, welcoming us into the glory he intends for us and our loved ones to share (Rev. 21:4).

"I am the resurrection and the life" (11:25). There is no clearer statement in Scripture of the significance of Jesus for us individually. He is the resurrection and the life. His is the power; he is the source. Those who believe in him may die physically, but they will live eternally. This is his promise to us if we will trust in Jesus as the resurrection and the life.

This truth points us toward the ultimate significance of the miracle. Jesus' claim to be the resurrection and the life was proven by the restoration of Lazarus. Jesus' deeds always backed up his words.

Today we can contemplate this miracle, finding in it a foreshadowing of what lies ahead. One day Christ will return and shout to our dead, "Come forth." Then we will arise, and together with the believers alive in that day, rise up to meet the Lord in the air (1 Thess. 4:16, 17).

Truly Jesus is the resurrection and the life.

JESUS CLEANSES TEN LEPERS *Luke 17:11–19*

Jesus healed ten lepers, but only one, a Samaritan, returned to give glory to God.

Background of the miracle. In the first century, the ancient Jewish hostility toward the Samaritans had been revived. The Samaritans were despised as offspring of pagan peoples brought into the territory of the old Northern Kingdom, Israel, by the Assyrians in the 720s B.C. The Samaritans claimed descent from the Jewish patriarchs, but this claim was angrily disputed by the Jews.

A little over 100 years before Jesus was born, John Hyrcanus had ruled in Judea and had destroyed the Samaritan temple on Mount Gerazim. In Christ's time, the Samaritans showed their hostility by refusing shelter to anyone traveling to Jerusalem (Mark 3:17). One of the most serious insults hurled at Jesus by the religious leaders was to call him a Samaritan (John 8:48).

Against this background, we understand Luke's observation that as Jesus was going to Jerusalem, he "passed through the midst" of Samaria and Galilee (Luke 17:11). The Greek word is *dia meson,* "along the border between" the two territories. Jesus apparently avoided the direct route to the Holy City from Galilee, which would have taken him through Samaria.

There, along the border of Samaria, ten lepers called out to Jesus and asked for mercy. At least one of these lepers was a Samaritan. In their misery Jew and Samaritan formed a bond that the healthy were unwilling to consider.

Parties to the miracle. The account identifies ten men who were lepers. Apparently most were Jews, as Jesus told them to show themselves to the priests. This action was prescribed for those who had been lepers but had become free of the disease. Only a priest could certify that a person had been healed. This assured the person could retake his or her place as a member of the community.

How the story unfolds. When Jesus entered an unnamed village, ten lepers—standing at an appropriate distance because of their uncleanness—cried out for mercy. Jesus told them to show themselves to the priests, and "as they went" (17:14) they were cleansed [healed]. One of the ten hurried back to thank Jesus and praise God when he realized he had been healed. And this man was a Samaritan. Jesus wondered aloud where the others were. Commending the foreigner's faith, Jesus sent the man on his way.

"As they went, they were cleansed" (Luke 17:14). The lepers trusted Jesus enough to set out to see the priests. They were cleansed "as they went."

Some believers hope God will give them "faith" so they can obey him. What a tragic misunderstanding. Faith is expressed in our obedience; as we obey God, he works in our lives.

"Were there not ten cleansed?" (17:17). Only one of those who realized he had been healed returned to thank Jesus, giving glory to God. Commentators have been sharply critical of the other nine. About the kindest thing said of them is that they were ungrateful. Others have wondered whether the nine were afraid Jesus might place demands on them if they returned. Still other interpreters have suggested that the nine, once healed, wanted nothing more to do with their benefactor.

The text doesn't explore the motives of the nine. Perhaps they were so eager to go home again that they didn't pause for even a moment. Whatever their motive, we are hardly in a position to condemn them. How often we have also taken our blessings for granted. Many of us are strangers to thanksgiving, just like these nine healed lepers.

"This foreigner" (17:18). The fact that the one who did return was a foreigner is significant. Jesus was drawing near the end of his earthly ministry. He had healed hundreds in Israel; yet his own people would soon join in the cries of "crucify him!" As history records, it was mostly foreigners who rejoiced in Israel's Christ and glorified him with their praise.

"Your faith has made you well" (17:19). The nine missed hearing Jesus' explanation of their healing. As the nine hurried to the priests, they may have assumed that it was their obedience that made them well. Perhaps they thought their willingness to undergo the ancient ritual examination was critical to their healing. Jesus had somehow made them well. But hadn't they played their role in their own healing?

The Samaritan knew better. It was Jesus himself who had brought about the cure. It was faith in Jesus which had channeled the power that flowed from our Lord. Faith in Jesus, demonstrated by doing as Jesus said, had made all the difference.

JESUS GIVES SIGHT TO BLIND BARKIMAEUS *Matthew 20:29–34; Mark 10:46–52; Luke 18:35–43*

While on the way to Jerusalem and the cross, Jesus stopped to heal a blind beggar.

Background of the miracle. There are two critical differences in the details given in the three gospel accounts of this miracle.

Mark indicates the miracle took place on the way out of Jericho, while Luke says the miracle occurred when Jesus was entering the city. But in the first century, there were two Jerichos: old Jericho, which was largely a ruin; and new Jericho, an attractive city built by Herod just to the south of the old town. Apparently the miracle took place on the border between the old and new cities, as Jesus was leaving one and entering the other.

Mark and Luke mention only one blind man, whom Mark identifies as Bartimaeus. Matthew indicates that Jesus healed two blind men. It is clear from the other details that the Gospel writers describe the same incident, so we can assume that Bartimaeus was the more prominent of the two. For a discussion of this type of supposed contradiction in the biblical text, see the discussion of the demoniac of Gadara, p. 198.

More significant than the supposed contradictions is the fact that this last of Jesus' healing miracles took place on his way to Jerusalem and the cross. In Matthew, this miracle concludes a major section dedicated to the theme of greatness.

Jesus' disciples had asked about greatness (Matt. 18:1). Jesus called a little child and taught, "Whoever humbles himself as this little child" is greatest in the kingdom of heaven (Matt. 18:4). After showing the disciples how to live together as God's little children (Matt. 18:5–35), Matthew records a series of incidents exposing the fallacy of seeking greatness through keeping the Law (Matt. 19:1–15), through humanitarian works (Matt. 19:16–29), and through relying on works rather than on God's grace (Matt. 20:1–19). Then, when two of the disciples sent their mother to ask Jesus for the most important posts in his coming kingdom, Jesus used the occasion to instruct them on true greatness.

The Gentiles thought of greatness as lording it over others. But, Jesus said, "Whoever desires to be first among you, let him be your slave—just as the Son of Man did not come to be served, but to serve, and to give His life a ransom for many" (Matt. 20:27, 28).

Immediately after this—while he was on his way to the cross and burdened with the awareness of his coming fate—Jesus paused in answer to the cry of the blind men and asked, "What do you want Me to do for you?" (Matt. 20:32).

How clearly this last healing miracle illustrated what Jesus had just taught his disciples. The truly great of God's kingdom set aside personal burdens and say to others "What do you want me to do for you?" Like Jesus, the great in God's kingdom give of themselves to meet other people's needs.

Parties to the miracle. The story in Matthew is told simply, with three major voices.

Jesus. In spite of his own heavy burden, Jesus stopped to meet the needs of two blind men.

The blind men. The blind men realized that someone special was passing by. When they learned it was Jesus, they cried out to him as "Son of David" and begged for mercy.

The crowd. The crowd tried to silence the blind men. Jesus was too important to be bothered by such as them! The crowd thus revealed a lack of concern for individuals which contrasted with the servant attitude exemplified by Jesus and to which he calls his followers.

How the story unfolds. Jesus was on his way to Jerusalem and the cross. Although the roads were filled with travelers heading to the holy city for Passover, an unusually large crowd was following him. When two blind men, one of whom was named Bartimaeus (Mark 10:46), realized that Jesus was near, they began to shout. Addressing Jesus by his messianic title as Son of David, they begged for mercy.

The crowd told them to be quiet, but they cried out even louder. Responding to

their cries, Jesus stopped and called them to him. At that, the crowd's attitude changed, and they told the blind men to cheer up. Jesus was waiting for them (Mark 10:49)!

Jesus asked the blind men what they wanted, and they told him they wanted their sight. Christ, again moved by compassion, touched their eyes (Matt. 20:34) and told them to receive their sight (Luke 18:42), indicating that their faith had made them well.

"They told him" (Luke 18:36). Luke describes the blind man's curiosity as he heard a large crowd passing by. We can almost hear him asking, "What's happening? Who is it?"

"Have mercy ... Son of David" (Matt. 20:31). Each account agrees that the blind man/men addressed Jesus as the Son of David. This was a messianic title, reflecting the conclusion reached by Bartimaeus and his companion that this Jesus, of whom they had heard many stories, was indeed the Messiah. He had power to help, so they cried out to him.

"Bartimaeus, the son of Timaeus" (Mark 10:46). Mark frequently provides details not mentioned by the other Gospel writers. In this miracle account, Mark alone reports the crowd's change of attitude (10:49), revealing that when Bartimaeus realized that Jesus was waiting for him, he discarded his outer cloak to hurry to Jesus (10:50). It is likely that he had spread the cloak over his knees so passersby could drop in coins.

In view of Mark's typical attention to such detail, we should not be surprised that he gave the name of one of the two blind beggars.

"What do you want Me to do for you? (Matt. 20:32). This one sentence sums up the servant attitude which Jesus displayed. This is the attitude which he desires for all who would be truly great in his kingdom.

"What do you want Me to do for you?" (Mark 10: 51). There is no question that Jesus knew the need and the cure. Why then did he ask this question?

Some suggest he wanted to increase the blind man's faith. But it is more likely a reflection of a teaching on prayer found in James 4:2: "You do not have because you do not ask." Prayer is to be specific. We are to identify our needs and bring them to Jesus, asking him to meet these needs.

It may be helpful for us when we pray to raise the question Jesus asked. What do we want God to do for us? We must not tell him how to meet the need. But we must define our needs, and then bring them to him.

"Jesus had compassion" (Matt. 20:34). Caring about others is essential if we are to be servants. Jesus was not acting a part. Unlike some whose claims to "feel your pain" is mere posturing, Jesus was deeply moved by the suffering of those in need. Servanthood is not technique, but a heart response to others which reflects Jesus' deep concern.

They followed Him (20:34). This comment most likely means that the blind men literally followed Jesus up the steep fifteen-mile trail from Jericho to Jerusalem, where Passover was about to be celebrated.

"All the people, when they saw it, gave praise to God" (Luke 18:43). The road to Jerusalem led through Jericho. Thousands of Jewish families would have passed along it on their way to celebrate the religious festivals in the Holy City. Bartimaeus and his blind friend were probably fixtures in Jericho, known and recognized by many.

This verse shows that servanthood brings praise to God. The people praised God when they witnessed the miracle. On the other hand, Jesus' servanthood did not protect him from that hostility from others which ultimately brought him to the cross.

The meaning of the miracle. Jesus' last miracle of healing is significant in several ways. The miracle shows what blessings were available if only Israel, like the blind men, had acknowledged Jesus as the Son of David. It also illustrates Jesus' servant attitude and serves as an example for us.

Through this miracle, we are also reminded that the key to claiming the blessings that God is eager to pour out is faith in Jesus Christ and his ability to meet our every need.

JESUS CURSES A FIG TREE *Matthew 21:17–22; Mark 11:12–14, 20–24*

Jesus cursed a fig tree whose leaves promised a fruit it had not produced.

Background of the miracle. Fig leaves appear about the same time as the fruit, or a little after. Thus the fact that this tree was in leaf should have indicated it was also bearing fruit, although it was not yet the season for figs (Mark 11:13). The tree's appearance promised something which it didn't deliver.

Most interpreters take this miracle as an acted-out parable. The fig tree represents Israel, which had the appearance of bearing fruit but which in fact was barren. Jesus cursed the tree not because of its failure to bear fruit but because its appearance was a lie. The tree's leaves advertised a fruitfulness that did not exist—just as Israel's outward honoring of God and his law advertised a relationship with the Lord which they didn't have.

When it was cursed by Jesus, the fig tree withered. Its appearance at last matched the reality of its fruitless state. How soon Israel would also wither. In A.D. 70, just a few short decades after this incident, the Romans destroyed Jerusalem. With its temple destroyed, the priesthood set aside, and its familiar worship patterns forever lost, the nation of Israel withered indeed.

While Matthew's arrangement of this account is topical, Mark provides a chronological account. Between the cursing of the fig tree and its withering, Jesus cleansed the temple—an event which showed the bareness of Israel's worship.

Parties to the miracle. The story mentions only Jesus, his disciples, and the fig tree.

Jesus. This is the only event in the Gospels in which Jesus used his power to destroy rather than to heal or restore. The withering of the fig tree reminds us that God is not only a God of grace but a God of judgment as well.

The disciples. The disciples were amazed when the tree that Jesus cursed withered away so quickly. Their question about how this was possible led to a brief teaching by Jesus on prayer.

The fig tree. The fig tree is an image of Israel, just like the vineyard of Isaiah 5:1–7 and the figs of Jeremiah 8:13 and 24:1–8. The "sin" of the fig tree was to make a show of fruitfulness when in fact it was barren, even as Israel's response to Jesus revealed the spiritual emptiness of God's people.

How the story unfolds. Jesus was on the way to Jerusalem the day after his triumphal entry when he saw a fig tree with leaves but no fruit. Jesus cursed the tree, declaring, "Let no one eat fruit from you ever again" (Mark 11:14).

In Jerusalem, Jesus entered the temple and drove out those who "bought and sold" in it. The temple was supposed to be "a house of prayer for all the nations," but God's people had made it a "den of thieves" (Mark 11:15–17). The scribes and chief priests wanted to kill Jesus, but they hesitated to act out of fear of the people.

The next morning when Jesus and his disciples were returning to the city, Peter pointed out the tree that Jesus had cursed the day before. It had withered away, "dried up from the roots" (Mark 11:20).

Jesus used the occasion to encourage his disciples to "have faith in God," and reminded them that with prayer, even the impossible could become a reality.

"Jesus went into the temple" (Mark 11:15f). The report of Christ's second cleansing of the temple (see John 2:13–17) is sandwiched between the two parts of the story of the fig tree. Jesus drove out the moneychangers and the merchants who were buying and selling in the temple court. The temple was supposed to be a house of prayer for all nations. But Israel's leaders had made it a "den of thieves."

After Jesus cursed a fig tree, it withered.

❖

The temple area referred to in this account was the outer court, or "court of the Gentiles." The priests supervised the merchants who sold sacrificial animals here and exchanged foreign coins for "temple currency." These businessmen were permitted to charge a fee of about 4 percent of the value of any money exchanged. But the high priestly family which controlled the temple at this time was known for its greed. Jesus' characterization of the market as a "den of thieves" suggests that these limits had been exceeded.

Even more serious, however, was the corruption of a place which God intended to be set apart as a "house of prayer for all nations" (Isa. 56:7). Israel's fig tree had leaves; its temple erected to the glory of God was one of the wonders of the ancient world. But the traffic in the temple court revealed that the practices of her people were barren indeed.

"Whoever says to this mountain" (Mark 11:22). The disciples, shocked at the rapid withering of the fig tree, stimulated a brief teaching on prayer. In the first century, any great difficulty or impossible task was frequently referred to as a "mountain." Jesus was speaking metaphorically, reminding his disciples that God was able to do what human beings cannot. We are thus to rely on him and bring life's challenges to the Lord. We can have complete confidence that God will deal with the greatest of our difficulties, even though a way out may appear to be as impossible as commanding a mountain to move itself into the sea.

The meaning of the miracle. The cleansing of the temple and Jesus' comments on prayer should not distract our attention from the miracle itself. The barren fig tree, whose leaves promised a fruit which the tree did not produce, was judged by Christ. It would never deceive hungry travelers again.

In a similar way, Israel would also be judged. Its way of life would wither when the temple and its sacrifices were taken away. A different form of Judaism would take the place of its familiar pattern of life and worship. Root and branch, the old would soon be gone.

JESUS RESTORES MALCHUS'S EAR
Matthew 26:51–56; Mark 14:46,47; Luke 22:50, 51; John 18:10, 11

When Peter struck a member of the mob that had come to take Jesus, he cut off part of the ear of a man named Malchus. Jesus touched the ear and healed it.

Background of the miracle. Jesus' last miracle before his death was performed on the night of his capture and trial, just hours before his crucifixion. A mob led by Judas arrested him on the Mount of Olives in the garden of Gethsemane.

Only John, who was from a wealthy family which maintained a large house in Jerusalem, names Malchus. He was "the" servant of the high priest, an important official in his own right and clearly a person whom John knew. It is ironic that Jesus' last miracle of healing was performed for an enemy who had

come with the mob to make sure Christ was arrested.

Parties to the miracle. The miracle is not the focus of the story, but it seems almost an aside. Judas led a mob to Gethsemane to take Jesus prisoner. Peter, named only in John's Gospel, resisted the arrest and struck out with his weapon, cutting off part of Malchus's ear. Jesus restored the ear, then told his disciples not to resist and left with the crowd as they went back to Jerusalem.

Jesus. Although he was being arrested, Jesus was clearly in command of the situation.

Peter. Frightened by the crowd, Peter drew a weapon and struck one of the mob that had come to take Jesus away.

Malchus. As an important official of the Jewish high priest, Malchus was probably in charge of the detail which had come to bring Jesus in for trial. He was accompanied by a mob carrying torches and weapons.

How the story unfolds. Jesus had finished a time of prayer and returned to his disciples when a mob led by Judas appeared. Judas pointed out Jesus. As the mob surged forward to seize him, Peter drew a weapon and struck at the group. He cut off part of the ear of the servant of the high priest, whom John identified as Malchus.

Jesus told Peter to put his sword back in its place. Jesus could have called legions of angels to defend him. But the Scriptures had to be fulfilled, so it was necessary that he be taken away.

"Drew his sword" *(Matthew 26:51).* The word for "sword" and "knife" are the same in Greek, so we can't be sure what kind of weapon Peter drew. It is clear that he attacked the crowd with it in an attempt to defend Jesus.

"Cut off his ear" *(26:51).* Mark uses the diminutive Greek word *otarion* for ear, suggesting that perhaps only the ear lobe was cut off. This would explain why Luke 22:51 indicates that Jesus healed the ear rather than reattaching it. In any case, this was a gracious miracle which he performed for an enemy.

"Put your sword in its place" (26:52). Luke 22:38 indicates the disciples had two swords, and 22:49 points out that other disciples were only awaiting Jesus' word to fight back. But Peter didn't wait for Jesus' command; he drew his weapon and struck! This was so like Peter.

Pacifists have argued for nonresistance from this passage, while their opponents have noted that Jesus told Peter to put his sword back, not throw it away. But this account of Jesus' capture is hardly one on which to base arguments over pacifism. Jesus himself said he could have called on legions of angels to fight for him, if this had been God's will.

Christ allowed himself to be taken so "the Scriptures be fulfilled, that it must happen thus" (Matt. 26:54).

The meaning of the miracle. This last miracle, taking place just before Jesus was arrested and sentenced to death, is a striking reminder. Christ was not *forced* to the cross. He was never overpowered by his opponents. He could have escaped the fate they intended for him at any time.

Jesus' last miracle was actually a warning to his accusers, who refused to believe his claims to be the Christ—in spite of the evidence of his signs and wonders. As Jesus warned them during his trial, "I say to you, hereafter you will see the Son of Man sitting at the right hand of the Power and coming on the clouds of heaven" (Matt. 26:64).

Those who refuse to accept healing at Jesus' hand will surely face his judgment.

WONDERS AT CALVARY

Jesus performed no miracle while on the cross, but his death was accompanied by wonders.

It is appropriate to note several wonders associated with the death of Jesus on the cross. These, like his miracles, were extraordinary events with a religious purpose caused by God.

The cross is one focus of fulfilled prophecy. It is a wonder indeed that hundreds of years before Jesus came to earth, his crucifixion was described in great detail.

Psalm 22 was acknowledged to be messianic long before Christ was born. It contains the following verses:

> "My God, My God, why have
>   You forsaken Me" (22:1).
>
> They shoot out the lip, they shake
>   the head, saying,
> "He trusted in the LORD, let Him
>   rescue Him;
> Let Him deliver Him, since He
>   delights in Him" (22:7, 8).
>
> They pierced My hands and My feet
>   (22:16).
>
> They divide My garments among
>   them,
> And for My clothing they cast lots
>   (22:18).

As we read the Gospels, we discover that each of these verses describes something that was said or something that happened at Calvary.

Isaiah 53 describes Jesus' death in the company of criminals (Isa. 53:9, 12), predicting that he would be buried in a rich man's tomb (Isa. 53:9). Psalm 34:20 predicts that none of Jesus' bones would be broken. This is a striking prediction, for the legs of the thieves with whom he died were broken to hasten their deaths (John 19:32, 33).

These and other prophecies fulfilled at Calvary on the day Jesus died are one of the wonders of God's Word. They remind us that the Cross was always a central element in God's plan and that the death of Jesus was decreed by the Father, not by human beings.

To find the meaning of the Cross, we must understand it not as a tragedy, but as the key to God's triumph over Satan, sin, and death.

The wonder of the torn veil. Matthew reports that at the moment of Jesus' death the veil of the temple was "torn in two from top to bottom" (Matt. 27:51). The same event is reported in Mark 15:38 and Luke 23:45.

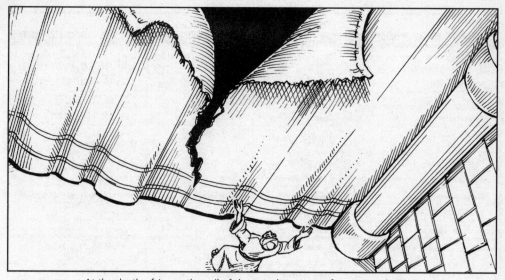

At the death of Jesus, the veil of the temple was torn from top to bottom.

❖

The veil that hung between the Holy Place and the Holy of Holies in the temple was a thick, woven tapestry of multiple colored strands. No known force could rip it apart.

The veil was also spiritually significant. Only once a year could the high priest go behind this veil—and then he carried sacrificial blood to sprinkle on the cover of the sacred ark of the covenant as an atonement for Israel's sins.

The writer of the book of Hebrews reveals that the veil which separated the two inner rooms of the temple indicated that "the way into the Holiest of All was not yet made manifest" (Heb. 9:8). The veil cut off not only the people but even the priests from direct access to God. It was a symbol of the reality that no avenue of approach to God existed in Old Testament times.

But with the death of Christ, a radical change took place. He took our sins upon himself and opened the way to God through his sacrifice. And so the writer of Hebrews declares, "Let us therefore come boldly to the throne of grace, that we may obtain mercy and find grace to help in time of need" (Heb. 4:16).

The wonder of the torn veil symbolizes the end of one age and the beginning of another. In this new age, all believers can enter the holiest of all boldly and with confidence, knowing that God's throne is a throne of grace for all.

The wonder of the opened graves (Matt. 27:52, 53). Matthew alone reports this extraordinary event. He indicates that an earthquake struck the area at the moment of Jesus' death, opening a number of graves. Many of the saints were restored to life and seen in Jerusalem after Jesus' resurrection.

The implications of this wonder are clear. Jesus' death brought life to some who had been dead. What a symbol of victory over death, and of the resurrection life that Jesus offers to all who trust him as Savior.

EASTER MIRACLES—AND BEYOND

Each Gospel devotes much of its space to the story of Jesus' trial and crucifixion. Yet each Gospel account ends on a note of triumph. Jesus has been falsely accused and foully murdered. Yet death cannot hold Jesus. In an unmatched exercise of the power of God, Jesus is raised from the dead!

The account of events on and beyond the first Easter focus our attention on a number of

RESURRECTION APPEARANCES			
Who Sees Him	**Where**	**When**	**Reference**
Mary Magdalene, Mary the mother of James, and Salome	At the tomb	Early Sunday morning	Matt. 28:1–10; Mark 16:1–8; Luke 24:1–12; John 20:1–9
Mary Magdalene	At the tomb	Early Sunday morning	Mark 16:9–11; John 20:11–18
Peter	Jerusalem	Sunday	Luke 24:34; 1 Cor. 15:5
Two travelers	Road to Emmaus	Midday Sunday	Luke 24:13–32
Ten disciples	Upper room	Sunday evening	Mark 16:14; Luke 24:36–43; John 20:19–25
Eleven disciples	Upper room	One week later	John 20:26–29; 1 Cor. 15:5
Seven disciples	Fishing in Galilee	Dawn	John 21:1–23
Eleven disciples	Galilee	Much later	Matt. 28:16–20; Mark 16:15–18
500 followers	Probably Galilee	Later	1 Cor. 15:6
James the apostle	Unknown	Later	1 Cor. 15:7
Disciples, leading women, Jesus' brothers, and others	Mount of Olives	40 days after the resurrection	Luke 24:46–53; Acts 1:3–14
Saul of Tarsus	Road to Damascus	Midday, years later	Acts 9:1–9; 1 Cor. 15:8

wonders associated with the Resurrection, which is the greatest wonder of all. As we look first at the associated wonders and then at the Resurrection itself, we realize how utterly central the bodily resurrection of our Lord is to authentic Christian faith.

WONDERS ASSOCIATED WITH THE RESURRECTION

The tomb's stone seal was rolled away (Matt. 28:2; Mark 16:1–3; Luke 24:1–2). The tombs of wealthy first century Jews like Joseph of Arimathea, where Jesus' body was placed, were hewn into rock cliffs. Such tombs generally had several niches carved into the rock, where the bones of several generations of the family could be stored. These tombs were sealed by large stone "wheels," which would be rolled along a track cut into the rock to seal the tomb. When on the first Easter morning several women set out for Jesus' tomb to wrap His body in linen strips interwoven with sweet-smelling spices, they worried. How could they roll away the heavy stone that sealed the tomb?

When they arrived at the tomb, they discovered the tomb already opened! Matthew tells us that an earthquake had jolted the stone from its track, and an angel had moved it away from the tomb's opening!

The guard posted at the tomb was unconscious (Matt. 28:4). The Jewish leaders had asked Pilate, the Roman governor, to put a military guard at the tomb. They remembered that Jesus had promised a return to life, and while they did not believe Him, they thought His disciples might try to steal the body.

But the appearance of the angel and the earthquake shocked the military guard into unconsciousness. Later, when they awakened, some of the guard reported what had happened to the chief priests. These religious leaders who had conspired to see Jesus executed then bribed the soldiers with "a large sum of money" to say that the disciples stole Jesus' body while they were asleep.

The leaders must also have promised the soldiers protection, for the penalty for a Roman soldier who slept while on guard was death. And, of course, if the disciples had actually stolen Christ's body while the soldiers slept, the soldiers could hardly have been credible witnesses. How would they know *what* happened, if they were asleep? Like most political cover-ups, this attempt to confuse the population about Christ's resurrection was destined to fail.

Angels informed visitors to the tomb that Jesus had risen from the dead (Matthew 28:3; Luke 24:4–7; John 20:12–13). This is a third wonder associated with the Resurrection. One or more angels appeared to groups of women who came to the tomb, and testified to Jesus' resurrection. In each case the angels appeared in their natural, radiant state, rather than as ordinary persons. There could be no mistaking the supernatural character of these witnesses to the raising of Jesus.

The undisturbed graveclothes (John 20:2–10). When Peter and John heard that Jesus' tomb was empty they ran to see for themselves. Peter stooped and stepped into the tomb and was stunned by what he saw.

In biblical times bodies were loosely wrapped in strips of linen, and a cloth was placed over the head of the deceased. What Peter saw was the cloths in which Jesus had been wrapped, still in the shape of the body around which they had been done up! But there was no body inside! Jesus had somehow passed through the grave cloths, leaving them as an empty husk!

The apostle John tells us that when he saw this, he believed (John 20:8)!

Mary saw Jesus Himself (John 20:12–18). Even after Mary had seen the angels at the tomb, she wept uncontrollably. She was still convinced that "they" had taken Jesus away.

Then through her tears Mary saw a figure standing nearby. Supposing him to be the gardener she asked the figure where the body of Jesus had been placed. Jesus then spoke only one word to Mary: her name. Immediately Mary recognized His voice.

Jesus appeared unrecognized to two disciples on the Emmaus road (Luke 24:13–35). Another striking incident is reported in Luke. As two disciples return to their home in Emmaus from Jerusalem they are joined by an unknown man. The man questions them, and when they share their vanished hopes that Jesus might have been the Christ, the man leads them through the Old Testament prophets, showing from Scripture that it was foretold that the Christ would suffer as Jesus had!

On arriving home the two travelers invited the stranger to take a meal with them. As the stranger broke the bread and gave thanks for it, in the traditional Jewish table blessing, they suddenly realized that their companion was Jesus Himself, raised from the dead. Jesus then disappeared, and the two hurried back to Jerusalem to tell the disciples that Jesus was alive.

Jesus appeared in a locked room (Luke 24:36–43; Mark 16:14). The text tells us that Jesus came to His disciples and spoke with them personally shortly after the Resurrection. Luke adds a fascinating detail. The room where the disciples had gathered was a locked room, where the disciples were hiding for fear of the religious leaders who had manipulated Jesus' death.

The sudden appearance of Jesus in the room is one of the proofs that the resurrection body is not limited in the way our mortal bodies are limited. Jesus appeared and disappeared at will, most likely freely crossing the

Faithful women were the first to discover Jesus' empty tomb.

barrier between the material and spiritual universes which no mortal can cross.

Jesus' resurrection body bore the marks of crucifixion in its hands and side (John 20:24–31). The disciple Thomas had not been present the first time Jesus appeared to the gathered disciples. He would not believe the report of the others that Christ had shown Himself to them, alive. Thomas bluntly stated that he would not believe unless he touched Jesus' hands and side, and confirmed that the One who now lived was indeed the same One who had been crucified.

Yet when Jesus did appear, and invited Thomas to touch His wounds, Thomas found he did not need this confirmation after all. Thomas knew Jesus, and fell down before him, confessing "My Lord and my God."

These events, each closely linked to that first Easter morning, were wonders indeed. Yet they pale in comparison to the event with which they are associated: the literal, bodily resurrection of Jesus Christ.

THE SIGNIFICANCE OF THE RESURRECTION: *Romans 1:4; 1 Corinthians 15*

Some contemporary "theologians" have argued that it doesn't matter whether the resurrection of Jesus was literal and historical or not. They claim that a "spiritual" resurrection is all that is required. What mattered is not whether or not Jesus' body was raised and transformed. What mattered is that the disciples *believed* that Jesus was raised. What mattered is that they experienced Him in a different way than when He lived among them.

But the Bible makes it very clear that the resurrection of Jesus was a literal resurrection of the material body, and that the Resurrection took place in space and time as a true historical event. Romans 1:4 reminds us that by His resurrection Jesus was "declared to be the Son of God with power." The Resurrection is the capstone miracle, which confirms once and forever Jesus' claim to be God the Son and Son of God.

The apostle Paul provides a thorough discussion of the Resurrection in chapter 15 of his first letter to the Corinthians. Tracing that discussion we gain some insight into both the nature of Jesus' resurrection, and its significance to our faith.

Christ's death, burial, and resurrection are all historical events prophesied in the Old Testament (1 Corinthians 15:3–4). This is significant, as prophecy which has been fulfilled has invariably been fulfilled literally. We can conclude from this that the death of Jesus was a real death, and the resurrection of Jesus was a real, historical resurrection.

Christ was seen alive after His resurrection by many witnesses who knew Him, and who could not have been deceived (1 Corinthians 15:5–11). Paul not only mentions the Twelve, but also some 500 others, most of whom were alive when Paul wrote the Corinthian letter.

Christ's was raised as the first of many (1 Corinthians 15:12–20). Christian faith promises resurrection to all who believe in Jesus. If Christ was not raised, this critical promise is an empty one. On the other hand, because Jesus did experience a bodily resurrection, our own future resurrection is assured.

The Resurrection is a critical element in God's eternal plan to destroy death itself (1 Corinthians 15:21–28). Adam's sin introduced death. Biblically "death" is not only the cessation of biological life; it is also that corruption of human moral nature which separates human beings from God and brings them under divine judgment. In dying Jesus paid the penalty for our sins. In His resurrection Jesus provided eternal life for those who believe in Him. When God's plan reaches its culmination believers will be resurrected also, and the last taint of sin and death will be forever done away.

The dynamic power of Jesus' resurrection life will accomplish the resurrection transformation of believers, that once again God may be all in all.

While mortal and resurrection bodies are related, the resurrection body is of a different order (1 Corinthians 15:35–48). The great apostle struggles to find analogies that will help us understand resurrection. In a real sense, we will never understand the glorious prospect God holds up to us until the final resurrection comes. Yet Paul does suggest a series of contrasts which helps us sense something of the transformation that took place when Christ was raised, and that will take place when we are raised from the dead.

Corruption vs. incorruption (1 Cor. 15:42). The natural body is subject to dissolution. The resurrection body is not.

Dishonor vs. glory (1 Cor. 15:43). The contrast is explained in the verse. Our natural body is weak and subject to all sorts of disabilities. The resurrection body is infused with power.

Natural body vs. spiritual body (1 Cor. 15:44). This contrast points out that our mortal body is governed by principles implicit in the material universe. In contrast, the resurrection body operates on principles that are supernatural, i.e., "spiritual."

Earthly source vs. heavenly source (1 Cor. 15:47–49). The first man, Adam, was molded from the earth, and his material body was infused with life by God. But Christ's origin is heaven itself, as is the origin of the transformation that produced His resurrection body. In the same sense the essence and origin of our resurrection bodies will be heavenly. In the resurrection "we shall also bear the image of the heavenly Man."

The bodily resurrection of Jesus is most certainly one of the three Grand Miracles of our faith, as described on pages 15 through 17 of this book. The literal, bodily resurrection of Jesus also serves as a miraculous confirmation of our own destiny, and as such is foundational to authentic Christian faith.

JESUS CAUSES A GREAT CATCH OF FISH   *John 21:1–14*

After his resurrection, Jesus appeared to his disciples by the Sea of Galilee and caused a great catch of fish.

Background of the miracle. This is the second miraculous catch of fish reported in the Gospels. The first was associated with the calling of the disciples as Jesus' followers (see p. 176). This extraordinary catch of fish is related to the recommissioning of Peter and Jesus' call to "follow Me."

Parties to the miracle. The parties to this miracle were the resurrected Jesus and his disciples, with the focus on Peter.

Jesus. This was the third time the disciples had seen Jesus following his resurrection. The other two took place in Jerusalem. This appearance was by the Sea of Galilee.

Peter. Back in Galilee, Peter took the lead and announced that he was going fishing (John 21:3). A man of action, Peter may have been unable to wait patiently for Jesus to come to them (see Matt. 28:7). Peter must have been uneasy as well. On the night before Jesus was crucified, Peter had denied the Lord three times.

Peter was so eager to see the Lord that he leaped into the water and swam to shore when Jesus appeared. Then he lingered behind to drag the full nets ashore and count the catch.

After a shared meal on the shore, Jesus spoke to Peter, asking three times about Peter's love for him. After each response, Peter was told to tend or feed Christ's sheep. Peter was thus recommissioned for the ministry to which all the disciples had been called.

But the spiritual significance of this miracle is not Christ's dialogue with his disciple. It is found in a miracle within the miracle.

How the story unfolds. The disciples had returned to Galilee. Peter announced he was going fishing, and the others went with him. Although they fished all night, they caught nothing.

Then as morning dawned, a person was seen on the shore. The figure called to them to cast their net on the right side of the boat. When the fishermen obeyed, they caught a school of large fish so heavy it could not be pulled into the boat.

At this point, John said to Peter, "It is the Lord!" (John 21:7). Peter grabbed his outer garment and leaped into the sea to swim to shore. The other disciples brought the boat into the shallows, dragging the heavy net. When they reached the shore, they saw that Jesus had a fire going, with bread and fish already laid on the fire.

Jesus instructed them to bring some of the fish they had just caught. The net was pulled on shore and the catch counted. They had caught 153 large fish. Christ called them to the meal, serving them the bread and fish he had prepared.

After this meal, the dialog with Peter occurred.

"They caught nothing" (John 21:3). The disciples were professional fishermen. But this night their best efforts were futile.

"Cast the net on the right side" (21:6). Some interpreters have suggested that Jesus could see from the shore the school of fish that the disciples could not. Given the conditions, and the fact that Christ himself was only an indistinct figure in the dawning light, this theory is as absurd as it is unnecessary.

Before his resurrection, Jesus had directed the path of fish in the seas (page 176). He was surely able to cause this school of fish to swim into the net of his disciples.

"A fire of coals there, and fish laid on it, and bread" (21:9). This is a miracle within the miracle. Jesus caused the disciples to catch fish. But before they brought their catch ashore, he was already preparing fish for them to eat—fish they had not caught, fish which Jesus obtained and prepared for his followers.

The significance of the miracle. The meaning of the miracle lies in three verses that speak of fish.

John 21:3 indicates the disciples caught no fish. Their best efforts were futile, even though they were expert fishermen.

John 21:6 reveals that by following Jesus' instructions they caught a "multitude of fish."

John 21:9 tells us that while the disciples were still out on the lake, Jesus was already preparing for them fish which they had not caught.

As the disciples set out on their mission to spread the gospel of the risen Christ, they left their old occupations. However skilled they were at these jobs, there was nothing more in them for persons called to guide Christ's church.

Jesus' instructions to the disciples to cast their nets in the path of a school of fish remind us that Christ is able to make us successful in any chosen pursuit, as long as we are obedient to him.

The meal Jesus served the disciples was a promise that they could rely on him to supply all their needs as they carried out their mission. This miracle within a miracle—Jesus' supply of fish which the disciples did not catch—was the most significant miracle of the two.

Both miracles speak to us today. We learn from one that our success depends on living by Christ's Word. And we learn from the other that we are free to obey him completely. We can rely on his ability to meet our every need.

CHAPTER 12

❖

MIRACLES OF THE APOSTLES

PROVING CHRIST'S POWER

Acts

Jesus was gone.

He had been raised from the dead, but within a few days Jesus returned to heaven. With Jesus gone, would miracles cease?

The answer of the book of Acts is, "No!" Even from heaven Jesus continued to perform miracles through His followers. Miracles performed by the apostles provided proof of their claim that Jesus is Lord, and proof that the power of Jesus is unlimited still!

MIRACLE CLUSTERS IN SCRIPTURE

As noted earlier, Scripture records several periods during which clusters of miracles took place. Typically these periods were marked by establishing miracles, which served to underline some great new revelation.

Thus, the ten great miracle plagues in Egypt, associated with the name Yahweh, demonstrated that the Lord was God, and that he was faithful to the covenant promises given earlier to Abraham. These miracles also established Moses as God's representative, who would unveil the next stage in God's eternal plan.

In a similar way, the next cluster of miracles, performed by Elijah in the eighth century B.C., were establishing miracles. King Ahab had launched an intensive campaign to make Baal worship the official religion of Israel. God's historic and written revelation were under direct attack. The miracles performed by Elijah, and particularly the miracle on Mount Carmel, demonstrated conclusively that the Lord is God, turning the tide against the advocates of Baal.

Each of these two clusters of establishing miracles was followed by a series of supportive miracles. The supportive miracles showed the continuing presence of the Lord, further confirming the revelation authenticated by the establishing miracles.

During the Exodus a number of miracles served this purpose, and miracles continued on through the time of the conquest of Canaan. God had promised Abraham that his descendants would occupy Canaan. The ten plagues established the Lord as God, and the later miracles revealed his continuing presence with his covenant people.

In the eighth century the miracles of Elijah again established that the Lord alone is God. The supporting miracles of Elijah's successor, Elisha, revealed the continuing presence of the Lord with his people, who had returned to him.

THE MIRACLES OF JESUS AND THE APOSTLES

The miracles of Jesus clearly fit the pattern and purpose of earlier clusters of miracles. A new aspect of God's eternal plan was being unveiled. The miracles of Jesus were establishing miracles. They proved that Jesus was God's spokesman as well as the promised Messiah.

Earlier miracles had proven that the Lord is God. Christ's miracles, and especially the Resurrection, proved that Jesus was the Lord.

But Christ had died and been raised, and had returned to heaven. So the question might well be raised, How could the presence of the risen Jesus be proven by those who set out on the new path that Jesus had revealed? In the past, establishing miracles had been followed by supporting miracles. It was the same with Jesus' miracles. The early days of the Christian church were marked by wonders and miracles performed by the apostles. As supporting miracles, these demonstrated the presence of Jesus with his followers, authenticating the movement Jesus founded as a work of God.

SUPPORTING MIRACLES IN THE BOOK OF ACTS

The book of Acts includes reports of 14 distinct wonders or miracles and references to others. The distinct wonders and miracles are:

The miracles of Jesus proved He was God's spokesman and the Messiah.

GENERAL REFERENCES TO MIRACLES IN ACTS

Many passages in Acts reveal that miracles, wonders, and signs accompanied the ministry of the apostles and others as the Christian church was established in Jerusalem, spread through Judea and Samaria, and ultimately radiated out into the wider Roman world.

We can sense how common miracles and wonders were in these early days by looking at the verses which give general descriptions of miracles during this period.

Then fear came upon every soul [in Jerusalem], and many wonders and signs were done through the apostles (Acts 2:43).

After being ordered to stop preaching, the apostles prayed,

"Look on their threats, and grant to Your servants that with all boldness they may speak Your word, by stretching out Your hand to heal, and that signs and wonders may be done through the name of Your holy Servant Jesus" (Acts 4:29, 30).

And through the hands of the apostles many signs and wonders were done among the people (Acts 5:12).

They brought the sick out into the streets and laid them on beds and couches, that at least the shadow of Peter passing by might fall on some of them. Also a multitude gathered from the surrounding cities to Jerusalem, bringing sick people and those who were tormented by unclean spirits, and they were all healed (Acts 5:15, 16).

And Stephen, full of faith and power, did great wonders and signs among the people (Acts 6:8).

And the multitudes with one accord heeded the things spoken by Philip, hearing and seeing the miracles which he did. For unclean spirits, crying with a loud voice, came out of many who were possessed; and many who were paralyzed and lame were healed (Acts 8:6, 7).

Then Simon himself also believed; and when he was baptized he continued with Philip, and was amazed, seeing the miracles and signs which were done (Acts 8:13).

Therefore they stayed there a long time [in Iconium], speaking boldly in the Lord, who was bearing witness to the word of his grace, granting signs and wonders to be done by their hands (Acts 14:3).

Then all the multitude kept silent and listened to Barnabas and Paul declaring how many miracles and wonders God had worked through them among the Gentiles (Acts 15:12).

God worked unusual miracles by the hands of Paul, so that even handkerchiefs or aprons were brought from his body to the sick, and the diseases left them and the evil spirits went out of them (Acts 19:11).

These were indeed supportive miracles, performed in Jesus' name. They made it plain to all that God was with these followers who proclaimed that Jesus was the Son of God. The new revelation introduced and established by the miracle-working Christ was further confirmed by a great number of supportive miracles performed by his followers.

THE ASCENSION OF JESUS *Acts 1:9–11*

The Ascension was Jesus' return to heaven, mentioned three times by Luke in his Gospel and Acts: Luke 24:50–51; Acts 1:2; and Acts 1:9–11. As the disciples watched in wonder, two angels joined them, promising that Jesus would come back "in like manner as you saw him go into heaven."

Jesus was taken up and received into a cloud (Acts 1:9). The miraculous departure of Christ contrasts with the Old Testament's report of Elijah's departure. That Old Testament prophet was swept up into heaven by angels, carried away in a fiery chariot (2 Kings 2:11). The description of Jesus' departure seems almost casual. One moment the resurrected Christ was blessing his disciples outside Bethany (Luke 24:51). And the next, he was taken up into the air and received into a cloud.

However, this departure was less casual than the description suggests. When associated with the miraculous, clouds have a special significance.

We're reminded of Luke 9, which describes Jesus' transfiguration in front of some of his disciples. Luke indicated that a cloud "overshadowed them" and that a voice speaking from the cloud announced, "This is My Beloved Son, hear him!" (Luke 9:34, 35). The cloud also reminds us of Jesus' words about himself and his return, "in the clouds with great power and glory" (Mark 13:26).

In each case, the image of the cloud is rooted in the Old Testament era, where a bright cloud symbolized the glory of God, the *shekinah,* which once filled the tabernacle and later filled the temple built by Solomon.

❖

Jesus was taken up into heaven.

Thus, the apostles' last glimpse of Jesus was of him being enveloped in a cloud which spoke of the divine presence. Even the manner in which Jesus was taken up was a powerful affirmation of his divinity.

Jesus was carried up "into heaven." The Greek phrase *eis ton ouranon,* "into heaven," is used in Luke 24:51 and repeated in Acts 1:10 and three times in Acts 1:11. It is clear that locating the risen Jesus in heaven was of central importance to Luke in reporting this wonder.

The message of the two angels further emphasizes this point. The angels told the watchers that "this same Jesus, who was taken up from you into heaven, will so come in like manner as you saw him go into heaven" (Acts 1:11). The angels' words established two things: Jesus was now in heaven and Jesus would return to earth.

The continuing emphasis on Jesus' location "in heaven" is the most significant feature of this first wonder described in the book of Acts.

Why Jesus' presence in heaven was so significant. The importance of establishing this point is reflected in a prayer offered by the apostles after a confrontation with the leaders who had conspired to have Jesus executed. The disciples prayed that the Lord would stretch out his hand to heal, and that signs and wonders might be done through the name of Jesus (Acts 4:30). Because he was in heaven, Jesus could now answer his disciples' prayers and act through them to perform fresh wonders on the earth!

In fact, the New Testament mentions a number of the present ministries of Jesus Christ.

- Jesus in heaven is preparing a place for us (John 14:2, 3).
- Jesus, as the vine, is the source of that spiritual vitality which enables us to bear fruit as we stay close to him (John 15:4, 5).
- Jesus, as head of the church, guides and directs us (Eph. 2:20, 21).
- Jesus, as our High Priest, sympathizes with our weaknesses and provides mercy

and enabling grace when we come to his throne of grace (Heb. 4:15, 16).

- Jesus, as our High Priest, intercedes for us, guaranteeing our salvation (Heb. 7:25).
- Jesus, as our advocate, represents us when we sin, pledging his own blood as the basis for our salvation (1 John 2:1, 2).

These and other ministries which Jesus performs for believers today make his living presence in heaven vital for us. And the wonder of the Ascension focuses our attention on the fact that Jesus lives, and that in heaven today he ministers to us and our needs.

THE WONDERS OF PENTECOST
Acts 2

The disciples had assembled in Jerusalem to wait, as Jesus instructed them, for "the Holy Spirit to come upon you" and provide the spiritual power required for their mission (Acts 1:8). On the day of Pentecost, 50 days after Jesus' resurrection, the Spirit swept into the room where the apostles and other believers in Jesus had gathered.

The day of Pentecost (Acts 2:1). This day fell on the fiftieth day from the first Sunday after Passover, and thus fifty days after the resurrection of Jesus. It was the day on which the first produce of the wheat harvest was presented to God. The Jewish rabbis had concluded from Exodus 19:1 that Pentecost was also the day on which God had given Moses his Law.

How significant that the Holy Spirit who would write God's law on the hearts of those who trust in Jesus (2 Cor. 3:6–8) should come on the anniversary of the day when the Law was given in written form. A new era began that day.

Visible signs of the Spirit's coming (Acts 2:2–4). The coming of the Spirit was marked with visible wonders:

And suddenly there came a sound from heaven, as of a rushing mighty wind, and it filled the whole house where they were sitting. Then there appeared to them divided tongues, as of fire, and one sat upon each of them. And they were all filled with the Holy Spirit and began to speak with other tongues, as the Spirit gave them utterance (Acts 2:2–4).

It was the combination of these three miraculous signs that marked the coming of the Spirit as a unique event in sacred history.

The "rushing mighty wind" (Acts 2:2). Wind is a symbol of God's Spirit in both the Old Testament and the New Testament. The Hebrew word *ruah* and the Greek word *pneuma* mean either wind or spirit, depending on the context.

The prophet Ezekiel had spoken of the wind as God's breath, blowing over the dry bones that represented Israel and filling them with new life (Ezek. 37:9–14). Jesus in speaking with Nicodemus had referred to the wind/spirit or meaning of *pneuma* to draw an analogy: "The wind blows where it wishes, and you hear the sound of it, but cannot tell where it comes from and where it goes. So is everyone who is born of the Spirit" (John 3:8).

John the Baptist had spoken of Jesus as One who "will baptize you with the Holy Spirit [wind] and fire" (Luke 3:16). There is little doubt that in describing the events of Pentecost, Luke saw in the rushing wind and tongues of fire the fulfillment of John the Baptist's prophecy.

Divided tongues, as of fire (2:3). Fire also has a long history as a symbol of the divine presence. The roots of this image are found in the appearance of the Lord to Moses in the burning bush (Ex. 2:2–5), in the cloudy-fiery pillar that led Israel through the wilderness, and in the fact that the Lord "descended upon [Mount Sinai] in fire." The tongue-like flames which burned over the head of each believer in the book of Acts was a clear, visible sign of the presence of God—this time the presence of the third person of the Trinity, the Holy Spirit.

They . . . began to speak with other tongues, as the Spirit gave them utterance (2:4). There is a clear

"Tongues, as of fire, sat upon each of them."

difference between the "other tongues" of Acts and the ecstatic utterances also called "tongues" in 1 Corinthians 12—14. In the 1 Corinthians passage, the tongues were unintelligible and the church needed an interpreter to understand what the speaker was saying (1 Cor. 12:10; 14:2, 5). In Acts, the wonder was that Jews from many foreign lands who had come to Jerusalem for the festival heard in their "own language in which we were born" (Acts 2:8, 11).

The lasting significance of the Spirit's coming. The Acts passage doesn't give a name to the Spirit's Pentecost activity. Acts does report that the disciples were "filled with" the Holy Spirit, an experience which was repeated on several occasions (Acts 4:8, 31). Later in Acts, however, the apostle Peter identified the initial experience and gave it a name.

Reporting the conversion of the first Gentile who became a Christian—a Roman centurion named Cornelius—Peter reported that "the Holy Spirit fell upon them, as upon us at the beginning. Then I remembered the Word of the Lord, how he said, 'John indeed baptized with water, but you shall be baptized with the Holy Spirit'" (Acts 11:15, 16). Peter's reference to "the beginning" in this context was clearly to the day

of Pentecost. And the ministry the Spirit exercised on that day was his baptizing work.

While believers in most Christian traditions speak of Pentecost in terms of the baptism of the Holy Spirit, Christians differ as to the meaning of that term. Yet this work of the Spirit was clearly defined in 1 Corinthians 12:13: "For by one Spirit we were all baptized into one body—whether Jews or Greeks, whether slaves or free—and have all been made to drink into one Spirit." The baptism of the Holy Spirit is thus that work of the Holy Spirit by which every believer is made a part of the body of Christ, linked forever to Jesus and through Jesus to every other believer in the Lord.

When the Spirit came on Pentecost, the church as the living body of Christ, a spiritual organism, was born (see 1 Cor. 10:16; 12:27; Eph. 4:12). After Pentecost, every believer has been joined to that spiritual body upon trust in the Lord.

The significance of the wonders that marked the Spirit's coming. While the three visible signs together served as the unique mark of the Spirit's coming, the focus of the text is clearly on the third sign—tongues.

As those from the western Roman world

Places represented on Pentecost.

❖

and from the east heard the Christians speaking in their own tongues, "they were all amazed and perplexed, saying to one another, 'Whatever could this mean?'" (Acts 2:12). The question was answered by the apostle Peter, who stood up and preached history's first gospel message. Peter quoted the prophet Joel, announcing that what the visible signs meant was that the promised age of the Spirit had actually arrived!

Peter quoted,

"And it shall come to pass in the
    last days, says God,
That I will pour out of My Spirit
    on all flesh" (Acts 2:17).

Peter continued to quote the passage, which promised a display of wonders, and concluded his quote with these words:

And it shall come to pass
That whoever calls on the name
    of the Lord
Shall be saved (Acts 2:21).

While a number of the signs mentioned in Joel are associated with the judgments linked to Jesus' second coming, Peter's emphasis was clear. The wonders of Pentecost marked the *beginning* of the last stage of God's plan for humankind. That stage, which continues to our own day, is marked by the vitalizing work of God's Holy Spirit and the promise of salvation to "whoever calls on the name of the Lord."

The wonders of the day of Pentecost established a link between the Old and New Testaments. They marked the initiation of an era predicted by the Old Testament prophets—a period in which each individual, Jew and Gentile alike, is faced with the necessity of making a personal decision about Jesus Christ.

THE HEALING OF A LAME MAN
Acts 3:1–26

Peter and John healed a man who had been a cripple from birth on their way to worship at the temple. The miracle amazed the other worshipers, who crowded around to listen as Peter seized the occasion to preach another evangelistic sermon.

Worship at the temple (Acts 3:1). The first Christians were observant Jews, who worshiped in the traditional ways and continued to practice their ancient religion. For many years Christians were simply known as practitioners of "the Way" (Acts 9:2). During this period Christianity was considered a sect of Judaism and not a separate religion. It was only as the gospel message spread in the gentile world that leaders like the apostle Paul had to struggle to define the lifestyle to which faith in Christ called believers.

So it was not surprising that the two apostles of Jesus were on their way to the temple "at the hour of prayer, the ninth hour" (Acts 3:1). Two principal daily services were held at the temple, one accompanying the morning and the other the evening sacrifice. It was the evening service the two intended to attend.

The lame man (3:2). The "lame man" was a cripple who had to be carried to the gate where he begged daily. The text emphasizes that he had been lame "from his mother's womb." This was no psychosomatic illness that could be "cured" by suggestion.

The lame man was probably familiar to those who had passed for years on their way to the temple. Many would have given him alms, which was considered a *mitzvah*, a meritorious act.

The fact that the lame man was well known as well as the serious nature of his disability contributed to the amazement of the people at his healing.

"In the name of Jesus Christ of Nazareth" (3:6). While passing by, Peter drew the attention of the cripple and announced that while he had no silver or gold, he would give what he had. In the name of Jesus, Peter told the man, "Rise up and walk."

The supportive miracles performed by the apostles were done in "the name of Jesus." That is, the apostles called on Christ to act and to demonstrate the power which he alone possessed.

There is a significant difference between the apostle's pronouncements of Jesus' name and the magical use of "names" in biblical times. For centuries magical formulas had included the supposed names of demons and deities, manipulating them to do the will of the sorcerer. This is the way some people interpret the healings in Acts. But an incident reported in Acts 19:13f makes it clear that this was not the case.

In Ephesus, Paul performed such stunning miracles in Jesus' name that a group of Jewish exorcists tried to cast out a demon using Christ's name. The demon then beat them

and chased them from the house, saying "Jesus I know and Paul I know; but who are you?" (Acts 19:15).

There was no magic involved in Peter's miracle of healing. The power of Jesus flowed through his servant and performed the miracle. These were supporting miracles indeed, revealing Jesus' presence with the leaders of the movement founded in his name.

"Entered the temple with them, walking, leaping, and praising God" (3:8). The complete healing of the crippled man was advertised by his actions. He was quickly recognized. Luke emphasizes the reaction of those who knew him. They were "filled with wonder and amazement" and were "greatly amazed" (Acts 3:10, 11).

There is a story that Thomas Aquinas once visited Pope Innocent II in Rome. Pointing out his riches, the pope said, "See, Thomas, the church can no longer say 'silver and gold have I none.'" Aquinas agreed. "True, holy father. Neither can she say, 'Rise and walk.'" This miracle reminds us that no Christian congregation should be more concerned with its facilities than with seeing the transforming power of Jesus at work in people's lives.

"Men of Israel . . ." (3:12). Peter used the occasion to address the crowd. It was not by Peter's or John's own godliness that the man was made to walk. The power was that of Jesus: "And his name, through faith in his name, has made this man strong, whom you see and know. Yes, the faith which comes through him has given him this perfect soundness in the presence of you all" (Acts 3:16).

Peter was not saying that the lame man had faith. He was not even claiming credit for his own and John's faith. Rather, Peter was saying that the *Jesus who was the object of their faith* had performed the miracle.

Peter then explained who this Jesus was. He was the one whom they had crucified but who had been raised again by God. He was the one predicted by prophets, whom God in faithfulness sent first to bless Israel. To have faith "in his name" was to have faith in him as the Scriptures defined him.

We must also accept Jesus on his own terms, as he is defined in the Word of God—not as he has been redefined by those who would keep the name but rob the person of his glory by viewing him as a good man or a simple Jewish rabbi. Jesus was and is the Christ, the Son of God; and for this reason alone power resides in his name.

The significance of the miracle. This was not the first of the confirming miracles worked by Jesus' followers (compare Acts 2:43). It was, however, the *defining* supportive miracle. All the miracles and wonders of Acts were performed through faith in the name of Jesus Christ. Each miracle demonstrated to all who saw the continuing presence of one whose own miracles had established him as the Son of God.

THE DEATHS OF ANANIAS AND SAPPHIRA   Acts 5:1–11

A couple eager to gain a reputation in the new Christian community sold some property. They kept part of the money for themselves but claimed the amount they brought to the apostles was the entire proceeds of the sale.

"Why has Satan filled your heart" (Acts 5:3). When Ananias brought the money to Peter, God revealed their dishonesty. Peter rebuked Ananias for an act which was in essence a "lie to the Holy Spirit." Ananias immediately collapsed and died. It is clear that Peter had no direct role in the death of Ananias. Ananias was struck dead by God.

"About three hours later" (5:7). In harmony with Jewish custom, Ananias was taken out and buried. Three hours later his wife came in. When she was questioned, she repeated the lie told by her husband (Acts 5:8). At that moment the men who had buried her husband returned, and Peter announced that they would bury her too. "Immediately" she also fell and died, and was buried beside her husband.

What was the sin of Ananias and Sapphira? Their plan to deceive the apostles and the church was a "lie to the Holy Spirit" (Acts 5:3). As such, the lie served "to test the Spirit of the Lord."

We need to remember that the purpose of confirming miracles and wonders was to demonstrate the continuing presence of God with his people. The events of the day of Pentecost (Acts 2) and the healing of the lame man (Acts 3), along with many other miracles (Acts 2:43), had demonstrated the living presence of God with this company which was committed to Jesus. The "lie to the Holy Spirit" by Ananias and Sapphira was a denial of God's presence—an act which put God to the test.

The significance of the miraculous deaths. In the critical early days of the church, the challenge issued by Ananias and Sapphira could not go unanswered. God struck the pair dead, confirming the reality of the divine presence within the Christian community.

The impact of the miracle (5:11–13). This miracle had its intended effect within and outside the church. Acts indicates that "fear came upon all the church and upon all who heard these things" (v. 11). We should not understand this fear as terror but as a deep, abiding awe. The reality of God's presence was impressed on Jesus' followers, and thus their faith was strengthened.

The miracle had an unusual effect on "the rest" of the people of Jerusalem as well. Acts 5:13 reveals that "none of the rest dared join them, but the people esteemed them highly."

Sometimes people have "joined the church" for reasons other than trust in Jesus as God's Son and Savior. When Jesus was on earth, many followed him not because they understood or accepted his claims but because he healed their diseases and fed them when they were hungry. The shocking deaths of Ananias and Sapphira sent a powerful message to anyone who might link themselves with the Christian movement without a real faith in Christ: it was dangerous to be a "pretend" Christian!

So while the people of Jerusalem had a high regard for the apostles and the followers of Christ, the movement never became "popular." The next verse reveals that while more and more people were added to the church, it was only those who "believed in the Lord" (Acts 5:14, NIV).

THE APOSTLES ARE MIRACULOUSLY FREED FROM PRISON   Acts 5:17–42

The flurry of miracles performed by the apostles after the death of Ananias and Sapphira (Acts 5:15) and their vigorous preaching of Christ aroused the anger of the Sadducees, who imprisoned the apostles.

They "laid their hands on the apostles" (Acts 5:18). The Sadducees were the priestly party in Judaism. They controlled the Levites, who served as the temple police. It was the temple police who arrested the apostles and put them in jail, where they would be tried by the Sanhedrin the next day.

"An angel of the Lord opened the prison doors" (5:19). The opening of the prison doors was not a miracle done by the apostles—but a miracle performed for them by an angel. For a discussion of the incident, see *Every Good and Evil Angel in the Bible.*

Luke provided specific details of this happening, so the miraculous nature of the release is clear. Acts 5:23 recounts the report of the detail of guards sent the next morning to bring the apostles before the Sanhedrin. "Indeed we found the prison shut securely, and the guards standing outside before the doors; but when we opened them, we found no one inside."

Reports of miraculous releases from prison in first-century literature. Jeremias has commented on the widespread popularity of legends in the ancient world which recount the opening of prison doors. Jeremias wrote,

The threefold repetition of the motif of the miraculous opening of prison doors in Ac., its distribution between the apostles in Ac. 5:19; Peter in 12:6–11, and Paul in 16:2ff, and the agreement with ancient

An angel released the apostles from prison.

❖

parallels in many details, e.g., liberation by night, the role of the guards, the falling off of chains, the bursting open of the doors, the shining of bright light, earthquake, all suggest that in form at least Lk. is following an established *topos* (*Jerusalem in the Time of Jesus,* p. 176).

While Luke wrote the most fluid Greek in the New Testament and was undoubtedly familiar with this literary convention, the content is always more important than the form. The important thing to remember is that the events Luke relates in Acts actually happened.

The apostles witnessed boldly (5:25). While the confused members of the Sanhedrin pondered this report, they were told that the apostles were now standing in the temple and teaching the people. The temple police then approached the apostles and politely asked them to appear before the Sanhedrin. The members of this supreme court of Judaism attempted to silence the apostles, who answered with boldness that they would obey God rather than men (Acts 5:29).

The court was restrained from killing the apostles by a Pharisee named Gamaliel, whose fame is known from rabbinic writings. Gamaliel pointed out that other messianic movements had died out. He suggested that they beat the apostles, command them not to speak in Jesus' name, and let them go. Hopefully this movement would also just go away.

The result was that "daily in the temple, and in every house, they did not cease teaching and preaching Jesus as the Christ" (Acts 5:42).

SAUL'S MIRACULOUS CONVERSION
Acts 9:1–20

A zealous young Pharisee named Saul saw a vision of Jesus while on the way to Damascus to seize Christians and return them to Jerusalem for trial.

❖

WAS SAUL RIGHT TO PERSECUTE CHRISTIANS?

There is no doubt that Saul felt justified in persecuting Christians. In Old Testament times, God had commended Phinehas for slaying a sinning Israelite (Num. 25:6–15). In more recent history, the Maccabees had shown their zeal for God by rooting out apostasy (compare 1 Macc. 2:23–28; 42–48). The writer of one of the Dead Sea Scrolls saw zeal against apostates as a natural expression of one's commitment to God. He wrote, "The nearer I draw to you, the more I am filled with zeal against all who do wickedness and against all men of deceit" (IQH 14:13–15).

There is no doubt that Saul the Pharisee felt justified in persecuting Christians. He also saw it as his religious duty—until that day on the Damascus road when Jesus spoke to him, and the foundation was laid for the transformation of Saul into the apostle Paul.

❖

The background of Saul's journey (Acts 9:1). Saul, who later became the apostle Paul, is pictured as "*still* breathing threats and murder against the disciples of the Lord."

Earlier Saul had taken part in the stoning of Stephen (Acts 7:58; 8:1). Following Stephen's death, nearly all the Christians were driven from Jerusalem (Acts 8:1). The "still" in 9:1 tells us that this crusade against Jesus' followers had not satisfied Saul. So Saul obtained letters from the high priest authorizing him to bind believers and return them to Jerusalem.

In the Roman Empire, ethnic groups were allowed to keep their own religions and their own systems of law. Letters from the High Priest as the head of the Sanhedrin, the supreme court of Judaism, would be recognized as authorizing the arrest of any Jew. Saul was on official business, and his business was the persecution of the church.

"Suddenly a light shone around him from heaven" (Acts 9:3). While on the road to Damascus, Saul was suddenly blinded by a bright light. He fell to the ground and heard a voice from heaven calling to him. The voice asked why Saul was persecuting the Lord. Saul, "trembling and astonished," could only ask, "Lord, what do you want me to do?"

When Saul arose, he was blind. His companions led him by the hand to Damascus, where he neither ate nor drank for three days.

"Ananias" (9:10). The vision on the road to Damascus was not the only miraculous element in Saul's conversion. God spoke in a vision to a believer named Ananias and sent him to Saul. Reassured by God that the hostile Saul was "a chosen vessel of Mine to bear My name before Gentiles" (Acts 9:15), Ananias went. When he reached Saul, Ananias laid hands on him and "immediately there fell from his eyes something like scales" (Acts 9:18). Saul got up and was baptized. After recovering his strength, Saul began to preach in the synagogues in Damascus that Jesus was the Christ, "the Son of God" (Acts 9:20).

The three accounts of Saul's conversion. Three accounts of Saul's conversion occur in Acts. They are found in Acts 9, 22, and 26. At first glance, the three accounts seem to conflict in important details. In Acts 9:3 and 22:6,

A bright light from heaven blinded Saul.

❖

the light radiated around Saul only; in Acts 26:13, it shone around everyone. Acts 9:4 says that Saul heard the voice, and 9:7 adds that his companions heard it as well. But Acts 26:14 indicates that Saul alone heard the voice.

The solution to this apparent contradiction lies in the fact that the Greek noun *phone* means both "sound" and "intelligible speech." What happened is that all saw the light that enfolded Saul. While Saul distinctly heard Jesus speak, his companions heard sounds they could not understand.

What everyone understood, however, was that something miraculous had happened. There had been a *bat qol*, the "daughter of a voice," or a "voice from heaven,"—a phrase used in the first century to indicate that God himself had spoken.

How stunned Saul was when the voice from heaven—obviously that of God—asked why Saul was persecuting him! Saul certainly didn't think he had been persecuting God! When the speaker identified himself as Jesus, everything Saul had believed was swept away.

The miracle convinced Saul that those believers he had been persecuting were right. By the time Ananias appeared, Saul was ready to commit himself to Jesus.

The significance of the miracle. The miraculous conversion and the restoration of Saul's sight foreshadowed the significance of Paul in the spread of the gospel. It also demonstrated the continuing active presence of Jesus, whose own miracles had established him as the Son of God.

PETER PERFORMS MIRACLES AT LYDDA AND JOPPA   *Acts 9:32–42*

The conversion of Saul was followed by a relaxation of the persecution of Christians. During this time, Peter traveled through Judea, Galilee, and Samaria. The book of Acts recounts two miracles which he performed.

The first miracle occurred in Lydda and the second in Joppa. These cities west of Palestine were populated by both Jews and Gentiles. The location suggests a further extension of the gospel message, laying a foundation for the conversion of the Roman centurion Cornelius. He would have heard of these nearby miraculous events.

"Jesus the Christ heals you" (Acts 9:34). The first miracle, which took place in Lydda, was the healing of a paralyzed man named Aeneas, who had been bedridden for eight years. Peter healed in the name of Jesus, and Aeneas "arose immediately."

"Tabitha, arise" (9:40). When a much-beloved woman in nearby Joppa died, the believers sent to Lydda for Peter. The woman's Hebrew name was Tabitha, while her Greek name was Dorcas. Both names mean "gazelle." She is described as a "disciple" (the only occurrence in the New Testament of the feminine form of the word) who "was full of good works and charitable deeds" (Acts 9:36). In response to the urgent request, Peter quickly traveled the ten miles to Joppa.

Peter prayed beside Tabitha's body, and then called on the dead woman to "arise." She opened her eyes and sat up. Peter led her out alive and presented her to the assembled widows and believers.

The significance of the miracles. These two miracles mimicked miracles performed by Jesus during his time on earth. They confirmed the continuing presence of Jesus with his followers, demonstrating that presence outside traditional Jewish territory.

These supportive miracles provided continuing proof of Jesus' power. As the restoration of Tabitha became known throughout Joppa, "many believed on the Lord" (Acts 9:42).

PETER'S DELIVERANCE FROM PRISON AND HEROD'S DEATH
Acts 12:1–25

Herod had executed the apostle James (Acts 12:2). The act pleased his Jewish subjects so much that he imprisoned Peter, intending to execute him after the Passover celebration. But the miraculous intervention of an angel in answer to the church's prayer freed Peter. This miracle was followed shortly afterward by a clear divine judgment against the king.

Who was the Herod of Acts 12? The Herod of Acts 12 was Herod Agrippa I, the grandson of Herod the Great of the Christmas story. Herod grew up in Rome as an intimate of the imperial family. Even so, he had to flee Rome at age 33 to escape his creditors. A few years later the emperor Caligula made him tetrarch of two northern Palestinian territories, with the right to be addressed as king. In A.D. 41, when Herod was 51, the emperor Claudius, a childhood friend, added Judea and Samaria to his territories, extending his rule over all the lands that had been ruled by his grandfather.

Herod Agrippa sought the support of his Jewish subjects. He played the part of an observant Jew, following every ritual rule. He moved the administrative seat of the province to Jerusalem from Caesarea and began to rebuild Jerusalem's northern wall. He was also able to prevent the emperor Caligula from erecting a statue of himself as a god in the Jerusalem temple.

It's not surprising that Herod saw suppression of Christians, a divisive element in Jerusalem, as a wise policy. When Herod executed the apostle James—who with his brother John was one of Jesus' earliest followers—the Jewish leaders were delighted.

To please them further, Herod seized Peter also. Herod was unable to have Peter brought to trial until after the Passover religious holidays. So Herod put Peter in a cell under heavy guard. Peter's execution would serve Herod's political purposes very well. Whether Peter had done anything to deserve death was immaterial.

Peter's prison (12:4, 5). Peter was imprisoned in the Fortress Antonia, just beyond the magnificent temple Herod the Great had spent 38 years and enormous sums to enhance. Important prisoners kept under guard were usually chained to one soldier. The political significance that Herod attached to Peter is seen in the fact that the apostle was "bound with two chains between two soldiers" (v. 5). In addition, guards were posted outside the locked cell door.

Herod's arrangements were futile. The Bible reports that "an angel of the Lord stood by him, and a light shone in the prison; and he struck Peter on the side."

Stories of angelic deliverance from prison were imbedded in the popular lore. Peter at first assumed he was dreaming. Peter saw the chains drop from his wrists. He could see the soldiers seated there, unmoving. He stooped to pick up the outer cloak he had used as a blanket as he slept on the stone floor. Peter even tied on his sandals, wrapping the leather thongs carefully around his leg.

Then Peter followed the angel. He passed the guards, still alert at their posts but totally unaware of Peter and his companion. He watched as the great iron gate that led out into the city swung open of its own accord. But it wasn't until they had walked some distance from the fortress and the angel had left that Peter realized this was no vision.

Peter's release was an answer to prayer (12:5). When Peter was imprisoned, many Christians gathered to pray. Even as Peter was being led from the prison, one group was praying in the home of Mary, the mother of John Mark. It was to this house that Peter walked that night.

In first-century Jerusalem, the wealthy lived in walled homes. Large gates were set in the outer wall. These were opened only on special occasions. Smaller doors were built into these large gates. It was on this smaller "door of the gate" that Peter knocked when he arrived at Mary's house.

That night a girl named Rhoda was serving as doorkeeper. It was her duty to respond to anyone who knocked. When she called out "Who?" the visitor responded, "It is I." The doorkeeper was expected to recognize the voice of a friend and would open the gate without actually seeing the person.

Rhoda recognized Peter's voice. But she was so happy that she neglected to open the door, running instead to tell the congregation inside the good news. The believers tried to calm her down, certain she must be wrong, but she kept on insisting.

The incident is encouraging for those who have the notion that our prayers are answered only if we have unshakable faith. The church was praying earnestly, but it was certain that Peter couldn't possibly be outside the door.

Peter's release from prison in answer to prayer was another miraculous confirmation of the presence of Christ with his people and also of Christ's power. Jesus even commanded angels to intercede for his own.

The miraculous death of Herod. The details and the timing of the subsequent death of Herod Agrippa I was portrayed as a miracle by Luke, and it was undoubtedly viewed this way in the early church.

Josephus, the first-century Jewish historian, gave an account of Herod Agrippa's death in his *Antiquities* (XIX, 343–50 [viii.2]). His account and Luke's narrative were clearly in-

dependent, but they are similar in structure and many details. Both make it clear that Herod was struck down as the crowds praised him as a god.

This way of honoring rulers was common in the Hellenistic world. For instance, an entry in a child's exercise book read: "What is a god? That which is strong. What is a king? He who is equal to the divine" (quoted in A. D. Nock's *Conversion*, Oxford, 1933, 91). Sacrifices in honor of kings often slipped over the already blurred line to become sacrifices made *to* the king. One first-century inscription honored King Antiochus I of Commagene as "The Great King Antiochus, the God, the Righteous One, the Manifest Deity."

In Judaism, however, this practice was viewed as a form of blasphemy. When Herod accepted the divine honors offered him, according to Acts, "immediately an angel of the Lord struck him, because he did not give glory to God" (12:23).

Luke provided a medical explanation in his comment that Herod was "eaten by worms." The king was probably killed by intestinal roundworms, which grow to a length of ten to fourteen inches. Clusters of roundworms can obstruct the intestine, causing severe pain. The sufferer will vomit up worms, but in a case so advanced will die an excruciatingly painful death.

Josephus gave a graphic description of Herod's demise. He wrote that Herod was "overcome by more intense pain. . . . Exhausted after five straight days by the pain in abdomen, he departed this life in the fifty-fourth year of his life and the seventh of his reign."

These two events, the release of Peter and the death of Herod, were connected by the angelic agency and linked in Luke's history. They were undoubtedly linked in the minds of first-century Christians. A pagan king who pretended to live as a pious Jew had threatened the existence of the early church. The angel that protected Peter from execution was also God's agent in carrying out the divine sentence of death passed on the persecutor.

The conclusion was inescapable: Jesus lived, and his presence hovered over the church even as his miracle-working power protected believers and threatened the lives of the enemies of his people.

THE BLINDING OF ELYMAS
Acts 13:4–12

On their first missionary journey, Paul and Barnabas preached on the island of Cyprus. When a renegade Jewish sorcerer opposed them, Paul struck him with blindness.

Paul's history. The miraculous conversion of Saul of Tarsus is described in Acts 9 (see p. 255). After his converson, Saul became such a fiery evangelist in Damascus that the Jews plotted to kill him, and he barely escaped with his life (Acts 9:22–25). He returned to Jerusalem, where he again spoke out so boldly that his life was endangered (Acts 9:26–29). The believers brought him to Caesarea and saw him off on a ship to his home city of Tarsus (Acts 9:30).

During the next several years, Saul studied the Scriptures and was given a deeper understanding of the implications of Christ's coming, death, and resurrection. Barnabas, who had befriended Saul in Jerusalem, eventually brought Saul to Antioch to help lead the gentile church in that city (Acts 11:19–28).

Some time later the Holy Spirit led the church at Antioch to send Saul and Barnabas on a mission to spread the gospel to other parts of the Roman Empire. Their first stop was in Cyprus, where they traveled and preached throughout the island.

Cyprus (Acts 13:4). The island of Cyprus was named for its primary export, *cyprium,* or copper. It had been annexed by Rome in 57 B.C. When the missionaries preached there, it was classified as a senatorial province, administered by a *proconsul* (Acts 13:7).

The missionaries landed on the east coast and traveled across the island, preaching first in the Jewish synagogues. Traveling west, the missionaries reached Paphos, the seat of the provincial government. The proconsul, Sergius Paulus, summoned Paul and Barnabas to question them about their message.

The Sergius Paulus family was prominent in the first and second centuries. Various members of the family have been proposed as the Sergius Paulus of this story. The governor's summons of the missionaries was likely motivated by his sense of responsibility to investigate any unusual happenings in his realm. However, Luke's account suggests that the governor was open to the Word of God that Paul preached (Acts 13:7, 8).

Elymas the sorcerer (13:6–8). We are told several things about this sorcerer, whose name in Hebrew was Barjesus (Son of Jesus, i.e., "the Deliverer"). First we know he was a Jew, but a renegade Jew. No traditional Jew would violate the proscription against occult practices in Deuteronomy 18 and seek a reputation as a *magos,* a "magician" or "sorcerer." He is also called a false prophet, not in the sense of foretelling future events but claiming to channel divine revelation. The statement that he was "with" the proconsul indicates he had gained some influence with him.

Elymas apparently saw Sergius Paulus's interest in the gospel as a threat to his position, so he "withstood" the missionaries, "seeking to turn the proconsul away from the faith" (Acts 13:8).

Paul's response to Elymas (13:9–11). The apostle openly condemned Elymas as a "son of the devil." Elymas was no Barjesus (deliverer). He was a *huie diabolou* (deceiver, or son of the devil)! As such, he was an "enemy of all righteousness" who was intent on perverting the "straight ways of the Lord." That is, Elymas was intent on twisting the truth.

Having exposed Elymas for what he was, Paul pronounced judgment. "You shall be blind, not seeing the sun for a time" (Acts 13:11). Luke makes it clear that this pronouncement was not an impulsive one. Paul was "filled with the Holy Spirit" (Acts 13:9) when he acted, and "the hand of the Lord" caused the blindness (Acts 13:11).

Some commentators have seen echoes of Paul's own temporary blindness in this judgment. Although both Saul and Elymas opposed Christianity, there was a significant difference between them. Elymas was a renegade Jew who had knowingly violated Old Testament Law; Saul was a Pharisee zealous for God's glory. The fact that the blindness of Elymas was temporary is a striking indication of God's grace.

A judgment miracle. The miracles performed by Jesus were "positive" miracles, involving restoration to health and well-being. Demons were cast out, the disabled were healed, the dead were restored to life. Even nature miracles such as those on the Sea of Galilee stilled storms rather than created them.

In contrast, several of the supportive miracles and wonders that demonstrated Jesus' continuing presence with his people were miracles of divine judgment. Ananias and Sapphira were struck dead when they conspired to lie and thus test the Holy Spirit. Herod Antipas was struck dead by an angel. Now Elymas, who resisted the preaching of the gospel to Sergius Paulus, was struck with blindness.

It is appropriate that all of Jesus' miracles were worked on behalf of people. But it is also appropriate that in the apostolic age the Lord supported the preaching of the gospel with both miracles of healing and miracles of judgment.

The outcome of the miracle (13:11, 12). When Paul pronounced judgment, Elymas "immediately" was blinded, and "he went around seeking someone to lead him by the hand." This phrase is significant. Elymas had to search for someone to lead him, because all would draw back! Elymas had been cursed by God, and all who knew would fear association with him.

What a reversal of fortunes. Elymas instantly lost all influence with others. Those who had honored him now feared him, and no one would have anything to do with him.

Luke revealed that the miracle had an impact on the proconsul of the island as well. Sergius Paulus "believed, when he saw what had been done" (v. 12). It is uncertain whether "believed" is used in the sense of being con-

Elymas was blinded for opposing the gospel.

❖

vinced that Paul was God's spokesman, or whether "believed" is used in the sense of having saving faith in Jesus. While the Sergius Paulus family is known from other documents, no evidence for or against a Christian branch of that family exists.

PAUL HEALS A CRIPPLE AT LYSTRA
Acts 14:8–20

In the Lycaonian city of Lystra, which had become a Roman colony in 6 B.C., Paul healed a cripple. The missionaries were hailed as gods, come down in the likeness of men.

A violent response to miracles and wonders (Acts 14:1–7). When Jesus performed his miracles, the people responded by giving glory to God. Many may not have accepted his messianic claims, but Christ's healings were met with approval and praise.

In Acts, as the gospel message spread into the Roman world, we see a different kind of response. Before going to Lystra, Paul and his missionary team had preached in Iconium.

Many people, both Jews and Greeks (i.e., non-Jews), believed. Luke tells us that the Lord bore witness to the message in Iconium by "granting signs and wonders" to be done by the apostles (14:3).

But most of the Jewish population resisted Paul and his message. The dispute spread so that the entire population of the city was divided. Finally, "a violent attempt" that involved the city officials, Jews, and Gentiles to "abuse and stone" the missionaries forced the missionaries out of Iconium.

The "signs and wonders" failed to create openness to the gospel. Just as the miracles of the Exodus had the effect of hardening the heart of Pharaoh (see page 68), these miracles of Paul seemed to polarize public opinion and intensify hostility to the gospel message.

The Healing in Lystra (14:8–10). After leaving Iconium, the missionary team moved on to Lystra. While preaching there, Paul noted that a disabled man was listening intently. Luke emphasizes the seriousness of the man's disability: he was "a cripple from his mother's womb, who had never walked" (Acts 14:10).

Luke also emphasizes another element in this healing. Paul perceived that "he had faith to be healed" (Acts 14:9). The observation is significant.

It implies divine revelation. "Faith" is not something that is observable. While the Bible does teach that faith will produce works, in this case the necessary time for faith's flowering was lacking. Paul was given insight by God to see into this hearer's heart.

It implies a spontaneous miracle. Paul had not planned to launch his ministry in Lystra with a miracle. But he perceived an awakened faith in his crippled hearer, so he responded spontaneously by commanding him to "stand up straight on your feet" (v. 10).

It implies a "family" miracle. When Paul perceived that the man had faith in Jesus, he called on him to stand. The man's faith was not the cause of the healing, although it was

the cause of his response to Paul's command. What seems significant, however, is that this was a family miracle, performed to meet the need of a new brother in Christ. It was not a miracle intended to authenticate Paul as God's spokesman.

The majority of New Testament miracles were family miracles. They were performed for those who had confidence in Jesus and who showed that confidence. We need to remember that the faith spoken of in such incidents is *not* faith in healing, but faith in Jesus. How gracious he is to his own.

The people of Lystra mistook Paul and Barnabas for gods (Acts 14:11, 12). What is most impressive about Luke's account of this miracle is the excitement of the onlookers. They shouted that "the gods have come to us in the likeness of men" (v. 11). Immediately the priest of Zeus prepared a sacrifice to offer to the two startled missionaries.

The details in passages of the Bible often refute the claims of critics. Luke's report of the reaction of the people of Lystra and their identification of Barnabas as Zeus and Paul as Hermes (Apollo) is one of those details that rings especially true.

The people of the area worshiped these two pagan gods. An ancient legend recorded by the poet Ovid (43 B.C.—A.D. 17) about fifty years before the missionarys' visit told of how these two deities visited the hill country of Phrygia where Lystra was located. The two gods came disguised as mortals looking for a place to stay and were turned away from a thousand homes.

Finally they were welcomed to the simple straw cottage of an aged couple. The homes of the inhospitable thousand were destroyed by the gods, while the cottage of the two old people was transformed into a golden temple. They were ordained priest and priestess of the temple and transformed into ever-living trees.

With this background, we can understand why the citizens of Lystra were so eager to honor "gods" noted for rewarding—and punishing!

"They tore their clothes and ran in among the multitude" (Acts 14:14). The people of Lystra had apparently been speaking in their own language. When the sacrificial animals [*taurous,* bulls] were brought out, the apostles realized what had happened and ran in among the crowd to stop them.

It is clear from later events that Paul's words to this crowd about the emptiness of idolatry and the goodness of the true God fell on deaf ears. When Jews from Iconium and Antioch arrived, the crowds not only turned against the missionaries but even stoned Paul, dragging him outside the city and leaving him for dead!

The miracle of healing had failed to open a door for the gospel. As in Iconium earlier, the miracle had only caused confusion and heightened antagonism against Paul and Barnabas.

Paul revived (19:20). Some have interpreted Paul's revival after the stoning as a miracle. But the text does not say that Paul was dead. It states that the people of the city dragged him outside and left him for dead. When the rest of his party gathered around him, Paul revived and got up. The next day they left Lystra for the nearby town of Derbe.

The significance of the miracle. On one level, the report of this and other miracles by Paul parallel the miracles of Peter, who had also healed a man who had been lame from birth (Acts 3; see p. 251). While Paul had not been one of Jesus' original disciples, he was personally called and commissioned by Jesus. The parallel between the miracles of Peter and Paul confirm his role as an apostle of equal authority to Peter and the others.

This miracle, however, like those performed by Paul in Iconium, highlights an important reality. Like the miracles of Moses in Egypt, these miracles hardened resistance to God's Word rather than producing faith.

It seems unwise to argue, as some do, that we should expect miracles to be performed by missionaries in territories where

the gospel is being introduced. The apostle Paul reminds us that faith comes by hearing, and hearing by the Word of God (Rom. 10:13–15). While a miracle was performed for a cripple who had faith, that miracle did not lead to the mass conversion of the crowd who listened to Paul without faith.

CASTING OUT A DEMON IN PHILIPPI   Acts 16:16–40

In Philippi Paul cast a demon out of a slave girl who told fortunes. Her angry masters incited a riot, and Paul and Silas were beaten and imprisoned. An earthquake opened the prison doors, leading to the jailer's conversion.

Fortunetellers in the New Testament world (Acts 16:16). Awe of the occult and a superstitious reliance on oracles was common in the first-century Hellenistic world. People with epilepsy were considered touched by the gods, and words they muttered in an epileptic episode were viewed as divine utterances. Cult oracles, like the Oracle of Delphi, inhaled fumes to put them in a trance. Their troubled mutterings were interpreted by priests, who recast them as cryptic or ambiguous proverbs which permitted several interpretations.

In Philippi, however, the apostles met a slave girl whose utterances were stimulated by a demon who possessed her. This girl's utterances were not muttered phrases but plain speech: "These men are the servants of the Most High God, who proclaim to us the way of salvation" (v. 17).

It's not surprising that a fortuneteller with a supernatural source of information, and especially one who spoke plainly, should earn her masters a significant income.

Paul exorcised the fortuneteller's demon (16: 17–18). Paul was annoyed by the fortuneteller's attention. For a few days he said nothing as she followed the missionaries around, screaming [*ekrazen*] her utterances. The demon-inspired words were not only tainted testimony; they received more attention than the gospel itself, as observers discussed her rather than Christ.

Finally, Paul commanded the spirit who possessed the girl to leave her.

The girl's owners incited the crowd against Paul and Silas (16:19–21). This first miracle freed the girl from the evil being who inhabited her. But it also stripped her of her powers, and this made her owners furious. Their hope of profit was gone; the girl was now useless to them. Their reaction was to strike out at Paul and Silas.

The angry owners of the slave girl aroused a mob by accusing Paul and Silas of being Jews who taught an illicit [unauthorized] religion. At this time, Jews made up about one-tenth of the population of the Roman Empire, and it was not illegal for Jews to seek converts. But a great deal of anti-Semitism existed in the first-century Roman Empire, in part because of the Jews' separatist ways and their religious beliefs. The girl's masters fanned the flames of this anti-Semitic sentiment by labeling Paul and Silas "these Jews," while appealing to their listeners' pride of "being Romans."

Paul and Silas were taken before the city magistrates and beaten (16:22, 23). The hostile mob dragged Paul and Silas before the city magistrates. Without questioning Paul and Silas, the magistrates tore off their clothes and ordered them flogged and imprisoned.

Paul and Silas imprisoned (16:23–24). The jailer rigidly followed the magistrates' order to keep the two men "securely." He not only put them in the *esotera*, the innermost cell in the prison, but he also placed their feet in stocks. These wooden instruments, anchored to the floor, were designed with several holes or notches, so the prisoner's legs could be forced apart and held in an unnatural position. Stocks were as much an instrument of torture as imprisonment, since it was impossible to avoid cramping. The fact that the apostles were immediately placed in stocks indicates that torture was intended.

❖

BIBLE BACKGROUND:

ROMAN PRISONS

Prisons have been excavated in various first-century Roman cities. Many references in literature of this era also provide insight into prison conditions. Prisons were frequently overcrowded, and prisoners slept on the floor wrapped in their cloaks (compare Acts 12:8; 2 Tim. 4:13). Hot in the summer, freezing in winter, with little or no ventilation, prisons were breeding grounds for disease. The stone cells were dark, admitting little light from outside. This was especially true in the most secure cells, like the one where Paul and Silas were left that night. The Greek word commonly rendered "dungeon" is *tenebrae*, which means "darkness." The apostle's stay in prison in Philippi was probably in complete darkness.

The darkness associated with prisons was viewed in ancient literature as one of their primary torments. An item in the *Theodosian Code* of A.D. 320 contained this word on prison reform:

> When incarcerated he [the prisoner] must not suffer the darkness of an inner prison, but he must be kept in good health by the enjoyment of light, and when night doubles the necessity for his guard, he shall be taken back into the vestibules of the prisons and into healthful places. When day returns, at early sunrise, he shall forthwith be led into the common light of day that he may not perish from the torments of prison [Cod. Theod. 9.3.1 (=Cod. Just. 9.4.1 [353 AD].

This item in the code explains how the other prisoners could listen to the two Christians singing hymns and praising God. Rather than double the guard at night, the Philippian jailer jammed all the prisoners into the most secure "inner prison" (v. 24) along with the two missionaries. This also explains why, after the earthquake, the jailer rushed first to the innermost cell of the prison, and how Paul could assure the jailer that none of the prisoners had escaped.

❖

Paul and Silas praised God in the prison (16:25). The reaction of Paul and Silas to imprisonment must have stunned their fellow prisoners. In spite of the pain of the untreated wounds and bruises received during the beatings, the two Christians spent the hours between sunset and midnight "praying and singing hymns to God."

By their actions, the two missionaries set a precedent that other believers in the Roman Empire were to follow. As the Christian message exploded across the empire, it began to threaten the social fabric. As the decades passed, both informal and official persecution of Christians developed. Many thousands were imprisoned, while others were martyred for their faith. The bright faith of these dedicated men and women is a reflection of that which led Paul and Silas to sing in the darkness.

As a later writer asked, "Well now, pagans, do you still believe that Christians, for whom awaits the joy of eternal light, feel the torments of prison or shrink from the dungeons of this world? . . . Dedicated as they are to God the Father, their brothers care for them by day, Christ by night as well." [Mart. Mar & James: 6.1, 3, 259 AD] The gloom of Roman dungeons was never able to extinguish the flame of faith—a faith that seemed to burn brighter in the darkness.

A miracle earthquake opened the prison doors (16:26–29). At midnight an earthquake hit. The foundations of the prison were shaken, the doors swung open, and everyone's chains were loosed.

The prison keeper rushed from his residence and saw the prison doors open. His suicide attempt reflects the fact that in the Roman Empire a jailer who let a prisoner escape was

Paul and Silas prayed and sang hymns in the Philippian jail.

to receive the penalty due the prisoner [see *Code of Justinian* 9.4.4] and that in Roman culture suicide was considered an honorable alternative. Suicide would prevent the forfeiting of all family assets in some cases, and a man who cared for his wife and children might kill himself to preserve their inheritance.

Before he could act, however, Paul shouted out, assuring the jailer that "we are all here" (v. 28). The jailer's reaction suggests that he had heard the missionary's message. He called for a light, carried it into the dark innermost cell, and fell trembling at Paul's feet.

The jailer and his household found Christ (16:30–34). The earthquake, miraculous because of its timing rather than its occurrence in this geologically unstable area, did not win the release of the prisoners by itself. Rather, the earthquake was interpreted by the jailer as proof that these men were indeed "servants of the Most High God." The words of the fortuneteller had not moved this practical retired soldier. But the earthquake compelled conviction. Shaken in heart as well as body, the jailer asked, "Sirs, what must I do to be saved" (v. 30).

Paul's answer has often been misunderstood. "Believe on the Lord Jesus Christ, and you will be saved" is direct and clear. But then Paul added "you and your household." What did he mean?

In the Roman world, the "household," or family, was not defined primarily by kinship but by dependence and subordination. Aristotle's *Politica,* 1,2,1 showed the same notion in Greek culture. He pointed out, "The household in its perfect form consists of slaves and freedmen." The head of the Roman household was responsible for—and expected some degree of submission from—his wife and children, his slaves, former slaves, hired laborers and tenants, clients, and sometimes even business associates.

It is not at all unusual in ancient literature to find references to an individual's "house" or "household," with the added phrase "and his wife and children." In the five times in Acts that Luke mentions "houses" (10:2; 11:14;

16:15; 16:31; 18:8), it is clear that the references are to individuals of relatively high social status and that the term encompasses more than the individual's immediate kin.

What did Paul imply, then? First of all, Paul was saying that the salvation by faith in Jesus Christ which he offered the Philippian jailer was not just available to him. It was available to everyone in the jailer's household, whatever his or her social status. The gospel is for adult and child, for master and slave, for high and low.

But Paul implied more. In the Roman world, the father as head of the household was responsible for carrying out religious rituals and maintaining a pious household. It was assumed that the family would practice the religion of the *pater familias,* the father [head] of the family.

With a few brief words, Paul reassured the Philippian jailer that responding to the message of Christ did not threaten the established social order! The Philippian jailer could accept Christ and the salvation he offered, confident that the gospel was for his whole household, and that his role in the family was not threatened by the new faith.

Ultimately, of course, each member of the household would accept or reject the gospel for himself or herself. But the influence of the head of the household was such that most would follow his lead and make a true heart-commitment to the Lord. This is exactly what happened in Philippi, for the jailer "rejoiced, having believed in God with all his household" (v. 34).

This incident had begun with the miracle of casting out a demon and continued with the miracle of a quake that opened doors. It concluded with the miracle of salvation experienced by the Philippian jailer and his household—perhaps the greatest miracle of all.

PAUL RESTORES THE LIFE OF EUTYCHUS   *Acts 20:7–12*

One night as Paul was speaking, a sleepy young man fell from a window and was killed. Paul restored him to life.

Paul's journey (Acts 20:1–6). The apostle Paul had determined to go to Jerusalem in time for the feast of Pentecost. Although he was in a hurry, Paul used every spare moment to teach in churches along the way.

Teaching in Troas (20:7–9). Paul and his friends spent seven days in Troas. On the Sunday before taking ship, Paul spoke to the believers "until midnight." Luke describes the setting. Paul taught in an upstairs room, lit by torches. The heat they generated and the lateness of the hour caused a young man named Eutychus to doze, finally "sinking into a deep sleep."

Eutychus's death (20:9). The "window" where Eutychus was sleeping was probably a slitted opening in the wall. He tumbled from this perch and, according to Luke the physician, who was present, "was taken up dead."

Paul restored Eutychus (20:10). Paul went downstairs, "embraced" Eutychus, and announced that "his life is in him." Some have taken this as a diagnosis rather than a miraculous restoration. However, Luke does not say that Eutychus "appeared" dead, but that he was dead. Luke wanted us to understand that Paul, like Peter, restored life to a person who had died.

Miracles of resuscitation. This miracle performed by the apostle Paul completes the series of resuscitation miracles recorded in Scripture. Seen together, there is compelling balance.

Resuscitation Miracles in the Bible		
1 Kings 17:21	Elijah	restored a widow's child
2 Kings 4:34–35	Elisha	restored a Shunamite's child
Mark 5:35–43	Jesus	restored Jairus's daughter
Luke 7:11–14	Jesus	restored a widow's son
John 11	Jesus	restored Lazarus
Acts 9:36–42	Peter	restored Dorcas
Acts 20:7–12	Paul	restored Eutychus

Thus, two Old Testament prophets raised the dead while two New Testament apostles raised the dead. In each of these four instances, the individual who was restored had died recently, probably within a few hours. Jesus, appropriately, restored the dead three times. And the third restoration, that of Lazarus, took place after Lazarus had been dead four days.

There were also two similar miracles mentioned in passing. A dead man dumped into Elisha's grave was restored to life when his body touched that prophet's bones (2 Kings 13:20–22). And when Jesus died on the cross, an earthquake opened a number of graves and "many bodies of the saints who had fallen asleep were raised" (Matt. 27:52).

The pattern of these miracles demonstrates a striking symmetry. Elijah and Elisha stand parallel with Peter and Paul. But Jesus remains supreme, both in the number of such miracles and in the level of difficulty displayed in the raising of Lazarus.

Scripture wants us to remember that Christ truly is the source of life. He who was the lifegiver as Yahweh of the Old Testament era is also lifegiver as Lord of the New Testament. Jesus is both Yahweh and Lord.

PAUL'S HEALING OF PUBLIUS'S FATHER   *Acts 28:7–10*

The last miracles recorded in Acts are healing miracles. They were performed by Paul while he was shipwrecked on the island of Malta.

The situation. Paul had been arrested in Jerusalem. Because he was a Roman citizen, he was transported to Caesarea, the seaport city which served as the Roman administrative center for Jewish lands. He remained under house arrest at Caesarea for two years. Finally, Paul exercised his right to be tried in Rome and officially "appealed to Caesar." Paul was then sent under guard on the long sea journey to Rome.

Caught in a terrible storm, the ship was driven aimlessly for two weeks before running aground on the island of Malta. Paul, encouraged by an angel, had promised that if everyone stayed with the ship, no lives would be lost. It happened as he said, and all 276 persons on board got safely to land.

On shore, Paul was bitten by a deadly snake as he carried wood to the fire they had built to warm and dry the ship's company. The natives, who observed the poisonous creature hanging from Paul's hand, assumed he was a murderer whom "justice does not allow to live" (Acts 28:4). When Paul showed no effects from the bite, the people of the island decided he must be a god.

Paul's healing ministry (Acts 28:7–8). The survivors were sheltered by the "leading citizen" of the island, Publius. Inscriptions from Malta suggest that "leading citizen" was an official title. The father of the leading citizen was ill. Again Luke, the physician, provides a medical diagnosis. He suffered from "a fever and dysentery."

Paul prayed, laid hands on him, and healed him.

The reaction to the healing miracle (28:9, 10). The response of the islanders was twofold. First, all the diseased of the island came to Paul and were healed. Second, the islanders "honored" the missionaries, and "when we departed . . . provided such things as were necessary."

What is notable, however, is what was *not* recorded. Luke does not state or even suggest that any conversions resulted from the miracles! In fact, there is no mention of any conversions on Malta at all.

The significance of the miracle. This account of Paul's miracle-ministry again parallels that of Peter. Like Peter, Paul restored the life of a person who was dead. Like Peter—who gained such a reputation as a healer that he attracted crowds—Paul also won a reputation as a healer and crowds of sick and diseased persons came to him.

Paul, like Peter, was an apostle, authenticated by God through miracles.

Peter's miracles were performed in Jewish territory, demonstrating the continuing presence of Jesus with the early Jewish Christians. But Paul's miracles were performed in gentile lands. And these supportive miracles showed Jesus' world-wide power and presence.

THE MIRACLES OF ACTS   *Summary and Review*

The book of Acts traced the history of the church from the ascension of Jesus through the next thirty years, up to the first imprisonment of Paul in Rome in approximately A.D. 62.

Luke built his history around the experiences of two leaders of the early Christian church—Peter and Paul. Peter, one of Jesus' original 12 disciples, preached the first gospel message to both Jews (Acts 2) and Gentiles (Acts 10). But most of Peter's ministry was to Jews in Jewish territory and in Jewish sections of cities of the Roman Empire.

Paul, on the other hand, was a reluctant convert, whose miraculous conversion transformed him into a committed missionary, dedicated to planting churches in Gentile lands. Paul's experience with Jesus commissioned him as an apostle, and he established churches in key cities in Roman Asia Minor and in Europe. Paul's letters to these churches stand, with the Gospels, as foundational Christian documents.

It is not surprising that Luke recorded miracles performed by both Peter and Paul. As we have noted, there is a pattern in the occurrence of the miracles recorded in Scripture.

First, they come in paired clusters. Second, they are associated with critical moments in the history of God's revelation of his purposes to humankind. Third, the first cluster in each pair (1) establishes a new body of truth, and (2) authenticates the person who introduces that body of truth as God's spokesman. Fourth, the second cluster in each pair demonstrates God's presence with those who accept and live by the new revelation.

The following chart compares these paired clusters, showing the function of the miracles in each period.

Exodus Miracles

Cluster One: The Plagues on Egypt

1. Yahweh is the God of Abraham, who keeps his covenant promises.
2. Moses is God's authentic messenger.

Cluster Two: Miracles in the Wilderness and Canaan

1. God is present to bless and judge his people when they live in accordance with Moses' Law.

Eighth-century Miracles

Cluster One: The Miracles of Elijah

1. Yahweh, not Baal, is the true God.
2. Elijah is God's authentic messenger.

Cluster Two: The Miracles of Elisha

1. God is present to bless a people who honor him as Lord.

First-century Miracles

Cluster One: The Miracles of Jesus

1. Jesus is the bringer of the promised new covenant which replaces Moses' Law.
2. Jesus is God's authentic messenger, the Messiah and Son of God.

Cluster Two: The Miracles of the Early Church

1. Jesus is present to bless those who accept him as Messiah and Lord.
2. Peter and Paul are God's authentic messengers, and their teachings are true.

When we think about how miracles touch the lives of believers today, we should begin with an understanding of the function of miracles in biblical times, as reflected in the chart above.

Miracles marked the introduction of a fresh revelation of God's purpose. And miracles authenticated as God's spokesmen the individuals whom God called to speak for him.

❖

MIRACLES PAST— AND FUTURE!

SIGNS AND WONDERS

The Epistles; Revelation

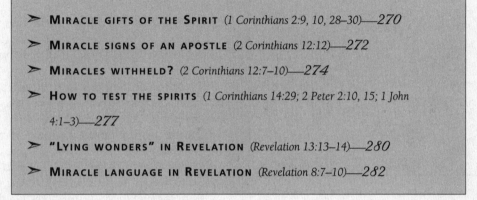

Another age of miracles is coming! The apostle Paul writes about it in 2 Thessalonians. The apostle John predicts it in Revelation. But these miracles are to be Satanic in origin. How can we tell the difference between real miracles and "lying wonders"? The New Testament epistles teach us many things about miracles. And Revelation provides a picture of future miracles.

REFERENCES TO MIRACLES AND WONDERS IN THE EPISTLES

The language of miracles occurs only eight times in the New Testament Epistles. Romans 15:19 refers to signs and wonders. The Greek word translated miracles (*dunamis*) occurs in 1 Corinthians 12:10, 28, 29 and in Galatians 3:5. "Miracles, signs and wonders" are used together in 2 Corinthians 12:2 and Hebrews 2:4. And 2 Thessalonians 2:9 speaks of "all power [*dunamei*, "miracles"], signs and lying wonders."

ROMANS 15:18, 19

I will not dare to speak of any of those things which Christ has not accomplished

through me, in word and deed, to make the Gentiles obedient—in mighty signs and wonders, by the power of the Spirit of God, so that from Jerusalem and round about to Illyricum I have fully preached the Gospel of Christ.

The context in which this verse appears. Romans 15:14 marks a change of subject in the letter. The apostle Paul moved from instruction and exhortation to share more personal matters. He reminded the church in Rome that he was writing to them as an apostle called by God to minister to Gentiles. Paul went on to share the passion which had motivated him, a passion to preach the gospel "not where Christ was named," but in lands where no one has yet heard the good news (Rom. 15:20). He mentioned "mighty signs and wonders" as miracles which the Holy Spirit had performed through him as evidence of Christ's calling to his ministry.

The interpretation of the verses. Paul appealed to miracles as evidence of a very special "grace given to me by God" (Rom. 15:15). The miracles which he has performed are divine

Paul wrote letters to churches he had established, and some he had never visited.

❖

proof of his position as a apostle of Jesus Christ.

1 CORINTHIANS 12:9, 10, 28–30

Gifts of healing by the same Spirit, to another the working of miracles (1 Cor. 12:9, 10). And God has appointed these in the church: first apostles, second prophets, third teachers, after that miracles, then gifts of healings, helps, administrations, varieties of tongues. Are all apostles? Are all prophets? Are all teachers? Are all workers of miracles? Do all have gifts of healing? (1 Cor. 12:28–30).

The context in which these verses occur. In 1 Corinthians 12—14, Paul took up an issue which had troubled the church in Corinth. The Christians there had taken the more obviously supernatural workings of the Holy Spirit through believers as evidence that those with such gifts were more "spiritual" than others. In fact, the Corinthians had fastened on the gift of tongues (speaking in an unintelligible "spiritual" language) as the premier indicator of a believer's closeness to the Lord.

In order to correct this misunderstanding, Paul taught in 1 Corinthians 12 that every believer has at least one spiritual gift. He pointed out these gifts were the method by which the Holy Spirit ministered through people to build up other believers. The exercise of any gift was an expression of the Holy Spirit's working, and spiritual gifts were distributed by the Spirit as he willed (1 Cor. 12:7, 11). According to Paul, this meant the gift a person had was *not* an indicator of spirituality (i.e., one's closeness to the Lord, or harmony with his will).

Paul then went on in 1 Corinthians 13 to show that the true indicator of spirituality is love, not the gift a person may possess.

Finally, in 1 Corinthians 14 Paul returned to the question of tongues. He pointed out that if gifts were to be ranked, this should be done on the basis of the contribution the gift makes to the edification of the body. On this basis, prophecy or teaching would be near the top of the list. Tongues would rank near the bottom because they are unintelligible and thus not edifying to others.

References to miracles and healings in the passage. The subject of this extended section of 1 Corinthians is not miracles or miraculous gifts. This makes their mention in the passage even more striking. Paul clearly assumed miracles and healings were not unusual events in Corinth. It seems the Corinthians had been experiencing both miracles and healings. Apparently, these were commonly recognized ways in which the Holy Spirit had been at work in this Christian community.

At the same time, it is perhaps significant that this is the only passage in Scripture in which both miracles and healings are spoken of in this way. In two other passages in which spiritual gifts are listed—Romans 12 and Ephesians 4—no reference to tongues, miracles, or healing occurs.

The almost casual references to miracles and healing as spiritual gifts in this passage, but not in other passages on gifts, raises an important question. Just what can we assume from the biblical evidence? And what can we *not* conclude?

Miracles and healings are valid spiritual gifts. It is clear from 1 Corinthians 12 that in Corinth at least the Holy Spirit did gift believers with the ability to perform miracles and to heal. As the Holy Spirit is free in his sovereignty to distribute gifts "as he wills" (1 Cor. 12:11), we have no basis for saying that the Holy Spirit cannot or will not distribute the same gifts in our own day—or any other time.

Miracles and healing gifts are referred to only in 1 Corinthians. This raises several questions. Why aren't these gifts mentioned in parallel passages on spiritual gifts? Why aren't healings mentioned in *any* other New Testament epistle as elements in Christian experience?

One possibility is that these gifts functioned in Corinth, but they did not operate in the other New Testament churches. This is certainly a possibility. There may have been

Jesus' miracles continued with His apostles.

unique factors which called for these gifts in Corinth but not, say, in the church at Ephesus. But we have no idea of what these factors might have been. And we have no reason to suppose that conditions in one city of the Roman Empire were radically different from the situation in another city.

In short, we simply don't know why these gifts are mentioned only in reference to Corinth. It's impossible to say why miracles and healings seem to have been performed by some Corinthian believers, and why no mention of miraculous healing is found in any other epistle.

Were miracles and healings for the first century only? First Corinthians 13:8, in speaking of the value of love, declares, "Whether there are prophecies, they will fail; whether there are tongues, they will cease; whether there is knowledge, it will vanish away." Some have argued from the reference to tongues "ceasing" that this gift operated only during the decades during which the church was founded.

Even though 1 Corinthians 13:8 says nothing about miracles or healings, those who hold this position argue that "tongues" represents all the supernatural gifts of 1 Corinthians 12 which were visible. Their conviction is that these supernatural gifts operated only in the period before the canon of Scripture was complete. With the writing of the last book of the New Testament, the need for the miraculous ended.

This is an interpretation which assumes more from the biblical text than is obvious. It is always a problem to build an important doctrine on a single verse of Scripture, especially when only indirect evidence and supposition support the interpretation.

A more serious objection to this position is that it tends to rule out the *possibility* of miracles, healings, or tongues in our day. In essence, it puts God in a box, declaring that the Holy Spirit cannot work today through believers in a method which he used in the first century. Any affirmation which places limits on God's freedom to act is suspect.

We really cannot limit the possibility of miracles, healings, and tongues to the first century or to the Corinthian community.

Miracles, healings, and tongues are a possibility in any age, including our own time. It is important to remember that agreeing such happenings are a possibility today is not the same as saying that miracles and healings are commonplace. Neither should we declare on the basis of the limited evidence we have that they happen infrequently. All we can affirm from the 1 Corinthians passage is that God can and does perform miracles, and that the Holy Spirit can enable believers as agents to perform miracles and to heal. Whether he chooses to do so in any given situation is entirely up to God.

2 CORINTHIANS 12:12

Truly the signs of an apostle were accomplished among you with all perseverance, in signs and wonders and mighty deeds [*miracles*].

The context in which this verse appears. Paul's second letter to the Corinthians contains an extended defense of his ministry. Paul's apostolic authority had been challenged in Corinth by persons representing themselves as leaders of the Jerusalem church and carrying letters of commendation to establish their "authority." In this most revealing of Paul's letters, the apostle shared freely the principles on which his new covenant ministry had been based.

Evidence of apostolic calling and authority (2 Corinthians 12:12). In these verses, Paul called his ministry "in signs and wonders and mighty deeds [*miracles*]" the "signs of an apostle." These were proof that "in nothing was I behind the most eminent apostles" (2 Cor. 12:11).

It is somewhat surprising that Paul called these wonder-working abilities "signs of an apostle." After all, Paul had spoken in 1 Corinthians 12 of such powers as gifts of the Holy Spirit, implying that ordinary believers might possess them. Yet it is clear from the book of Acts that the ministries of both Peter and Paul were often marked by miracles, especially healing miracles. This may indeed be the difference. The apostle worked many such miracles, and thus was authenticated as God's spokesman. The number, frequency, and function of gift-miracles may have been significantly less.

Conclusions. All we can conclude from this passage is that the ministry of Jesus' 12 apostles and Paul were marked by the performance of miracles and wonders. We have no information on how common non-apostolic miracles were in the New Testament era.

GALATIANS 3:5

Therefore he who supplies the Spirit to you and works miracles among you, does he do it by the works of the law, or by the hearing of faith?

The context in which this verse appears. In the book of Galatians, Paul wrote to a congregation which had been led astray concerning the role of faith and works. Paul's careful argument in the book demonstrated that salvation is by faith alone, and that the Law given by Moses had no role in establishing personal relationship with God.

Paul also argued that the believer relates to God by being responsive to the Holy Spirit, not by keeping the Law. The Galatians received the Holy Spirit by faith and not by "the works of the law" (Gal. 3:2). Why then would they imagine that progress in the Christian life comes by making an effort to keep God's law rather than by walking in the Spirit (Gal. 5:25) and letting the Spirit produce in us his own unique fruit (Gal. 5:22, 23)?

The reference to miracles in Galatians 3:5. Here, as in 1 Corinthians 12, the passage in which miracles are mentioned is not *about* miracles. Paul referred to miracles, *as though the Galatians were familiar with them.* In fact, the text spoke of working "miracles among you" as though miracles were even commonplace occurrences.

Clearly in the experience of at least two New Testament Gentile churches, miracles seem to have been more or less expected.

While we cannot generalize from this to conclude that miracles were commonplace in all the New Testament churches, this text—along with similar comments in 1 Corinthians 12—is certainly suggestive. Yet we cannot generalize from the experience of the churches in Acts and the Epistles by declaring that miracles *ought* to be found in churches of our day.

HEBREWS 2:4

God also bearing witness both with signs and wonders, with various miracles, and gifts of the Holy Spirit, according to his own will.

The context in which this verse appears. The book of Hebrews was written to demonstrate to Jewish believers the superiority of the new covenant initiated by Jesus to the old covenant introduced by Moses. In Hebrews 1, the author carefully established the superiority of Jesus to angels. The reason for this was that the Jews believed angels had been mediators of the Law given on Mount Sinai.

In chapter 2 of Hebrews, the writer drew an initial conclusion. If the "word spoken through angels" was binding, and every transgression was punished, how much more dangerous it was to neglect the great salvation first spoken by the Lord himself (Heb. 2:3).

Miracles confirmed the message spoken by Jesus. Hebrews 2:4 points out that the words spoken by Jesus were confirmed by God himself. The miracles, signs, and wonders Jesus performed were God's witness to him and to the truths he revealed.

This reference views miracles as authenticating signs, which confirmed the One who performed them as God's spokesman, and which served as the divine stamp of approval on what Jesus said and did. This reference refers back to the ministry of Jesus on earth. It is not relevant to the questions of modern miracles or to questions about the role of miracles in first-century Christianity.

2 THESSALONIANS 2:9

The coming of the lawless one is according to the working of Satan, with all power [*dunamis,* "miracle"], signs and lying wonders.

The context in which this verse appears. In his second letter to the Thessalonians, Paul corrected certain misunderstandings about the future. Some believers in the church had assumed that Jesus' second coming had already taken place. Paul described what would happen when Jesus did return—openly and accompanied by mighty angels—to punish and judge the unbelieving world (1 Thess. 1:7–10).

In chapter two, Paul pointed out that this day could not possibly have happened yet because certain events must precede Jesus' return. In particular, a "lawless one" [the Antichrist] would be revealed. There would be no mistaking his appearance because it would be marked by a new age of miracles! But this time, the extraordinary events would be caused by Satan rather than God! In judgment, God will send a "strong delusion" (2 Thess. 2:11) on those who have rejected Christ. They will be convinced by the "lying wonders" of Satan and follow the Antichrist in the great rebellion against God which precedes Jesus' return.

The implications of 2 Thessalonians 2:4. In previous chapters of this book, we have noted that clusters of miracles are associated with the introduction of significant new revelations from God. Groups of miracles have clustered around the Exodus story and the 40-year ministry of Moses in the 1400s B.C. They have clustered around the ministries of Elijah and Elisha in the 700s B.C. And they have clustered around the ministry of Jesus and the founding of the church.

What Paul suggests in 2 Thessalonians is that a fourth cluster of miracles lies ahead. But this cluster of miracles will involve "lying wonders" performed by Satan to deceive mankind into following the Antichrist in open rebellion against the Lord.

Implications of Paul's teaching in 2 Thessalonians. The first implication is that God is not the only one who can cause extraordinary events. Satan also seems to have the power to perform what we call miracles. Throughout biblical history, God has been the one who performed signs and wonders, but we must be open to the likelihood that "lying" wonders have been part of pagan religious experience.

We must also be aware that no miracle *in and of itself* is necessarily God's work. We need something more than miracles—or perhaps other than miracles—to show that a person or teaching is approved by God.

This is an issue that we will take up in the next chapter on miracles in the book of Revelation. For now, it is enough to note that we must be careful not to take miracles or wonders alone as sufficient authentication of anyone who claims to be God's spokesperson.

SITUATIONS WHICH MIGHT HAVE BEEN RESOLVED BY MIRACLES BUT WERE NOT

Our review of references to miracles and wonders in the Epistles has established several things.

First, miracles and signs and wonders did authenticate the ministry of Jesus (Heb. 2:4) and serve as authenticating signs for those with apostolic authority (2 Cor. 12:12).

Second, healing and miracles are also identified as spiritual gifts which God the Holy Spirit distributes. These clearly functioned in the Corinthian church, even though neither healing nor miracles is found on other New Testament lists of spiritual gifts.

Third, in letters to both the Corinthians and the Galatians the apostle Paul referred to miracles in such a way that it is clear they were familiar if not common occurrences in these congregations. But these miracles (*dunamis,* works of power) clearly did not have the same function as the numerous miracles which authenticated Jesus and then Peter and Paul as God's spokesmen.

Fourth, a new thought is introduced in 2 Thessalonians 2:4. Extraordinary events may be "lying wonders" caused by Satan rather than God. The experience of a miracle in and of itself is not sufficient proof that God's hand is involved—or that a person credited with performing miracles is God's servant.

But we have not yet established whether we should expect miracles in our day. The evidence from references to miracles in the Epistles is inconclusive on this point. So we need to look for additional evidence and ask other questions. One of the most important questions we can ask is, Did believers *expect* miracles when they had problems?

BELIEVERS AND THEIR SICKNESSES

Believers and their illnesses. Several passages speak of sickness among New Testament Christians. How did the writers of the Epistles deal with sickness? Four passages are particularly helpful in answering this question.

Paul's thorn in the flesh (2 Corinthians 12). Paul was troubled by a "thorn in the flesh." Most commentators believe this was a chronic illness of some kind, and many take it to refer to an eye disease. Paul tells us that his problem was a "messenger of Satan to buffet me" (2 Cor. 12:7).

Paul relates that he pleaded with the Lord three times, asking for healing (2 Cor. 12:8). But God told Paul "no," reminding the Apostle that God's strength is expressed through human weakness. Paul then stopped praying for the "thorn" to depart, and chose to praise God for his infirmity.

The life-threatening illness of Epaphroditus (Philippians 2:25–27). Epaphroditus, a close friend of Paul's, had come to visit the apostle, bringing an offering from the church at Philippi. While he was with the apostle, Ephaproditus became sick "almost unto death." This "brother, fellow worker, and fellow soldier" of Paul's did recover, which Paul credited to the mercy of God (Phil. 2:27).

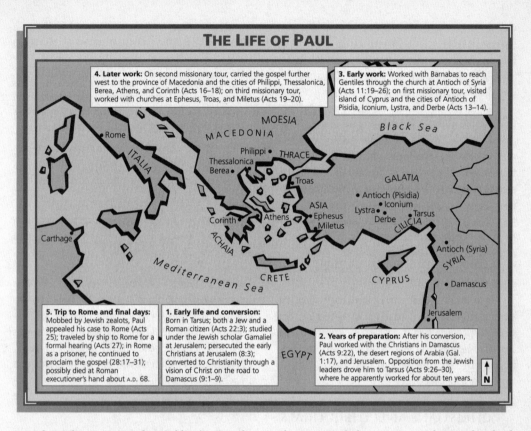

THE LIFE OF PAUL

4. Later work: On second missionary tour, carried the gospel further west to the province of Macedonia and the cities of Philippi, Thessalonica, Berea, Athens, and Corinth (Acts 16–18); on third missionary tour, worked with churches at Ephesus, Troas, and Miletus (Acts 19–20).

3. Early work: Worked with Barnabas to reach Gentiles through the church at Antioch of Syria (Acts 11:19–26); on first missionary tour, visited island of Cyprus and the cities of Antioch of Pisidia, Iconium, Lystra, and Derbe (Acts 13–14).

5. Trip to Rome and final days: Mobbed by Jewish zealots, Paul appealed his case to Rome (Acts 25); traveled by ship to Rome for a formal hearing (Acts 27); in Rome as a prisoner, he continued to proclaim the gospel (28:17–31); possibly died at Roman executioner's hand about A.D. 68.

1. Early life and conversion: Born in Tarsus; both a Jew and a Roman citizen (Acts 22:3); studied under the Jewish scholar Gamaliel at Jerusalem; persecuted the early Christians at Jerusalem (8:3); converted to Christianity through a vision of Christ on the road to Damascus (9:1–9).

2. Years of preparation: After his conversion, Paul worked with the Christians in Damascus (Acts 9:22), the desert regions of Arabia (Gal. 1:17), and Jerusalem. Opposition from the Jewish leaders drove him to Tarsus (Acts 9:26–30), where he apparently worked for about ten years.

Timothy's chronic stomach trouble (1 Timothy 5:23). In his first letter to Timothy, Paul gave his younger protégé advice on many matters. One of the most mundane pieces of advice was about Timothy's chronic stomach trouble, a common complaint in the first-century world where the water supply was often tainted. Paul's advice was, "No longer drink only water, but use a little wine for your stomach's sake and your frequent infirmities." That is, mix some wine in the water you drink to purify it.

James' advice concerning the sick (James 5:14–15). In his epistle, James, the brother of Jesus, said, "Is anyone among you sick? Let him call for the elders of the church, and let them pray over him, anointing him with oil in the name of the Lord. And the prayer of faith will save the sick, and the Lord will raise him up. And if he has committed sins, he will be forgiven." One interpreter commented on these verses:

This passage linking prayer, sickness, church elders, anointing with oil, and confession of sins has fascinated Christians throughout the ages.

Several things are clear from the text. (1) Prayer is needed when sickness comes. (2) One role of the elders of a church is to pray for the sick. (3) Prayer is primary, an active verb, and anointing with oil is secondary, expressed as a participle. (4) Oil was the most common ingredient in ancient medical treatments, and the verb describing its use (*aleipho*) means to "smear on" rather than the sacramental "to anoint" (*chrio*). Thus the passage teaches applications of both prayer and normal medical treatments. (5) "Confession" is important if sin should happen to be the cause of the sickness, and thus the sickness is disciplinary. (6) Since confession and prayer are associated with good health, it is important for Christians to be sensitive to sin, confess their sins to each other, and pray for each other (The *Bible Reader's Companion*, Chariot/Victor, 875).

Conclusions. It is clear from this brief survey that the normal approach in the first century when a Christian became sick was to come to

God in prayer and ask the Lord for healing. At the same time, the believers utilized the normal medical treatments available at the time. This is essentially the way most Christians today deal with sickness.

What is significant is that Paul did not perform a miraculous healing of either Epaphroditus or Timothy. Neither James nor Paul advised calling someone with the gift of healing or miracles when a brother fell sick. Instead, both advised prayer and medical treatment.

It seems from these facts that—in spite of the references to miracles in 1 Corinthians 12 and Galatians 3—it was neither typical nor "normal" to expect miracles or healings when Christians fell ill.

It is undoubtedly true, however, that the early Christians looked to and relied on the Lord to provide healing when sickness struck. But the healing they looked to God for was apparently what we would call "natural" healing—a normal recovery.

CHRISTIANS AND THEIR TRIALS

One of the things we realize if we read the New Testament carefully is that the early Christians didn't have an easy life. Their faith in Christ carried them through their sufferings. Most of them didn't expect deliverance through instant miracles.

Paul's account of his own sufferings (2 Corinthians 11:23–28. Earlier we looked at the Acts 16 description of Paul's miraculous release from prison in Philippi. It would be easy to assume that whenever the apostle was in difficulty, God simply performed a miracle and got his servant out of the uncomfortable situation. But Paul's own description of his life as a missionary quickly dispels any such impression:

Are they ministers of Christ?—I speak as a fool—I am more: in labors more abundant, in stripes [i.e., beatings] above measures, in prisons more frequently, in deaths often. From the Jews five times I received forty stripes minus one. Three times I was beaten with rods; once I was stoned; three times I

was shipwrecked; a night and a day I have been in the deep, in journeys often, in perils of waters, in perils of robbers, in perils of my own countrymen, in perils of the Gentiles, in perils in the city, in perils in the wilderness, in perils in the sea, in perils among false brethren; in weariness and toil, in sleeplessness often, in hunger and thirst, in fastings often, in cold and nakedness (2 Cor. 11:23–27).

Surely Paul was subject to intense pressures and danger. And just as surely, Paul did not expect or experience miracles to deliver him from these problems.

Peter's advice in view of coming persecutions (1 Peter). Peter's first epistle shows a great sensitivity to believers who are "grieved by various trials" (1 Peter 1:6). Nowhere in this letter did Peter offer any hope of miraculous interventions. Rather Peter told believers to commit themselves to a godly lifestyle and remember that Christ "suffered for us, leaving us an example, that you should follow his steps" (1 Peter 2:21). Peter even spoke of situations in which Christians do what is right, but suffer anyway (1 Peter 3:14f). In fact, Peter quite bluntly says,

Beloved, do not think it strange concerning the fiery trial which is to try you, as though some strange thing happened to you; but rejoice to the extent that you partake of Christ's sufferings, that when his glory is revealed, you may also be glad with exceeding joy (1 Peter 4:12, 13).

It should be clear from Paul's experience and from these words of the apostle Peter that Christians were not promised daily miracles. In fact, even when they faced extreme difficulty, the early Christians did not expect nor were they encouraged to expect miraculous deliverance.

Passages like these could be multiplied. But it is clear from this brief survey that miraculous deliverance from difficulties was not the norm in the early church. Whatever we may think of contemporary miracles, Scripture does not support the idea that we should expect them as commonplace. Rather, we are to trust the Lord, expecting him to provide the strength to live godly lives in and through our trials.

A miraculous earthquake freed Paul and Silas from the Philippian prison.

AUTHENTICATION OF GOD'S SPOKESMEN IN THE EPISTLES

We've seen that one function of the miraculous in Scripture was to mark individuals as authentic spokesmen for God. This was true in Old Testament times, and it was true of Jesus, Peter, and Paul as well.

AUTHENTICATION OF GOD'S SPOKESMEN IN OLD TESTAMENT TIMES

The Old Testament provided four tests by which a person who claimed to speak for God could be authenticated. Deuteronomy 18 taught that God's true prophets would be an Israelite (Deut. 18:18), who would speak in Yahweh's name (Deut. 18:19). In addition, whatever a true prophet spoke in the name of the Lord would "happen or come to pass" (Deut. 18:22). If a prophet's predictions did not come true, he could be ignored. He did not speak for the Lord.

The fourth test, in Deuteronomy 13:1–2, makes it clear that even the miraculous was not a sufficient test. What the prophet says must also be in harmony with God's revealed word.

If there arises among you a prophet or a dreamer of dreams, and he gives you a sign or a wonder, and the sign or the wonder comes to pass, of which he spoke to you, saying, 'Let us go after other gods— which you have not known—and let us serve them,' you shall not listen to the words of that prophet (Deut. 13:1–3).

This fourth test is important because it highlights the possibility that a fulfilled prediction, a sign, or a wonder might not come from God.

AUTHENTICATION OF GOD'S SPOKESMEN IN THE NEW TESTAMENT EPISTLES

There are several passages in Scripture which state principles for distinguishing God's authentic spokesmen from false teachers. Not one of these passages mentions miracles, signs, or wonders as valid authenticating signs.

A theological test. The apostle John in his first letter gives Christians a theological test. In chapter four John warned Christians to "test the spirits, whether they are of God; because many false prophets have gone out into the world" (1 John 4:1). John affirmed, "Every spirit that does not confess that Jesus Christ has come in the flesh is not of God" but is of the Antichrist (1 John 4:3). Belief in Jesus as God the Son incarnate is a theological test which Christians are always to apply to those who claim to be God's messengers and ministers.

This same emphasis is seen in 2 Peter 2:11, where false teachers are described as those who deny the Lord who bought them.

A lifestyle test. Both Jude and Peter described the personalities of false prophets and false teachers. They were bold and arrogant (2 Peter 2:10; Jude 16), they despised authority (2 Peter 2:10; Jude 3), they followed the corrupt desires of the sinful nature (2 Peter 2:10; Jude 4, 19), and they loved money and wealth (2 Peter 2:15; Jude 12).

These lifestyle descriptions contrast sharply with the lifestyle appropriate for Christian leaders, as given by the apostle Paul in 1 Timothy 3:1–9 and Titus 1:5–9.

A discernment test. In addition to these tests which help to identify false prophets and teachers, the early church was to rely on Spirit-led discernment to test specific teachings. In 1 Corinthians 14, Paul turned to the topic of orderly worship in a church meeting where all were welcome to participate. After establishing rules for the exercise of the gift of tongues, Paul said, "Let two or three prophets speak, and let the others judge" (1 Cor. 14:29). The word *judge* means to distinguish, to discern, to evaluate, and thus to judge. The "others" mentioned here were the elders of the church who had the responsibility of guarding the congregation.

This function was especially important in the early church, as the New Testament canon had not been completed. This meant there was no written revelation against which to measure the teachings of those who claimed to speak for the Lord.

Conclusions. It is significant that while the New Testament Epistles showed a deep concern for distinguishing true and false prophets and teachers, not one passage even suggested a miracle test like that for Old Testament prophets. Instead, the Epistles provided theological, lifestyle, and discernment tests to be used by the early Christians.

It seems clear that miracles and wonders simply were not considered to be authenticating tests which could be applied in local church settings. While "signs and wonders and mighty deeds [*miracles*]" were understood to be "the signs of an apostle" (2 Cor. 12:12), they were not expected of the itinerant teachers and evangelists who traveled from church to church across the Roman Empire.

MIRACLES AND WONDERS IN THE EPISTLES: A SUMMARY

Our review of references to miracles in the Epistles has led to several conclusions.

First, miracles and signs and wonders did authenticate both the ministry of Jesus (Heb. 2:4) and did serve as signs authenticating those with apostolic authority (2 Cor. 12:12).

Second, healings and miracles were identified as spiritual gifts which God the Holy Spirit distributed. These clearly functioned in the Corinthian church, even though neither healings nor miracles are found on other New Testament lists of spiritual gifts.

Third, in his letters to the Corinthians and the Galatians the apostle Paul's references to miracles implied that in both congregations these were familiar if not commonplace experiences. Yet such miracles (*dunamis*, works of power) did not have the same function as the numerous miracles which authenticated Jesus—and then Peter and Paul—as God's spokesmen.

When we raised the question of how the Epistles described dealing with sickness, we found a surprising fact. When the apostle Paul or his close friends became sick, Paul did not perform a healing miracle, or call for a person with the gift of healing. Paul simply prayed and, like the apostle James, recommended medical treatment.

In the same vein, the apostle Paul in 2 Corinthians 11 recounted his many trials. In none of them did the apostle expect or rely on miraculous deliverance. Similarly, 1 Peter's guidance on how Christians were to meet persecution and suffering made no mention of calling for or expecting miraculous divine intervention.

We find a similar pattern if we examine how the early church distinguished between true and false prophets and teachers. While the Epistles provided doctrinal and lifestyle tests, and expected Christians to exercise Spirit-led discernment, there is no evidence at all that miracles or wonders were means by which authentic messengers of God could be distinguished.

When we take all the evidence of the Epistles together, we are forced to conclude that miracles were not common in the apostolic age, nor were they normative for vital Christian churches.

While God can and does perform miracles, Christians apparently are not to *expect* miracles when faced with sickness or troubles. Instead, we are to meet life's trials with faith in Christ, finding in him the strength to endure and to overcome.

INTERPRETING THE BOOK OF REVELATION

Church history records a variety of ways in which the book of Revelation has been understood by Christians.

Revelation as a book of prophecy. The early church fathers saw Revelation as a book of prophecy. They linked its teachings with those of the Old Testament prophets and with Jesus' statements about the future, as recorded in Matthew 24 and Luke 13. During these early centuries Revelation was understood to describe future events which would surely take place on earth.

For instance, Justin Martyr drew from Revelation when he wrote, "I and as many are orthodox Christians, do acknowledge that there shall be a resurrection of the body, and a residence of a thousand years in Jerusalem, adorned and enlarged, as the prophets Ezekiel, Isaiah, and others so unanimously attest" (*Ante-Nicene Fathers,* Vol. I, 239).

Irenaeus, another church father who was also a famous missionary, gave this picture of the future as held by the early church. Again, this vision of the future incorporates information found in Revelation with the vision of the Old Testament prophets:

When the Antichrist shall have devastated all things in the world, he will reign for three years and six months, and sit in the temple at Jerusalem; and then shall the Lord come from heaven in clouds, in the glory of the Father, sending this man, and those who follow him, into the lake of fire (*Ante-Nicene Fathers,* Vol. I, 560).

The understanding of Revelation as prophecy destined to be literally fulfilled was maintained through the first four hundred years of church history.

Revelation as an allegory. About A.D. 390, a leader of the African church, Tyconius, allegorized Revelation. He assumed that the visions recorded in Revelation referred symbolically to hidden spiritual truths. The allegorical view of Revelation dominated until about A.D. 1200.

Revelation as a chronological document. Joachim of Fiore divided history into three ages—of the Father, Son, and Holy Spirit. Joachim divided Revelation according to this scheme. The Reformers adopted this chronological approach, and identified the Antichrist of chapter 13 and the harlot of Revelation 17—18 with the papacy and Rome. Catholic scholars were quick to respond and argue that the Antichrist was an individual who would appear at some future time. Yet neither Catholics nor Protestants attempted to relate the book of Revelation to the Old Testament prophets, as had the early church fathers.

Modern approaches to interpreting Revelation. In modern times, two views of Revelation predominate. Some hold the view of the early church, considering Revelation a prophetic description of things to come. Others continue to take revelation primarily as an allegory, filled with symbolism but powerfully conveying the truth that God is sovereign and that he will triumph at history's end.

MIRACLES IN THE BOOK OF REVELATION

Whatever approach we take to interpreting Revelation, we must be struck by two things about references to wonders and miracles in this fascinating book.

The first is that when the language of miracles is used, it describes extraordinary events produced not by God but by Satan or demonic powers. The second is that this book is filled with descriptions of extraordinary acts of judgment executed by angels at God's direction.

"LYING WONDERS"

Lying wonders were predicted by the apostle Paul. In writing to the Thessalonians, Paul presented a decisive argument to prove that Christ's second coming had not yet occurred. Paul wrote in his second letter to this church that "that Day will not come unless the falling away comes first, and the man of sin [the Antichrist] is revealed, the son of perdition, who opposes and exalts himself above all that is called God or that is worshiped, so that he sits as God in the temple of God, showing himself that he is God" (2 Thess. 2:3, 4). In making this statement, the apostle linked his teaching to Old Testament prophecies by Daniel (see Dan. 11:31; 12:11) and to Christ's own description of the future (Matt. 24:15f).

Paul then went on to state that "the coming of the lawless one [again, the Antichrist] is according to the working of Satan, with all power, signs and lying wonders" (2 Thess. 2:9). The appearance of this great enemy of God, a person who is energized by Satan himself, will initiate history's fourth great age of miracles.

We've seen that at pivotal points in history, fresh revelations by God of himself and his plans have been marked by clusters of miracles. What Paul is saying is that when a fourth age of miracles dawns, they will be worked by Satan and not God! They will be wonders. But they will be lying wonders, for God will not be their source. And the person they seem to authenticate will be Satan's man and not the Lord's.

These lying wonders are further described in the book of Revelation. When we scan Revelation for the language of miracles, we find the biblical words for miracles, signs, and wonders occur in the following verses.

Revelation 13:13, 14. "He performs great signs, so that he even makes fire come down from heaven on the earth in the sight of men. And he deceives those who dwell on the earth by those signs which he was granted to do in the sight of the beast."

The context of these verses. Revelation 13 introduces "the beast," an individual who is named the Antichrist only in 1 John 2:18 and 4:3. This individual is given political power and authority by "the dragon," another name for Satan (Rev. 20:2). The first beast, or Antichrist, is supported by "another beast." This second individual, identified as the "false prophet" in Revelation 16:13 and 19:20, is the one who performs the "great signs" described in this passage.

The purpose of the false prophet's signs. The miracles performed by the false prophet are in support of the Antichrist. These miracles help to convince humanity to worship both "the dragon who gave authority to the beast" and the Antichrist (Rev. 13:4, 15). They also help to consolidate his political power (Rev. 13:15–18).

There is no doubt, as reflected in the quotes from Justin Martyr and Irenaeus above, that this passage reflects the early church's understanding of Revelation 13.

Revelation 16:13, 14. "And I saw three unclean spirits like frogs coming out of the mouth of the dragon, out of the mouth of the beast, and out of the mouth of the false prophet. For they are spirits of demons, performing signs, which go out to the kings of the earth and of the whole world, to gather them to the battle of that great day of God Almighty."

The context of these verses. John's next mention of lying wonders is of demons "performing signs." Here as throughout the Old and New Testaments, "signs" are miracles which serve to authenticate a messenger and/or his message.

Again, the language of the verse has deep roots in the Old Testament. The phrase "that great day of God" is a constant theme of the Old Testament prophets. One interpreter notes that

this phrase, along with its shorter version, "that day," occurs often in the OT prophets. It always identifies a critical period of time during which God personally intervenes in history, directly or indirectly, to accomplish a specific purpose which fulfills his announced plan for the ages. Most often the events of "that day" take place at history's end, as in Isaiah 7:18–25 (The *Bible Readers' Companion*, Chariot/Victor, 413).

For instance, there are 45 references to the "day of the Lord" or "that day" in Isaiah. In each case, it refers to a time of judgment as history reaches a climax (see Isa. 13:9–13; 24:1–23; 32:1–20; 63:1–6).

The purpose of these demon-produced signs. It is clear from the text that the purpose of the signs mentioned in Revelation 16:13, 14 is to guarantee the allegiance of the nations of earth for a final great struggle against God. Reading a few verses further, we see that the place where the final battle is to occur is named Armageddon (Rev. 16:16).

Revelation 19:20. "Then the beast was captured, and with him the false prophet who worked signs in his presence, by which he deceived those who received the mark of the beast and those who worshiped his image. These two were cast alive into the lake of fire burning with brimstone."

The context of the verse. Earlier uses of the language of miracles in Revelation is associated with the appearance of two individuals called "beasts" and identified as the Antichrist and a false prophet. These two are portrayed as agents of Satan, who gives the false prophet the power to do "lying wonders." These lying wonders are miracles which mimic the works of God but are actually works of Satan.

This cluster of miracles produced by Satan's henchmen is used to consolidate the political power of the Antichrist and to deceive humanity into worshiping him as a god. The miracles are also used to guarantee the allegiance of earth's nations to Satan as history's terminal battle, Armageddon, approaches.

The outcome of the battle. Chapter 19 of Revelation describes Christ's conquest of Satan and his armies. The victory is decisive and total, and Jesus is established as King of kings and Lord of lords (Rev. 19:16). The Antichrist and the false prophet are cast into a "lake of fire," a place which we know as "hell."

The miracles which will accredit those who will lead humanity into history's climactic rebellion against the one true God will be lying wonders indeed.

DIVINE JUDGMENTS

The most striking feature of Revelation is its vivid descriptions of divine judgment poured out on earth. If we understand miracles as extraordinary events caused by God with a religious purpose, the great judgments described in Revelation are certainly miracles.

Before we look at several of these miracles, we need to understand something important about the language of this powerful but difficult-to-understand book of the Bible.

THE APOCALYPTIC LANGUAGE OF THE BOOK OF REVELATION

The *American Heritage Encyclopedic Dictionary* defines *apocalyptic* as "of or pertaining to a prophetic disclosure or revelation" and "portending violent disaster or ultimate doom." It is common these days to assume that all such language is symbolic or metaphorical. However, while there clearly are symbolic elements, the critical problem in understanding the apocalyptic literature of the Bible is lack of vocabulary.

An image of divine judgment (Revelation 8:7–10). The apocalyptic visions of Revelation begin with Revelation 4. John introduces them by telling us that an angel called him up into heaven, where the angel would "show you things which must take place after this" (Rev. 4:1). Thus, John tells us that what he describes is to take place in the future, and that he sees the future from the viewpoint of heaven, not earth. From that viewpoint, John not only can observe events on earth but he can also see their heavenly cause.

In chapter 8 of Revelation, John describes seven angels being given seven trumpets. As each trumpet is sounded, another judgment strikes the earth and its population. From the vantage point of those on earth, only the effect will be experienced. John, in heaven, sees both the cause and the effect.

In Revelation 8:7–10, John describes the effect caused by the sounding of the first three trumpets:

The first angel sounded: And hail and fire followed, mingled with blood, and they were thrown to the earth. And a third of the trees were burned up, and all green grass was burned up. Then the second angel sounded: And something like a great mountain burning with fire was thrown into the sea, and a third of the sea became blood. And a third of the living creatures in the sea died, and a third of the ships were destroyed. Then the third angel sounded: And a great star fell from heaven, burning like a torch, and it fell on a third of the rivers and on the springs of water.

It is clear from this sample that we can't really tell just what John is describing. Is the "great star" a massive meteorite? What could "something like a mountain burning with fire" possibly be? And what does John mean by hail and fire mixed with blood?

It is easy to dismiss this language, or to consider it strictly metaphor, just because we can't imagine what John is talking about. No wonder many interpreters assume this language can't be taken literally.

A contemporary example. Before we consider whether the language of Revelation is "literal," we need to try an experiment. We need to imagine ourselves among the first colonists to land in America. We disembark from our tiny ship and set out to carve a home in the wilderness. We build log shelters, struggle to clear land on which to grow crops, and huddle together in winter around flickering fires.

Now let's suppose that suddenly we were transported hundreds of years into the future. There we are shown three scenes of the twentieth century. We are shown a television program depicting Americans landing on the moon. We are shown a Los Angeles freeway, with cars zipping by. And we are shown the Dallas–Fort Worth airport, with jets landing and taking off.

Now let's suppose that we awaken. Stunned and awed by what we've seen, we try to share these realities with our fellow colonists. What would we say? What words would we have to use to enable them to visualize what we have seen? Remember, we can only use the vocabulary of our own time. And we can only compare the things we are trying to describe with things that are familiar to us and our companions.

I suspect that—given these limitations—what we said or wrote would sound very much like John's description in Revelation of the events which he witnessed. Our report of what we had seen would sound, well, apocalyptic. Or at the very least, we would be accused of using symbolic language and metaphor. Nevertheless, what we described would be real to us. And in this sense, our depiction would be "literal."

The issue in understanding apocalyptic language is not whether it can be taken "literally," if by *literally* we mean that the writer is describing as actual events what he has observed. The problem is that the vocabulary available to describe what one sees in apocalyptic literature is so limited by the writer's time and place that we cannot tell what is being described.

If John had been a twentieth-century man, would he have called the burning star that falls from heaven a meteorite? Or would hail and fire mingled with blood have become the eruption of a string of volcanos? We simply do not know.

What we do know is that whatever events John is describing, they represent extraordinary events caused by God. And we know that in Revelation these events have a clear and distinct religious purpose. They are elements of God's judgment on a sinful humanity which has rejected the gospel of grace, and which prefers Satan's ways to those of the Lord.

THE OUTCOMES OF THE DIVINE MIRACLE; JUDGMENTS DESCRIBED IN REVELATION

The miracle-judgments do not produce faith (Revelation 6:15–17). We've noted earlier in this book that miracles tend to confirm faith in believers, but at the same time they tend not to produce faith in unbelievers. As miracle judgment followed miracle judgment in the time of Moses, Pharaoh's heart became more and more hard. In spite of the wonderful miracles Jesus performed, which identified him as the Messiah, Israel rejected and crucified him rather than extended a welcome.

It should be no surprise, then, that the miracle judgments of Revelation also fail to produce faith in those who experience them. In a telling passage, John describes the reaction of individuals who recognize the divine origin of the judgments. Rather than turn to God for forgiveness, they "hid themselves in the caves and in the rocks of the mountains, and said to the mountains and rocks, 'Fall on us and hide us from the face of him who sits on the throne and from the wrath of the Lamb!' " (Rev. 6:15, 16).

In another passage John writes, "But the rest of mankind, who were not killed by these plagues, did not repent of the works of their hands, that they should not worship demons, and idols of gold, silver, brass, stone and wood, which can neither see nor hear nor walk. And they did not repent of their murders or their sorceries or their sexual immorality or their thefts" (Rev. 9:20, 21).

The judgment miracles of Revelation are just this—judgment miracles. They are not intended to call human beings to God, but to punish those who have refused to heed his call in Christ, and who have remained committed to a lifestyle of sin.

The miracle judgments are preparation for history's end (Revelation 20—22). The book of Revelation ends with Christ triumphant, the sinful dead judged, and a new heaven and earth created by the Lord. The sin which plagued the first creation has been dealt with at last. Those who trusted Christ are now the joyful inhabitants of a new and perfect universe. Those who turned their backs on God and refused to respond to his gospel have been dismissed to the lake of fire.

The grand drama is over, and justice and love have been vindicated. As the contemporary worship songs affirm, "Our God rules."

IMPLICATIONS OF THE LYING WONDERS AND DIVINE JUDGMENTS

As we have explored what the Bible says about miracles, we've noted a consistent pattern. Miracles come in paired clusters. As new revelation is introduced or old revelation reaffirmed, there is first of all a cluster of establishing miracles. These authenticate a divine messenger and validate his message. The establishing miracles are followed by a cluster of supportive miracles, which demonstrate the presence of God with those who have responded to the new revelation. This pattern can be seen in each of the three historic ages of miracles in the fourteenth century B.C., the eighth century B.C., and the time of Christ and the apostles.

But the pattern is broken in the Bible's fourth age of miracles, which lies in the future.

The first cluster of miracles of that time are indeed establishing miracles. But they are lying wonders, energized by Satan, intended to establish the Antichrist as the world's political and religious ruler.

What happens then is a cluster of judgment miracles caused by God. Rather than support the claims of the Antichrist established by the first cluster of miracles, these judgment miracles demolish those claims, even as they demolish the pretensions of the Antichrist and the false prophet.

In the battle of miracles, God is shown to be supreme. This is Revelation's great and final contribution to Scripture's teaching on miracles.

❖

MIRACLES TODAY

God Working in and Through Us

MIRACLE: An extraordinary event caused by God for a religious purpose.

If this defines a biblical miracle, are such miracles for today? The author suggests, probably not. But he believes that God does perform compassionate miracles today—and anonymous miracles as well. There is no doubt that God can perform such miracles today. And there is good reason to believe that He does!

BIBLICAL MIRACLES: NOT FOR TODAY

We must say this hesitantly. It's always presumptuous for a mere human being to announce what God will and will not do. God is Sovereign, and free to act in any way he chooses and at any time.

With this caveat, let me explain what I mean by saying biblical miracles are not for today. As we have seen, biblical miracles occur in history in paired clusters. These clusters of miracles were intended to introduce or reaffirm significant truths revealed by God.

The first cluster of miracles in each pair are *authenticating* miracles, which validate the new revelation. They also clearly identify the individual who coveys the new revelation as God's spokesman. This first cluster of miracles is followed by another cluster of miracles

which are *supportive* miracles. These miracles demonstrate the living presence of God with those who welcome and follow the path marked out by the new revelation.

Historically, the agents of the authenticating and the supportive miracles have differed. Moses was God's agent for the authenticating miracles of the Exodus and many of the supportive miracles; Joshua was the agent of additional supportive miracles. Elijah was God's agent for authenticating miracles in the 700s B.C.; Elisha was God's agent for the supportive miracles. Jesus was God's agent for the authenticating miracles of the first century; Peter and Paul were his primary agents for the supportive miracles.

We should not expect this kind of miracle cluster in our day. The New Testament has completed God's revelation of his plans and purposes, and no new revelation is to be expected. In fact, the apostle Paul in 2 Thessalonians and John in Revelation make it clear that the next cluster of miracles to occur will be "lying wonders," worked by Satan to validate a false revelation. Rather than being followed by supportive miracles, the "lying wonders" will be followed by a series of devastating judgment-miracles poured out on an unrepentant humanity by God.

It is for this reason, and with this understanding of the role and function of miracles in Scripture, that we conclude that biblical miracles are not for today.

GOD DOES PERFORM MIRACLES FOR BELIEVERS TODAY

Although what we have called "biblical miracles" are not for today, we must also conclude that God really does perform miracles for believers today.

Christ's miracles revealed God's compassionate nature. One of the most beautiful truths expressed by the miracles performed by Jesus is that they were expressions of God's compassionate nature. It is true that the miracles Christ performed were exactly the kinds of miracles that the Old Testament prophets associated with the Messiah and the messianic age. Thus Jesus' miracles served to authenticate his claim to be Israel's promised deliverer. Yet the kinds of miracles predicted and performed were by their nature compassionate.

Isaiah wrote of the messianic age when God would come to save his people:

> Then the eyes of the blind shall
>   be opened,
> And the ears of the deaf shall be
>   unstopped.
> Then the lame shall leap like a
>   deer,
> And the tongue of the dumb sing
>   (Isa. 35:5, 6).

How easy it would have been for God to choose other kinds of miracles as authenticating signs. He could have made mountains leap, or blinded his enemies. Instead, God chose miracles of compassion to mark his Messiah, demonstrating the loving compassion of One who cares deeply about human beings.

The Gospel writers recorded on 14 separate occasions that Jesus had compassion on the persons for whom he performed miracles. The miracles of Jesus stand as a permanent monument to the compassion and love of God.

Modern Christians report miracles of compassion performed by God. Paul Prather was a skeptic about miracles. In his book, he told of an experience that began to change his outlook:

My father was a Southern Baptist preacher as well as a school teacher and, for several years, an administrator at a Baptist college. My mom, a housewife, was an equally staunch Baptist. In those days some Southern Baptists, including my parents, held the theological view that the age of miracles had ended in the first century with the death of the original apostles. They looked askance at other Christians who acted as if God was very much in the miracle business today, such as the ragged Pentecostals who met in a small, white frame building on the poorer end of one town where we lived.

Our understanding of miracles changed in 1976, while I was a ne'er-do-well student at the University of Kentucky. By the time cancer was discovered, it had invaded my father's entire body: his head, a kidney, his bones. First, doctors operated on a tumor on his skull. They opened him up and stitched him shut after removing only enough tissue for a biopsy. Surgery wouldn't do the job, they'd known as they saw the tumor. Dad's neurosurgeon told me a few minutes afterward that the cancer had spread so far that they could draw marrow from any bone in his body and it would be malignant.

And then something happened that I still find hard to grasp. One day I visited my father in his hospital room. He told me that God had spoken to him as he was praying. The Lord had told him he was going to be healed. I can't remember exactly what I thought, except that I was puzzled and sad. My father didn't normally claim to have received divine revelations regarding faith healings, or anything else (*Modern-Day Miracles,* 1996, pp. 8, 9).

Prather went on to tell how the cancer vanished before his father had received a single medication. A kidney tumor which had been clearly visible on X-rays disappeared. Bone marrow tests returned negative. His team of doctors sent their findings to another hospital, assuming they had missed something or that his dad had never had cancer. The doctors at the other hospital agreed with the original diagnosis. Prather's father had had cancer. Then he didn't. Twenty years later, Prather wrote in his book,

God still performs healing miracles, but believers can't claim them as their right.

❖

Say what you want, but my father told me what was going to take place before it happened: God had said he intended to heal Dad. Then, apparently, God did just that. I bear witness that I saw what I believe to have been a miracle (p. 9).

Others bear witness to similar happenings. Extraordinary things, for which there seems to be no explanation but God, do occur. Doctors may speak of "spontaneous remission." But many who experience such things call them miracles and give God and prayer the credit.

Certainly this experience and many others like it are in complete harmony with what we know of the power and compassion of our God.

But what about those who are not healed or delivered? One of the troubling things about what we might call "miracles of compassion" is that not everyone who is sick or in need experiences a miracle. In our survey of the New Testament Epistles, we saw that even men of faith such as Paul and James did not expect or claim miracles as their right. Instead, they advised prayer and normal medical treatment.

Some would say that whether a person is granted a miracle depends on his or her faith. If we believe strongly enough, God will supply the miracle. Aside from the fact that texts used to support this position are misinterpreted, this teaching makes God dependent on us rather than us dependent on God. Ultimately, this position pictures a God who is captive to human beings—who must behave in a certain way if we have enough faith, pray believing, purge ourselves of sins, or meet some other condition.

The fact is that God is sovereign, and his freedom to act is not dependent on anything that any human being does. The reason why God seems to provide miracles for some and not for others is a mystery to us, hidden in his inscrutable will.

How are we to respond to this mystery? We have an example in the three Hebrews who faced Nebuchadnezzar's fiery furnace with quiet faith. Like them, we are to appeal to the Lord, and then say with confidence, "Our God whom we serve is able to deliver us from the burning fiery furnace, and he will deliver us from your hand, O king. But if not, let it be known to you, O king, that we do not serve your gods, nor will we worship the gold image which you have set up" (Dan. 3:17, 18).

Our God is able to deliver.

But if not . . . we will continue to trust only him.

In God's hands. The June 29, 1996, edition of the *St. Petersburg Times* carried a story on parents whom the writer described as having "a faith that has no limits." The article told the poignant story of Fred and Lu Langstone, whose 18-year-old son suffered a massive heart attack and was in a coma. The article reported:

"We are just struggling parents who trust their God in hard times," said Fred Langston. "This is the darkest valley I could ever walk."

"I would have never thought I could have lived through this," said Lu Langston. "I have watched and read about others and wept and sobbed. But I know where my strength comes from."

This was after the family got jolted at 7:30 Wednesday when a neurologist at University General Hospital in Semanole told them their son, Leighton, suffered from a brain hernia. With a swelling, there was no penetration of blood to the brain.

No one has ever survived a similar condition.
"From the standpoint of one doctor," said Fred Langston, "it means there is absolutely no hope. This would be a first and won't happen unless God does something on a par with the parting of the Red Sea."

The family asked for a second opinion and called in another neurologist Wednesday night. The neurologist confirmed the findings of the other specialist. It is possible they might take Langston off life support today. He still will have a tube that feeds him food and water and keeps his throat clear.

Leighton Langston, 18, a high school soccer star, suffered a massive heart attack Friday and has been in a coma ever since. Tuesday evening, he turned his head toward his dad's voice but showed no such signs Wednesday.

"A lot of people think what we are is all about religion," said Fred Langston. "If it were just about religion, we would not have made it through Friday night. This is about the knowledge of God and an ongoing relationship with him that is sustaining."

The 75 to 100 young people who have spilled into the hospital's halls are witness to this.

"People will say how they [the Langstons] need to get a little reality," said Cameran Brenner. "They just don't understand what they say all leads back to God. They really make you want to believe. When you drive down the street, you start crying.

Then you realize, 'Why should I cry when they are so strong.'

"I'm Jewish," said Doug Bird, "but I went to their prayer service [at Pasadena Presbyterian Church in St. Petersburg], and it is something I have never seen before in my life. So many people coming together, singing and praising Jesus.

"You would cry, even if you were a complete stranger."

Tuesday night, the third of such gatherings in the chapel drew 300 for a 9:30 service. It wasn't until 6:45 that someone suggested it.

The scene was repeated Wednesday, even though the service didn't begin until after 10 P.M.

"This thing just wipes you out," said Fred Langston, "but you keep drawing on the resources of a loving Lord and he'll get you through."

Fred and Lu Langston were not granted a miracle. Leighton died. And why one is saved by a miracle and another is not is something that we simply cannot explain. All we can do is remember that our God is a God of love and compassion. And trust that what he chooses to do is best, for reasons we may never know.

Does God perform miracles of compassion in our day? May he perform miracles for other reasons of his own? Of course God does, and he can.

But when we ask whether we are to *expect* miracles, or whether we have any basis on which to claim miracles as our right, the answer must be "No." Our relationship with God is no guarantee of miraculous intervention. But as Fred and Lu Langston discovered, "the knowledge of God and an ongoing relationship with him . . . is sustaining" indeed.

ANONYMOUS MIRACLES

One of the great convictions that Christians have shared across the ages is that God is sovereign. God is at work in history and in our individual lives.

Recently I ran across a saying penned by an unknown writer: *Circumstances are God's way of doing miracles anonymously.* What the author wants us to contemplate is that God is always at work in the circumstances of our lives. When we suffer a serious illness and respond to medical treatment, God is no less involved than when our healing cannot be "explained" by doctors. God works through the natural as well as the supernatural to show his grace to us.

Recently my wife was pondering the unusual events that led up to our meeting and subsequent marriage. She made a list of all the unusual things that had happened in her life that had brought her to the place where our paths crossed. These included moves from one part of the country to another, two personal tragedies, the wise advice of a Christian counselor, and a number of other experiences. She realized again that if any of the things she listed had not happened as they did, she would either never have met me or she would not have been attracted to the qualities she had come late to value.

To Sue, this series of events which many would dismiss as "coincidences" were no less a cause of wonder and amazement than if we had both been guided by an audible voice to a meeting place, and told by that voice that God intended us to marry. The path that brought us together seemed to her to bear the mark of the miraculous. And rightly so.

For us, and for you as well, God has often performed his miracles anonymously. He has worked through circumstances in which only the eye of faith can see his hand.

And it is with the eye of faith that we are to look not only at Scripture, but at our daily lives as well. In the Word of God, we meet the author of history's grand miracles. He is the Creator, at whose Word the universe sprang into being. In Jesus, God the Son became incarnate, entering our world to live among us as a human being and die for mankind's sins. In the grand miracle of the Resurrection, Jesus was displayed to all as the Son of God with power—history's living and coming Lord.

When we know him and appreciate his power and love, doubt disappears. The miracles of Scripture and the anonymous miracles which fill our lives become occasions of wonder, awe, and praise.

And we affirm, together, that our God truly is a miracle-working God.

❖
EXPOSITORY INDEX

An expository index organizes information by topic and guides the reader to Bible verses and book pages which are critical to understanding the subject. It does not list every verse referred to in the book, but seeks to identify key verses. It does not list every mention of a topic in the book, but directs the reader to pages where a topic is discussed in some depth. Thus an expository index helps the reader avoid the frustration of looking up verses in the Bible or the book, only to discover that they contribute in only a small way to one's understanding of the subject.

This expository index organizes references to miracles and wonders by topic. Topics and subtopics are identified in the left-hand column. Key Bible verses and passages are listed in the center column under "Scriptures." The far right column identifies pages in this book where the topic is covered.

In most instances, several of the key verses in the "Scriptures" column will be discussed on the book pages referred to. Very often additional verses will be referred to on the pages where the topic is covered. Our goal is to help you keep in focus the critical Bible verses and passages. Similarly, the book pages referred to are only those which make a significant contribution to understanding a topic, not every page on which a topic may be mentioned.

Please note that material under sub-topics is sometimes organized chronologically by the sequence of appearance in Scripture, and sometimes alphabetically, depending upon which organization will be most helpful in understanding and locating information.

TOPIC	SCRIPTURES	PAGE(S)
ABSENCE OF MIRACLES, IMPLICATIONS		
For the sick	2 Cor. 13; Phil. 2:25–27; 1 Tim. 5:23; James 5:14–15	274–276
For those undergoing trials	2 Cor. 11:23–28; 1 Pet. 1:6; 2:21; 4:12, 13	276
ATTACKS ON MIRACLES		17–19
Early Jewish		17
Early pagan		17–18
Spinoza		17–18
Hume		18–19
Paulus		19
Bultmann		19
Contemporary		19–20
AUTHENTICATING ROLE	Deut. 13:1, 2; 18:18–22	157–158, 277–278

❖ SCRIPTURE INDEX

(Bible references are in boldface type, followed by the pages on which they appear in this book.)

THE EVERYTHING IN THE BIBLE SERIES

Every Angel in the Bible (ISBN: 0-7852-4533-2)
Explore an unseen world inhabited by agents of God and Satan.
The most complete contemporary exploration of every angelic appearance from
Genesis to Revelation. More than 100 drawings, charts, and maps, along with
comprehensive Expository and Scripture Indexes, focus on specific instances of
angelic appearances and what the Bible teaches through them.

Every Man in the Bible (ISBN: 0-7852-1439-9)
Share the lives of the men who shaped our faith and our world.
Meet the men God used to tell His story. The significant contributions of
patriarchs, prophets, and kings, as well as the men around Jesus, are explored
and explained. Even more, the men of the Bible are portrayed as real people
whose flaws often betrayed them, yet who found in their personal relation-ship
with God the strength to achieve great things.

Every Miracle in the Bible (ISBN: 0-7852-4531-6)
Examine the mighty works of God in time and space.
Richards takes you on a grand tour of all the Bible's truly "extra-ordinary events
caused by God." This book will help you understand the amazing miracles and
wonders of the Bible and strengthen your faith in a God who cannot be bound by
time and space. Richards explains each miracle's significance in God's unfolding
revelation.

Every Name of God in the Bible (ISBN: 0-7852-0702-3)
Understand who God is through His names, titles, and images.
Humanity has come to understand God more fully by way of the names, titles,
and images used to identify Him in the Bible.
  - *Names* – Yahweh, Sovereign Lord, Eternal God
  - *Titles* – Creator of heaven, God of truth, God of justice
  - *Images* – Fortress, Potter, Father
Richards expands our view of Jesus and the Holy Spirit by examining terms
applied to them in both the Old and New Testaments.

Every Prayer in the Bible (ISBN: 0-7852-4534-0)
Learn to follow God's patterns for confession, petition, and intercession.
An in-depth examination of prayer throughout the Scriptures. Journey through
the Old and New Testament to strengthen and empower your times of
communion with God as you learn to appropriate His promises and follow His
biblical patterns for worship, confession, petition, and intercession.

Every Promise in the Bible (ISBN: 0-7852-4532-4)
Find comfort and strength in God's unshakable commitments.
Richards demonstrates that God is a keeper of His word, trustworthy and
dependable to fulfill everything He has promised. A helpful compilation of
"Words to Count On" provides hundred of beloved expressions of faith and
confidence in God as recorded by the biblical writers.

Every Woman in the Bible (ISBN: 0-7852-1441-0)
Discover all the women of the Bible and how they lived.
This comprehensive reference book explores the individual life and contribution
of each woman who appears in Scripture. Building upon the most up-to-date
scholarship, it provides powerful vignettes exploring the character of Bible
women and draws healing and helpful lessons for today.

COMING SOON:

Every Teaching of Jesus in the Bible (ISBN: 0-7852-0703-1)